SHAKESPEARE AND THEATRICAL PATRONAGE IN EARLY MODERN ENGLAND

During the past quarter of a century, the study of patronage–theatre relations in early modern England has developed considerably. This, however, is the first extensive, wide-ranging, and representative study of patronage as it relates to Shakespeare and the theatrical culture of his time. Twelve distinguished theatre historians address such questions as: What important functions did patronage have for the theatre during this period? How, in turn, did the theatre impact upon and represent patronage? Where do paying spectators and purchasers of printed drama fit into the discussion of patronage? The authors also show how patronage practices changed and developed from the early Tudor period to the years in which Shakespeare was the English theatre's leading artist. This important book will appeal to scholars of Renaissance social history as well as those who focus on Shakespeare and his playwriting contemporaries.

PAUL WHITFIELD WHITE is Associate Professor of English at Purdue University. He is the author of *Theatre and Reformation: Protestantism, Patronage, and Playing in Tudor England* (1993), and editor of *Marlowe, History, and Sexuality* (1968) and *Reformation Biblical Drama* (1992).

SUZANNE R. WESTFALL is Professor of English and Theatre at Lafayette College. She is the author of *Patrons and Performance: Early Tudor Household Revels* (1991), and articles on patronage and household theatre.

To our sons
Dylan James Putzel and William Sebastian White

SHAKESPEARE AND THEATRICAL PATRONAGE IN EARLY MODERN ENGLAND

EDITED BY

PAUL WHITFIELD WHITE AND
SUZANNE R. WESTFALL

CAMBRIDGE
UNIVERSITY PRESS

PUBLISHED BY THE PRESS SYNDICATE OF THE UNIVERSITY OF CAMBRIDGE
The Pitt Building, Trumpington Street, Cambridge, United Kingdom

CAMBRIDGE UNIVERSITY PRESS
The Edinburgh Building, Cambridge CB2 2RU, UK
40 West 20th Street, New York, NY 10011-4211, USA
477 Williamstown Road, Port Melbourne, VIC 3207, Australia
Ruiz de Alarcón 13, 28014 Madrid, Spain
Dock House, The Waterfront, Cape Town 8001, South Africa

http://www.cambridge.org

First published 2002

Printed in the United Kingdom at the University Press, Cambridge

Typeface Baskerville Monotype 11/12.5 pt   *System* LaTeX 2ε   [TB]

A catalogue record for this book is available from the British Library

ISBN 0 521 81294 1 hardback

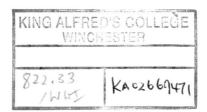

Contents

Illustrations

Contributors

LEEDS BARROLL, Professor of English, University of Maryland, Baltimore County

DAVID M. BERGERON, Professor of English, University of Kansas

DAVID BEVINGTON, Professor of English, University of Chicago

MARY BLACKSTONE, Professor of Theatre, University of Regina

ANDREW GURR, Professor of English, University of Reading

ALEXANDRA JOHNSTON, Professor of English, University of Toronto

ALEXANDER LEGGATT, Professor of English, University of Toronto

SALLY-BETH MACLEAN, Executive Editor of Records of Early English Drama, University of Toronto

MILLA RIGGIO, Professor of English, Trinity University, Hartford

MICHAEL SHAPIRO, Professor of English, University of Illinois, Urbana

SUZANNE R. WESTFALL, Professor of English and Theatre, Lafayette College

PAUL WHITFIELD WHITE, Associate Professor of English, Purdue University

Shakespeare and theatrical patronage in early modern England

Paul Whitfield White and Suzanne R. Westfall

During the past quarter of a century, the study of patronage/theatre relations in early modern England has grown immensely, partly because of the sharp increase in archival research and data collection relating to theatrical culture, and partly because of new methodologies and innovative approaches. Yet despite a number of distinguished studies focusing on individual patrons and writers and on patronage in general, the field remains without an extensive, wide-ranging, and representative study of patronage as it relates to Shakespeare and the theatrical culture of his age. In seeking to fill that void, this volume's twelve theatre historians address such questions as: What important functions did patronage have for the theatre during this period? How, in turn, did the theatre impact upon and represent patronage? In what ways do patronage, political power, and playing intersect? How did patrons and theatre artists mutually affect one another's sense of personal and professional identity? Where do paying spectators and purchasers of printed drama fit into our discussion of patronage? In what ways did patronage practices change and develop from the early Tudor period to the years in which Shakespeare was the English theatre's leading artist?

In the opening chapter, Suzanne Westfall endeavors to contextualize our study; she observes that patronage is not easily defined, especially with reference to an art form as multifaceted and socially complex as the theatre. Her discussion of the history of patronage theatre studies from Victorian times onward demonstrates the many ways in which the term has been used within the theatrical context. She argues that while nineteenth- and early twentieth-century archivists and historians published and commented insightfully on a wealth of records relevant to the royal and aristocratic sponsorship of drama, the study of patronage in general and theatrical patronage in particular has benefited significantly during the last quarter of the twentieth century from methods of inquiry and insights brought to the discussion by scholars who seem far afield from traditional theatre studies, among them Clifford Geertz, Michel Foucault, and Wolfgang Iser, from the respective disciplines of anthropology, cultural history, and reception theory. Now a more interdisciplinary and theoretically sophisticated undertaking, the study of theatrical patronage has moved beyond its early preoccupation with royal and noble sponsorship of playing; it now explores the positioning and mediating role of theatre within a complex web of interdependent, though often discordant, relationships crossing class and regional boundaries and involving kinship ties, political loyalties, and economic transactions. Westfall also shows that recent approaches to the topic have changed our view of "theatre" itself from the conventional generic confines of dialogue-centered spectacle to encompass, at one end of the spectrum, a variety of performance – masques, processions, and other quasi-dramatic entertainments – to, at the other end, drama sold and read in printed texts.

Westfall's discussion sets the stage for several clusters of essays, the first of which concentrates on Shakespeare, his immediate theatrical milieu and the publication of his plays. In "The King's Men's king's men: Shakespeare and folio patronage," David Bergeron turns to the 1623 Folio to show that theatre's entry into book publishing, like the emergence of commercial playgoing, complemented and sometimes competed with, but did not undermine, the practice of aristocratic patronage, and thereby increased the opportunities available to playwrights for support. Indeed, Bergeron indicates that the "king's men" addressed in the Folio's "Epistle Dedicatory," Lord Chamberlain William Herbert and his brother Philip, Gentleman of the King's Bedchamber, were among the Jacobean court's most active patrons of both book publishing and the public stage, and that the Lord Chamberlain, himself, was clearly instrumental in creating opportunities for theatrical artists within the printing industry, intervening on their behalf with the Stationers' Register and patronizing Jonson's *Works* of 1616 (a major event in legitimating drama as serious writing). Furthermore, Bergeron shows that, like their fellow actor Edward Alleyn who knew a thing or two about manipulating noble patrons (as Andrew Gurr's essay will later relate), the two King's Men behind the 1623 Folio, John Heminge and Henry Condell, had the future in mind in seeking Philip Herbert's patronage in addition to William's, since the younger brother was predicted to become (and in fact became in 1626) their next boss as Lord Chamberlain. Yet in their "Address to the Variety of Readers," the editors appeal assiduously for the support of book buyers, since the fate of the Folio largely rested in their hands.

The Folio editors were also aware of rival claims to the buying public's patronage, presenting themselves as rescuers of the plays from the stolen, maimed, and fraudulent versions also available on the print market.

Paul Whitfield White's chapter on "Shakespeare, the Cobhams, and the dynamics of theatrical patronage" explores a range of patronage-related issues that link Shakespeare and his fellow players to the Elizabethan Lords Cobham, particularly to William Brooke, tenth Baron Cobham, during his Lord Chamberlaincy between August 1596 and March 1597. White challenges one-dimensional accounts of Cobham as antitheatrical – evidence shows that he was actually well-qualified to administer court festivities during the years leading up to his appointment – or as an impartial/indifferent Lord Chamberlain. In an important letter virtually ignored by theatre historians, Robert Jones, the Earl of Essex's secretary, shows that Cobham was active in overseeing and intervening in court festivities, though in a manner that clearly upset members of the Essex faction, and probably also the players – Shakespeare's company it turns out – whose 1596/97 holiday season performance at court was interrupted by a staff-waving Lord Chamberlain. An analysis of the implications of this document for the theatre and politics of Cobham's Lord Chamberlaincy leads to questions about the complex web of patronage relations Shakespeare's company found itself in during the late 1590s, about playwright/player criticism of patrons (as manifested in the second *Henriad* and *Merry Wives of Windsor*), the conflicts and tensions between major figures in the patronage system (the Lord Chamberlain and his deputy the Master of the Revels), and the role of patronage drama in factional politics at court. The production of a series of Oldcastle plays by Lord Admiral Nottingham's Men, beginning with *The History of Sir John Oldcastle, Lord Cobham*, may tell us something about the broader functions and effects of patronage drama on the Cecil–Cobham/Essex rivalry at the end of Elizabeth's reign.

The intriguing question of Shakespeare's links to the Essex circle is further considered by Leeds Barroll in the following essay, although for Barroll power-brokers like the earls of Southampton, Pembroke, and Rutland, along with the Countess of Bedford, were drawn to the theatre by the sheer pleasure it could provide; politics had little, if anything, to do with it. In "Shakespeare, noble patrons, and the pleasures of 'common' playing," Barroll reappraises the rationale behind aristocratic sponsorship of the drama. While many assume that the nobility retained players simply for "magnificence," for social status, or because they were interested in staging polemical battles, Barroll explores aristocratic taste as a motive for hiring players and supporting playwrights. Beginning with a discussion of the "carnival" atmosphere of public court occasions, when the aristocracy might be constrained, by custom, to entertain strangers and be entertained by a variety of questionable characters, Barroll moves on to discuss the types of plays he believes that the aristocracy actually enjoyed and admired. During the Christmas season, Barroll argues, aristocrats were expected to associate with the commoners, including the "common" player, who did not command the same status as the court minstrel or painter. But some aristocrats, like the extended Sidney and Spenser families, the Essex and Derby/Oxford circles, seem to have supported players because their own literary tastes led them to, because they took pleasure in, theatrical performance. Most significantly, Barroll brings to our attention the fact that many women, including the Dowager Countesses of Derby and Pembroke, were instrumental in maintaining the family player troupes after their husbands died, shepherding their entertainers to new patrons. His thorough examination of the complex family relationships between and among patrons reveals once again that theatrical patronage was multifaceted and multi-purpose.

The next group of essays expands our discussion chronologically and geographically, tracing the nature and development of theatre/patronage relations at the royal court and in various provincial centers from the late fifteenth through the early seventeenth century. In "'What revels are in hand?' Marriage celebrations and patronage of the arts in Renaissance England," David Bevington and Milla Riggio focus on a type of occasion that necessitated extravagant patronage of the arts: aristocratic marriage celebrations. By comparing the wedding festivities for three of Henry VII's children (Prince Arthur in 1501, Princess Margaret in 1502, and Princess Mary in 1508) to those for James I's daughter Elizabeth over a century later (1613), they highlight several significant points of continuity and change concerning the nature of court patronage for such occasions and the role of the artists commissioned to produce the festivities. If advancing the dynastic ambitions of the royal family was a shared ideological function of the disguisings, masques, and plays designed for both early Tudor and early Stuart royal marriages, Bevington and Riggio observe a pronounced shift in the roles and attitudes of court-based artists. Specifically, the largely anonymous artists commissioned for the wedding festivities under Henry VII subsumed individual identity and expression in the higher political interests of their patrons who, while allowing some measure of artistic freedom, maintained tight control over the political contents of such entertainments.

In marked contrast a century later, court entertainers for Princess Elizabeth's wedding – Campion, Chapman, and Beaumont among them – were more conscious of their identities as artists of reputation who used their creations to comment on patronage, to advance aesthetics, and to criticize their patrons. Their work, the essay concludes, is characterized by a conflicted and ambivalent attitude towards the patronage of the governing class, reflecting a shift in literary focus from text to author.

Alexandra F. Johnston, editor-in-chief of the Records of Early English Drama project that has collected and published so many of the archives that are revolutionizing the study of Renaissance theatre, considers a different type of patron, the entire city of York. Through a detailed examination of the relationship among the city authorities, the confraternities, and the plays, Johnston traces the polemical and economic factors that led eventually to the demise of the Corpus Christi cycle in York. "The city as patron: York" also investigates an issue that Mary Blackstone pursues in the essay that follows – the relationship between crown and local authority. While many had long supposed that Tudor hegemony and Tillyard's "great chain" had enforced national interest on local populations, Johnston and Blackstone find that the politics of local patronage are far more complex. Johnston's investigation of fifteenth-century local patronage also speaks to the final essay in this volume, Alexander Leggatt's "The audience as patron: *The Knight of the Burning Pestle*." While most of the essays in this volume concentrate on patronage by the baronial class, these two are concerned with the merchant, professional, and artisan classes. The craft guilds of York and their brother businessmen in London one hundred years later affected the theatre differently, but just as significantly as did the Earl of Northumberland in his court. As we consider how patronage and power interrelated, it is vital that the "public" part of the equation be fully appreciated.

In "Theatrical patronage and the urban community during the reign of Mary," Mary A. Blackstone shifts our attention to the mid-sixteenth-century reign, precisely midway between the early Henrician and Jacobean termini of Riggio and Bevington's work, marking quite different conditions of theatrical patronage at court. Yet Blackstone, drawing on models of political power and subjection developed by Michel Foucault and Charles Phythian-Adams, extends the discussion far beyond the royal court to explore the complex array of patronage networks in the provinces, where locally based power structures overseen by town corporations and noble magnates sometimes worked in conjunction, sometimes at odds, with each other and with the central government. Theatrical entertainment functioned in several significant ways within this patronage system. In the final analysis, Blackstone proposes that unlike her brother and her father, Queen Mary inefficiently utilized patronage, theatrical and otherwise, to win broad-based noble and popular support for her policy of reunification with Rome and her marriage to Philip of Spain. The pronounced rift between her and "the temporal nobility" who refused to return church lands is addressed in the touring troupe interlude, *Health and Wealth.*

As the first essay in our final section on patrons, players, and audiences, Andrew Gurr's chapter on "Privy Councilors as theatre patrons" draws us into the heart of Elizabeth's reign when the Queen's chief political advisors at court virtually dictated the course of professional playing in and around London during a time of rapidly developing theatrical conditions, fierce opposition from the London Corporation, and division within the Privy Council itself. Gurr argues that despite the Council's official reason for protecting weekday performances of the adult companies – to prepare them for the Queen's annual entertainments at court – individual councilors, most notably Thomas Howard and Henry Carey, worked behind the scenes as well as up front to secure a place for the players in the London area. Howard and Carey adroitly used the patronage system with its kinship ties and political networking to carry out a policy that aimed to provide the Queen with the best possible theatrical entertainment at court, prevent amphitheatre closings, and exercise the dominance of their own companies (the Lord Admiral's Men and Lord Chamberlain's Men) in London during the mid-to-late 1590s. In addition to demonstrating the continuing power of aristocratic patrons after the advent of commercialism, Gurr shows the political resourcefulness of clients such as James Burbage and Edward Alleyn who divided their allegiances among two or more stage patrons in a period of intense rivalry to attract the status and protection that went with aristocratic sponsorship.

The next two chapters give more attention to individual acting companies and their relationship with aristocratic patronage. Following up on her work with Scott McMillin on *The Queen's Men and their Plays,* Sally-Beth MacLean analyzes the historical records relating to Leicester's Men, a company employing some of the nation's most important theatre producers – James Burbage, Robert Wilson, John Laneham – that first formed as Lord Robert Dudley's Men near the beginning of Queen Elizabeth's reign. Like Blackstone, MacLean is concerned with touring patterns, since the Queen's Men were, perhaps, the most widely traveled of the troupes in the 1580s. Her work (including detailed itineraries and maps) investigates the relationship between patron and player troupe by studying private and municipal accounts, asking some of the same questions that Leeds Barroll poses about patronage and taste. To what extent did the personality of the patron, or his pursuit of power, affect the repertoire, itinerary, and profits of the performers he maintained? As MacLean demonstrates, by using the Records of Early English Drama collections, we can begin to piece together a more detailed model of how and where player troupes actually operated. By linking texts with troupes, we can also begin to decode the intricate workings of ideology and patronage theatre.

Michael Shapiro adds a new dimension to our study in his consideration of patronage of the children's companies, which he shows, like other patronized entertainers, to have undergone a number of complicated developments from the early Tudor era through the first decade of James I when they fell into decline. Shapiro cites the royal performances of the Westminster grammar school boys during the 1560s to illustrate the traditional pattern of gift-exchange patronage in which the school offered plays (along with elaborately decorated manuscript copies) to the Queen as reward for her patronage of the school, the foundation of which she restored at her accession. Challenging the theory that the Paul's boys and Children of the Chapel Royal rapidly developed into crass commercial ventures during Elizabeth's reign, Shapiro proposes that gift-exchange patronage remained important, and that the income gained from box-office returns in their own playing venues may not be a simple instance of profiteering on the part of such masters as Westcote, Mulcaster, and Ferrant, but rather the necessary means to fund elaborate entertainments that they presented in tribute to Elizabeth. At the same time, the directors of such troupes sought court patronage for traditional reasons: advancement at court (John Lyly and the Earl of Oxford) and protection from enemies (Westcote, the Catholic master at Paul's). Shapiro acknowledges, however, that if the boys remained part of a ritualized gift-exchange system right to the end, their exploitation for commercial advantage was intensified during the early years of the new century when Paul's boys and the Blackfriars company fell into the hands of astute entrepreneurs who capitalized on the London playgoers' taste for satire and controversy.

As David Bergeron shows in the collection's second chapter, Heminge and Condell's "Address to a Variety of Readers" in 1623 tacitly acknowledges the theatre community's financial dependence on the general public's patronage, even if it comes many years after the fact and applies to drama in print. The implications of that dependence so far as it applies to commercialized spectatorship in the so-called "private" as well as public playhouses of London concerns Alexander Leggatt in the collection's final essay, "The audience as patron: *The Knight of the Burning Pestle*." As Leggatt demonstrates, Beaumont, Jonson, and other playwrights expressed an acute anxiety about the potential loss of artistic and interpretive control in an environment where regular playhouse patrons, by virtue of paying for dramatic fare, believed they were entitled to dictate its nature. The irony, of course, is that, as Bevington and Riggio reveal, theatre artists never had it so good in terms of artistic license; never before had accomplished writers enjoyed such unrestricted freedom to work apart from royal and aristocratic patronage. And yet, in *The Knight of the Burning Pestle*, Beaumont's raucous burlesque of playhouse audiences, we are presented with the dramatist's worst nightmare: spectators climbing onto the stage to protest a play only moments after it begins, and demanding that the actors perform a different one suiting their tastes and expectations. Leggatt argues that the play explores several problems raised by the audience as a demanding collective patron: the often unavoidable disparity between authorial intention and audience reception, the difficulty of reconciling the playwright's and players' desire for a carefully crafted artistic experience with a popular audience's demand for cheap jokes and sensationalism, and the inability to keep everyone happy when the spectatorship is demographically mixed and ideologically diverse. Like other essays in the volume, Leggatt's piece dwells on the need for patrons, as well as artists, to reinforce their sense of identity through the theatrical experience; and it explores the divisions and breakdowns within patron–client relationships. Whether we are talking about propaganda or taste in dramatic fare, artists often failed to deliver what patrons, aristocratic and popular, expected. *The Knight of the Burning Pestle* provides us with a tellingly rich and ironic example of this both in reality (it turned out to be a theatrical bust) and in its representation of failed relations between play producers and playgoers.

As much as it may be commonplace now to claim that all drama in early modern England operated within the confines of patronage, the essays in this volume attempt to fully explore that assertion. In some instances, as illustrated by the wedding masques at Henry VII's court, anonymous artisans and writers seem to have unselfconsciously labored to advance the dynastic claims of the monarch, in others they may have attempted to assert their autonomy in the face of the demands of paying spectators. Yet playwrights and players have always perceived themselves as expendable, and in early modern England where this was acutely felt patronage was a constant concern; the frequency with which the drama itself displays and interrogates this condition is a telling indication of how seriously all members of society felt it. It is our hope that these assembled essays not only demonstrate the crucial importance of patronage for the study of Tudor and early Stuart drama, but that they contribute to the ongoing research of other scholars for many years to come.

Inspired by a seminar we co-directed at the Shakespeare Association of America annual meeting of 1993, this book has accumulated many debts of gratitude during its near-decade in the making. Not the least of these is owed to the distinguished group of writers who generously accepted our invitation to contribute to this volume. Their spirit of cooperation, not to mention an almost saintly level of patience and faith in this project, was essential in seeing it develop through several phases of expansion and revision to final production. Our gratitude is also extended to several institutions which have been generous in providing financial support, including the Lafayette College Advanced Research Council, the Purdue Research Foundation, and the Purdue Medieval Studies Committee. We would like to thank our readers at Cambridge University Press for suggesting corrections and revisions which significantly improved the manuscript. Finally, for reading all or significant parts of the manuscript and offering timely advice and encouragement, we are especially grateful to Steven Putzel, Patricia Donahue, and Paula Leverage.

Note on supplementary website: For readers interested in pursuing further the topic of *Shakespeare and Theatrical Patronage in Early Modern England*, we refer them to http://icdweb.cc.purdue.edu/~pwhite/patronage, which features supplementary materials, particularly maps and appendices pertaining to Chapters 6, 7, and 9.

Theories and histories

CHAPTER I

"The useless dearness of the diamond": theories of patronage theatre

Suzanne R. Westfall

> At the political center of any complexly organized society (to narrow our focus now to that) there is both a governing elite and a set of symbolic forms expressing the fact that it is in truth governing. No matter how democratically the members of the elite are chosen (usually not very) or how deeply divided among themselves they may be (usually much more than outsiders imagine), they justify their existence and order their actions in terms of a collection of stories, ceremonies, insignia, formalities and appurtenances that they have either inherited or, in more revolutionary situations, invented. It is these – crowns and coronations, limousines and conferences – that mark the center and give what goes on there its aura of being not merely important but in some odd fashion connected with the way the world is built. The gravity of high politics and the solemnity of high worship spring from liker impulses than might first appear.[1]

Clifford Geertz, although speaking as an anthropologist about the structures of cultures, could well have been describing the way patronage and patronage theatre functioned in Shakespeare's England. The structure of Elizabeth's court affirms what Geertz notes – that, regardless of veiled factionalism, the Tudor elite, and indeed the national culture affected an image of patriotic unity. But the key word here is "affected." In actuality, this solidarity was performative; while appearing to reaffirm the hegemonic spirit, sometimes performances were transgressive, sometimes polemical, sometimes downright treasonous. For example, in 1595 the Earl of Essex, to use Paul Hammer's term 'upstaged' the Queen at her own Accession Day celebrations. In an entertainment probably written by Francis Bacon, Essex ostensibly demonstrated his devotion to the Queen, but actually emphasized his own power, which so displeased the Queen that she said "if she had thought there had been so much said of her, she would not have been there that night, and so went to

---

[1] Clifford Geertz, *Local Knowledge: Further Essays in Interpretive Anthropology* (New York: Harper Collins, 1983), 124.

bed." Nevertheless, the entertainments were "much comended" by the audience.[2]

These representational encodings so thoroughly permeated public life as to be inextricable from it. From the cult of Diana, the virgin queen, so frequently invoked by John Lyly,[3] to plays that criticized the Queen for refusing to marry or name an heir; from the ostentatious ceremonies of the Order of the Garter, to squabbles over precedence at table, as those consummate actors Woolsey and Buckingham enacted at the Field of the Cloth of Gold; from the coded insignia of the College of Heralds, which often provided a subtext to tournaments that modern readers can barely discern, to civic ceremonies blatantly portraying political figures as gods, goddesses, and holy virtues – or priests and monks as demons and vices; to the fictional hierarchies and royal characters of the Renaissance playwrights – early modern social life was filled with what Sir Thomas More called "kynges games, as it were stage plays, and for the more part plaied vpon scafoldes."[4]

Studies of literary patronage have always been somewhat more plentiful and more sophisticated than those dedicated to dramatic or theatrical patronage. Many more scholars were interested in Shakespeare's "dramatic poetry," in his relationship with Southampton, in identifying the dark lady of the sonnets, or in fantasizing about his "real" identity, than in figuring out precisely how or why the Lord Admiral made use of his players. Many more were interested in Edmund Spenser's attempts to attract powerful patrons than were examining John Bale's relationship with Cromwell. But in the new century, this landscape is rapidly changing.

In order to examine *performance*, today's scholars have embraced the interdisciplinary approaches Geertz suggests from the anthropologists' realm, approaches that must inform any cultural inquiry these days, early modern theatre history in particular. Patronage of the theatre, in particular, must be explored from a variety of perspectives, for the anthropologist views the patron–client relationship through a very different lens than does the theatre historian. There is a difference (though perhaps not so

---

[2] Paul E. F. Hammer, "Upstaging the Queen: The Earl of Essex, Francis Bacon and the Accession Day celebrations of 1595," in David Bevington and Peter Holbrook (eds.), *The Politics of the Stuart Court Masque* (Cambridge: Cambridge University Press, 1998), 41–66.
[3] For a recent overview of royal court entertainments, see Graham Parry, "Entertainment at Court," in John D. Cox and David Scott Kastan (eds.), *A New History of Early English Drama* (New York: Columbia University Press, 1997). Parry discusses Lyly on pp. 197–98. See also John Astington, *English Court Theatre 1558–1642* (Cambridge: Cambridge University Press, 1999).
[4] Thomas More, *The History of Richard III*, vol. 2 of *The Complete Works of Sir Thomas More*, ed. Richard Sylvester (New Haven: Yale University Press, 1963), 80–81.

great as we might think) between a Yoruba villager and a seventeenth-century English craftsman, between Hrothgar the ring-giver of *Beowulf* and the CEO of an American corporation. To be sure, patronage remains vividly with us in a number of incarnations, all demonstrating to various degrees the pragmatic nature of the beast, and the ideology of generosity: in Moscow, Sicily, Beijing, and Chinatowns, various Mafia-like organizations continue to structure themselves around the *patrone*; Bill Gates and Ted Turner raise philanthropic largess to new heights; corporate logos are splashed across sports complexes and PBS programming; Britain at least establishes an official National Theatre, but the Tory government cuts its largess to save money; and in America the NEA withholds funds effectively to silence or censor artists.

Not only is theatre itself an interdisciplinary art, but it also comprises several ideological binaries that necessitate such a broad view. It is both public and private, text (sometimes) and context, literary art and plastic art, commodity and the labor that produces it – labor that encompasses the carpenters, tailors, writers, actors, designers, and moneyed patrons. In addition, patronage theatre produces so much more "product" than mere text; it also delivers spectacle, visual art, music, throngs called spectators, celebratory mood, and movement. By drawing from theory developed during the last century in many different disciplines, we can better comprehend the conditions and contexts of "patronage theatre," for the artists and patrons of the early modern period were engaged in an elaborate semiotic that reflected, reinforced, and in a way created the power of the aristocratic class. Hence, my title "The useless dearness of the diamond," a concept Foucault used to explore how and why a lovely, but perfectly unnecessary bit of crystallized carbon could become such a numinous symbol, such a treasured object.

I model my term "patronage theatre" on Robert Evans's description of the spectacularly successful poet/playwright Ben Jonson. As Evans says,

I do not, for instance, want to call Jonson a "poet dependent on patronage," ... [for] it stresses his dependency in a manner that fundamentally simplifies the complex nature of his relations with superiors. I want to suggest that he was a writer whose life and works were radically conditioned by a culture rooted in hierarchical relations, and by using "patronage" as an adjective throughout this book, I want to imply that patronage during the English Renaissance was more than a matter of economic give-and-take, that it was basic to the period's life and psychology and crucially shaped Jonson's attitudes and experience.[5]

[5] Robert Evans, *Ben Jonson and the Poetics of Patronage* (Lewisburg: Bucknell University Press, 1989), 9. Evans provides one of the most thorough surveys of the literature on patronage theatre. See p. 269, nn. 1 and 2.

Shakespeare and Jonson have been focal points for patronage studies for some time;[6] Jonson and his sometime partner Inigo Jones in particular provide a wildly sensational, aesthetically complex and, most importantly, well-documented occasion of patronage at the court of King James. But Evans's observations, I believe, extend beyond Jonson (as unique an artist as he may be), to encompass patronage theatre in general during the sixteenth and seventeenth centuries.

In the following pages my purpose will be to frame patronage studies, to focus on ways in which theatrical patronage in Tudor England "connected with the way the world is built," as Geertz puts it. Rather than providing an exhaustive historical overview, I will focus on a discussion of theoretical approaches, and show how the combination of post-structuralist theory and careful archival collection has affected the field. From the historical, biographical, and bibliographic scholars who have edited source documents from the turn of the last century through the present, to the contemporary theorists and philosophers who have given us newly ground epistemological lenses through which to view the subtexts (or the "micropolitics" as Evans calls it) of patronage theatre, the parameters of patronage studies as a field of inquiry within cultural studies have changed considerably. Here, I would like to explore – and perhaps challenge – conventional conceptions of theatrical patronage, and to discuss some of the more prominent critical and theoretical studies of patronage, a remarkably interdisciplinary field to which historians (intellectual, social, art, theatre, and music), anthropologists, sociologists,

---

[6] What Evans did for Ben Jonson as a "patronage poet," Alvin Kernan does for William Shakespeare in *The Playwright as Magician* (New Haven: Yale University Press, 1979), and more recently in *Shakespeare, The King's Playwright: Theater in the Stuart Court 1603–1613* (New Haven: Yale University Press, 1995). While Kernan is decidedly anti-new historicist, he nevertheless concurs with most scholars about the recursive nature of patronage, that it shapes and is in turn shaped by political realities (see pp. 184–85). Donna B. Hamilton also focuses on patronage in *Shakespeare and the Politics of Protestant England* (Lexington: University Press of Kentucky, 1992). Of the many books about Jonson's life, art, and relationship with the court, a few very important works focus extensively on the function of patronage in Jonson's career. See, for example, Stephen Orgel, *The Jonsonian Masque* (Cambridge, MA: Harvard University Press, 1965), or *The Illusion of Power: Political Theater in the English Renaissance* (Berkeley: University of California Press, 1975), or, with Roy Strong, *The Theater of the Stuart Court; Including the Complete Designs for Productions at Court, for the most part in the Collection of the Duke of Devonshire, together with their Texts and Historical Documentation* (Berkeley: University of California Press, 1973); Leah Marcus, *The Politics of Mirth: Jonson, Herrick, Milton, Marvell and the Defense of Old Holiday Pastimes* (Chicago: University of Chicago Press, 1986); John Gordon Sweeney, *Jonson and the Psychology of Public Theater: To Coin the Spirit, Spend the Soul* (Princeton: Princeton University Press, 1985); Jonathan Haynes, *The Social Relations of Jonson's Theater* (New York: Cambridge University Press, 1992); David Scott Kastan and Peter Stallybrass (eds.), *Staging the Renaissance: Reinterpretations of Elizabethan and Jacobean Drama* (New York: Routledge, 1991); J. R. Mulryne and Margaret Shewring (eds.), *Theater and Government Under the Early Stuarts* (Cambridge: Cambridge University Press, 1993).

psychologists, archaeologists, and literary critics have made significant contributions.

Theatre history is a unique discipline, far different from its sister, literary history. In his essay "Theater History as an Academic Discipline," Ron Vince suggests that "historical investigation as normally practiced proceeds in two stages: the collection, organization, and description of data, selected on the basis of hypotheses or assumptions either conscious or unconscious; and the interpretation of data at the level of 'cultural–historical integration,' a concept drawn from the science of archaeology."[7] And indeed, during the nineteenth and early twentieth centuries, scores of gentleman-scholars dedicated themselves to the pleasant and profitable occupation of fulfilling the first part of this process. Following in the footsteps of chroniclers like John Stowe and Edward Halle, they pored over the archives and personal papers of various members of the British gentry and aristocracy. Publishers such as the Malone Society, the Roxburgh Club, the various volumes of the *Victoria Histories* of each shire, as well as local history journals like the *Antiquarian Repertory* printed these studies (often for limited memberships), frequently including invaluable quotations from unpublished letters and account books, biographies or family histories, and occasionally drawings or blueprints of manors that no longer exist.

Certainly no Marxists, these historiographers seem to have felt a profound nostalgia and hence a need to preserve a record of English life (particularly aristocratic life) as reinforcement for the politics of empire. Few comment critically on the materials they were collecting and publishing; rather than contextualizing or analyzing their discoveries, they were content to preserve and to pass on to posterity records of the public and private lives of members of the upper classes, and occasionally, like Joseph Strutt,[8] the customs and entertainments of the lower. That indefatigable burrower in archives, John Payne Collier, was so obsessed with this activity that he produced a dozen monographs dealing with manuscript records, frequently resorting to forgery in order to produce abundant source materials.[9] Although these publications were not called at the time "patronage studies," such antiquarian works clearly began to

---

[7] R. W. Vince, "Theater History as an Academic Discipline," in Thomas Postlewait and Bruce A. McConachie (eds.), *Interpreting the Theatrical Past* (Iowa City: University of Iowa Press, 1989), 1–18; 14–15.

[8] Joseph Strutt, *The Sports and Pastimes of the People of England: Including the Rural and Domestic Recreations* (London: W. Tegg, 1855).

[9] A. Freeman, "Scholarship, Forgery, and Fictive Invention: John Payne Collier," *Library* 15.1 (March 1993), 1–23.

collect information on the subject which would develop, beginning with
E. K. Chambers and W. W. Gregg, into more detailed studies of social
history, cultural studies, and most important here, theatre history.

While biographical and historical approaches to literature reigned
during the nineteenth to early twentieth centuries, drama was perceived,
for the most part, as a seductive bastard child of literature. During
the thirty plus years in which New Criticism was the predominant
methodology, most critics (with notable exceptions such as Nicoll, Nagler,
Wickham, Hardison, Styan, and Brockett) turned their attention almost
exclusively to the dramatic texts, which may have contributed significantly to *literary* history, but was almost disastrous for *theatrical* studies.[10]
For many years, theatrical activities that lacked dramatic text (such as
pageantry, ceremony, folk dramas, and rituals) were largely ignored,
although some, like Wickham and Anglo continued to analyze these
forms.[11] Teachers focused on teaching Shakespeare's plays as poetry, or
"theatre of the mind," and scores of medieval plays (interludes, moral
plays, mysteries, miracles, and moralities) were pronounced "primitive"
and "boringly didactic," primarily because any cultural or performative
context was utterly ignored in favor of textual analysis.

At the same time, however, scholars like E. K. Chambers had begun
to focus a different kind of attention on performance, and in the context of historical studies of medieval and Renaissance drama, to take a
keen interest not only in collecting and printing information from private, civic, and ecclesiastical accounts of theatrical activity, but also in
describing the contexts of performance in the specific period. Theatre
historians still begin with Chambers, and the data he collected (printed,
ironically, in appendices) continues to be central to modern scholars
who reassess his conclusions based on additional data as well as on different assumptions. Recent publications, such as the Records of Early
English Drama volumes and *Newsletters*, reflect the priorities of these
modern scholars, making what was once thought material for appendices
into primary concerns. This painstaking and vital information-collecting
and publication – as well as the tabulation of plays (Stratman), writers,

---

[10] I distinguish here between "drama," the page, and "theatre," the stage. More and more over
the past two decades it has become obvious that many theatrical activities were unscripted,
and consequently we have to refer to other sorts of documents than dramatic texts in order to
analyze these activities. Ceremonies, disguisings, the offerings of tumblers, minstrels, and fools –
all these constitute theatre and are crucial to our understanding of early modern culture, yet
none of them can be documented by scripts, and few of them were even described by audience
members, though they were very frequently noted in financial accounts.

[11] Glynne Wickham, *Early English Stages*, 3 vols. (London: Routledge and Kegan Paul, 1959), and
Sydney Anglo, *Spectacle, Pageantry, and Early Tudor Policy* (Oxford: Clarendon Press, 1969).

acting companies (Murray and Gurr), catalogues of theatrical activities (Lancashire),[12] and detailed studies of individual troupes (Blackstone, McMillin, and MacLean) – present us with rich hoards that are mined in various ways by those interested in patronage studies. Firmly based on records, chronicles, and histories, our considerations can now move to process and context, particularly as we turn from the theatrical event itself to the conditions affecting its creation.

But as scholars and critics turn to these contextual matters, databases, indexes, catalogues, and publisher's backlists continue to list books that concern patronage, even literary or theatrical patronage, under the category "social history," that hybrid of history and sociology that gives a home to many cultural studies that have no other label to claim them. Reflecting (or perhaps causing?) this categorical displacement is the fact that the phenomenon of patronage continues to be approached from a great number of theoretical perspectives: biographical and historical critics may have led the way, but feminist, Marxist, new historicist, cultural materialist, semiotic, structuralist, deconstructionist, and psychoanalytic critics have also made significant contributions. To complicate matters further, in Shakespeare's England patronage could originate from a number of different sources and motivations: aristocratic, ecclesiastical, educational, and civic. All these groups had specific political agendas, and all used performance at different times in different ways and for different purposes.

Before continuing to survey theoretical attitudes, it may be helpful to examine a few definitions of the term "patronage," starting with the standard *Oxford English Dictionary* formulation. Early references, from the thirteenth-century *Sir Gawain* through Wycliffe, Lydgate, and of course Spenser show that already patronage was thought of in terms of ownership and protection. Wycliffe seems to sound early a Protestant alarm that would remain unheard for three centuries when he cautioned that "crist and his apostlis techen vs to lyuc beter þan þes patrouns of þes newe ordris." A patron could also be thought of as one who "supports with his custom a commercial undertaking," a meaning Ben Jonson had in mind when Volpone disguised as a mountebank salutes his audience as "my worthy patrons." By the latter half of the sixteenth

[12] See, for example, Ian Lancashire, *Dramatic Texts and Records of Britain: A Chronological Topography to 1558* (Toronto: University of Toronto Press, 1984); Carl J. Stratman, *Bibliography of English printed tragedy, 1565–1900* (Carbondale: Southern Illinois University Press, 1966), and his *Bibliography of Medieval Drama*, 2nd edn., 2 vols. (New York: Frederick Ungar, 1972); John Tucker Murray, *English Dramatic Companies, 1558–1642* (New York: Houghton Mifflin, 1910); and Andrew Gurr, *The Shakespearian Playing Companies* (New York: Oxford University Press, 1996).

century, this meaning of "patron" was becoming more and more important, as theatre became more and more commodified, as the patronage of
the public theatre vacillated between aristocratic patrons and the paying
public.[13]

We all know that Shakespeare was a member of the Lord Chamberlain's Men and later the King's Men, signaling for some critics a renewed
interest in and commitment to theatre patronage in the royal household.
But during the earlier part of the last century, few literary critics were
interested in pursuing exactly what such patronage entailed, particularly
in relationship to the so-called "public" theatre. It has become commonplace for writers to acknowledge that virtually all players (or at least those
who wished to be exempted from the acts against vagrancy) wore the livery of a patron, but most did not speculate on precisely what that patronage meant either to the player or to the aristocrat who acted as patron.
Did the relationship imply political protection? Guarantee economic se-
curity? Indicate simple largess? From the historian's perspective, Werner
Gundersheimer states the case succinctly: "The political and social or-
derings in European societies in the Renaissance are mirrored in their
structures of patronage. Could Shakespeare's awareness of this point have
led him to prefer the support of the London crowds to that of a single
patronus?"[14] Had Gundersheimer been a theatre historian he would have
realized that Shakespeare did not "prefer" either elite or public support,
he enjoyed both simultaneously. Guy Fitch Lytle is more specific in his
definition: "Patronage in the sixteenth century was an inherited muster
of laws, properties, obligations, social ligatures, ambitions, religious activities, and personal decisions that kept a complex society working."[15]

Stephen Orgel has led us through the complexities of aesthetics and
personality in his studies of Inigo Jones and Ben Jonson at the court of
James I,[16] while David Bergeron has examined the social and political
life of James's family, and how that life was reflected and refracted in contemporary plays.[17] But few theatre historians have been as bold as have
social and political historians. For example, Gundersheimer, focusing on

[13] See the essays by Michael Shapiro and Alexander Leggatt in this volume.
[14] Werner Gundersheimer, "Patronage in the Renaissance: An Exploratory Approach," in Guy
Fitch Lytle and Stephen Orgel (eds.), *Patronage in the Renaissance* (Princeton: Princeton University
Press, 1981), 3–23; 23.
[15] Guy Fitch Lytle, "Religion and the Lay Patron in Reformation England," in *Patronage in the
Renaissance*, 65–114.
[16] Stephen Orgel, *The Illusion of Power.*
[17] David Bergeron, *Shakespeare's Romances and the Royal Family* (Lawrence: Kansas University Press,
1985), and *Royal Family Royal Lovers* (Columbia: Missouri University Press, 1991).

Italy, begins his article "Patronage in the Renaissance: An Exploratory Approach" with the sweeping statement that "Patronage, broadly defined as 'the action of a patron in supporting, encouraging, or countenancing a person, institution, work, art, etc.,' has been clearly established as one of the dominant social processes of pre-industrial Europe." He further asks, "Can there be a Renaissance society without patronage?"[18] Art historians, particularly those who study Italy, would be quick to answer this question in the negative. And we cannot forget the observations of a fundamental text in early modern social history, Machiavelli's *The Prince*:

> A prince also should demonstrate that he is a lover of talent by giving recognition to men of ability and by honouring those who excel in a particular field ... He should, besides this, at the appropriate times of the year, keep the populace occupied with festivals and spectacles.[19]

More and more we are realizing that early modern England was indeed formed by interlocking patterns of patronage–client relationships, a network that bound Privy Councilor to Queen, and local government to central, as Richard Dutton has explained.[20]

These patronage networks, weaving communities together from the kitchen scullions in the great households of noble men and women to the Bishops in their palaces and the Monarch on her throne, seem to create a hierarchy rather like that described by Tillyard in his *Elizabethan World Picture*, a work that has been widely discredited in the past thirty years.[21] The intertwining system of patronage does indeed create a hierarchy, but Renaissance men and women did not assume the order to be either natural or divinely inspired, as Tillyard proposes. Rather, they understood this hierarchy to be fluid and reactive; patrons shift their relationships with those above and those below them, constantly adjusting system equilibrium. The creation of the Queen's Men from the *crème de la crème* of other competing companies in 1583, so ably explored by McMillin and MacLean, is a clear representation of such adjustment, with far-reaching causes and consequences.[22]

[18] Gundersheimer, "Patronage in the Renaissance," 3–4.

[19] Niccolo Machiavelli, *The Prince*, ed. and trans. Peter Bondanella (Oxford: Oxford University Press, 1984), 76.

[20] Richard Dutton, *Mastering the Revels: The Regulation and Censorship of English Renaissance Drama* (Iowa City: University of Iowa Press, 1991); Linda Levy Peck, "Court Patronage and Government Policy: The Jacobean Dilemma," in *Patronage in the Renaissance*, 27–46; 31.

[21] Eustace Mandeville Wetenhall Tillyard, *The Elizabethan World Picture* (London: Chatto and Windus, 1943).

[22] Scott McMillin and Sally-Beth MacLean, *The Queen's Men and Their Plays* (Cambridge: Cambridge University Press, 1999).

Perhaps the most violent (in all senses of the word) example of the reorganization of patronage networks is the English Civil War, in which Oliver Cromwell's iconoclasts (I use the word in its original sense – destroyers of icons) demonstrated quite vividly their contempt for the signs of patronage. Although most Protestant reformers, including Calvin and Luther, had supported social hierarchies while razing ecclesiastical ones, Cromwell's armies demolished and despoiled a variety of the arti- facts of patronage, from noblemen themselves to their homes to religious artwork, visual and visceral manifestations of patronage of the arts as well as "graven images." And in their most revolutionary attack on the pa- tronage systems that had entangled and oppressed them for so long, they "defaced" the supreme icon, the fountainhead of patronage, the King.

Martin Butler has focused on this period, scrutinizing the theatre scene of 1632–42, and pointing out that, far from retreating into fantasy entertainments as has so often been thought (Foucault's "uselessly dear diamonds"), theatre during this period was in fact intensely political, and that various patrons with particular agendas at court were using the theatre, as they had for so many years, as another front on the battlefield for the hearts and minds of the people, as another way of knitting country interests to court. He is particularly interested in the heterogeneity of Caroline audiences, which he characterizes as "crossed by a network of friendship and kinship the extraordinary complexity of which must have made the environment at once public and intimate."[23] Once again, this complexity mirrors the structure of the patronage system. These observations have also been made by Paul Whitfield White in *Theatre and Reformation*, and in this volume Mary Blackstone reiterates Butler's ideas about the variety of audience responses to polemical theatre.

These scholars, seventy years after Chambers, have begun to exploit his groundbreaking work in *The Mediaeval Stage* and *The Elizabethan Stage* in very different ways, to review and rethink traditional approaches to theatre history, and to investigate cultural history and political contexts, a direction Chambers himself had indicated in his *Notes on the History of the Revels Office under the Tudors* in 1906.[24] Glynne Wickham, for example, building on Chambers, produced *Early English Stages* and *The Medieval Theatre*,[25] works that consider theatre history in the broader context of

---

[23] Martin Butler, *Theater and Crisis 1632–42* (Cambridge: Cambridge University Press, 1984), 133.

[24] E. K. Chambers. *The Elizabethan Stage*, 4 vols. (Oxford: Clarendon Press, 1923); *The Mediaeval Stage*, 2 vols. (Oxford: Clarendon Press, 1903); *Notes on the History of the Revels Office under the Tudors* (London: A. H. Bullen, 1906).

[25] Glynne Wickham, *Early English Stages* and *The Medieval Theatre* (Cambridge: Cambridge University Press, 1987).

social, economic, and art history and therefore turn serious attention to the uses and functions of patronage. At about the same time, source-document collecting, collating and publishing itself began to experience a renaissance. Following in the footsteps of the Malone Society, the Records of Early English Drama Project (REED) began an ambitious program to construct an inventory, shire by shire, of the public and private records of the United Kingdom, sifting through millions of references to extract references to dramatic texts and theatrical activities. This project, more than any other scholarly endeavor, has provided models and materials to extend our studies of theatre. So, by the eighties and nineties, scholars ready to emulate and exploit REED volumes frequently return to those nineteenth-century antiquarians who preserved precious information that would serve many of our new endeavors.

We have learned that from the very beginning of the Tudor dynasty, as early as Henry VII's Burgundian wedding revels at his newly-formed court,[26] theatre and theatre artists had been used by patrons and had themselves used patrons in a variety of complex fashions; both parties could, to use Stephen Greenblatt's term, "self-fashion" through the sign systems of both theatrical art and socio-political ideologies. Indeed, the fundamental structures of patronage, politics, and maintenance were so intrinsic to the culture of Tudor England, that all, from the servants to the sovereigns, were creatures of the paradigm, which, through overdeterminism rather than through the base/superstructure model suggested by Tillyard, forged their social and political relationships and penetrated their very psychology. In "Politics and Community in Elizabethan London," Frank Foster points out that virtually all power and exchanges of wealth functioned through various strata of patronage.[27] Theatre in this period functions as what Althusser calls "ideological state apparatuses," or ISAs – social institutions (ecclesiastical, familial, educational, legal, and cultural) that legitimize the state and the sovereign, that predispose rather than coerce the public to subscribe to "socially acceptable ideas,"[28] making these ideas seem natural rather than constructed.

[26] Anglo's study, *Spectacle, Pageantry and Early Tudor Policy* provides a thorough and thought-provoking survey of royal entertainments at the turn of the sixteenth century, combined with a cultural studies approach that demonstrates clearly how theatre and ideology have been, since the earliest Tudor monarch, comfortable bedfellows. See also Alistair Fox, *Politics and Literature in the Reigns of Henry VII and Henry VIII* (Oxford: Blackwell, 1989).

[27] Frank Foster, "Politics and Community in Elizabethan London," in Frederick Cople Jaher, ed. *The Rich, the Well Born, and the Powerful: Elites and Upper Classes in History* (Chicago: University of Illinois Press, 1973).

[28] Louis Althusser, "Ideology and Ideological State Apparatuses," in *Lenin and Philosophy and Other Essays* (London: New Left Books, 1971), 127–86.

But rather than Althusser's notion of a hegemonic, monolithic system of ISAs, what we seem to have in Tudor England are a multiplicity of ISAs, sometimes competing, sometimes confederated, created by various patrons in order to promote a range of religious, social, and political platforms.

Even within the early modern period itself, the ideology of patronage in England changed greatly, suggested by the fact that an unpatronized player in the sixteenth century could be prosecuted under the vagrancy laws, yet by the eighteenth century Dr. Johnson could complain to Lord Chesterfield that a patron was "one who looks with unconcern on a man struggling for life in the water, and when he has reached ground encumbers him with help."[29] Even though Samuel Johnson undervalued patronage, Ben Jonson made a very fine living as the official author of court entertainments for his patron James I. Dr. Johnson's antipathy notwithstanding, patronage was, for seventeenth-century writers, a fundamental necessity. As Kernan puts it:

Ninety percent of all published books appeared with a dedication to an actual or a prospective patron. In late Tudor times about 250 works were dedicated to Elizabeth I alone and similar numbers to her favorite, the earl of Leicester, and her secretary William Cecil, Lord Burleigh. Over a twenty-year period at the end of the sixteenth and the beginning of the seventeenth centuries there were 80 dedications to the Sidney and Herbert families, the most generous literary patrons of their age. In a time when there were too many writers and too few patrons, the search for patrons never ceased.[30]

One of the dedications to Leicester, a very active patron of theatre, describes specifically the special relationship of artist to patron: "Neither Princes maye live cleare and known to posteritie wythoute the penne and helping hande of learned Arte, neyther men excelling learning, woulde be either in lyfe reputed or spoken of after death, withoute the countenaunce, defence, and patronage of noble Peeres."[31] We must, of course, acknowledge the performative nature of these sorts of sycophantic appeals. In contrast, many artists, Jonson and Shakespeare among them, had far more critical attitudes toward patronage; the patronage artists in *Timon of Athens* are parasites, as are Volpone's retained entertainers.

---

[29] James Boswell, *Life of Johnson*, 2 vols. (Oxford: Oxford University Press, 1924). Unlike Ben Jonson, Samuel Johnson had nothing positive to say about patronage. In *The Vanity of Human Wishes* he includes patrons in the "ills the scholar's life assails," and in the preface to his *Dictionary* defines a patron as "commonly a wretch who supports with insolence and is paid with flattery."

[30] Kernan, *Shakespeare*, 171.   [31] Ibid., 177.

And indeed, by the end of Charles I's reign, the patronage system had become so corrupt that it led to public disdain.[32]

One of the richest theoretical sources for patronage studies has been anthropological study. Almost since the beginning of anthropology as a discipline, kinship systems, and patron–client relationships have formed an integral part of the anthropological and sociological literature, fundamental to the primal cultures and corporate structures they study. Up until the late sixties, however, literary critics often overlooked this work, perhaps because they were reluctant to view so-called "first-world" cultures like the British and the American as analogous to the primal "third-world" cultures that form most ethnographies. Potlatch (ritualized gift-giving), after all, is a far cry from largess or office politics. Or is it?

Studies like S. N. Eisenstadt and L. Roniger's *Patrons, Clients, and Friends: Interpersonal Relations and the Structure of Trust in Society* tend to make many of the same observations about ancient and modern cultures in Europe, Asia, and South America that I make here about early modern England. Among the basic characteristics of patron–client relationships, for example, they explain:

The interaction on which these relations are based is characterized by the simultaneous exchange of different types of resources – above all, instrumental and economic as well as political ones (support, loyalty, votes, protection) on the one hand, and promises of reciprocity, solidarity and loyalty on the other. Ideally, a strong element of unconditionality and of long-range credit is built into these relations … It is often very strongly related to conceptions of personal identity (above all of personal honour, personal value or face-saving) and of obligations, and it is also evident in the presumed existence in such relations of some, even if very ambivalent, personal "spiritual" attachment between patron and clients. At the same time, relations established between patron and clients are not fully legal or contractual; they are often opposed to the official laws of the country and they are based much more on "informal" – although very strongly binding – understandings. Despite their seemingly binding, long-range, almost (in their ideal portrayal) life-long, endurance, patron–client relations are entered into, at least in principle, voluntarily, and can, officially at least, be abandoned voluntarily … Last and not least patron–client relations are based on a very strong element of inequality and of differences in power between patrons and clients.[33]

---

[32] Jaher, *The Rich, the Well Born, and the Powerful*, III, 163. This volume provides a particularly valuable study from an historic and sociological perspective of the patronage network and its abuses.

[33] S. N. Eisenstadt and L. Roniger, *Patrons, Clients, and Friends: Interpersonal Relations and the Structure of Trust in Society* (Cambridge: Cambridge University Press, 1984), 48–49.

This definition of patronage clearly applies to the relationships among the monarch, the ruling classes, and their maintained servants, both noble and common, as I have described at length elsewhere.[34] Noble patrons exchanged money and/or protection for art, and prided themselves on the number and quality of retainers they maintained, a pride that frequently led to excessive ostentation for which they were sometimes called to account. Further, as Paul Whitfield White has demonstrated, the patron–client relationship was also often characterized by shared political and religious beliefs. We have known for years that "bilious Bale" and his "felowes" worked for Thomas Cromwell during the 1530s, with his virulently anti-Catholic *Kynge Johan*, performed at Canterbury in the household of Archbishop Cranmer, forming almost a model of the political use of the stage. Bale's other extant plays, *Three Laws*, *God's Promises*, *Johan Baptystes Preachyng*, and *The Temptation of Our Lord* clearly toe the royal and Cromwellian party line, whilst the titles of the lost plays (*Concerning the Deceptions of the Papists*, *On the Papist Sects*, *The Knaveries of Thomas Becket*, for example) leave little to the imagination about Bale's religious opinions.[35]

Of course the religious card could be played both ways. John Lyly, who counted the Catholic Earl of Oxford among his patrons, seems to try to temper the Queen's attitudes by recommending tolerance toward Catholics in *Endymion* and *Midas*.[36] Sir Richard Cholemeley's players, who performed *King Lear* and *Pericles* for the household of Sir John Yorke circa 1609–10 got into serious trouble with the Star Chamber for their recusant interpretations of plays, suggesting that Shakespeare's plays might be construed in ways sympathetic to the sufferings of the northern Catholics.[37] Just two years later, the same Sir John was once again in hot water for harboring priests and sponsoring a seditious interlude as well as a forbidden saint's play at his household; these revels seem to create public space for recusant festivity, including fireworks, lightning, thunder, and the expulsion of known anti-Catholics who later testified

---

[34] Suzanne Westfall, *Patrons and Performance: Early Tudor Household Revels* (Oxford: Clarendon Press, 1990), 87.

[35] Paul Whitfield White, *Theatre and Reformation: Protestantism, Patronage and Playing in Tudor England* (Cambridge: Cambridge University Press, 1993), 12–27.

[36] David Bevington, "Lyly's *Endymion* and *Midas*: The Catholic Question in England," *Comparative Drama* 32 (1998), 26–46.

[37] Mashahiro Takenaka, "The Cholemeley Players and the Performance of King Lear in Yorkshire in 1609–10," paper given at Lancastrian Shakespeare Conference, Lancaster University 21–23 July 1999. See also *Star Chamber Accounts* (London: Public Record Office), Stack 18 19/10, fos. 51–56.

that the Church of England had been ridiculed.[38] Even Shakespeare has been claimed as a playwright at least sympathetic to the recusancy, with patronage ties to the Houghton family.[39]

And, of course, the relationships were fluid, as artists negotiated for more generous or powerful patrons, or abandoned those whose star had fallen. For example, when Essex fell from the Queen's grace, those he maintained in his offices and through his power quickly scrambled for safe ground, taking on other patrons in an attempt to re-stabilize their own lives.[40] As Kernan points out, "Robert Greene addressed 16 different great ones in his 17 published books, while Thomas Lodge tried 12 patrons in the period 1584–96."[41] On the other side of the contract, aristocratic patrons would seek to attract men and women who could serve them well, gathering more power as they gathered more retainers within their spheres of influence. In some cases, successful artists could play patrons off against one another. The Bassano family gathered as much as they could from Henry VIII (including residence in the Charterhouse, which had been harvested by the king at the dissolution), before heading back to more lucrative and prestigious employment with the Doge of Venice, then returning after Henry granted the family a monopoly for trading in Gascon wine.[42]

Grace E. Goodell, in "Paternalism, Patronage, and Potlatch: The Dynamics of Giving and Being Given To," elaborates on the anthropological perspective. Besides providing a comprehensive review of ethnographies that address this phenomenon, she carefully distinguishes between paternalism, which robs clients of freedom, autonomy, choice, and responsibility (a type of patronage that seems to characterize British behavior toward colonial populations), and patronage *per se*, which offers "mutually binding obligations, [in which] the patron and client can hold one another accountable." This sense of patronage seems more useful in the theatrical context, when we are considering not only the market value of the artifact, but also the increasing autonomy of the artists in the later Tudor period as they acquired public as well as private patrons. In addition, Goodell believes that this reciprocity allows the client to

---

[38] Phebe Jensen, "Recusancy, Festivity and Community: The Simpsons at Gowlthwaite Hall," paper given at Lancastrian Shakespeare Conference, Lancaster University, 21–23 July 1999.

[39] E. A. J. Honigmann, *Shakespeare: The "Lost Years"* (Totawa, NJ: Barnes and Noble, 1985); Eric Sams, *The Real Shakespeare: Retrieving the Early Years, 1564–1594* (New Haven: Yale University Press, 1995); Park Honan, *Shakespeare: A Life* (Oxford: Clarendon Press, 1999).

[40] See the essay by Leeds Barroll in this volume.   [41] Kernan, *Shakespeare*, 171.

[42] Westfall, *Patrons and Performance*, 87.

"initiate service to his patron, obligating the latter to respond. This gives the client political leverage." Later Goodell echoes Eisenstadt's perception that "the patron is accessible to his client; the latter plays off patrons, shops around for new ones, if need be, goes over one patron's head to *his* patron, or acquires more leverage by becoming a patron to others himself."[43] Once again we can see that these perceptions apply with equal validity to the history of theatrical patronage.

Goodell's explanation of potlatch as a "redistributive mechanism" that "hinges on common values" which "enables it to bind giver and receiver, who cosponsor the giving" seems to describe accurately the social concept of largess; she goes on to discuss more altruistic giving (analogous to almsgiving in the noble households) and the boasting associated with potlatch, which recalls the "flyting" matches of the court, and certainly pertains to aristocratic jockeying for position and precedence.[44] In her engaging study *Cultural Aesthetics: Renaissance Literature and the Practice of Social Ornament*, Patricia Fumerton connects this redistribution of wealth more concretely to early modern England and to art. Through her analysis of all sorts of gift-giving, from miniatures to banquet foods to children in marriage, Fumerton shows that the confusion here of objects, values, contracts, and sexes (establishing the further etymological link between 'generosity' and 'gender') characterizes all systems of gift. For the gift ring is a complete cultural experience that through the act of donation at once generates, expresses, and contains every aspect of the community: economic, legal, social, political, religious, and – not the least – aesthetic.[45] Ideology, hegemony, political hierarchy – all these are served by networks of patron–client gift exchange.

The words of Clifford Geertz, with which I began this inquiry, suggest how conflicted and problematic the relationships among artists and their patrons tended to be, and how dependent all were on the symbols and icons of power to convey to audiences a specific aesthetic or ideology, whether idiosyncratic to a particular patron or general to prevailing philosophies of the Crown. In their quest to convince all sorts of audiences that "whatever is, is right," both patrons and artists conjured Foucault's "three great functions" (political, aesthetic, and economic power) to strut and fret upon the stage. And here the "whatever" could indeed be a

[43] Grace E. Goodell, "Paternalism, Patronage, and Potlatch: The Dynamics of Giving and Being Given To," *Current Anthropology* 26:2 (Apr. 1985), 247–66, 252–53.

[44] Goodell, "Paternalism, Patronage, and Potlatch," 256–57.

[45] Patricia Fumerton, *Cultural Aesthetics: Renaissance Literature and the Practice of Social Ornament* (Chicago: University of Chicago Press, 1991), 35.

particularly loose and floating signifier, from the religious polemics of John Bale's *Kynge Johan*, to the consequences of regicide (surely a particularly resonant issue for James I) in Shakespeare's *Macbeth*, to the divine right of hierarchy in Heywood's seemingly innocuous *Play of the Weather*. For early modern patronage theatre was almost always both didactic and conspicuously consumptive, the embodiment of Foucault's concept of the "useless dearness of the diamond."[46]

Geertz further challenges us in his essay "Blurred Genres: The Refiguration of Social Thought," of which the title alone indicates the predominant methodology and aim of patronage studies for the last twenty years. Writing about the increasingly interdisciplinary methodologies of his own discipline, Geertz suggests that

> some of those fit to judge work of this kind [analyzing cultures as "theatre states"] ought to be humanists who reputedly know something about what theatre and mimesis and rhetoric are, and not just with respect to my work but to that of the whole steadily broadening stream of social analysis in which the drama analogy is, in one form or another, governing. At a time when social scientists are chattering about actors, scenes, plots, performances, and personae, and humanists are mumbling about motives, authority, persuasion, exchange and hierarchy, the line between the two, however comforting to the puritan on the one side and the cavalier on the other, seems uncertain indeed.[47]

The invitation Geertz extends here, even in his allusion to the English Civil War, that violent intermission in the pageant of English theatre history, calls attention to the uniqueness of performance and the ubiquity of theatrical metaphors; scores of theatre historians have responded to this call.

Ten years before the publication of *Local Knowledge*, Michel Foucault had produced his seminal studies *The Archaeology of Knowledge*, *The Order of Things*, and *Discipline and Punish*, inaugurating our fascination with the substructures of power and power relationships, particularly as they apply to the commodification of art and labor. This work (though unappreciated by many Marxists, who object to the diminishment of *agency*), which views historical discontinuity in such an innovative manner, influenced Stephen Greenblatt when he came to write *Renaissance Self-Fashioning*, the volume that gave many of us in literary and theatrical studies a local habitation and a name – "new historicism" – that has complicated and of course problematized the interdisciplinary studies of the period, and has,

---

[46] Michel Foucault discusses the interplay of *"Basileus, Philosophos, and Metallicos"* as fundamental to the organic structure of art in *The Order of Things* (New York: Vintage Books, 1970), 167, 173.

[47] Geertz, *Local Knowledge*, 30.

in some sense, established cultural studies as a theoretical configuration. As H. Abram Veester somewhat aggressively puts it:

As the first successful counterattack in decades against this profoundly anti-intellectual ethos [traditionalists, conventional scholarship], the New Historicism has given scholars new opportunities to cross the boundaries separating history, anthropology, art, politics, literature, and economics. It has struck down the doctrine of noninterference that forbade humanists to intrude on questions of politics, power, indeed on all matters that deeply affect people's practical lives – matters best left, prevailing wisdom went, to experts who could be trusted to preserve order and stability in "our" global and intellectual domains. New historicism threatens this quasi-monastic order.[48]

I find it somewhat ironic that the "gentleman scholars" to whom I refer above, who collected information for local history publications, also frequently "cross[ed] the boundaries separating history, anthropology, art, politics, literature, and economics," perhaps because they did not perceive (as clearly as we assume *we* do) those boundaries. Nevertheless, Veester's point has some validity in the province of theoretical analysis. Whereas, he maintains, "old historicists" are deterministic and monolithic, emphasizing causality and considering history as a continuous "flow," new historicists acknowledge that history is actually a series of discontinuous strata, of diachronic events symptomatic of rupture and discontinuity. Consequently, new historicists invest as much interest in contiguous phenomena as traditionalists do in focusing narrowly on artifacts (mostly in the form of dramatic texts) from within the assumptions of their specific disciplines. This new historical attention to "local knowledge," to the deconstruction of the hegemony and the dispersal of power, rather than the more traditional and Tillyardian view of unified or at least singular political and artistic visions, leads new historicists to acknowledge that power "circulates," as Greenblatt puts it. These critics decenter their materials and approach them with interdisciplinary methodologies, a fitting response to Geertz's challenge. Nevertheless, as Foucault cautions us against "presentism," we, like the anthropologist gone "native," find it difficult to represent the past accurately because we must constantly strive to recover it from within the prisons of our own paradigms.

Just as New Criticism inspired a pedagogy that shifted us from the philological, historical, and biographical approaches of the previous

[48] H. Abram Veester (ed.), *The New Historicism* (New York: Routledge, 1989), ix. This volume provides a spirited discussion of various aspects of New Historicism.

century, the present retreat from New Criticism shifts literary criticism to make room for new theoretical approaches, thus allowing us to challenge the primacy of the dramatic text and to concentrate on the social, historical, and political contexts of patronage theatre. This shift has been revolutionary for theatrical studies, since so many of us are finding that cultural history and contextual materials significantly increase our understanding of early modern theatrical events, and allow us to broaden our definitions of theatre from the limitations of playtexts to other performative occasions. Theatre history, so recently severed from its Siamese twin literary history, also has need, however, of methodologies more suited to the analysis of the discourses of the stage. Vince summarizes the problem:

> theater history has seldom had a very high profile; those who profess it have seldom enjoyed a status independent of their academic appointments either in literature departments, where the predominant values and methods are literary, or in departments of theater ... For much of the present century, theater researchers have struggled to distance themselves from literary critics and literary historians, to establish their discipline on the fact of theatrical performance rather than on that of dramatic text.[49]

As Vince clearly points out, until recently many critics considered that "performance is ancillary rather than integral to the drama"; and unfortunately, many still labor under this misconception. Many also assume that the absence of dramatic text indicates the absence of drama, and fail to seek sources and resources that might indicate the conditions and contexts of performances. In this respect, the work of theatre historians resembles that of social historians, art historians, and music historians. We find evidence for our reconstructions not in scripts alone, but also in financial accounts, chronicles, archaeological digs, letters, biographies, local histories, legal documents, paintings, and sculpture. In addition, because of the visual, aural, and kinesthetic nature of performance, we must also consider music and dance history, as well as the arts of engineering and science, since all of these contribute toward the *mise en scène* and the physical production.

Furthermore, theatre differs from literature in the ephemeral and intensely social nature of the stage. It is certainly understandable that literary critics would feel discomforted by the elusive nature of theatre, by the fact that the conditions of performance, from commission to

---

[49] Vince, "Theater History," 1–18.

reception, cannot and are not meant to be reproduced. Though some argue that this historicity affects literary texts as well, it is undeniable that the printed literary text is the primary artifact, while the primary theatrical text, written on the wind as it were, leaves no tangible trace. In addition, while the literary artifact may be privately shared between patron and patron artist, the theatrical event, from beginning to end, is a communal, social occasion. Although it may be written by one person, it cannot be fully realized without the assistance of many artists and the reception of an audience.[50]

In fact, many social rituals require no written script, but are nevertheless essential to the theatre historian, particularly in patronage studies. Ceremonies (such as weddings, coronations, elevations to nobility, funerals), religious and civic processions, military parades, folk pageants, and dances all comprise theatre. Many of these occasions require the participation of theatre artists and technicians to build, costume, manage, enact, and design (if not compose or script) the event – theatre artists who manipulate audience expectations and responses to create the same suspense, wonder, and catharsis that more traditional plays affect. And, as critic after critic has shown, these social and ceremonial occasions feed structures, styles, and ideas back into the public theatre in a symbiotic relationship.

These differences between literary history and theatrical history make our work in theatrical patronage fundamentally different from the work of other scholars in patronage studies. In some senses, theatre scholarship entails not only the reconstruction of the performance (if that is indeed ever possible), but also reconstructions of the venues and auspices, as well as the social and political conditions of production. Since we also include audience reception and response, we must conclude that no performance is recoverable, that each and every production of a script is a unique event, a different play. Theatre, paratheater, metatheater – all these must inform the work of theatre historians. A. M. Nagler, author of the fundamental collection *A Source Book in Theatrical History* and one of the formative figures in the discipline, disagrees:

We are engaged neither in historical philology nor in the study of literature, neither in folklore nor in sociology. The styles of performance and their more or less plausible reconstructions, these are our primary concern, and I shall be honored if this be called a purist's stance.[51]

---

[50] For information about the oft-ignored craftsmen who helped create the revels, see the chapter entitled "Artists and Artisans" in John Astington, *English Court Theatre*.
[51] A. M. Nagler, *The Medieval Religious Stage* (New Haven: Yale University Press, 1976), xi.

While Nagler might resist interdisciplinarity, insisting on the uniqueness of theatre history as a discipline, most of today's scholars recognize that we have need of various interdisciplinary techniques and that we often study many of the same artifacts as do folklorists and philologists. So theatre history is drawn further from traditional literary criticism and becomes perhaps a sub-discipline within cultural studies.

After New Criticism redirected theatre historians away from theatrical biographies, and after post-modern approaches began to refocus our attentions beyond the New Critical limitations of the "work," the dramatic texts, we began to redefine our studies, to concentrate much more closely on the complexities of the theatrical texts. Simultaneously, interdisciplinary interests led to many fresh approaches to our studies. Marxist, psychoanalytic, anthropological, semiotic, new historical, and feminist theories adapted, inspired, and tested alternative approaches from wider perspectives; scholars began to contextualize materials as cultural studies that would help us to consider not only the works of art we study, but the people who produced and received them. In addition to the all-important play and playwright, such subjects as patrons, venues, occasions, money, contracts, costume stocks, musicians, and visual artists began to take center stage in critical and theoretical work. That prolific playwright "Anonymous" (or perhaps Anonyma?) became more and more interesting as a clear signal that authority rested not just in authorship during the early modern period, but also in aristocrats, ecclesiastics, schoolmasters, and guilds as creators of theatrical art. Consequently, critics and historians began investigating auspices and political allegory as clues to the workings of theatrical patronage.[52]

Many have been too quick to mistake the blueprint (the dramatic text) for the whole structure (the theatrical text), perhaps since so many generations of critics, teachers, and readers have privileged the dramatic text; we must, after all, access history chiefly through documents, and playtexts seem the most basic documents. In the tendency to elevate the historical, philological, and philosophical aesthetics of the dramatic

---

[52] See, for example, Thomas W. Craik's "The Political Interpretation of Two Tudor Interludes: *Temperance and Humility* and *Wealth and Health*," *Review of English Studies* 4 (1953), 98–108, and *The Tudor Interlude* (Leicester: Leicester University Press, 1958); William Harris's "Woolsey and Skelton's *Magnyfycence*," *Studies in Philology* 57 (1960), 99–122; Gwen Ann Jones, "The Political Significance of the Play of *Albion Knight*," *Journal of English and German Philology* 17 (1918), 267–80; Ian Lancashire, "The Auspices of *The World and the Child*," *Renaissance and Reformation* 12 (1976), 96–105, "Orders for Twelfth Day and Night circa 1515 in the Second Northumberland Household Book," *English Literary Renaissance* 10 (Winter 1980), 7–45, and *Two Tudor Interludes: "The Interlude of Youth," "Hick Scorner"* (Baltimore: Johns Hopkins University Press, 1980).

texts, scholars often ignore the visual, aural, and kinesthetic aesthetics of the theatrical texts (not to mention the science and engineering required to physically produce the theatrical event), and consequently underestimate the art in many ways: to consider it popular rather than high culture; to assume that since it was ephemeral it was simplistic; to marginalize the performance artists (especially in comparison to the privileging of the composing artists, even as we do today); and to fault rather than to celebrate the gaps and indeterminacies of the medium, to use McLuhan's term. But as the dramatic text found that it now had to share the limelight with performance text, various structuralist and post-structuralist theorists began to give us the language with which to talk about the non-verbal systems of the stage and to encourage the exploration of various other "texts" from finances to fashions. Clothes (or masks, or sets, or roles, or *venues*) do indeed "make" the man, we are indeed what we seem to be, and the theatre analogies so common to our lives (as well as to *Macbeth* and *Hamlet*) are found to be more than "mere shows," as Geertz suggests, but rather ritualistic enactments of the social constructions of reality.

We have to go further afield in the history of literary theory to note the philosophers who began formulating aesthetic theories that would be more useful to theatre theorists, some of whom base their analyses solely on social phenomena and patterns that inform theatre but remain without scripts.[53] Mikhail Bakhtin's *Rabelais and His World* (published in Russian in 1965, and translated into English in 1968), and later *The Dialogic Imagination* (which appeared originally in 1975), got us thinking about *carnivale* and the socio-political implications of comic performance, an approach that Michael Bristol later turned with great effectiveness on Renaissance theatre history.[54] Jesters, clowns, the Feast of Fools, and Boy Bishops, to which E. K. Chambers had collected references in the 1920s, were raised in status from marginalized players of (often deprecated) "folk" festivals to ritual actors in the social contract.

Bakhtin's and Bristol's work challenges us to think more seriously about the political construction and exploitation of transgressive performances, like the Queen's (rather than Ben Jonson's) *Masque of Blackness*, when the Queen, desiring some exotic (and erotic?) fantasy, requested Ben Jonson to compose a masque in which she and her ladies could

[53] Roy Strong's illustration-rich *Art and Power* (Berkeley: University of California Press, 1973) is a particularly good representation of an analysis of non-textual performances.

[54] Michael D. Bristol, *Carnival and Theater: Plebeian Culture and the Structure of Authority in Renaissance England* (New York and London: Methuen, 1985).

appear "all paynted like Blackamores face and neck bare," inspired perhaps by the spectacle of Africans dancing "naked in the snow in front of the royal carriage" at her own wedding.[55]

Our study of *carnivale*, transgression, and the structure of authority has also finally put to rest the "big bang" theory of the development of medieval theatre – that the ecclesiastical authorities, once thought of as the monolith of theatrical patronage, expelled theatre from the nave to the marketplace because of its excessive use of the comic. Rather, recently published records have shown that other patrons, including aristocrats, schools, and civic organizations, had long served as patrons of theatre, and perhaps it was the increasing competition among patrons, the beginnings of the replacement of the feudal system with incipient capitalism based heavily on patronage politics, that encouraged actors to market their commodities in more lucrative and rewarding (and perhaps multiple) ways. We can also now dispense with Part II of the Big Bang, the shrinking and cooling of the theatrical "universe" from the provinces to London, from private auspices to public. In 1981 Glynne Wickham concluded that from 1530 to 1580 a "paralysing blight settled on country districts, so local practitioners with centuries of local expertise in play-making, acting, and production techniques behind them were trapped into having either to abandon these pleasurable and dignified social pursuits, or else to transfer to London, on a full-time professional and commercial basis, taking their skills with them." He continues, claiming that there was a substantial "decline in local theatrical activity . . . leaving only the residual folk-customs associated with the agricultural year as pale shadows of the epic dramas and memorable theatrical occasion that formerly had been the common heritage of the whole nation – 'bare, ruined choirs/where late the sweet birds sang'." But by 1990, REED records and the studies they engender show clearly that touring players and private revels were not in decline; in contrast, the Queen's Men seem to have spent as much, if not more, time in the "bare ruined choirs" as in the city.[56]

Theatre historians also seize upon the science of semiology, pioneered by Peirce and Saussure, then extended to the notion of expectation horizons by Roman Jakobson, Roland Barthes, and Umberto Eco, to provide

---

[55] Kim F. Hall, "Sexual Politics and Cultural Identity in *The Masque of Blackness*," in Sue-Ellen Case and Janelle Reinelt (eds.), *The Performance of Power: Theatrical Discourse and Power* (Iowa City: University of Iowa Press, 1991), 4; *Ben Jonson*, ed. Charles Hereford and Percy Simpson (Oxford: Clarendon Press, 1925), 449.

[56] Wickham, *Early English Stages*, III, 60–61. See also McMillin and MacLean, *The Queen's Men*.

us with a vocabulary and methodology for analyzing and interpreting gesture, *mise en scène*, costume, intonation, and blocking – the visual and aural signs of performance. Wolfgang Iser and Hans-Robert Jauss encourage us to consider the other inhabitants of the *locus* and *platea*, so we pay much more attention to audience reception and response, adopting (and adapting) ideas presented in their discussions of literary texts for use in analyzing performance text. Ann Jennalie Cook, for example, in *The Privileged Playgoers of Shakespeare's London*, extends the fundamental work of these theorists, conveniently summarizing the socio-historical approaches that focus on patronage and patriarchy as it applies to Elizabethan theatre.[57]

At the same time that Stephen Greenblatt was suggesting modifications for historical criticism within literary studies, Guy Fitch Lytle and Stephen Orgel produced the interdisciplinary study *Patronage in the Renaissance*, the first volume to focus specifically on the social practice of patronage and the various manifestations of its function in politics, art, literature, and theatre. Ten years later, a special number of *The Yearbook of English Studies*, subtitled *Politics, Patronage and Literature in England 1558–1658*, edited by Cedric C. Brown and reissued in an American edition entitled *Patronage, Politics, and Literary Traditions in England 1558–1658*, brought literary patronage studies into the 90s, including many articles that focused specifically on theatre and theatrical patronage. As the articles by Paul Whitfield White, Kathleen E. McLuskie, Margot Heinemann, Deborah C. Payne, and M. D. Jardine clearly demonstrate, theatre is indeed different from its sister arts, and legal documents from the period make this crystal clear. Painting was not licensed. Poetry was not forbidden by Royal Proclamations and Statutes of the Realm at certain times and places (though certainly various cases of censorship and book burning occurred). Music was rarely previewed by mayors or court officials to be sure that there was no offense in it. And the practitioners of those arts were rarely arrested, stocked, forbidden to play, or railed against in the pulpit. Here, then, is another crucial difference between patronage of the theatre and patronage of other sorts: since theatre required official policies to control it, clearly it carried a potential threat. Theatre once wielded an immense power to both reflect and shape political discourse, as well as the propensity to influence a huge and diverse audience, factors that make theatre perhaps more potentially threatening than the printed volume, which

---

[57] Ann Jennalie Cook, *The Privileged Playgoers of Shakespeare's London 1576–1642* (Princeton: Princeton University Press, 1981).

was never intended for mass simultaneous consumption, particularly by "commoners."[58]

Feminist criticism has also inspired some of the most refreshing discoveries in patronage studies, for it has given women a significant role in artistic production in early modern England. We have known for ages that women were forbidden to act on the stage, except at the two social extremes – as vaudeville-type traveling entertainers and court fools[59] or as noble dancers in court masques and disguisings. We have also never identified, until Aphra Behn, a woman playwright who earned her living through her art. But we do know that several women, including seven queens (Katharine of Aragon, Anne Boleyn, Jane Seymour, Mary Tudor, Elizabeth, Anne, and later Henrietta Maria), served as patrons to player troupes, artists, and playwrights who created court entertainments. Queen Elizabeth's tastes were certainly taken into account by artists destined to perform for her (or at least by the patrons of those artists who had their own patron-client interests to consider). David Bergeron has identified, through dedications of dramatic texts, at least fourteen women who served as patrons.[60] David Roberts has continued this exploration in *The Ladies: Female Patronage of Restoration Drama*, showing that the tradition of female patronage was strong enough to outlast the interregnum interlude, for even after the government closed the theatres in 1642, the women of the Cavendish household produced their domestic theatrical *The Concealed Fancies*.[61] Noble women such as Susan Vere, Countess of Montgomery, Lady Anne Herbert, and Lady Mary Wroth performed in masques.

Women could participate in private household entertainments in a variety of ways. Many, like Margaret Beaufort, mother of King Henry VII and patron of the poet/playwright John Skelton, headed their own households and therefore acted as patrons to poets and performers within

---

[58] I use the past tense here in a somewhat despairing tone, since theatre in North America today (perhaps with the exception of Québécois performance) seems to carry precious little political or even sociological threat, the Pulitzer Prize for Tony Kushner's *Angels in America: A Gay Fantasia on National Themes* notwithstanding. Susan Sontag seems to have had an experience with *Waiting for Godot* in Sarajevo that might compare with the power of Elizabethan theatre to tap the social consciousness of large audiences. In Africa, theatre is being used to educate people about health and contraception; particularly in third-world countries where social structures are under tremendous stress, theatre continues to be a potent force.

[59] Westfall, *Patrons and Performance*, 91.

[60] David Bergeron, "Women as Patrons of English Renaissance Drama," in *Patronage in the Renaissance*, 274–90. See also Barbara Lewalski, "Re-writing Patriarchy and Patronage: Margaret Clifford, Anne Clifford, and Aemilia Lanyer," in Cedric C. Brown (ed.), *Patronage, Politics and Literary Traditions in England: 1558–1658* (Detroit: Wayne Stage University Press, 1991), 59–78.

[61] David Roberts, *The Ladies: Female Patronage of Restoration Drama* (Oxford: Clarendon Press, 1989).

them. Lady Honor Lisle went shopping in 1538 and purchased the text of an interlude called *Rex Diabole*, then presumably produced it for her household.[62] Denied roles in the civic and public theatre, women sang, played musical instruments, spoke text, and danced in disguisings and masques. Matilda Makejoy, one of the very few female minstrels on record, entertained the royal court with dances and acrobatics in the early fourteenth century. Aemilia Lanyer, feminist poet and (at least to A. L. Rowse) Shakespeare's "dark lady," was a member of the recorder-playing Bassano family who served Henry VIII, enjoying with them the monopoly on Gascon wine and the confiscated London monastery, Charterhouse.[63]

And, of course, women often provided the theme and point of entertainments, as countless prologues and epilogues demonstrate. It would be impossible for me to list the innumerable compliments to Elizabeth that trod the boards during her reign, but I will indulge in a couple of the more extreme examples. John Lyly, who held a post in the household of Queen Elizabeth's Lord High Treasurer, William Cecil, Lord Burghley, was also under the patronage of Edward de Vere, Earl of Oxford; his *Endymion*, drawing freely from Eliza's identifications with Diana and the moon, has always been considered a thinly veiled compliment to the chastity of Queen Elizabeth and the devotion of her courtiers, as have many of his other classically influenced plays.[64] The extremely artificial end to George Peele's *The Araygnement of Paris*, in which the prize golden apple rolls to the Queen's feet, demonstrates just how blatant appeals to feminine influence might be.[65] Through the power of patronage and purse strings, a few women did indeed affect the theatrical art of their era. And in more indirect fashion, women in the audience, both public and private, served as patrons, a situation satirized in quite controversial style in *The Knight of the Burning Pestle*.

With this brief discussion of an exceedingly intricate phenomenon as backdrop, I would like now to revisit etymology, to recontextualize the word "patronage." *The Oxford English Dictionary* recognizes the complexity of the term in its prologue to the definition of "patron":

[62] *Letters and Papers, Foreign and Domestic, of the Reign of Henry VIII*, ed. John Brewer, James Gairdner, and R. H. Brodie, 21 vols. (London: HMSO, 1862–1918), Addenda ii, ii.ii, no. 1362.
[63] David Lasocki, "Professional Recorder Playing in England 1500–1740," *Early Music* 10.1 (Jan. 1982), 23–28.
[64] David Bevington, "Lyly's *Endymion* and *Midas*," 26–46.
[65] Andrew Von-Hendy, "The Triumph of Chastity: Form and Meaning in *The Arraignment of Paris*," *Renaissance Drama* 1 (1968), 87–101.

patronus had the senses of protector and defender of his clients (viz. of individuals, of cities, or provinces) . . . an advocate or defender before a court of justice, or, generally, of any person or cause . . . also that of exemplar, pattern. Most of these senses are represented in the English *patron*.

The *Dictionary* proceeds then to define the term patron in thirteen ways (including as a verb, "to patron") ranging from its roots in the Latin *pater* (a link that anthropologists and feminists in particular find resonant for its paternalistic overtones) to its ecclesiastical, legal, and maritime denotations. Most pertinent to my discussion here is the third sense:

'One who countenances, supports, or protects' (J): one who takes under his favour and protection, or lends his influential support to advance the interests of some person, cause, institution, art or undertaking; *spec.* In 17th and 18th century the person who accepted the dedication of a book. (Always implying something of the superior relation of the wealthy or powerful Roman patron to his client.) Now a chief sense.

What this definition omits is as problematic as what it includes, for patronage systems and networks, both in anthropological studies and in historical studies, are far more intrinsic to social and governmental structures than simple "favor" and "protection" might imply. Indeed as Richard Dutton has made quite clear in *Mastering the Revels*, patronage systems to a great extent actually formed the Elizabethan government, from the patron-based alliances of the countryside gentry, through those of the Privy Councilors, directly to the Queen. Through a detailed study of source documents, Dutton suggests a very complex relationship among the royal court, the aristocratic patrons, the Master of the Revels, and the theatre producers and writers.[66] Rather than reproducing the traditional image of the Privy Council as a bunch of censors determined to control theatres and persecute playwrights, Dutton argues quite reasonably that the Master of the Revels and the producers of theatre enjoyed a comfortable and lucrative relationship; it was neither profitable nor productive for either party to antagonize the other. In addition, Dutton suggests that complex lines of patronage served not just as channels of artistic discourse, but also as the warp and woof of political life. Consequently theatrical patronage, rather than being some serendipitous arrangement to escape legal prosecutions and provide aristocrats with a hobby, formed

[66] Dutton, *Mastering the Revels*.

an integral part of the socio-political fabric of the sixteenth and seventeenth centuries. Linda Levy Peck goes so far as to state that "historians have emphasized the importance of patronage practices to the stability of monarchy," and to speculate that the Civil War may have been brought on by James I's inability to properly maintain and manage the patronage networks.[67]

Peck here continues a discussion that has preoccupied historians, particularly social historians, whose work often overlaps with that of theatre historians. Other fundamental contributions to the discipline include Wallace MacCaffrey in "Place and Patronage in Elizabethan Politics,"[68] and Malcolm Smuts, who further explores the breakdown of patronage networks under Charles II in "The Political Failure of Stuart Cultural Patronage."[69] Recent studies by McMillin, MacLean, and Gurr have continued in this vein, providing thorough, careful analysis of records newly available, "biographies" of player-troupe companies that expose the patronage subtexts more clearly. For the first time, we are beginning to understand how patrons used their players, both aesthetically and politically. We can begin to associate particular plays with particular patrons, to trace the movements of player-spies and emissaries, and to examine how religious and political polemics were presented in the country at large.[70]

Historians have produced a great deal of the literature on patronage, including biographies of individual aristocrats and analyses of their households too numerous to mention. One of the earlier, and now somewhat dated studies of the changing relationship between noble patrons and the structure of Elizabethan government is Lawrence Stone's *Crisis of the Aristocracy, 1558–1641*,[71] which explores in detail the "evolution" of

---

[67] Peck, "Court Patronage," 27.

[68] Wallace MacCaffrey, "Place and Patronage in Elizabethan Politics," in S. T. Bindoff, J. Hurstfield, and C. H. Williams (eds.), *Elizabethan Government and Society: Essays Presented to Sir John Neale* (London: University of London, Athlone Press, 1961), 95–126.

[69] Malcolm Smuts, "The Political Failure of Stuart Cultural Patronage," in *Patronage in the Renaissance*, 165–87.

[70] McMillin and MacLean, *The Queen's Men*, 22–24; Alan Haynes, *Invisible Power: The Elizabethan Secret Service, 1570–1603* (Stroud: Sutton Publishing, 1992). Sally-Beth MacLean and Alan Somerset have also constructed a marvelous website that makes patronage data easily available at www.utoronto.ca/patrons. David J. Kathman's admirable biographical index to Elizabethan Theatre is at http://www.clark.net/pub/tross/ws/bd/kathman.htm. The publisher has used its best endeavors to ensure that the URLs for external websites referred to in this book are correct and active at the time of going to press. However, the publisher has no responsibility for the websites and can make no guarantee that a site will remain live or that the content is or will remain appropriate.

[71] Lawrence Stone, *Crisis of the Aristocracy, 1558–1641* (Oxford: Clarendon Press, 1961).

English culture from feudalism, when theatre was a prominent form of largess and education (perhaps to the point of propaganda), through what Stone calls "bastard feudalism," when theatre was, as I have discussed in *Patrons and Performance*, a means of ensuring political and aesthetic control through household lines, to embryonic capitalism, when theatre was rapidly becoming commodified and patronage shifted to include not only the upper strata of society but also, and frequently simultaneously, the general public.

I do not mean to suggest, however, that theatre happens only from the top down. Throughout these times we also see an intertwining line of popular theatre, as Michael Bristol has pointed out so clearly in *Carnival and Theatre*, a line that frequently intersects patron theatre in such activities as the Feast of Fools and the various "vaudeville" entertainers at any aristocratic fête, or the imitations of folk theatre in the masquerades of the royal court, such as Henry VIII's fondness for dressing up, most likely without much sense of irony, like Robin Hood. By the end of the sixteenth century, obviously, these lines had intertwined so that companies like Shakespeare's clearly had two patrons – both the monarch and the paying public. In some cases these two patrons worked at cross purposes, but in most cases they appeared to be quite comfortable as bedfellows, implying that aristocratic patronage offered perquisites that the public could not, and that the public offered economic rewards that the patrons were (if we can believe, for example, in Queen Elizabeth's frugal habit of getting others to pay for her entertainment) reluctant to distribute.[72] Perhaps the epitome of Queen Elizabeth's economic cunning is that she got the public to pay, through their admission fees to the ever-touring Queen's Men, to hear the political spin that she, Leicester, and Walsingham desired to broadcast.

As I trust this discussion has shown, studies of theatrical patronage recontextualize all the labor and motivation that created the theatre of the sixteenth and seventeenth centuries. I am aware that my overview here has been brief and selective, as I had confessed it would be at the start. For every work I have touched on here, scores of volumes left unmentioned continue to explore the intriguing connections between theatrical art and the people who produced and consumed it. Most important, shifting our analytical lenses to considerations of patronage, as the volume you hold does, permits us a fresh look at some old commonplaces, opens the doors

---

[72] Kathleen E. McLuskie and Felicity Dunsworth, "Patronage and the Economics of Theater," in *A New History of Early English Drama*, 423–40. See also Alexander Leggatt's essay in this volume.

to new players in the theatre game, and allows us to reassess so many relationships – between men and women, between public and private, between provincial and city, between artists and producers, between baronial and royal courts, between Catholics and puritans. All the world (or at least all of England) is indeed a stage, not just the London playhouses. And behind every painted drop, within each miraculous devise, we find patrons with a very worldly-wise sense of theatre and the power it could wield.

Shakespearean patronage

CHAPTER 2

The King's Men's king's men: Shakespeare and folio patronage

David M. Bergeron

Possibly as early as 1620, two actors of the King's Men, John Heminge and Henry Condell, spearheaded efforts to collect Shakespeare's plays and publish them in a handsome folio volume. Although Jonson's 1616 Folio clearly had an impact on this decision, the actors nevertheless produced a unique book: the first collection in English exclusively containing plays in a folio format. This project seems all the more remarkable when we recall that at this point Shakespeare, the King's Men's principal playwright, had died in 1616, and Richard Burbage, the company's principal actor, in 1619. This risky venture needed support and stature; this the King's Men sought by dedicating the Folio to two of the King's men: William Herbert, Earl of Pembroke and Lord Chamberlain, and his brother, Philip Herbert, Earl of Montgomery and Gentleman of the King's Bedchamber.

My subject focuses on the Epistle Dedicatory and the Address "To the great Variety of Readers." For some reason – perhaps the result of renewed interest in historical issues – commentators in the past decade have paid special attention to the preliminary matter of the Folio. In widely varying contexts, scholars such as Leah Marcus, Margreta de Grazia, Douglas Lanier, Martin Elsky, and I, have examined the material that introduces us to the Folio's texts. Marcus, for example, discusses the apparatus in terms of how it corresponds to other books of the period and what this preliminary material sets out to accomplish.[1] De Grazia argues that the "preliminaries are thus organized to publicize the functions on which the Folio depends: publishing, patronage, purchase, performances, and acclaim."[2] Lanier and Elsky both in different ways cite the introductory material as an approach to the larger questions of the

---

[1] Leah Marcus, *Puzzling Shakespeare: Local Reading and Its Discontents* (Berkeley: University of California Press, 1988); see especially 2–25.
[2] Margreta de Grazia, *Shakespeare Verbatim: The Reproduction of Authenticity and the 1790 Apparatus* (Oxford: Clarendon Press, 1991), 21–22.

construction of authorship.[3] And I have looked at the Epistle and Address as calling attention to problems of reading and interpretation.[4]

I want to put the focus on patronage. I will argue that through the Epistle and Address the 1623 Folio stands on the patronage fault line between past and future, between aristocratic and commercial support, between what McLuskie would call the "use value" system and the "exchange value" system.[5] The Folio comprises both systems, and the Epistle and Address signal this stance. The medieval and early Renaissance pattern of courtly and aristocratic patronage still lives, even if Shakespeare and his fellow writers do not reside in the great houses of noblemen. On the other hand, printing has opened a world previously only dreamed of, in a sense liberating writers from the constraints of aristocrats. A reading public emerges which by its purchases expands a new world of commerce that corresponds to what has already been happening in the theatre with its paying audiences. The Folio therefore stands at a particularly propitious and auspicious moment, asserting the existence of competing and complementary worlds of patronage.

A number of years ago, Alvin Kernan argued that Shakespeare in the Sonnets offers an image of the failure – considered inevitable – of the aristocratic system of patronage.[6] Shakespeare depicts the necessary turning of the poet from patronage to the marketplace, specifically toward a new career in the theatre. Kernan writes: "But the real failure of patronage in the *Sonnets* results from the inability of the institution and the courtly type of poetry it fostered to take into account the realities of human nature and the complexities of human relationships." This joins such matters as "the untrustworthiness of patrons, the intense competition among rival poets to attract patrons by means of novel styles, the difference between the social status of patron and poet, and the failure of poets and patrons to establish a situation of mutual understanding and support." Therefore, in Kernan's view, patronage moves "from the great house to the public theater."[7] This reductive conclusion obscures

[3] Douglas Lanier, "Encryptions: Reading Milton Reading Jonson Reading Shakespeare," David M. Bergeron (ed.), in *Reading and Writing in Shakespeare* (Newark: University of Delaware Press, 1996), 227–35; Martin Elsky, "Shakespeare, Bacon, and the Construction of Authorship," in *Reading and Writing in Shakespeare*, 252–54.
[4] David M. Bergeron, "Introduction: Reading and Writing," in *Reading and Writing in Shakespeare*, 13–15.
[5] Kathleen E. McLuskie, "The Poets' Royal Exchange: Patronage and Commerce in Early Modern Drama," *Yearbook of English Studies* 21 (1991), 53–62.
[6] Alvin B. Kernan, *The Playwright as Magician: Shakespeare's Image of the Poet in the English Public Theater* (New Haven: Yale University Press), 1979.
[7] Kernan, *The Playwright as Magician*, 37.

a more complex arrangement, as I will be arguing. If the "great house" serves as the synecdoche for the range of aristocratic patronage, then clearly no complete break occurs. The theatre and book publication provide writers with additional options without shutting them off from aristocratic support.[8] I do not think that we have to choose between the image of, say, Chaucer in the service of John of Gaunt and a fledgling playwright hawking his wares to an acting company.

More recently, Kernan has returned to the subject of patronage, finding King James to be Shakespeare's patron, as the book's title implies: *Shakespeare, the King's Playwright*. In a sense, this new book extends the argument that writers, Shakespeare in particular, indeed moved from the great house to the theatre. But this position takes an ironic twist because Kernan now argues for Shakespeare's indebtedness, reliance on the King's patronage. We have come full circle: the theatre now serves the royal patron. We have arrived at the greatest house of them all: the court. In the palace, Kernan writes, "Shakespeare, whose roots still lay in the public theater ... takes a place among the age's great patronage playwrights."[9] His body of work "becomes one of the master oeuvres of European patronage art."[10] Shakespeare serves Stuart ideology. Therefore, to cite one example, "Shakespeare fulfilled his patronage contract in *Coriolanus* with elegant and highly wrought theater," a "treatment of the crisis of the Stuart aristocracy."[11] In such an approach Prospero and Shakespeare blend into one person. Kernan suggests: "It must have been one of the great moments of English theater when Prospero turned that night to the king and queen sitting in their State ... to speak one last time for the bending author and ask his royal patron for his release from service."[12] This perspective begs several questions, even as we acknowledge evidence of obvious royal support for the dramatist and his acting company. Kernan's two books certainly illustrate the complexity of the subject and the difficulty of being precise about patronage's operation and effect. If in the first book we move from the great house to the theatre, in the second we move from the King's Men to the King's Man.

But such a seeming evolution obscures the actual working of the patronage system, which does not finally derive solely from the King. Heminge and Condell in fact dedicate the Folio to the Herbert brothers,

[8] See my article, "Patronage and Dramatists: The Case of Thomas Heywood," *English Literary Renaissance* 18 (1988), 294–304.

[9] Alvin B. Kernan, *Shakespeare, the King's Playwright: Theater in the Stuart Court 1603–1613* (New Haven: Yale University Press, 1995), xxii.

[10] Kernan, *Shakespeare*, xxiii.   [11] Ibid., 148.   [12] Ibid., 168.

TO THE MOST NOBLE
And
INCOMPARABLE PAIRE
OF BRETHREN.

William
Earle of Pembroke, &c. Lord Chamberlaine to the
Kings most Excellent Maiesty.

AND

Philip.
Earle of Montgomery, &c. Gentleman of his Maiesties
Bed-Chamber. Both Knights of the most Noble Order
of the Garter, and our singular good
LORDS.

Right Honourable,

*Hilst we studie to be thankful in our particular, for
the many fauors we haue receiued from your L.L.
we are falne vpon the ill fortune, to mingle
two the most diuerse things that can bee, feare,
and rashnesse; rashnesse in the enterprize, and
feare of the successe. For, when we valew the places your H.H.
sustaine, we cannot but know their dignity greater, then to descend to
the reading of these trifles: and, while we name them trifles, we haue
depriu'd our selues of the defence of our Dedication. But since your
L.L. haue beene pleas'd to thinke these trifles some-thing, heereto-
fore; and haue prosequuted both them, and their Authour liuing,
with so much fauour: we hope, that (they out-liuing him, and he not
hauing the fate, common with some, to be exequutor to his owne writings) you will vse the like indulgence toward them, you haue done
A 2   vnto*

1. "Epistle to the Herbert Brothers." From the 1623 edition of Shakespeare's
Comedies, Histories, and Tragedies (a) A2 recto (b) A2 verso

The Epistle Dedicatorie.

vnto their parent. *There is a great difference, vvhether any Booke choose his Patrones, or finde them* : *T his hath done both. For, so much were your L. L. likings of the seuerall parts, vvhen they were acted, as before they vvere published, the Volume ask'd to be yours. We haue but collected them, and done an office to the dead, to procure his Orphanes, Guardians; vvithout ambition either of selfe-profit, or fame : onely to keepe the memory of so worthy a Friend, & Fellow aliue, as was our* SHAKESPEARE, *by humble offer of his playes, to your most noble patronage. Wherein, as we haue iustly obserued, no man to come neere your L.L. but vvith a kind of religious addresse ; it hath bin the height of our care, vvho are the Presenters, to make the present worthy of your H.H. by the perfection. But, there we must also craue our abilities to be considerd, my Lords. We cannot go beyond our owne powers. Country hands reach foorth milke, creame, fruites, or what they haue : and many* Nations (*we haue heard*) *that had not gummes & incense, obtained their requests with a leauened Cake. It vvas no fault to approch their Gods, by what meanes they could : And the most, though meanest, of things are made more precious, when they are dedicated to Temples. In that name therefore, we most humbly consecrate to your H.H. these remaines of your seruant Shakespeare ; that what delight is in them, may be euer your L.L. the reputation his, & the faults ours, if any be committed, by a payre so carefull to shew their gratitude both to the liuing, and the dead, as is*

Your Lordshippes most bounden,

IOHN HEMINGE.
HENRY CONDELL.

1. (*cont.*)

not to King James. In order to assess this example of aristocratic patronage, I want first to look consciously at the typography and topography of these preliminary pages that make up the Epistle and the Address. Through such a perusal we can see without yet looking at the content of these items that they complement and compete with each other. They therefore constitute a wonderful visual image of the tension that exists among the different systems of patronage.

As we move from the impressive, and by now well-known, title page with its engraving of Shakespeare, we come immediately to the Epistle Dedicatory, which at the top of its first page has a pleasant ornamental border, which recurs on the contents page and at the beginning of the first play, *The Tempest*. This first page also has generous spacing with its own preliminary matter before it arrives at the text proper. The printer has placed the text in italic type, granting it elegance. The closing and the names of Heminge and Condell occur, however, in roman type in order to distinguish them from the text. Overall, the topography suggests care and generous spacing, including precise centering of the opening material.

By contrast, the Address has a more modest appearance, starting with the restrained ornamental border. We notice that the printer here has chosen roman type for the text, relieved only by the italics of the heading and the closing names of Heminge and Condell. Judged only by appearance, this item seems the obverse of the other: complement and contrast. The thirty-nine lines of text in smallish font neatly and compactly fit on one side of the sheet, in contrast to the thirty-eight lines of the Epistle that spill over two pages. For the Address the printer has made a conscious choice to make one page suffice, although the verso of the page remains blank. By design, I suggest, these two preliminary items go together; paradoxically, their differences in fact link them visually and typographically.

The names "William" and "Philip" stand at the center of the opening of the first page, and they rest typographically on a base of titles. This stylistic prominence underscores the importance of these two men, designated as "the Most Noble and Incomparable Paire of Brethren."[13] If we knew nothing about the Herbert brothers, we might initially sense their significance because of their titles and their connection to the King: William, Earl of Pembroke, "Lord Chamberlaine to the *Kings most Excellent Maiesty*"; and Philip, Earl of Montgomery, "Gentleman

[13] Throughout I cite the 1623 Folio edition, which I have slightly modernized, as found on sigs. A2–A3.

of his Maiesties Bed-Chamber." In addition, both "Knights" serve as members "of the most Noble Order of the Garter." They look for all the world like a pair of King's men to whom a pair of King's Men have chosen to dedicate this collection of plays. I do not share Leah Marcus's view that the Epistle Dedicatory exhibits "slippage" because the dedication pays little attention to the King. She writes: "the dedicatory epistle aborts its incipient placement of Shakespeare's collected plays within an official Stuart context."[14] And she adds that the Herbert brothers stand as "independent agents, not intermediaries with the king."[15] But the brothers' identification on the page links them explicitly to the King, and they function within his orbit.

I find intriguing the "&c." that follows the titles of Earl of Pembroke and Earl of Montgomery. What does "&c." mean? I see it paradoxically as both expansive and elliptical. Readers have the task of filling in the imagined and constructed blank. I will suggest some of the possibilities that "&c." might include. To begin, we could talk about the Herbert brothers as nephews of Sir Philip and children of Mary Sidney, Countess of Pembroke, therefore inheritors of an exceptionally rich literary heritage that extends through their kinsman George Herbert. The brothers functioned as major patrons of literary artists (more on that below). Philip Herbert served as a member of parliament in 1604, and the next year James created him Earl of Montgomery. In 1615 he became High Steward of Oxford University, and in 1617, Keeper of Westminster Palace. He also accompanied James on the nostalgic trip to Scotland in 1617. After the Folio publication, Philip became a member of the Privy Council in 1624 and Lord Chamberlain in 1626. Because of his dashing and handsome looks and because of his fascination with dogs and horses, he early in James's English reign became the King's "favorite," although he never secured the status and rewards that this entailed for Robert Carr and later George Villiers. Perhaps we can more accurately regard Philip as "semi-favorite." But we find this interesting incidental note to State Papers in April 1623 in a directive from Secretary Conway to the Lord Treasurer: "The King wishes him to consider the enclosed suit of the Earl of Montgomery, whom His Majesty, from his great affection for him, would be glad to satisfy."[16] Thus several months before the Folio publication Philip Herbert obviously still enjoys the King's good favor.

[14] Marcus, *Puzzling Shakespeare*, 106–07.   [15] Ibid., 108.
[16] *Calendar of State Papers Domestic, 1619–1623* (London, 1858), x, 552.

William Herbert inherited their father's title as Earl of Pembroke, but in 1604 James made him Lord Lieutenant of Cornwall and in 1605, Warden of the Forest of Dean. By 1611, William had become a member of the Privy Council. With the fall of Carr, William became Lord Chamberlain on 23 December 1615, a position that he held until he relinquished it to his brother. In 1617, he became Chancellor of Oxford University, a post that he took seriously and served until his death in 1630. James appointed Pembroke as Lord Lieutenant of both Somerset and Wiltshire in 1621; these posts gave him increased political clout.

In a word, we can readily expand what "&c." might imply. Michael Brennan rightly suggests that by 1616 "the Herbert brothers were widely recognized as being among James's most intimate advisers and friends."[17] Desperately ill and fearing death in 1619, James "commended to the Prince [Charles] many of the lords, as Buckingham, for his love to himself ... and especially the Lord Chamberlain."[18] Brennan adds: "By the early 1620s, Pembroke's influence at court and in Parliament was at its height."[19] Small wonder, then, that Heminge and Condell chose the Herberts as dedicatees of the Folio; they tapped supporters of the arts and men of considerable political influence. Purchasers of the Folio would doubtless know these brothers as earls, and they may have been able to fill in the "&c." with their own suggestions. Whatever else it may mean, "&c." implies familiarity. To refer to the Herberts as "most noble and incomparable" rings with truth.

Philip Herbert, who seems to have lived somewhat in the shadow of his elder brother, nevertheless has a distinction never attained by William: namely, Gentleman of the King's Bedchamber. Neil Cuddy cites the Duke of Newcastle, who recalled that "'William earl of Pembroke, that most excellent person, [did] labour as for his life all the reign of King James ... to be of the Bedchamber and could never obtain it.'"[20] James frustrated his desire, although rewarding Philip with this honor. Cuddy has argued persuasively for the increasing political importance of this group within the King's entourage: "... the Bedchamber displaced the Privy Chamber as the focus of the monarch's private life ... The balance of power swung away, increasingly, from the Privy Council and a

[17] Michael Brennan, *Literary Patronage in the English Renaissance: The Pembroke Family* (London: Routledge, 1988), 167.
[18] *Calendar of State Papers Domestic, 1619–1623* (London, 1858), x, 33.
[19] Brennan, *Literary Patronage*, 171.
[20] Neil Cuddy, "The Revival of the Entourage: The Bedchamber of James I, 1603–1625," in David Starkey (ed.), *The English Court from the Wars of the Roses to the Civil War* (London: Longman, 1987), 173–225; 195.

bureaucrat-minister towards the Bedchamber and the royal favourite."[21] The Gentlemen, Grooms, and Pages of the Bedchamber had the closest direct contact with the King, including taking care of his physical needs and private ablutions. James chose Philip in 1603 to become a Gentleman of his Bedchamber – an extraordinary honor since typically the other Gentlemen were Scots. Cuddy observes: "The Bedchamber itself was the most important substantive product of the political settlement of the succession: given these origins, it is unsurprising that it continued to be of central political importance during the reign."[22] Robert Cecil, for one, watched his power diminish as the Bedchamber rose in significance. It became an elitist and exclusive operation, controlling access to the King's person. Philip Herbert got to watch first Robert Carr and then George Villiers gain control of the Bedchamber's power and operation. Heminge and Condell surely knew what they were doing when they called attention to Philip's prestigious position in the King's Bedchamber.

In the long run, William Herbert exercised the greater power as Lord Chamberlain, the post that he held in 1623 at the time of the Folio. Clearly he had desired this post for some time. Writing nearly two years before Pembroke got the appointment, John Chamberlain reports to Sir Dudley Carleton on 20 January 1614: "the voyce runs now that yf the earle of Suffolke be Treasurer the Lord Knolles shalbe Lord Chamberlain, which to me is very improbable, and wold be too great a distast to the earle of Pembroke, who looks duly for yt when yt falls and yf he shold fayle, wold thincke his long service and diligent waiting yll rewarded."[23] This important post oversaw all dramatic entertainments, including sanctioning the printing of dramatic texts under the Master of Revels, who reported to the Lord Chamberlain. Herbert therefore had to plan and direct the progresses of James, oversee the lodgings at the various royal palaces, receive foreign ambassadors, and plan dramatic entertainment at court. The white staff of office helped distinguish the Lord Chamberlain. Many people repaired to him for favors, especially concerning appointments. Brennan reports: "It has been calculated that Pembroke's total stipend, comprising his salary, diet allowance, livery, brokerage and other fees, came to over £4,800 a year, one of the highest declared incomes enjoyed by a court official."[24]

A taste of Pembroke's duties as Lord Chamberlain can be gleaned from perusing the *Calendar of State Papers Domestic*; one also sees in these

---

[21] Cuddy, "The Revival of the Entourage," 173. [22] Ibid., 177.
[23] *The Letters of John Chamberlain*, ed. Norman E. McClure, 2 vols. (Philadelphia: American Philosophical Society, 1939), I, 502.
[24] Brennan, *Literary Patronage*, 137–38.

collections how often the names of the Herbert brothers occur. To cite
items only from the crucial year of 1623, one finds this directive from
the Lord Chamberlain to Secretary Conway, dated 23 March 1623,
concerning the "fitting up of St. James's Palace for the Infanta" as
"the most pressing point, as her side will have to be enlarged, the oratory
built, and the whole palace refurnished, the furniture there being too
mean for their Highnesses; the expense will be heavy."[25] This refers to
the anticipated arrival of the Infanta of Spain, whom Prince Charles
intends to marry and whose person he seeks in Spain at this moment.
Nothing came of this, as we know, and Pembroke came increasingly to
oppose "the Spanish Match." On 15 May 1623, Pembroke sends a directive to the Justices of the south parts of Wiltshire: "Many disorders arise
from pilfering vagabonds having no place in which, either to be set to
work or punished, nearer than Devizes. Urges them to fix on some convenient place for building a house of correction, to give ease to the county,
now oppressed with the insolencies of vagabond multitudes."[26] Such
tasks seem a long way from arranging for some dazzling and spectacular
court masque. But these episodes offer a clear picture of the nitty-gritty
that attended the office of Lord Chamberlain.

Several events suggest Pembroke's dutiful concern for the welfare of
the King's Men. He records his affection for Richard Burbage in a letter
written to Viscount Doncaster, 20 May 1619, shortly after Burbage's
death, reporting on a "great supper" for the French Ambassador:
"And even now all the company are at the play, which I being tender
hearted could not endure to see so soon after the loss of my old acquaintance Burbage."[27] As Brennan reports of the King's Men: "In 1617 some
of their members went into the provinces and, using copies of letters
patent belonging to their parent company, set up a group which tried to
pass itself off as the real royal company."[28] The Lord Chamberlain intervened, ordering that these actors be apprehended and be sent to him. In
1619, at the request of Heminge, "he insisted that the King's Men should
continue to receive their accustomed allowances, even though Lionel
Cranfield, the new Master of the Wardrobe, wished to cut them."[29]
In May 1619, Pembroke wrote to the Stationers' Company forbidding
them to print corrupt and unauthorized texts of plays that belonged to
the King's Men. In a word, Pembroke took seriously his duties as Lord
Chamberlain and sought to protect the interests of the King's Men.

[25] *Calendar of State Papers Domestic*, x, 536.   [26] Ibid., 584.
[27] Quoted in Henry Brown, *Shakespeare's Patrons and Other Essays* (London: J. M. Dent, 1912), 66.
[28] Brennan, *Literary Patronage*, 139.   [29] Ibid., 140.

A measure of his preoccupation with the office and his family's political standing comes from his ongoing insistence that his brother Philip
succeed him in the post. The King dangled various offices in front of
William, but he would never accept unless the King also guaranteed that
Philip would become Lord Chamberlain. In a letter to Dudley Carleton,
10 August 1618, John Chamberlain takes note of this situation: "We talke
still of a new Treasurer and the Lord Cooke is in some consideration, but
the most generall and likely voyce goeth with the Lord Chamberlain, who
seemes nothing fond of yt unles he might leave his place to his brother
Mongomerie."[30] A similar comment crops up in a letter of 8 January
1620.[31] Dick Taylor observes: "By 1623, then, it was well established
at court that Pembroke would only relinquish his chamberlain's staff to
his brother, who, although in competition with other court stars, still
had enough standing with James and Buckingham to make Pembroke's
promotion of his cause valid and realistic."[32] The transfer finally took
place in 1626 when Pembroke became Lord Steward. Heminge and
Condell in their Folio dedication obviously have their eyes on the present
and future Lord Chamberlain as they write.

In addition to their political stature, this incomparable pair of brethren
actively supported the arts through their patronage. William especially
encouraged literary production. In an excellent study of this topic, Dick
Taylor concludes: "Thus in the roster of Pembroke's acquaintances
among the poets, few names of any importance from the early seventeenth century are missing."[33] Ben Jonson emerges as one of the most important for whom Pembroke served as patron. Jonson told Drummond
that the Earl sent him twenty pounds every New Year's Day for the purchase of books. In 1619 Oxford University conferred the M.A. on Jonson,
thanks to Pembroke's recommendation. When Jonson got in trouble for
his part in *Eastward Ho*, he wrote a letter to William Herbert: "Neither
am I nor my cause so much unknowne to your Lordshipp, as it should
drive mee to seeke a second meanes, or dispaire of this to your favoure.
You have ever been free and Noble to mee, and I doubt not the same
proportion of your Bounties, if I can but answere it with preservation
of my vertue, and Innocence."[34] Jonson acknowledges the King's anger

[30] *Letters of John Chamberlain*, II, 168.   [31] Ibid., 281.
[32] Dick Taylor, Jr., "The Earl of Montgomery and the Dedicatory Epistle of Shakespeare First
Folio," *Shakespeare Quarterly* 10 (1959), 123.
[33] Dick Taylor, Jr., "The Third Earl of Pembroke as a Patron of Poetry," *Tulane Studies in English* 5
(1955), 41–67; 66.
[34] *Ben Jonson*, ed. C. H. Herford and Percy and Evelyn Simpson, 11 vols. (Oxford: Clarendon Press,
1925), I, 199–200.

and pleads for help: "Most honor'd Earle, be hastie to our succoure. And, it shall be our care and studye, not to have you repent the tymely benefit you do us, which we will ever gratefullye receive and Multiplye in our acknowledgment." Not surprisingly, Jonson dedicates his *Catiline* (1611) to Pembroke. In such an ignorant time, Jonson writes, he craves "to stand neare your light: and, by that, to be read. Posterity may pay your benefit the honor, and thanks; when it shall know, that you dare, in these Jig-given times, to countenance a legitimate Poeme."[35] He appeals to Pembroke's "judgment" which enables him to "vindicate truth from error. It is the first (of this race) that ever I dedicated to any Person." Jonson honors Pembroke by repeating this dedication in his 1616 Folio in which he also dedicates his *Epigrammes* to William Herbert. He writes that he expects "protection of truth, and libertie, while you are constant to your owne goodnesse."[36] Given Jonson's own Folio and his close involvement with Pembroke, we experience no surprise in seeing Jonson at work in the prefatory material of Shakespeare's Folio. Heminge and Condell thus successfully bring together patron and poet in constructing their volume in honor of Shakespeare.

Writers of at least twelve other books or translations dedicate them jointly to the Herbert brothers, most of them prior to 1623. Of these works only the Folio is a dramatic text. These writers seek patronage and protection, and they recognize the advantage of dedicating their texts to these King's men. I choose several examples to illustrate the range of the dedications and to show some connections to Shakespeare's Folio. In 1607 Richard Carew dedicates his edition of Estienne's *A World of Wonders* to the Herberts: "I could see none [diamonds] more resplendent, and consequently fitter to be placed in the Frontispice of this worke . . . then your two Lordships."[37] Calling the brothers "bountiful benefactors," Carew asks the rhetorical question: "And if it be a true saying, *Temples are to be dedicated to the Gods, and bookes to good men*; to whom may I better dedicate this Apologie, then to your good Lordships." The image of "temples" and consecration finds an important place in the Heminge and Condell dedication. Carew praises the Herberts' connection to the Sidney heritage, as do a number of writers; and he closes by wishing them health of body, peace of conscience, increase of honor, and length of days.

---

[35] Ben Jonson, *Catiline* (London, 1611), sig. A2–A2v.
[36] Ben Jonson, *The Workes of Benjamin Jonson* (London, 1616), 767–68.
[37] Henri Estienne, *A World of Wonders: Or An Introduction to a Treatise Touching the Conformitie of Ancient and Modern Wonders* (London, 1607), sig. 4v.

Leonard Digges, who contributes a poem "To the Memorie of the deceased Authour Maister W. Shakespeare" to the Shakespeare Folio, dedicates his translation of Cespedes's *Gerardo* to the Herberts in 1622. (Edward Blount, famous for his involvement with the publishing of the Folio, serves also as publisher of the Digges book.) In the heading of the dedication, Digges calls attention to Pembroke's office of Lord Chamberlain and to Montgomery's membership in the Order of the Garter. Explaining why he has translated this work, Digges then connects to the Herberts: "Now, that I presume to offer my weake endevours to the view and protection of both your Lordships, I shall no way despaire of a pardon; since the world, that takes notice of your Noble Goodnesse . . . gives me assurance, that . . . I shall be esteemed."[38] Digges signs himself "a devoted Servant."

Addressing the Herberts as "Knights of the Honourable Order of the Garter," William Shute, in his translation of Fougasses's history of Venice (1612), waxes eloquent about the function of books; these same books need protection by patrons. Books, Shute claims, extend fame, "being the clearest Oracles to the living, and faithfullest Heralds to the dead." He adds: "Bookes (the only issue, wherein our Wives cannot defraude us) though they be often canceld by Time, yet in every next impression find a new being."[39] Shute's witty image combines the matter of parentage with book publication ("impression"). He addresses the Herberts: "Hence I have extracted a hope, that your Lordships might be pleased to pardon my gratefull and humble presumption, in consecrating my Labours to your Names." Like the book itself, the Herberts' names "shall shine to Posteritie." Again, we encounter the idea of consecration.

As publisher, Edward Blount dedicates Ducci's *Ars Aulica* (1607) to William and Philip. He seems not to know how this book got translated, except by a kind of fate; nevertheless, he knows that it needs protection. Therefore, he seeks the Herberts, "who from your owne practise in Court can cleereliest judge of his [its] arte. You, whose individuall and innated worths, besides my particular dutie, challenge this so equall Patronage."[40] Blount claims to be "most humbly devoted to your honors." Thus by examining these several dedications, we not only see the obvious appeals to the Herberts' patronage; but also witness an emerging constellation

---

[38] Cespedes y Meneses, *Gerardo the Unfortunate Spaniard*, made English by Leonard Digges (London, 1622), sig. A2v.

[39] Thomas de Fougasses, *The Generall Historie of the Magnificent State of Venice*, trans. William Shute (London, 1612), sig. A2–A2v.

[40] Lorenzo Ducci, *Ars Aulica or the Courtiers Arte* (London, 1607), sig. A4v.

of images and people, all of which surface in the Shakespeare Folio: temples, issue, consecration; Jonson, Blount, Digges.

We have no information that lets us know how often these King's men may have gone to watch performances of the King's Men, but we do know something about their intense involvement with drama. Taylor says of William: "The realm, however, in which he shone most brilliantly and splendidly was that of the theatrical arts."[41] The same could be said of Philip. Their father patronized an adult acting company, and their mother translated drama. The Herbert brothers have an impressive record of performance in court masques – not surprising given their position at court and William's patronage of Jonson and Inigo Jones. Both of the brothers performed in the first masque of the Jacobean court: Daniel's *The Vision of the Twelve Goddesses*, performed on 8 January 1604. They typically served as masquers or dancers; such was Philip's role in Jonson's *Hymenaei* (5 January 1606). They both danced in Campion's *Lord Somerset's Masque*, performed on the occasion of the marriage of Frances Howard, Countess of Essex, to Robert Carr, Earl of Somerset (26 December 1613). Philip had earlier that year participated in Campion's *The Lord's Masque*, presented on the evening of the wedding of Princess Elizabeth to Frederick, Elector Palatine (14 February).

In the astonishingly successful masque *The Gypsies Metamorphosed*, written by Jonson and performed first in August 1621 at the estate of the Earl of Buckingham at Burley, William Herbert has the distinction of being a guest singled out to have his fortune told by one of the gypsies. The character Jackman says to the Lord Chamberlain: "You are a good man"; "And faithful you are."[42] Jackman further underscores Pembroke's involvement with the arts: "You know how to use your sword and your pen, / And you love not alone the arts but the man: / The Graces and Muses everywhere follow / You, as you were their second Apollo." Records indicate the Herbert brothers' involvement with other masques as well, and they regularly took part in tournaments and tilts. Therefore, from whatever angle we approach the subject, the incomparable pair of brethren seem logical and completely worthy candidates for the Folio's dedication. Small wonder that in the heading Heminge and Condell refer to them as "our singular good lords."

[41] Dick Taylor, Jr., "The Masque and the Lance: The Earl of Pembroke in Jacobean Court Performances," *Tulane Studies in English* 8 (1958), 21–53; 21.
[42] Quotations come from Ben Jonson, *Masques and Entertainments*, ed. Henry Morley (London: G. Routledge, 1890), 268.

Because the author of the plays printed in the Folio no longer lives, Heminge and Condell seek patronage not so much for the person as for his "remaines." They urge the Herbert brothers to be patrons for "Shakespeare" rather than Shakespeare. The emphasis therefore falls on this text and the hope that the patrons will lend luster to this enterprise and by their stature endow this book with additional merit. Such defines aristocratic patronage for as far back as we can trace it. As Jonson wrote in his dedication to *Catiline*, Heminge and Condell also hope that this collection will be read by the light of the noble lords. Such light may shine far into the future.

But Heminge and Condell engage a fair amount of their rhetorical strategy in documenting the past: namely, the brothers' past favors. Therefore, the epistle proper begins: "Whilst we studie to be thankful in our particular, for the many favours we have received from your L.L." The Herberts have "prosequuted" the texts and Shakespeare "with so much favour." They add: "For, so much were your L.L. likings of the severall parts, when they were acted, as before they were published, the Volume ask'd to be yours." Past favors, of course, offer historically one of the principal reasons for seeking additional patronage from aristocrats. As the discussion above documents, these King's men evidenced much support for the King's Men and drama.

Heminge and Condell adopt a suitably modest persona. After all, they write to lordships from the position of being mere actors. They insist that they have but collected the plays without regard for ambition, self-profit, or fame: "onely to keepe the memory of so worthy a Friend, & Fellow alive, as was our Shakespeare, by humble offer of his playes, to your most noble patronage." The actors have no particular authority: "We cannot go beyond our owne powers" – hence the need for patrons. If any "faults" appear in the texts, consider them "committed, by a payre so carefull to shew their gratitude both to the living [the Herberts], and the dead [Shakespeare]." Modesty may account for the somewhat curious way that Heminge and Condell at the beginning raise the issues of "rashnesse in the enterprize, and feare of the successe." Dedicating the Folio to the Herberts can scarcely be deemed "rash" – prudent and shrewd perhaps, but not rash. Fearing success must refer to the worry about the fate of the book. They cannot imagine that the Herberts would "descend to the reading of these trifles." And yet they add a bracing recognition: "while we name them trifles, we have depriv'd our selves of the defence of our Dedication." Exactly. Self-effacement could call these plays "trifles," or perhaps an exalted aesthetic sense that cannot take plays seriously. Our humble opinion, Heminge and Condell seem to say, can regard the plays as trifles; but when we recall the lordships' delight in and support of these plays, then they assume greater value. Rhetorically, Heminge and Condell probably choose "trifles" as a recognizably loaded term that can easily be dismissed.

The "parent" metaphor permeates the dedication. Heminge and Condell write: "you will use the like indulgence toward them [texts], you have done unto their parent [Shakespeare]." As de Grazia observes: "The dedication to Pembroke and Montgomery refers to the plays as children who have lost their natural parent and need a legal surrogate."[43] This role the Herberts fulfill. The actors have "done an office to the dead, to procure his Orphanes, Guardians." De Grazia adds: "Thus the dedicatory epistle represents the contents of the Folio as a family, all issuing from the same parent and entitled to his sustaining legacy."[44] As other dedications note the Herbert brothers' literary parentage, so here Heminge and Condell decide to make them substitute parents, protecting Shakespeare's progeny.

Not surprisingly, given what we saw in some of the other dedications to Pembroke and Montgomery, the religious image resonates strongly here. Heminge and Condell have "justly observed, no man to come neere your L.L. but with a kind of religious addresse." This they intend to do also: "to make the present worthy of your H.H. by the perfection." They come with what they have, as the homespun image of "country hands" makes clear. Religion works two ways: first, reverential awe with which they approach the patrons; and second, religious sanction for the Folio itself. "It was no fault to approch their Gods, by what meanes they could," Heminge and Condell write. And they enunciate this principle: "And the most, though meanest, of things are made more precious, when they are dedicated to Temples. In that name therefore, we most humbly consecrate to you H.H. these remaines of your servant Shakespeare." As the Herbert brothers transform into temples, so the act of consecrating this text elevates it and makes it worthy. One could say that Shakespeare has been canonized. His "remaines" may refer either to his corpse or to his corpus of work. Either way, he and his plays gain transcendental stature. The transubstantiation of Shakespeare leads to these texts. In a sense, the religious rhetoric logically extends the parental metaphor. These lords, these temples, evoke all the cultural adulation given to noble aristocrats – a clear instance of the older system of patronage at work.

---

[43] De Grazia, *Shakespeare Verbatim*, 37.   [44] De Grazia, *Shakespeare Verbatim*.

A linguistic sign of reverence appears in Heminge and Condell's consistent failure to name Pembroke and Montgomery within the epistle's text. Instead, they regularly refer to the lords as "H.H." (Honors) or "L.L." (Lordships). If the noblemen had not been named in the heading of the epistle, we might not know to whom Heminge and Condell refer. They sign their names as "Your Lordships most bounden," reflecting indebtedness, obligation. The bonds that exist among Shakespeare, Heminge and Condell, and Pembroke and Montgomery suggest a triangular boundary. Within those bounds aristocratic patronage functions, protecting and supporting the writer's trifles until they can be consecrated through dedication to Temples. The well-wrought dedication becomes the greatest remains.

As suggested earlier, the Address "To the great Variety of Readers" by its typography alone contrasts with the Dedication. It opens another world of patronage: the future in which readers and purchasers of books provide support and financial reward for writers, rendering less important the practice of aristocratic patronage. The commercial marketplace becomes crucial, as Heminge and Condell already hint at. They see the wave and way of the future. One wonders if the opening sentence of the Address signals the transition from aristocrat to mere readers: "From the most able, to him that can but spell." In any event, Heminge and Condell evoke the exchange value system of patronage: in a monetary transaction the reader gains a copy of the book with which the reader can do whatever he or she desires. In its simplest form, purchase completes patronage. This comes with a sobering recognition: "the fate of all Bookes depends upon your capacities" – no wealthy, well-placed aristocrat to lead a rescue. "Whatever you do, Buy."

Purchase empowers the reader to exercise judgment: "Judge your sixe-pen'orth, your shillings worth, your five shillings worth . . . or higher." The Shakespeare Folio costs one pound, which buys a large measure of potential judgment. These plays, Heminge and Condell argue, have already passed a judgment, that made by theatre audiences: "these Playes have had their triall alreadie." They have been sanctioned, "quitted rather by a Decree of Court." Heminge and Condell negotiate skillfully the terrain between performance and publication.

In fact, the final paragraph of the Address focuses on editorial matters, beginning with the recognition that the actors function as substitutes for Shakespeare, he who did not live to oversee his writings. Heminge and Condell have assumed "the office of their care, and paine, to have collected & publish'd them." They make a kind of parental claim. Their

To the great Variety of Readers.

From the moſt able, to him that can but ſpell: There you are number'd. We had rather you were weighd. Eſpecially, when the fate of all Bookes depends vpon your capacities : and not of your heads alone, but of your purſes. Well! It is now publique, & you wil ſtand for your priuiledges wee know : to read, and cenſure. Do ſo, but buy it firſt. That doth beſt commend a Booke, the Stationer ſaies. Then, how odde ſoeuer your braines be, or your wiſedomes, make your licence the ſame, and ſpare not. Iudge your ſixe-pen'orth, your ſhillings worth, your fiue ſhillings worth at a time, or higher, ſo you riſe to the iuſt rates, and welcome. But, what euer you do, Buy. Cenſure will not driue a Trade, or make the Iacke go. And though you be a Magiſtrate of wit, and ſit on the Stage at *Black-Friers*, or the *Cock-pit*, to arraigne Playes dailie, know, theſe Playes haue had their triall alreadie, and ſtood out all Appeales ; and do now come forth quitted rather by a Decree of Court, then any purchas'd Letters of commendation.

It had bene a thing, we confeſſe, worthie to haue bene wiſhed, that the Author himſelfe had liu'd to haue ſet forth, and ouerſeen his owne writings ; But ſince it hath bin ordain'd otherwiſe, and he by death departed from that right, we pray you do not envie his Friends, the office of their care, and paine, to haue collected & publiſh'd them ; and ſo to haue publiſh'd them, as where (before) you were abus'd with diuerſe ſtolne, and ſurreptitious copies, maimed, and deformed by the frauds and ſtealthes of iniurious impoſtors, that expos'd them : euen thoſe, are now offer'd to your view cur'd, and perfect of their limbes; and all the reſt, abſolute in their numbers, as he conceiued thē. Who, as he was a happie imitator of Nature, was a moſt gentle expreſſer of it. His mind and hand went together : And what he thought, he vttered with that eaſineſſe, that wee haue ſcarſe receiued from him a blot in his papers. But it is not our prouince, who onely gather his works, and giue them you, to praiſe him. It is yours that reade him. And there we hope, to your diuers capacities, you will finde enough, both to draw, and hold you : for his wit can no more lie hid, then it could be loſt. Reade him, therefore ; and againe, and againe : And if then you doe not like him, ſurely you are in ſome manifeſt danger, not to vnderſtand him. And ſo we leaue you to other of his Friends, whom if you need, can bee your guides : if you neede them not, you can leade your ſelues, and others. And ſuch Readers we wiſh him.

A 3 .   *Iohn Heminge.*
                 Henrie Condell.

2. "To the great Variety of Readers." From the 1623 edition of Shakespeare's *Comedies, Histories, and Tragedies*

editorial practices, they argue, help drive out "diverse stolne, and surrep-
titious copies, maimed, and deformed by the frauds . . . of imposters."
Good money drives out bad in this economy. Not only have Heminge and
Condell perfected the texts; but they have also perfected Shakespeare's
image with a creative piece of myth-making: Shakespeare, the "happie
imitator of Nature," the one who did not blot his papers. They serve his
memory and add the disingenuous claim: "it is not our province . . . to
praise him." Instead, in the circulation of judgment the reader assumes
this task. Heminge and Condell admonish: "Reade him, therefore; and
againe, and againe: And if then you doe not like him, surely you are
in some manifest danger, not to understand him." The "them" of the
Epistle Dedicatory has become the "you" of the Address. "You" as reader
and purchaser can compete with aristocrats in differing systems of patronage. Heminge and Condell idealistically imagine a community of
readers busily reading, interpreting, and understanding the texts: "such
Readers we wish him." The "him" has to be "Shakespeare," the now
collected, consecrated, and canonized text.

Heminge and Condell, whose authorship of the Dedication and
Address has been questioned,[45] have nevertheless succeeded in working both sides of the street. They understand the necessity for these
two competing and complementary systems of patronage. They have
skillfully positioned the Folio to reap the advantages of aristocratic
and market-place patronage. In an ironic twist, these preliminary matters remain in all four seventeenth-century editions of the Folio, even
though Pembroke had died before the Second Folio, and Montgomery
before the Third. Therefore, the Epistle Dedicatory increasingly has
vestigial value and relevance; on the other hand, one could argue that
the Address to readers continues to have vitality and pertinence. In the
eighteenth century and subsequent centuries the Epistle and Address
either vanish from complete editions of Shakespeare or appear only
as ancillary documents. But in 1623, they underscore the struggle for
patronage and two actors' astute understanding of how to launch and
perpetuate Shakespeare's remains.

---

[45] See W. W. Greg, *The Shakespeare First Folio* (Oxford: Clarendon Press, 1955), 17–18. Greg leans
   toward Jonson as possible author of these items, although he admits there may be no compelling
   reason to deny the authorship by Heminge and Condell.

CHAPTER 3

Shakespeare, the Cobhams, and the dynamics of theatrical patronage

Paul Whitfield White

The reputation of William Brooke, tenth Baron Cobham, has not fared well with either mainstream historians or theatre/literary scholars of the early modern period. Neither the *DNB* nor the *Who's Who in Shakespeare's England* even bothers to give him an entry, despite his being a politician of some influence at Queen Elizabeth's court, a distinguished patron of letters, and Shakespeare's second Lord Chamberlain.[1] If mainstream historians have underestimated Cobham's importance (as his only modern biographer David McKeen maintains), theatre scholars have misleadingly represented him as either a papist sympathizer who betrayed the throne or a puritan zealot who betrayed the theatre, when it is entirely plausible that he was neither.[2]

As is well documented, the significance of the Cobham family for Shakespeare studies is that William Brooke's term as Lord Chamberlain in 1596/97 and his son Henry's succession to the Barony in March 1597 coincide with the widely accepted dating of *1 Henry IV* and *The Merry Wives of Windsor*, two plays which, apparently, so offended the Cobhams that Shakespeare and his company were compelled to change the names of Oldcastle (fourth Lord Cobham and revered Protestant martyr) to Falstaff in *1 Henry IV*, and Brooke (the Cobham family name) to Broome in *Merry Wives*. On these matters, most critics agree. Where they part company, however, is on whether Shakespeare deliberately slighted the

---

[1] See David McKeen, *A Memory of Honour: The Life of William Brooke, Lord Cobham*, 2 vols. (Salzburg: University of Salzburg, 1986), 173. Like other students of the Cobhams, I am much indebted to McKeen's copiously documented and absorbing biography, even if I disagree with him on several points. See also Alan Palmer and Veronica Palmer, *Who's Who in Shakespeare's England* (New York: St. Martin's Press, 1981). Illustrating Cobham's considerable reputation as a literary patron is the dedication to him of Holinshed's *Chronicles*, 2nd edn., and Harrison's *Description of England*.

[2] See Alice-Lyle Scoufos, *Shakespeare's Typological Satire: A Study of the Falstaff-Oldcastle Problem* (Athens, OH: Ohio University Press, 1979); E. K. Chambers, *The Elizabethan Stage*, 4 vols. (Oxford: Clarendon Press, 1923).

Cobhams and, if so, under what circumstances and why. Various theories have been offered. Shakespeare's company satirized the Cobhams to please their patron, George Carey, whose hopes to succeed his father as Lord Chamberlain were dashed by the elder Brooke's appointment, and who later competed with the younger Brooke who wished to succeed *his* father in office; to please Shakespeare's literary patron Southampton and his mentor the Earl of Essex, who hated the Cobhams; to avenge the elder Cobham, William Brooke, for his negligent handling of theatrical affairs as Lord Chamberlain. Of course, gaining some measure of independence from ruling-class patrons by virtue of their success in the popular amphitheatres, the players may not have been put up to satirizing the Cobhams by any ruling-class patron. Conversely, at least in the case of *1 Henry IV*, they may not have done it at all, unwittingly offending the Cobhams by simply taking the name Oldcastle from an earlier box-office success, *The Famous Victories of Henry V*.

Whatever happened, the careers and reputations of Lord Chamberlain Cobham and his son, the eleventh Baron Cobham, Henry Brooke (himself a little-known sponsor of court entertainment), are important for the study of late Elizabethan theatrical patronage, and it is within this context that I wish to examine their interaction with the late Elizabethan theatre community, and particularly with Shakespeare's company. As Lord Chamberlain from 8 August 1596 to his death on 5 March 1597, William Brooke was, next to the Queen herself, *the* most powerful theatrical patron in England, and yet very little is known (though speculation abounds) about his handling of theatrical affairs and his relationship with the nation's premier acting troupe. My first concern below is to examine a much overlooked document illuminating Cobham's conduct as Lord Chamberlain on a specific occasion at court during the winter theatre season in 1596/97. I will then revisit what critics have called "the Oldcastle controversy" as a focal point for discussing several patronage-related issues: playwright/player criticism of patrons, the conflicts and tensions between major figures in the patronage system (the Lord Chamberlain and his deputy the Master of the Revels), and the role of patronage drama in factional politics at court. Finally, the production of a series of Oldcastle plays by Lord Admiral Nottingham's Men, *The History of Sir John Oldcastle, Lord Cobham*, not to mention several other plays, may tell us something about the broader functions and effects of patronage drama on the Cecil–Cobham/Essex rivalry at the end of Elizabeth's reign.

I

In 1925, E. K. Chambers published in *The Review of English Studies* several documents which he discovered too late to include in *The Elizabethan Stage* (1923). Among them is a letter from one Edward Jones, French secretary at Queen Elizabeth's court, to William Brooke during his tenure as Lord Chamberlain.[3] This letter, which reports an extraordinary incident involving the Lord Chamberlain during a play performance at Whitehall, has received virtually no attention from theatre historians. I quote it in full because I think it not only gives us a glimpse of William Brooke conducting his official duties as Lord Chamberlain at a court play (performed by Shakespeare's company as we shall see below), but also because it may cast some further light on the disputed relationship between the Elizabethan Lords Cobham (William and his heir, Henry) and the Oldcastle affair of the mid-to-late 1590s.

Your L. hath done me some disgraces which greive me so much as I must complayne thereof to your L. And that which greiveth me most is the publicke disgrace which your L. gave me at the play on Sunday night not only before many of my frendes that thought your L. did me wronge but in the hearinge of my wife who beinge with childe did take it so ill as she wept and complayned in the place, for I cam to her but to aske her how she did & not to stay there, and your L. liftinge up your staffe at me, called me sirra and bide me gett me lower saucy fellowe besides other wordes of disgrace. All which though I bear patiently at your L. handes, yet because [it] seemes to proceede of some spightfull informacion of me which I am loth sholde harbor in your L. opinyon, I beseech your L. to give me leave to say that I knowe noee cause why your L. or any other sholde despise me. For my birth I am indeed one of the meanest of my kindred, but yet not base: but well descended as many honorable persons the L. Keper, the Erle of Essex, the Countesse of Warwicke and others of good quality in the courte to whom I am allyed doe knowe. My educacion hath been allwayes like a gentleman both here in Englande and biyonde the seas, and such as hath bene so made knowne to her Maiestie by divers of her counsell as her Maiestie was pleased to knowe me & thinke me worthy to serve her, as Sir John Stanhope can witnesse, Sir Robert Cecill also was present when her Maiestie of her selfe named me for secretary for the French tonge. Besides my life hath been honest and my behavior respective, and I thank God I am noe begger (though the worse by a 1000L by means of your L. crossinge of me). These things I speak not in vayne glory for alas they are but meane things and agreable to the poore countenance I carry, but to lett your L. knowe that I deserve not so much your displeasure or skorne. Therefore I beseech your L.

---

[3] E. K. Chambers, "Elizabethan Stage Gleanings," *Review of English Studies*, o.s., 1 (1925), 75–77; 76–77. To my knowledge, except for McKeen, *A Memory of Honour*, 652–54, students of the Cobhams and of the Oldcastle affair have failed to examine this document.

cancell your ill opinyon of me and forbeare to despise me or to disgrace me till your L. shall see me doe any thinge indiscretely or unworthy a gentleman. I could have procuredd many either of the counsell or the nobility to deal with your L. herein and to be mediators for your favor but it shall be needles if your L. will be pleased to take this in good parte at my handes which I protest is meant only to remove your L. ill opinyon from me and to prevent further disgrace, this beinge the gratest that ever I received in my life and most unworthily. And so I pray God to prosper your honor. Your L. in all humbleness.

Edw. Jones

Court records, along with circumstantial evidence, enable us to determine with some confidence the date of the performance Jones alludes to here, its location, and the acting company on hand. The only two known plays staged on Sundays at the royal court during Cobham's tenure in office in 1596/97 took place on 27 December 1596, and 6 February 1597. In both cases, Shakespeare's company performed; indeed they were the only troupe called to court that winter play season, performing four times during Christmas in the Great Chamber at Whitehall, and one month later traveling with the court up to Richmond to contribute two plays to the Shrovetide festivities. Since Cobham was no longer active at court after the unexpected death of his daughter at the beginning of February 1597, the occasion about which Jones writes must have been on 27 December. It took place in the Great Chamber at Whitehall, which, having less than half the floor space of the palace's Great Hall, provided a more intimate setting for royal entertainment.[4]

Jones is writing to Cobham to complain about his embarrassing altercation with the Lord Chamberlain at that Sunday evening performance. Apparently, he and his wife were not seated together, and because she was "with childe," Jones writes, he "cam to her but to aske her how she did & not to stay there" while the play was in progress, at which point Cobham approached Jones with his white staff (in this instance not used merely as a symbol of his office as Lord Chamberlain), calling him "saucy fellowe besides other wordes of disgrace" and commanding him to "get . . . lower." This last remark might suggest that Jones was visually as well as audibly distracting the court audience's attention. Yet the Lord Chamberlain may have been ordering Jones to return to his "lower" assigned place, perhaps the standing area on the hall floor, his wife – widowed recently to a sergeant-at-arms, we learn – having secured a place on one of the scaffolded degrees reserved "for Ladys & the Kings

---

[4] See Chambers, *The Elizabethan Stage*, IV, 110, 165; John Astington, *English Court Theatre 1558–1642* (Cambridge: Cambridge University Press, 1999), 51, 234–35.

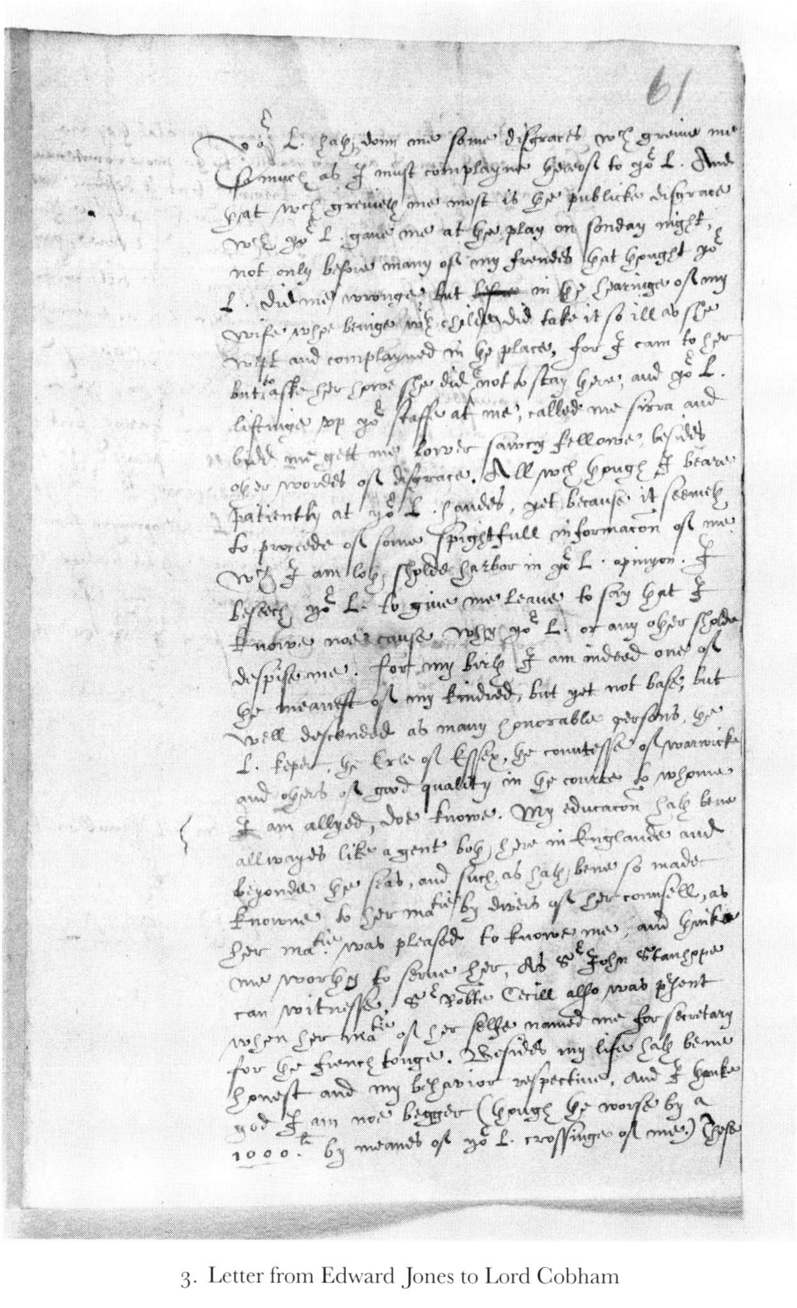

61

Yo[r] L. hath done me some disgrace w[ch] greiveth me
so much as I must complayne thereof to yo[r] L. And
that w[ch] greiveth me most is the publicke disgrace
w[ch] yo[r] L. gave me at the play on sonday night,
not only before many of my frendes that thought yo[r]
L. did me wronge, but ~~[illegible]~~ in the hearinge of my
wife who beinge wth childe did take it so ill as she
wept and complayned in the place, for I cam to her
but to aske her howe she did not to stay there; and yo[r] L.
liftinge up yo[r] staffe at me, called me sirra and
badd me gett me lower sawcy fellowe, beside
other wordes of disgrace. All w[ch] though I beare
patiently at yo[r] L. handes, yet because it seemeth
to proceade of some spightfull informacon of me
w[ch] I am loth should harbor in yo[r] L. opinyon. I
beseche yo[r] L. to give me leave to say that I
knowe no cause why yo[r] L. or any other should
despise me. For my birth I am indeed one of
the meanest of my kindred, but yet not base; but
well descended as many honorable persons, the
L. Keper, the Erle of Essex, the countesse of warwicke
and others of good quality in the courte to whome
I am allyed, doe knowe. My educacon hath bene
allwayes like a gent[l] both here in Englande and
beyonde the seas, and such as hath bene so made
knowne to her ma[tie] by divers of the counsell, as
her ma[tie] was pleased to knowe me, and thinke
me worthy to serve her, as S[r] John Stanhope
can witnesse, & S[r] Robte Cecill also was present
when her ma[tie] of her selfe named me for secretary
for the Frenche tongue. Besides my life hath bene
honest and my behavior inoffensive. And I thanke
god I am not begger (though the worse by a
1000[li] by meanes of yo[r] L. crossinge of me.) These

3. Letter from Edward Jones to Lord Cobham

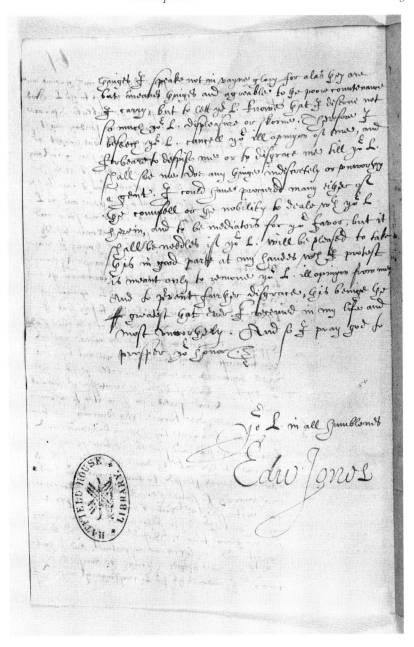

servants" at royal entertainments.[5] Presiding over and maintaining
order at royal court performances was a routine function of the Lord
Chamberlain, and indeed a special "standinge" was constructed by the
Office of the Works in the Hall and the Great Chamber at Whitehall
from which he kept watch on the audience as well as the play. Contemporary accounts indicate that he was not above using his white staff to
discipline, and usher from the auditorium if necessary, unruly playgoers,
the troublemaking Ben Jonson among them a few years later.[6] But in
this instance Cobham's intervention created the very disturbance it was
designed to prevent. If the indecorous display between the two men was
not enough to divert the Whitehall spectators' attention, then the weep-
ing and complaining of Jones's pregnant wife certainly did. It was an
incident that must have disrupted the players as much as it distracted the
audience. This is "the gratest [disgrace] that ever I received in my life
and most unworthily," Jones exclaims. His reason for writing, his letter
concludes, is to remove Cobham's "ill opinyon" of him and "to prevent
further disgrace."

What we know about Jones suggests that there may be more to the
letter than this, and indeed more to Cobham's outburst at the play.
A year-and-a-half earlier, the French secretary was married considerably above his station to the widow of Richard Branthwayt, a sergeant-
at-arms whose son, on his father's death, became a ward under the
mastership of Lord Burghley. Around this time, Burghley granted the
Branthwayt wardship to none other than Lord Cobham, his close
friend of more than thirty years. Cobham's biographer, David McKeen,
speculates that the thousand pounds Jones claims he lost due to "your
L. crossinge me" is the value of that wardship.[7] But this may not have
been the only reason for tension between the two men. Named "secretary
for French tonge" by Queen Elizabeth, an appointment opposed by
Cobham's now powerful son-in-law, Robert Cecil, Jones had also served
in the office of Vice Chamberlain Thomas Heneage during Henry
Hunsdon's long term as Lord Chamberlain until Heneage's death in
1595. More significantly, in August 1596, about four months before this

---

[5] Quoted by Astington, *English Court Theatre*, 84. Astington offers an extensive discussion of court
audiences on 161–88.

[6] See Astington, *English Court Theatre*, 91, 110 (and references cited there), 176–77; and Chambers,
Elizabethan Stage, I, 39.

[7] McKeen, *A Memory of Honour*, 652–53. It is, of course, quite possible that Jones is speaking fig-
uratively to emphasize the extent of his loss. One thinks of Hamlet's remark to Horatio, "I'll
take the ghost's word for a thousand pound." For this account of Jones, I am indebted to
McKeen.

performance, he became secretary to the Earl of Essex, who for some time had made no effort to hide his hatred for Cobham's heir, Henry Brooke, and who had had a run-in with the senior Brooke over foreign affairs. This may explain Jones' fear that the Lord Chamberlain's action "seemes to proceede of some spightfull informacion of me." Cobham's humiliating public rebuke should be seen within this context. Unfortunately, we cannot be sure of the play in question that night, but it is noteworthy that the one Shakespearean work repeatedly assigned to this winter season, *The First Part of Henry IV*, depicted in its earliest productions Cobham's Lollard ancestor, Sir John Oldcastle, second Lord Cobham, as a degenerate buffoon.[8] If indeed *1 Henry IV* was performed that eventful Sunday evening, then the Lord Chamberlain clearly had another reason to be indignant!

II

In the latter half of 1596, the position of Shakespeare's company in relation to governing-class patrons was a complicated one. Even though they had the exclusive privilege of appearing at court this winter season – in all they performed six times – the troupe no longer wore the livery of the Lord Chamberlain. This is noted in the Chamber Accounts, where on 26 December 1596 fifty pounds was paid to "John Hemynge and George Bryan s[e]rvuantes to the late Lorde Chamblayne and now s[e]rvuantes to the Lorde Hunsdon."[9] The "late Lorde Chamblayne" was Henry Carey, first Baron Hunsdon, who died the previous summer, on 23 July 1596. Hunsdon's death must have been a major blow to the company. He had served his players well, as he had the theatrical community at large since assuming the Chamberlaincy in 1585, as Andrew Gurr demonstrates elsewhere in this volume. The Queen's first cousin and a war hero whose greatest moment came in leading the royal army to a decisive victory against the rebels in the Northern Uprising of 1569, the elder Carey would have appreciated the dramatization of a similar defeat of the northern earls in *1 Henry IV*. If written after his death, "It would not have been difficult for the shrewd businessmen of the company to introduce

---

[8] For example, A. R. Humphreys (ed.), *The First Part of Henry IV*, Arden Shakespeare (London: Methuen, 1960), xiii–xiv; David Bevington (ed.), *Henry IV, Part 1* (Oxford: Clarendon, 1987), 9; Robert Fehrenbach, "When Lord Cobham and Edmund Tilney 'were att odds': Oldcastle, Falstaff, and the Date of *1 Henry IV*," *Shakespeare Studies* 18 (1986), 87–101; Gary Taylor, "William Shakespeare, Richard James and the House of Cobham," *Review of English Studies*, n.s., 38 (1987), 334–54.

[9] Chambers, *Elizabethan Stage*, IV, 165.

their new play as homage to their dead lord."[10] Nevertheless, the weeks immediately following Carey's death may have been very anxious ones for Shakespeare's troupe. Observing the numerous other recent troupes which "broke" when their noble patrons died, the players could not be certain that Hunsdon's heir, George Carey, would continue the family patronage, especially since he failed to succeed his father in office as Lord Chamberlain, as he clearly had hoped to do and, indeed, was led to believe he would by Robert Cecil, who told him he would not "fayle of succession" to his father's high office.[11] Needless to say, Carey did continue the sponsorship of his father's company, as early as 1 August, when on touring the provinces due to the London plague they appeared in Faversham, Kent, as "my Lord Hunsdowns plaiers," for which they were paid a modest sixteen shillings.[12]

The younger Hunsdon, who succeeded William Brooke as Lord Chamberlain in March 1597 and thereafter took his place on the Privy Council, remained the company's nominal patron through the remainder of Queen Elizabeth's reign. In conjunction with Lord Howard of Effingham, he maintained the duopoly of his own company with the Admiral's Men set in 1594 by his father and Howard, and yet, if on the whole a supportive patron, he was not above signing his name to the neighborhood petition blocking James Burbage's plan to open the second Blackfriars Playhouse to provide a winter venue for the Hunsdon troupe in the fall of 1596. Like Cobham, Hunsdon lived virtually next door to the new playhouse in the Blackfriars precinct, and he probably did not want to put up with noisy playgoers and the accompanying traffic of coaches and horses, although he may also have known that the new playhouse violated the agreement which his father as Lord Chamberlain had made with the Lord Mayor for no playing venues to open within the city walls.[13]

Hunsdon continued to provide Shakespeare's troupe with the family name and livery, but his sponsorship had its limitations, as the Blackfriars' petition reveals, and their privileged treatment at court owed probably less to his influence in late 1596 than to their already established reputation as the nation's premier troupe. If it goes without saying that the Queen, herself, favored Shakespeare and his fellow players, we should

---

[10] Peter Thomson, *Shakespeare's Professional Career* (Cambridge: Cambridge University Press, 1992), 122.

[11] Letter from Cecil to Carey, 25 July 1596; cited in Charles Nicholl, *A Cup of Newes: The Life of Thomas Nashe* (London: Routledge and Kegan Paul, 1984), 249.

[12] Andrew Gurr, *Shakespearean Playing Companies* (Oxford: Clarendon Press, 1996), 303.

[13] Ibid., 65–67.

nevertheless not underestimate the roles of Lord Chamberlain Cobham, and his deputy, Edmund Tilney, Master of the Revels, in securing their place at court and in the London community at large. Cobham's appointment as Lord Chamberlain is sometimes thought to have been unexpected, if not inappropriate, for an aging courtier puritanically inclined and with little interest or experience in theatrical entertainment.[14] Yet these assumptions are mistaken. As early as November 1594 when the sixty-eight-year-old Henry Carey was in declining health, he filled in as "L. Chamberlain," according to one piece of court correspondence, and in the following spring he served as "ceremonial lieutenant to the sovereign" in the Knights of the Garter festivities.[15] Better known is the fact that he patronized a traveling acting company early in his career, from 1563 through 1571.[16] Whether or not he colluded with the London Corporation against urban and suburban playing, as some evidence suggests (more on this below), there is every reason to believe Cobham was an experienced administrator of festivities at court, coordinating arrangements amongst the offices of the Revels, the Works, and the Wardrobe in producing the various pageants and plays demanded by the Queen and her circle in the winter season of 1596/97. To the extent that he arranged for Shakespeare's company to perform at the royal palaces that season, he was their royal court patron, and one they could not do without. It is nevertheless one of the ironies of the Oldcastle controversy that Cobham would give exclusive privilege during his tenure as Lord Chamberlain to the company which was perceived to defame his family reputation, and at the expense of the players instrumental in rehabilitating that reputation a few years later, the Lord Admiral's Men.

But no less significant for the company's well-being was the Master of the Revels, Edmund Tilney. Facilitated in office by Thomas Howard, to whom he was related, and receiving an exclusive patent to license all plays and playing places back in 1581, Tilney was, by 1596, an experienced political veteran of the theatre and a power to reckon with in the London theatrical community. Officially a deputy of the Chamberlain's

---

[14] See E. A. J. Honigmann, "Sir John Oldcastle: Shakespeare's Martyr," in John W. Mahon and Thomas A. Pendleton (eds.), *"Fanned and Winnowed Opinions": Shakespearean Essays Presented to Harold Jenkins* (London: Methuen, 1980), 118–32; 125; J. Dover Wilson, "The Origin and Development of Shakespeare's *Henry IV*," *Library* 26 (1945), 13.

[15] McKeen, *A Memory of Honour*, 629–31.

[16] Giles Dawson (ed.), *Records of Plays and Players in Kent 1450–1642*, Malone Society Collections VII (Oxford: Oxford University Press, 1965), 14, 138; J. T. Murray, *English Dramatic Companies 1558–1642*, 2 vols. (1912; reprint, New York: Russell, 1963), II, 82.

office, he as much dealt directly with the Privy Council as with his immediate superior, as when he was commanded by the Council in 1583 to choose the twelve best actors in the nation to form the Queen's Men.[17] Considering the Lord Chamberlain's many other pressing responsibilities at court, Tilney appears to have been given quite extraordinary discretionary powers. He was not a patron in any traditional sense, since the companies and impresarios like Henslowe and Burbage paid *him*, but as was typical of many patron/suitor arrangements, the Revels Master and the companies needed each other, and it was in Tilney's interests to look out for the players as much as to exercise authority over them. It seems likely, therefore, that in the winter of 1596/97 when Cobham was settling in to his new position, Tilney and the theatre leaders felt closer to each other than either did to the recently appointed Lord Chamberlain. Ideally, the Revels Master served the interests of the Lord Chamberlain, but it must not have always worked out that way and, as we shall see shortly, Tilney and Cobham appear to have had a falling out during the period they worked together.

We should not exclude other influential figures at court who may have exercised influence over Shakespeare's company. Much has been made of the connections with the Essex circle: Shakespeare's literary dedications to the Earl of Southampton who, by 1596, was a close advisor to Essex; the admiring allusion to Essex by the Chorus in *Henry V*; the payment by the Earl's followers to stage *Richard II* on the eve of the failed rebellion in February 1601. The Earl himself, who sponsored an acting company in the 1590s and was apparently an enthusiastic playgoer, seems also to have been familiar with Shakespeare's "Falstaff" plays (more on this below), so while the evidence is circumstantial, it is not unreasonable to suppose that the players, like so many of the younger generation in the 1590s, identified with and supported the charismatic Earl and his reformist agenda in the face of the current gerontocracy dominating the government.[18] What *is* clear is that Shakespeare and his company found themselves inexorably caught up in the factional politics at court dividing Essex and his followers from the Cobhams, who bonded closely with the Cecils.

[17] Scott McMillin and Sally-Beth MacLean, *The Queen's Men and Their Plays* (Cambridge: Cambridge University Press, 1998), 10. For more on Tilney as Revels Master and his symbiotic relationship with the players, see Richard Dutton, *Mastering the Revels: The Regulation and Censorship of English Renaissance Drama* (Iowa City: University of Iowa Press, 1991), 41–116, esp. 96.
[18] On Essex's company, see Gurr, *Shakespearean Playing Companies*, 170–71. On watching plays, see Chambers, *Elizabethan Stage*, I, 220.

The demands, influences, and restrictions which court patronage brought to bear on Shakespeare's company in the mid-1590s need to be balanced against the level of autonomy and independence the troupe achieved by virtue of its economic success in the amphitheatres and in provincial playing venues on tour. By the 1590s, playwrights and players had no doubt developed their own viewpoints on such matters as religion, politics, and the theatre, and there is no reason to doubt that they voiced those personalized opinions on stage. Moreover, in the environs of the public theatres, the players were subject to the demands and tastes of popular audiences who financed their careers and, in the case of the fortunate few such as Shakespeare himself, made them prosperous. Thomas Dekker, in *The Gull's Horn-Book*, spoke for his fellow dramatists and actors when he frankly admitted that drama is a commodity exchanged for payment, with audiences as the "Muses." "The theatre," he exclaimed, "is your poets' Royal Exchange upon which their Muses – that are now turned to merchants . . . barter away that light commodity of words for a lighter ware than words – plaudits . . . Your gallant, your courtier and your captain had wont to be the soundest paymasters . . . when your groundling and gallery commoner buys his sport by the penny and like a haggler is glad to utter it again by retailing."[19]

III

It is with these complex patronage relationships in mind that we should reconsider the so-called "Oldcastle controversy," with its central perplexing question of what precise role Shakespeare and his company played in this controversy, as evidenced by the supposed defamation of the Cobham family name and ancestry in *1 Henry IV* and *Merry Wives of Windsor*. The broad outlines of this controversy are familiar but bear briefly repeating here. When Shakespeare's *1 Henry IV* was first performed, probably in mid-to-late 1596, that great comic worldling we know as Sir John Falstaff was named Sir John Oldcastle. Audiences in London and beyond may have known this character from Shakespeare's chief dramatic source, the old Queen's Men's *Famous Victories of Henry V*, yet Oldcastle, the fourth Lord Cobham, was also a widely known historical figure, a Lollard leader who, according to Catholic apologists and sympathizers, died a heretic to the true Church and a traitor to the English monarchy. While some

---

[19] Thomas Dekker, *The Gull's Horn Book*, quoted in Kathleen McLuskie, "The Poets' Royal Exchange: Patronage and Commerce in Early Modern Drama," *Yearbook of English Studies* 21 (1991), 53–62.

Protestants also saw Oldcastle somewhat disfavorably as a forerunner of Puritan separatism, he was more generally hailed by mainstream Protestantism as a godly man who heroically died for his faith.[20] This is how he is perceived in the second edition of Holinshed's *Chronicles*, dedicated to Lord Cobham. Indeed, in direct contrast to the charming figure of vice Shakespeare developed him as, the more strident Protestant chronicles such as Foxe's influential and popular *Acts and Monuments* canonized Oldcastle as a pre-Reformation saint and model of Christian piety, courage, and loyalty to the Crown.

The Elizabethan Cobhams were not in the direct line of descent from Oldcastle, since Sir John married into the family in 1408 and only became Lord Cobham thereafter, but they proudly regarded him as their ancestor. That William Brooke, or his son, the inheritor of his title, were offended by what they perceived to be a smear on their family honor is clear from a letter by one Richard James some twenty years after the fact. James writes:

> In Shakespeare's first show of harry the fifth, the person with which he undertook to play a buffoon was not Falstaff but Sir John Oldcastle, and . . . offence being worthily taken by personages descended from his title (as peradventure by many others also who ought to have him in honorable memory) the poet was put to make an ignorant shift of abusing Sir John Falstaff, a man not inferior of virtue, though not so famous in piety.[21]

It is safe to say, therefore, that under pressure from the Brookes, either the elder Cobham or his son Henry Brooke, the inheritor of the family title, Shakespeare dutifully changed the name to Falstaff. Other names were changed as well, those of the old knight's companions, Russell and Harvey (who also had prominent descendants at court), who became Peto and Bardolph.[22] At what point performances of the play started using the name Falstaff is unclear. However, the revision turns up in the first printed quarto of *1 Henry IV* in February 1598, possibly rushed out to press to appease the family, and in the Epilogue to *2 Henry IV* a disclaimer is tacked on after the prayer to the Queen which usually concludes it,

---

[20] On the Lollards' associations with radical puritanism in late Elizabethan England, see David Kastan, *Shakespeare after Theory* (New York: Routledge, 1999), 100–01. Kastan is mistaken, I think, in arguing that late Elizabethans came to identify Oldcastle primarily with puritan radicals. Both the Drayton-Munday-Hathaway-Wilson *Oldcastle* play, as well as John Weever's poetic tribute *A Mirror of Martyrs*, carefully distinguish Oldcastle from the separatists and other extremists, placing him in the mainstream of serious Protestantism. See E. A. J. Honigmann, *John Weever: A Biography of a Literary Associate of Shakespeare and Jonson* (New York: St. Martin's, 1987), 34.

[21] Cited in Peter Corbin and Douglas Sedge (eds.), *The Oldcastle Controversy: Sir John Oldcastle, Part 1 and The Famous Victories of Henry V* (Manchester: Manchester University Press, 1991), 10.

[22] See Bevington (ed.), *Henry IV, Part 1*, 5.

stating, "Oldcastle died a martyr, and this is not the man." It may have been around this time that Henry Brooke demanded that revisions be made to two other plays which allegedly defamed the Cobhams, specifically *Merry Wives of Windsor*, where "Brooke," the pseudonym taken by Mistress Ford's jealousy-consumed husband, was changed to Broome, and *2 Henry VI*, where a whole section of a scene implicating Eleanor Cobham, wife to the "good duke" Gloucester, in treason, is expunged from the text in the 1623 folio edition.[23] The damage, however, had already been done, with court gossip identifying the younger Cobham, Henry Brooke, with the Oldcastle/Falstaff character. The controversy dragged on through 1599 when, in October or November, the rival Admiral's Men condemned Shakespeare's treatment of Oldcastle as "forged invention" in the Prologue to its own dramatic production of *Sir John Oldcastle*.

Whether or not Shakespeare and his company deliberately offended the Cobhams is a question which has divided critics, and in one sense it is beside the point, for whatever intentions the company had, playgoers, at least those at court, *interpreted* the Oldcastle character as a deliberate send-up of the tenth or the eleventh Lord Cobham, or both, as will be discussed at further length later. The question of intention, however, is a significant one, for it comes to bear on the possible relationships Shakespeare and his company had with their patrons and it raises the additional question of whether the players engaged in criticism of persons in authority who, directly or indirectly, functioned as their patrons.

I would like to begin addressing this question by reference not to *1 Henry IV* but rather *The Merry Wives of Windsor*, for however much critics dispute whether the offense to William Brooke was intended in *1 Henry IV*, there is a wide consensus that the younger Cobham is definitely targeted in *Merry Wives*. The allusions to Oldcastle persist (for example, the Host rather curiously responds to an inquiry about Falstaff's whereabouts in Act 4, Scene 5, with, "Sir John, there's his Castle, his standing bed"), but more brazenly the family name itself is directly invoked in a context of ridicule. For the jealous Master Ford, in pursuit of Falstaff, who he is convinced has cuckolded him, assumes the identity of another would-be adulterer named Brooke. Extensive topical references link *Merry Wives* to the Feast of the Garter in April 1597, when the patron of Shakespeare's company, George Carey, was elected a new Knight of the Garter. As

[23] See T. W. Craik (ed.), *Merry Wives of Windsor* (New York: Oxford University Press, 1989); Andrew S. Cairncross (ed.), *The Second Part of King Henry VI*, Arden Shakespeare (1957; reprint, London: Routledge, 1988), app. 4.

with the name change of Oldcastle to Falstaff, the revision of "Brooke" as "Broome" in the folio edition deprives the play of much punning and topical significance. A brook, of course, may be crossed by a ford, and it is brook in this sense that Falstaff puns on when, on his first meeting with the disguised Ford, he says "Call him in. / Such Brooks are welcome to me, that o'erflows such liquor."[24] We assume that the object of this satire is Henry Brooke, since his father died on 5 March 1597, a month or so before the Feast of the Garter and before George Hunsdon finally secured the highly sought-after office of the Lord Chamberlain.

Why did Shakespeare and his company make light of the Brooke name in *Merry Wives*? It may simply be a case of the players, now safely under Carey's protection as the newly instituted Lord Chamberlain, getting back at the overly sensitive Brookes for forcing Shakespeare to change Oldcastle's name to Falstaff when no offense was deliberately given, perhaps after, or possibly even before, the previous winter season showing of *1 Henry IV* at court with Lord Chamberlain Cobham (and Edward Jones?) in attendance.[25] The reading certainly would give topical resonance to the comedy's opening exchange where Shallow heatedly complains to his cousin Slender about Falstaff's defaming his name:

SHALLOW: Sir Hugh, persuade me not; I will make a Star Chamber matter of it; if he were twenty Sir John Falstaffs, he shall not abuse Robert Shallow, Esquire.
SLENDER: In the country of Gloucester, Justice of Peace, and Coram.
SHALLOW: Ay, cousin Slender, and Custalorum.
SLENDER: Ay, and Ratolorum too; and a gentleman born, Master Parson, who writes himself 'Armigero' in any bill, warrant, quittance, or obligation – 'Armigero'.
SHALLOW: Ay, that I do; and have done any time these three hundred years.

(1.1.1–11)

As Janet Clare remarks, "Shallow's indignant reaction and comic exposition of his ancient lineage could conceivably have been written as a parody of the Brookes' reaction to the assumed slight upon their ancestry."[26]

It is not insignificant that a parody of the Cobhams' aggrandizement of their family's lineage, and particularly its ties to Oldcastle, shows up in another play performed by the Lord Chamberlain's Men in September 1598: Ben Jonson's *Every Man in his Humour* (with Shakespeare apparently

---

[24] Craik (ed.), *Merry Wives of Windsor*, 2.2.141–43.
[25] See Taylor, "William Shakespeare, Richard James, and the House of Cobham."
[26] Janet Clare, *'Art made tongue-tied by authority': Elizabethan and Jacobean Dramatic Censorship* (Manchester: Manchester University Press, 1990), 79.

in the cast). There, Cob, the water-bearer, boasts of his lineage drawn from "the harrot's books" (that is, Herald's Books) where his ancestor is shown to be "a mighty great cob," "my great-great-mighty-great-grandfather."[27] In a more explicit reference to Sir John Oldcastle, the fourth Lord Cobham, and the saint's day honoring his grisly martyrdom (first proposed by John Foxe in *Acts and Monuments*), Cob says "A fasting day no sooner comes, but my lineage goes to rack; poor cobs, they smoke for it, they are made martyrs o' the gridiron, they melt for passion." As David McKeen has shown, this is not overreading the text; other plays of the period mock the Elizabethan Cobham barony's complex formula of connecting themselves with Oldcastle by depicting characters who boast that Sir John Oldcastle was my "great Grand-father" and "my great-grandfathers fathers Uncle."[28]

With two comedies staged by the Lord Chamberlain's Men taking side-jabs at the Cobhams, it is quite conceivable that Hunsdon himself might have taken personal satisfaction in the topical satire. Despite the fact that the elder Cobham may have been the logical choice to succeed Hunsdon's father as Lord Chamberlain in August 1596, the forty-nine-year-old George Carey could not have been happy to be passed over for this appointment in favor of Cobham, especially considering the hints from Cecil that he was in line for it. Moreover, Carey competed with the younger Cobham for several offices vacated by the latter's father upon his death in March 1597: the Lord Warden of the Cinque Ports and the Lord Lieutenancy of Kent (which Cobham secured).[29] If Brooke, himself, did not have his eye on the Chamberlaincy at this time as well, we know that he lobbied vigorously for the appointment when George Carey fell ill in 1601. He may have been maneuvering for the office the previous summer when he hosted an entertainment and accommodated the Queen overnight in his Blackfriars mansion following a wedding. After supper on 6 June a lavish mask of eight Muses was shown and followed by dancing in which the Queen herself participated.[30]

Interestingly enough, only three months earlier and almost certainly in his own Blackfriars residence literally right next door, Lord Chamberlain Hunsdon was entertaining a distinguished guest of his own, the Flemish

[27] Ben Jonson, *Every Man in His Humor*, ed. Gabriele Bernhard Jackson (New Haven, Yale University Press, 1969), 1.4.14–18. See also Nicholl, *Cup of News*, 247–48; and Scoufos, *Shakespeare's Typological Satire*, 246–62.

[28] McKeen, *A Memory of Honour*, 24.

[29] See Nicholl, *Cup of News*, 249–50, and references cited there.

[30] Chambers, *Elizabethan Stage*, I, 169.

ambassador Louis Verreyken, with a play described as "Sir John Oldcastle."[31] As most scholars surmise, this must have been *1 Henry IV* – perhaps with Oldcastle's name revived for this private event – since it was performed by the Lord Chamberlain's Men. Apart from the Queen who favored him (possibly in deference to his mother who was among her closest friends until her death in 1591) and several prominent ladies of the court linked to him romantically during the nineties, the ambitious Henry was intensely disliked at court. Essex was particularly vocal in his hatred for the Baron, reportedly calling him "the Sycophant ... even to the Queene her selfe."[32] Hunsdon might have shared some of this dislike, and hence the provocative use of the Brooke family name in the Shakespeare and Jonson comedies of 1598, and a repeat send-up of the Baron in the private showing of *1 Henry IV* at his home two years later.

IV

But did this deliberate debunking of the Brookes, Carey-inspired or otherwise, pre-date *Merry Wives*? Was the comedy's satire merely re-taliation for the Brookes' oversensitive reading of *1 Henry IV* in which no offense to the Cobhams was intended, as Gary Taylor argues? Or was it possibly an extension of the deliberate satire which was more subtly developed in the former history play?

   The character of Oldcastle/Falstaff in *1 Henry IV*, and in *2 Henry IV* for that matter, raises two issues: one concerning the historical Oldcastle and the other concerning the living Cobhams, and I believe it is important, at least for the moment, to keep them separate and distinct. Both have implications for the study of patron–player relations, for in parodying Oldcastle, *1 Henry IV* risked offending Puritan-leaning officials at court and their constituencies; not the least important of these lords were the Earls of Pembroke and Essex, sometimes identified as Shakespeare's patrons.[33] And in burlesquing William Brooke, the company would, in effect, have been insulting the official who arranged their performances at court.

   In my mind, there can be little doubt that through his portrayal of Oldcastle in *1* and *2 Henry IV* Shakespeare voiced considerable unease

---

[31] Reported in a letter by Rowland Whyte; see Chambers, *Elizabethan Stage*, I, 220.
[32] McKeen, *A Memory of Honour*, 436.
[33] See Donna Hamilton, *Shakespeare and the Politics of Protestant England* (Lexington: University Press of Kentucky, 1992).

with the more extreme tendencies of late Elizabethan puritanism. In the play, Sir John's old-age debauchery and treasonable offenses both before and after going to war call into question hagiographic treatments of the Lollard leader popularized in Foxe's *Acts and Monuments* and other chronicles. Those more militantly Protestant publications strained credulity to the limit by praising him not merely as a model of Christian piety but a loyal subject of the Crown as well. Shakespeare's contemporaries would have picked up the numerous subtle and not-so-subtle references in the play's dialogue to Oldcastle's treasonable offenses and their punishment. In the play-acting scene of 2.4, for example, Hal describes him as "a roasted manningtree ox" (447), a rather grisly allusion to the Lollard's form of death in which he was suspended by chains around the waist from the gallows and consumed by the fire that even destroyed the scaffold. Catholic accounts of Oldcastle, which Shakespeare generally favors, railed against him as a traitor who fermented revolt and in fact probably instigated the Lollard rebellion in 1414, after which Oldcastle's steward was arrested. This seems closer to the truth than the accounts of Bale and Foxe which go to some lengths to defend the Lollard reformer's allegiance to Henry V right to the end. Yet the play's satire goes deeper, for in jesting tones, Sir John repeatedly speaks the language of the conscience-stricken puritan ("Monsieur Remorse" as Poins calls him [1.2.106–7]), who alternately longs for and despairs of repentance (1.2.91–94; 3.3.1–10), mutters about hellfire to Bardolph whom he likens to "the son of utter darkness," fears he is "one of the wicked" and not called to grace (1.2.91; 5.1.128–29), and so on. It is not surprising, therefore, that while many contemporaries undoubtedly found Sir John endearing and amusing (including the Queen, evidently), some serious-minded Protestants of the period were seemingly offended by Shakespeare's characterization. They certainly would have endorsed, if not contributed to, the Cobham family's insistence that Shakespeare make the name change to Falstaff, resulting in missed puns, irregular meters, and lost topical significance in the surviving text.[34]

Yet Shakespeare was not doing anything particularly new with this kind of anti-puritan satire, and he certainly knew that it would delight his popular patrons at the Theatre and Curtain. Kristen Poole has shown how Oldcastle/Falstaff's mock-puritan cant and burlesque staging derive

---

[34] See Gary Taylor, "The Fortunes of Falstaff," *Shakespeare Survey* 38 (1985), 85–100. References are to Bevington (ed.), *Henry IV, Part 1*.

from the government-sponsored pamphlets and stage propaganda of the anti-Marprelate campaign of the late 1580s.[35] And here we should keep in mind that the *Famous Victories*, from which Shakespeare originally took his Oldcastle character, was a play of the Queen's Men who engaged in anti-puritan satire during the Marprelate controversy.[36] David Bevington has noted the attributes of Falstaff's character taken from Tarleton's comic routine, his "fondness for mock-serious reforming cant, his satiric depiction of psalm-singing Puritans, his use of extemporaneous wit to joke his way out of difficult situations."[37] All of these would have appealed to regular playgoers, many of whom might have remembered the Queen's Men's play.

Naturally, in Shakespeare's "metamorphosing the most renowned member of the Cobham family, the Protestant martyr, into a penniless adventurer and buffoon,"[38] it is understandable that the Lords Cobham might be offended. Yet three things ought to be kept in mind as we consider the question of the satire in *1 Henry IV*. First, the Master of the Revels and his superiors "allowed" for a fair amount of criticism in plays, and here one could argue that Shakespeare was critiquing the Protestant idealization of Oldcastle, of which the Cobhams no doubt were leading proponents.[39] It certainly was not the first time that important dignitaries were, or believed they were, represented and satirized on stage. Back in 1528, Cardinal Wolsey jailed two actors in the Fleet Prison for falsely representing him in an Inns of Court play; in 1561 an eyewitness claimed he saw King Eric of Sweden and Robert Dudley represented in one of the *Gorboduc* dumbshows; a Star Chamber record reveals a case in which Dudley was impersonated on stage; Francis Bacon claims he was targeted in a version of *Richard II*, and the list goes on and on. Richard Dutton suggests that such satire, including actual impersonation of contemporaries, was the norm rather than the exception in the drama, and that the Master of the Revels and other authorities simply could not keep track of the number of offenses. Only in the most flagrant of instances, and in times of intense political crisis (for example, the Marprelate controversy, the Essex rebellion, the *Isle of Dogs* production – which Charles Nicholl believes was another Cobham debunking) were

---

[35] See Kristin Poole, "Saints Alive! Falstaff, Martin Marprelate, and the Staging of Puritanism," *Shakespeare Quarterly* 46 (1995), 47–75.
[36] See McMillin and MacLean, *The Queens Men*, 53–55.
[37] Bevington (ed.), *Henry IV, Part 1*, 32–33.   [38] Honigmann, "Sir John Oldcastle," 120.
[39] On this matter with respect to Shakespeare's company, see particularly Leah Marcus, *Puzzling Shakespeare: Local Reading and Its Discontents* (Berkeley: University of California Press, 1988), 148–52; and Dutton, *Mastering the Revels*, 96.

the offenders arrested and punished.[40] It is additionally noteworthy that throughout his history plays, Shakespeare had turned many prominent figures from the past with living descendants into dramatic creations without much concern for "historical accuracy." In the case of Lord Stanley, Earl of Derby under Richard III, he departed from standard chronicle accounts to give a flattering, favorable portrayal, possibly to please Lord Strange, whose company staged his plays in the early 1590s.[41] In other instances, including some in *1 Henry IV* itself, he changed the time period of historical characters (Hotspur, for example) or collapsed two personages into one (Mortimer) with no evident complaint from their living contemporaries.

In the case of the Cobhams and Shakespeare's *1 Henry IV*, nevertheless, we need a motive, an explanation, of why Shakespeare would engage in such risky satire. Two explanations have been offered by critics, though they are not necessarily mutually exclusive. The one relates to Cobham's handling of theatrical affairs while Lord Chamberlain and his differences with that other crucial authority who determined the players' fate, the Master of the Revels, Edmund Tilney.[42] Cobham's predecessor, Henry Carey, first Lord Hunsdon, along with Carey's son-in-law, Lord Admiral Howard of Effingham, and his cousin, Tilney, had steered the players through some stormy periods during the previous decade when they controlled theatrical affairs, and in the last two years had given the leading companies some measure of stability by placing them in their own resident playhouses, the Theatre and the Rose respectively, and by giving them exclusive rights to perform at court. Following the death of Hunsdon in July of 1596, however, some evidence suggests that the City Corporation stepped up its efforts to ban playing from the London area for good. This is suggested by a well-known statement by Thomas Nashe around August or September in a letter to William Cotton, himself a servant of George Carey, Shakespeare's new patron. Despite the plague which shut down the suburban playhouses, Nashe reports that he stayed in London with the hope of a "harvest . . . by writing for the stage and for the presse." No such luck, however. "The players as if they had writt another Christs tears, ar piteously persecuted by the L. Maior & the aldermen." Nashe may have been thinking specifically about Carey's

---

[40] On Wolsey and the *Gorboduc* production, see Paul Whitfield White, "Politics, Topical Meaning, and English Theatre Audiences 1485–1575," *Research Opportunities in Renaissance Drama* 34 (1995), 41–54; 47 and 48. For the other instances, see Dutton, *Mastering the Revels*, 127–36. On Cobham and *The Isle of Dogs*, see Nicholl, *A Cup of News*, 242–56.

[41] Honigmann, *Shakespeare: The "Lost Years"* (Totowa, NJ: Barnes and Noble, 1985), 63–64.

[42] This argument is developed in Dutton, *Mastering the Revels*, 102–08.

own troupe, the one he hoped to pen plays for, when he adds that
"however in their old Lords tyme they thought there state setled, it is now
so uncertayne they cannot build upon it."[43] Quite literally, Hunsdon's
new company could not build on their investment, since before they had
a chance to move into their new public playhouse in Blackfriars, the
Privy Council, under Cobham's watch, sided with the precinct's neighborhood petitioners and prohibited it from opening. Much has been
made of the fact that Cobham himself, who had previously leased the
theatre property and at the time occupied another wing of the former
friary, did not sign the lease, and thereby indicated either neutrality or
opposition to the petition.[44] However, as Andrew Gurr has observed,
the Lord Chamberlain did not *need* to sign it, indeed it may have been
inappropriate for him to have done so, since as a member of the Privy
Council he was in receipt of the document, if not the leading authority
on the Council to address the issue at hand.[45]

Another piece of evidence has recently been cited to suggest that
Lord Chamberlain Cobham had a falling out with Tilney, who, as we
have seen, had enjoyed the privileged and lucrative position of licensing
plays and play venues since 1581. In a letter to William More which has
been dated with some certainty to 1599/1600, Tilney reports a dispute
over a subsidy with one Thomas Vincent who has sent him the "most
Arrogantist letter that Euer I receuid only for finding fault therwith, and
yett haue I reciuid diuerss braue letters from the last Lord Chamberlayne
When he and I were att odds."[46] This "last Lord Chamberlayne" must
be Cobham, since his successor through 1599/1600 was George Carey,
the second Lord Hunsdon. The letter has led Richard Dutton to suspect
that Tilney colluded with Shakespeare's company in an effort to embar-
rass the new Lord Chamberlain who interrupted the Hunsdon/Howard
line of controlling theatrical affairs at court from at least the mid-
1580s through to the end of Elizabeth's reign. Dutton suggests that
as Revels Master, Tilney licensed *1 Henry IV* knowing full well of the
Oldcastle/Cobham parallel and how it would play out in public.[47] Tilney
could hardly have failed to see the family connection; he had just finished
writing a book on the genealogy of England's leading families, including
the Falstaffs and the Brookes. And, of course, he must have also let pass

---

[43] Nashe's letter to Cotton is reproduced in Nicholl, *Cup of Newes*, Document 10 (between pp. 274
and 275); see also 236–37.
[44] See particularly McKeen, *A Memory of Honour*, 650–51.
[45] Gurr, *Shakespearean Playing Companies*, 282–83.
[46] Fehrenbach, "When Lord Cobham and Edmund Tilney 'were att odds.'"
[47] Dutton, *Mastering the Revels*, 101–07.

the slight to the Brookes in *Merry Wives* in the spring of 1597 and in *Every Man in His Humour* a year-and-a-half later.

Dutton is the first to admit that this hypothesis is highly conjectural, and one still needs to explain why a company, even if it could defend itself by arguing that the character in question died nearly two hundred years earlier and that the Revels Office expressed no objection, would risk insulting a powerful court official such as the Lord Chamberlain who, as it turns out, gave them the exclusive privilege among professional companies to perform at court in 1596/97. This assumes, of course, that *1 Henry IV* dates from Cobham's tenure in office, which means that the play was probably not performed, at least in the London area, before November 1596, since from late July through October the playhouses were closed due to the plague and possibly for other reasons, justifying the Lord Mayor's prohibition. This brings us to the second theory explaining the supposed lampooning of the Cobhams in *1 Henry IV*. According to E. A. J. Honigmann, the play was written sometime during the first half of 1596 before the elder Hunsdon's death and Cobham's succession to office, a period when neither event could have been seriously anticipated by Shakespeare and when the playwright and his company produced the play to please the Earl of Essex who was approaching the height of his power (reached after his victory at Cadiz that summer) and would take satisfaction in seeing his rivals, the Cobhams, ridiculed.[48] We have already observed how the enmity between the Essex circle and the Cobhams impinged on the performance at Whitehall in December of 1596. Following Leslie Hotson and finding further support from McKeen's recent biography of the Cobhams, Honigmann demonstrates that the mutual hatred of Essex and both Lords Cobham ran deep, was openly expressed, and dated from 1595 or earlier through to the 1601 rebellion when the Earl's band of followers could be heard shouting in the London streets that Cobham and his co-conspirator Raleigh "would have murdered the Earl in his bed."[49] In the early months of 1596, therefore, Shakespeare "could not anticipate that Lord Cobham would become Lord Chamberlain, and therefore felt he might take a liberty with Cobham's celebrated predecessor which would amuse Southampton and Essex."[50] What makes this argument more than mere speculation is that the connection between Shakespeare's comic buffoon and the younger Brooke became a familiar joke at court, and it was Essex and his associates

[48] Honigmann, "Sir John Oldcastle."
[49] Leslie Hotson, *Shakespeare's Sonnets Dated* (London: Macmillan, 1948), 149.
[50] Honigmann, "Sir John Oldcastle," 124–25.

who, if not the source of it, certainly seemed to be enjoying it most. In February 1598, the Earl concluded a letter to Robert Cecil saying, "I pray you commend me allso to Alex. Ratcliff and tell him for newes his sister is maryed to Sr Jo. Falstaff." The gossip circulating at court was that Ratcliff's sister, Margaret, was involved with Henry Brooke, whom Essex identifies with Falstaff, formerly known as Oldcastle, and the association was sufficiently widespread that the Earl could count on Cecil, Brooke's brother-in-law, getting the joke. A year later in July 1599 when Southampton was with Essex in Ireland, his wife the Countess wrote to him making the same identification.[51]

This court gossip is important evidence, but not because it supports the notion that Shakespeare intended the Oldcastle/Cobham identification to be made in *Henry IV*, nor that Essex had anything to do with his creating the character. What it does prove is that the identification was made by audiences who attended the play. Ironically, if the Cobhams insisted on the name change, which seems certain, they may have unwittingly validated and perpetuated the topical reading of Shakespeare's plays, one which saw the fictional penniless adventurer and buffoon as representing members of their own family. It now appears that the "Oldcastle controversy" had taken on a momentum and dynamic of its own, drawing the Lord Chamberlain's Men into the factional politics which dominated the latter years of Elizabeth's reign, reinforcing the acrimony between these rival parties and patronage networks surrounding the monarchy.

My own reading of events and texts suggests that while Shakespeare and the Lord Chamberlain's Men may have entered the fray of court politics in the late 1590s, the company did not consistently adopt any political or religious allegiance. Shakespeare was too much of a pragmatist and his company managed to balance a range of demands made by their various patrons at court and in the commercial playhouses. It seems that they did engage in the satire against the Cobhams but this was always incidental and peripheral to their role as entertainers. This may not always have been the case with the Lord Admiral's Men, now known as Nottingham's Men to reflect their patron's elevation to the earldom, who with the launching of their own rival *Oldcastle Play* at the Rose in November of 1599 reaffirmed an identity with London's puritan-leaning audiences. This play, and almost certainly its non-extant sequel, were as close as one could get to Protestant propaganda in the theatre, as a comparison with Shakespeare's "Oldcastle" plays will demonstrate. That the play was explicitly answering the false depiction of the Lollard

[51] See Hotson, *Shakespeare's Sonnets Dated*, 153–56; Dutton, *Mastering the Revels*, 103.

hero in Shakespeare's drama is proclaimed by the Prologue: "It is no pampered glutton we present, / Nor aged counsellor to youthful sin."[52] The Admiral's Men's play championed the Foxian representation of Oldcastle as a godly, brave, and loyal servant of the Crown. The timing of the play is interesting. Shakespeare's Globe had recently been built on Bankside a few streets away from the Rose, perhaps opening with *Henry V* which had so optimistically anticipated Essex's triumphant return from Ireland. Now in November, with Essex back home in disgrace facing charges of treason and cowardice, the Lord Admiral's Men seized the opportunity to stage a play honoring as a valiant warrior and godly Christian the ancestor of Essex's hated enemy at court, the man Essex repeatedly stated was out to destroy his reputation and even murder him.

If Henslowe was simply exhibiting sharp business acumen in taking some attention away from his competitors down the street at the newly opened Globe, he may also have received backing from a higher authority, namely Charles Howard, Lord Admiral and by this time the Earl of Nottingham, as Andrew Gurr (following Leslie Hotson) has suggested in Chapter 8. The Lord Admiral became a political ally of Henry Brooke, the younger Cobham, when the latter became engaged to his daughter, the widowed Countess of Kildare.[53] Moreover, by 1599, the Lord Admiral had become estranged from Essex, who vehemently objected to Howard's being granted the Earldom of Nottingham for achievements Essex claimed for himself, namely the sacking of Cadiz in the summer of 1596. It stands to reason, then, that Howard and Cobham would have supported a play rehabilitating the memory of Cobham's martyred ancestor and in turn enhancing his own reputation, after an extended period of public ridicule, partially at the hands of the Essex faction. Indeed, they may have financially contributed to its production. For the script of *Sir John Oldcastle* and its planned sequel, Henslowe paid its authors, Munday, Drayton, Hathaway, and Wilson, a bonus of ten shillings recorded "as a gift."[54] There is reason to believe that this gift came from an outside party, not unlike the thirty shillings gift paid by the followers of Essex to the Lord Chamberlain's Men to stage *Richard II* in 1601.

Whatever the case, Lord Admiral Nottingham's Men further advanced the Cobham cause by idealizing the portrait of Eleanor Cobham in John Day and Henry Chettles' *The First Part of the Blind Beggar of Bednall Green*, a historical folk drama set in the same period as Shakespeare's

---

[52] References are to the edition in *The Oldcastle Controversy*, 40.
[53] Hotson, *Shakespeare's Sonnets Dated*, 157–60.   [54] Gurr, *Shakespearean Playing Companies*, 245.

2 Henry VI, and to which it served as an answer of sorts. Following Foxe, who predictably broke with the pre-Reformation tradition which treated Lady Eleanor as a witch and a traitor (the model for Shakespeare's Eleanor), Chettle and Day portray her as an innocent pursued by the wicked Cardinal Winchester, and it is only through the goodness of Duke Humphrey of Gloucester, whom she marries, that the Duchess escapes the clutches of the devious prelate. Henslowe paid the playwrights five pounds and ten shillings for the play in May 1600 and, like *Oldcastle*, its success sparked a sequel, indeed two sequels, neither of which survive. In following the Foxian narrative, no doubt, these plays traced her career to martyrdom at the hands of a corrupt church.[55] The Admiral's troupe, along with the other companies Henslowe managed at the Rose and later at the Fortune, established an identity with the more advanced Protestant party by staging a series of plays based on Protestant heroes, many also modeled directly on the biographical narratives in Foxe's *Acts and Monuments*. These "elect nation" plays, as they have been called, included *Sir Thomas Wyatt*, *Robert Earl of Huntington*, *When You See Me You Know Me*, and *The Whore of Babylon*.

v

The Oldcastle controversy illustrates ways in which the nature and dynamics of theatrical patronage changed from the middle years of the sixteenth century. Back then, playing companies, closely tied to their patrons' households, performed only intermittently during the year and advanced their patrons' interests and reputation. Following the advent of commercialism in the theatres of London during the 1570s, companies gained some measure of autonomy and self-identity apart from their patrons yet managed to combine economic self-interest and artistic integrity with an ideological commitment to their patrons, as Scott McMillin and Sally-Beth MacLean have convincingly shown in their study *The Queen's Men and Their Plays*. This political alignment, it seems to me, extended into the next century with the Henslowe companies, especially around the close of the century with the Lord Admiral's or Nottingham's Men. Yet in the 1590s, we see the Lord Chamberlain's Men emerging as a company that managed, with Shakespeare as their leader, some degree of autonomy, at least to the extent that they could possibly

---

[55] John Day, *The Blind Beggar of Bednall Green* (London: Pollard and Dring, 1659). See Scoufos, *Shakespeare's Typological Satire*, 154–65, who discusses this and other Elizabethan accounts of Eleanor Cobham.

resist or subvert the views of court patrons. Ironically, however, the rich signifying potential of Shakespeare's plays, particularly his history plays, make them perhaps more vulnerable to topical controversy than those of his rivals. The theatrical controversy involving the Elizabethan Lords Cobham offers more sophisticated insights into the relationship between patronage and professional theatre. If Shakespeare and his fellows did intend to satirize the Elizabethan Cobhams, then we have a case of where an acting company was sufficiently independent to criticize, perhaps subvert, the reputations of their own governing-class patrons. But even if no satire was intended, then we have an instance of where a company's play content is subject to the whims of topical interpretation by certain playgoers, in this instance the Essex faction, who used the Oldcastle/Falstaff character to attack their enemies. The final insight that the Oldcastle controversy provides is that Shakespeare's text has been used as a means of reinforcing antagonism and political opposition between factions at the royal court.

CHAPTER 4

Shakespeare, noble patrons, and the pleasures of "common" playing

Leeds Barroll

Every student of the early modern period in England is familiar with the fact that members of the nobility or of the gentry, and even other persons of money and influence in many cases, supported the arts. They contributed occasional or sustained financial support to – or even found suitably respectable employment for – poets, musicians, painters, and also men of learning who, though not artists, undertook, as did John Florio, such formidable intellectual tasks as the translation of all the *Essais* of Michel de Montaigne. What is not so clear, however, is the extent to which these moneyed members of society considered public plays by professional actors to be worthy of the same quality of support – of patronage. Before the creation of that canon of Elizabethan public plays (starting in the 1580s?) now considered to be artistically significant, no public plays seem to have been valued so greatly that they prompted the interest of the rich and educated. Perhaps for this reason, acting "interludes" on the stage for pay had not endowed the participants with the social respectability enjoyed by an artist such as Holbein, nor did the profession of playing seem to imply in any actor the degree of learning (and thus potential gentility?) held either by a man of letters from the educated class, or even by musicians, composers, or painters, the difficulty of whose attainments were perhaps more obvious to the moneyed neophyte than was the practice of the actor. Indeed, for reasons beyond the scope of what is planned here, players, as is well known, were equated with the vagabond class.

All this being so, the purpose of this essay is to inquire into the extent to which players – and playmakers – might have been patronized at all: to consider whether dramatists and the actors of their plays can be added to the company of other artists, of scholars, and of translators. The question seems worth asking because an answer – positive or negative – may help to define the extent to which public drama had an impact either by impressing educated donors, or by creating some social aura that induced the rich to want to associate themselves with what had heretofore been the productions of persons legally considered little better than vagrants.

But then, one might wish to urge that another kind of evidence staring us in the face is the names of such companies in the early 1570s as "The Queen's Servants," and, at the beginning of the Jacobean era, The King's Servants, The Queen's Servants, and The Prince's Servants. Surely the concept of patronage is implicit in such grand nomenclature. And, of course, the host of nobles whose names identify such Elizabethan companies as The Earl of Leicester's Servants, The Earl of Essex's Servants, Lord Strange's Servants, and so on, might suggest, one would think, a rather steady groundswell of patronage bearing up Tudor and early Stuart public drama. But to argue for the unproblematic aristocratic support of the drama on the basis of nomenclature alone frequently entails making assumptions about the structure of the early modern English state which are not borne out by relevant historical documents.

Briefly to summarize the basis of this problem: present-day historicism by no means envisages the peerage and the Crown as comprising one seamless social garment. Rather, recent discussions about the early modern state argue that state power should not be conceived as a close alliance of interests between crown and peerage; on the contrary, because of their large local holdings and great local authority, members of the peerage might or might not share aims with the centralizing power inherent in the Crown – or for that matter, with each other.[1] If this is indeed the case, then the question of the nomenclature of the early acting companies poses questions, not answers: specifically, do the names of these late Tudor and early Stuart playing companies imply that public playing was initially supported by the peerage as a group; and further, at the accession of James, did the Crown, as many recent literary discussions of the subject suggest, actually seize some of these playing companies, strip them of their peerage associations, and stamp royalty upon their commercial identities for some (obscure) monarchic purpose?

Any thoroughgoing response to these questions, given their profound social implications for the period, lies outside the scope of this essay. Instead, my interest here is in a more limited inquiry into what circumstances seem to have governed several specific associations of noble and/ or rich patrons with public drama. On occasion, these circumstances,

---

[1] For recent studies of this matter, see Perez Zagorin, *Rebels and Rulers: 1500 1660*, 2 vols. (Cambridge: Cambridge University Press, 1982), I, 74–75; Charles Tilly, *Coercion, Capital, and European States, AD 900–1990* (Oxford: Oxford University Press, 1990), 30, 137–43.

which may be more or less complex, do suggest that a partiality to public drama was the incentive for aristocratic patronage, but even in these cases, the purposes for which individual members of the nobility intervened in the public theatre vary considerably, and rarely have to do with the cachet that such association supposedly lent them.

Because of the extremely low caste into which documented legislation placed public players in the 1570s, the circumstances according to which monarch or noble and common plays would encounter one another at all were theoretically problematic, although they were also in a sense socially inevitable.[2] The hermeneutic challenge here for literary historians is to recognize, first, that the mingling of players with nobility or royalty enacted an exceptional relationship among constituencies: specifically, the coming together of aristocratic figures with a group not only devoid of royal, noble, or gentle blood, but also only recently – since the 1570s – exempted from embodying the homeless and lawless fringes of the English state. While carnival as communal celebration is one concept that seems to legitimize a social miscegenation in which servants, rather than dutifully obeying a noble's bidding, become, at least temporarily, the social cynosure – watched and listened to more or less quietly by an assemblage of rich, ranked, and often royal auditors – such inter-constituency gestures need also to be viewed as a reaffirmation: an enactment of the order of things as understood not only by monarch and nobility, but also by those they considered their underlings.

That is to say, there were particular ideological circumstances other than some generally aristocratic love of drama that might bring these common playing companies to the royal palace in the first place. These circumstances were the designated periods of formalized "revelry": the times of Christmas and Shrovetide. Then the monarch and his or her inner circle shared in an interchange in which the ruler joined earls, countesses, and certain powerful barons and their well-connected wives to participate in the ritualized joy occasioned by the season. At these times of official gladness in which expensive New Year's gifts were exchanged between monarch and peerage, not only was there feasting but also arranged entertainment, and this entertainment included plays. But the impact of such drama on the larger life of the court was necessarily limited because, as important as these festivals were – these revels of Christmas, New Year's, Twelfth Night, and Shrovetide which often saw

---

[2] This essay will often emphasize the term "common" in connection with the actors not as an authorial evaluation but as a reminder of public players' perceived social status in the period.

players performing at court – they were by no means the only court celebrations. Equally important and equally absorbing to the court were occasions such as the monarch's Accession Day, or the annual feast of the Knights of the Garter, or Whitsunday, celebrations which, in contrast to the revels of Christmas, might almost be deemed solemnities. And, significantly, these occasions were not marked by plays at all. Accession Day saw the quasi-medieval tournament or tilting so loved by such nobles as the Earl of Essex and his friends, while Whitsunday seems inevitably to have been associated with bear-baiting which had been brought to the royal palace on this day since at least 1574.[3]

The variety of entertainment viewed by the court may thus caution us against a sense of the predominance of drama as a consideration in the state. Indeed, in a letter written on Whitmonday, 1600, an observer noted of Queen Elizabeth that

Her Majesty is very well; this day she appoints to see a Frenchman who danced on the rope in the Conduit Court. Tomorrow she hath commanded the bears, the bull, and the ape to be baited in the tiltyard. Upon Wednesday she will have solemn dancing.[4]

What is missing here, obviously, are plays. And, in fact, plays were tied only to those formalized periods of revelry between Advent and Shrove Tuesday. Throughout the reign of Elizabeth and for most of the time spanned by this study – that is, from 1590 to 1611 – plays paid for by the Crown and viewed by the monarch ceased entirely between Ash Wednesday and the following Christmas, an interval of eight or nine months, except for the rare visit of a foreign monarch or a royal wedding.[5] The Crown's appetite for drama, therefore, seems to have been a specifically seasonal one. Indeed, in the end, when one considers the role of "the arts" *vis-à-vis* the Crown, music and musicians seem – statistically, at least – to have held greater value for the royal court than "players of interludes." Musicians commanded annual salaries from the Crown and were used all year in a variety of circumstances.[6] One might also make a strong argument for the social importance at court of skilled

[3] See *Dramatic Records in the Declared Accounts of the Treasurer of the Chamber 1558–1642*, ed. David Cook and F. P. Wilson, Malone Society Collections VI (Oxford: Oxford University Press, 1962, for 1961).

[4] See *Manuscripts of the Lord de L'Isle and Dudley Preserved at Penshurst Palace*, 6 vols., ed. C. L. Kingsford and William A. Shaw (London: HMC, 1936), II, 194.

[5] As in the visit of the King of Denmark in the summer of 1606: see Leeds Barroll, *Politics, Plague, and Shakespeare's Theatre* (Ithaca, NY: Cornell University Press, 1941), 147–50.

[6] See some of the studies cited in Leeds Barroll, "Looking for Patrons," in Marshall Grossman (ed.), *Aemilia Lanyer: Gender, Genre, and the Canon* (Lexington: University Press of Kentucky, 1998), esp. 36–38.

portrait painters with their direct access to their subjects, and of musicians, painters, dancers: fictional incidents in *The Taming of the Shrew* will readily come to mind. Such persons outside of the peerage, with their unique talents, could well aspire, like John Florio, Anna of Denmark's Italian master, to be personal tutors of nobility or even royalty. But there are no records, at least no extant ones, that show royalty or nobility receiving private lessons in acting!

Once the period of revelry arrived, Christmas or Shrovetide, the sovereign or the noble, even if uninterested in the arts, did, however, become something of a patron of drama – at least for the duration of the season. The Crown paid the playing companies to perform plays at this time, expenditures that the royal treasury had been recording for every Christmas back to before the very birth of any Elizabethan dramatist writing in the 1590s. Four years before Shakespeare himself was born, for example, the actors in the company of Robert Dudley, future Earl of Leicester, were paid for presenting "interludes" before the Queen in the Christmas season.[7] The longevity of this tradition, in fact, tells us something more than a story about mere court tastes. Obviously, whatever performances were presented in those earlier times were not from scripts written by a Marlowe, a Shakespeare, or a Ben Jonson. Thus one is led to wonder how a courtly audience familiar from grammar school with the Latin classics, with Terence and Plautus especially, and with such writers as Chaucer, Petrarch, and Boccaccio, might have been responding to play performances of the 1560s, 1570s, or even earlier.

The answer, it seems to me, is that in such circumstances, the quality of "common plays" was ultimately irrelevant – even though welcome when present. This irrelevance stems from the very purpose of such occasions both for sovereign and noble alike. That is, in the appropriate holidays that offered even to peers a release from the pressures of government – Christmas and Shrovetide (and often Allhallowtide) – the formal "revelry" also seems to have operated as the expression of an ideology important to the self-image of the peerage and wealthy gentry. This had to do with the aristocratic concept of "magnificence," that quasi-Aristotelian virtue so carefully exemplified by Edmund Spenser's Prince Arthur in *The Faerie Queene* and so misunderstood by Shakespeare's Timon of Athens. On the private level "magnificence" had to do

---

[7] For my prior discussion of this matter, see Barroll, "Drama and the Court," in Clifford Leech, T. W. Craik, et al. (eds.), *The Revels History of Drama in English* (London: Methuen, 1975), 4–8.

with the display that nobility was expected to furnish in accordance with status in the peerage. William Harrison put the matter rather baldly:

In England no man is commonly created baron except he may dispend of yearly revenues £1000, or so much as may fully maintain and bear out his countenance and port. But viscounts, earls, marquises, and dukes exceed them according to the proportion of their degree and honor. But though by chance he or his son have less, yet he keepeth this degree; but if the decay be excessive and not able to maintain the honor sometimes they are not admitted to the upper house in the Parliament although they keep the name of lord still.[8]

On appropriate occasions, such as the anniversary of the birth of the Savior, "magnificence" required a display of generosity in accordance with this aristocratic wealth, a generosity extended not only to one's retainers but even to those outside of one's household circle and of lower standing. This was the quality that Ben Jonson praised in Sir Robert Sidney when the poet, perhaps exaggerating to make his point about Sidney's magnificence, observed in "To Penshurst" that here, at this great house, every day, farmers and peasants received the same food in hospitality as did kings:

> whose liberal board doth flow,
> With all that hospitality doth know!
> Where comes no guest, but is allow'd to eat,
> Without his fear, and of thy lord's own meat:
> Where the same bread, and beer, and self-same wine,
> That is his Lordship's shall be also mine.
> And I not fain to sit (as some this day
> At great men's tables) and yet dine away.[9]

The case for such aristocratic comportment even towards players was apparently understood in the text of *Hamlet*, where we gather that what I have been calling "magnificence" is tantamount to what Hamlet demands of Polonius in his description of how the visiting players were to be treated. Asked to see that the traveling actors are hospitably bestowed, Polonius replies: "My lord, I will use them according to their desert." Hamlet responds:

[8] William Harrison, *The Description of England*, ed. Georges Edelen (New York: Dover Publications and Washington: The Folger Shakespeare Library, 1994). Edelen uses the 1587 text, but for his intentional omissions from copy see his vii–ix.

[9] See *Ben Jonson*, ed. C. H. Herford and Percy and Evelyn Simpson, 11 vols. (Oxford: Clarendon Press, 1947), vii.96. 59–66. I have modernized the spelling.

God's bodkin, man, much better: use every man after his desert and who shall scape whipping? Use them after your own honor and dignity – the less they deserve, the more merit is in your bounty. (2.2.527–32)

It was, in the end, perhaps the same magnificence – along with the appropriate show of Christian charity – which promoted the inclusion of poor men in the elaborate funeral processions of such figures as Sir Philip Sidney and, ultimately, the Queen herself.

The acme of such gentle behavior was the Christmas season when the beneficent noble demonstrated the quality of his or her Christian *caritas* to all, no matter how lowly the beneficiary, magnificence thus making manifest the noble's humility and sense of ontological undeserving as he or she sought to imitate, in the Christmas season, Christ's own cosmic condescension to humankind. Even a wealthy member of the gentry such as Sir John Harington, for instance, during the Christmas season of 1595/96 at his great house, Burleigh-on-the-Hill, entertained two hundred relatives and private guests in the several days before Christmas, but between Christmas Eve and Twelfth Night he supplied food and amusement to as many as nine hundred visitors, regardless of social standing, from neighboring county towns and hamlets.[10]

The visits of professional actors to court at the time of Christmas revelry and Shrovetide "carnival" were, I would argue, very much a function of this notion of magnificence. At Christmas the sovereign as often as not made a journey to a central palace such as Whitehall or, later, Hampton Court, and, never having been instructed that he or she was participating in the significant literary history of English Renaissance Drama, gathered the nobility together in an atmosphere of general holiday activities. Noble weddings often took place at this time between the middle of December and the middle of January; such individual celebrations were especially popular during the reign of James I, and complemented with dinners designed to include foreign ambassadors in this holiday hospitality. Apparently, it was appropriate at these occasions to make room for the dutiful performances of common men only a few steps away from being classified as vagabonds. Again, the comic exaggerations of a seasoned player (Shakespeare) may nonetheless have resonated with the class distinctions of the court as we observe *Pyramus and Thisbe* tolerated as part of Theseus' wedding-celebration in *A Midsummer Night's Dream*, or the thoughtless young male nobles of his *Love's Labor's Lost* (Q: 1598) being chidden for the discourteous manner in which they receive the

---

[10] See Gustav Ungerer, "Shakespeare in Rutland," *Rutland Record* 7 (1987), 242–48.

homely, local pageant of *The Nine Worthies*, presented to them by fearful amateurs of a lower class.

Admittedly, King James, presumably displaying this kingly generosity of spirit towards such lowly subjects at court on St. Stephen's night in 1606, was splendidly rewarded (if he realized it) by seeing *King Lear*. But who knows what, in the name or spirit of the same magnificence, Queen Elizabeth (herself a translator of Boethius' *Consolations of Philosophy*) may have endured from the common players in the Christmases of 1561 through 1580, a period in which she was also summoning companies of gentle youth from the great public schools to present plays of Terence and Plautus in Latin on occasions when even foreign diplomats were present? Still, quality, at least on the former occasions, was not the primary concern. Tolerance and benignity towards the halting Latin welcomes of country justices (again as implied in *Love's Labor's Lost*), adulatory coronation poems by city poets, long Latin speeches by Cambridge scholars, rustic plays by a Bottom the Weaver – tolerance towards these often fumbling manifestations of duty were the obligations of greatness. And, at Christmas, magnificence smiled in this time of universal charity when common men, and often common children as in 1586, approached the presence of their sovereign in offering the art of the underclass, after which a palace official rewarded the group as a whole with fees that over a span of forty years (occasional gratuities excepted) never, however, rose above the ten pound mark.

Nevertheless, as previously observed, the productions of common players were not singled out at the expense of other entertainments from members of the same social class, since the monarch, perhaps concerned with a sense of social equity, watched more than plays. This even-handedness of magnificence was demonstrated in its hospitality to a variety of underclass activities such as the bear-baiting on Whitsunday and other feats that seem to have monopolized certain holidays.[11] In addition to common players, there were common acrobats, common bearkeepers, common gymnasts, common swordsmen, common dancers. Indeed, this sense of the condescending obligations of magnificence seems to have been so deeply inscribed in aristocratic ideology that adherence to this ideal may well explain what might otherwise seem

[11] See, for example, the entry for Whitsunday 24 May 1607 in *Dramatic Records in the Declared Accounts*, 45:194a. In 1607, as a sampling, we may note that there were three bear-baitings and four lion-baitings before the royal family between August 1606 and March 1608, all such instances occurring in the spring or summer (cf. 48:[1] 233a). Each such baiting garnered £5 per palace-visit as opposed to the £10 paid to players.

to us to have been instances of appalling insensitivity on the part of both Queen Elizabeth and King James.

The occasion for Queen Elizabeth's possibly callous behavior was 24 February 1601, Shrove Tuesday, the day she signed the warrant re-ordering Essex's execution for the following morning. Whatever her personal distress about the matter may have been, on that evening of the 24th the Queen watched a Shrovetide performance by a group of common players, Shakespeare and his fellows.[12] Instead of regarding this event as suggesting either Queen Elizabeth's indifference to Essex's impending death, or her solipsistic desire to enjoy a play at a time when Essex was praying for his soul in the Tower, we should, I think, understand it as an expression of her duty as monarch. We deal, I suggest, with the Queen's need to maintain, on one hand, the flavor of the Shrovetide entertainment that traditionally involved her accessibility to loyal, lower-class player-subjects, and, at the same time, to deny any appearance of anticipatory court mourning for the death of a traitor.

King James's situation, on another such occasion, may have been even more difficult. Because of the devastatingly unexpected death of their eighteen-year-old son and heir, Henry Prince of Wales, in November 1612, both the King and the Queen (who was said to be prostrated) remained in seclusion well into Christmas – until as late as 30 December. However, on 1 January 1613, with the Queen still in seclusion, James made his appearance. In celebration, presumably, of the new year, he presided over the revels and watched a group of professional child players perform *Cupid's Revenge*.[13] With the Queen Consort still so affected by Henry's death that she remained in her Christmas-season seclusion, the King subsequently viewed five additional plays. Again, this kind of holiday ritual had to go on – or, to put it more carefully, plays at court at this time evidently represented the Crown's effort to resume the Christmas revels however difficult the circumstances. Moreover, a resumption of normal court activities would seem to have been necessary as precursor to the long-planned and unexpectedly delayed state wedding between James's daughter and the man representing England's strategic interests on the continent.[14] Plays seemed to go with the season,

---

[12] This was, we recall, the same group implicated in the pre-rebellion performance of *Richard II*, a fact emphasizing, I think, the perceived irrelevance of common players to matters of high plotting.

[13] See *Dramatic Records in the Declared Accounts*, 54–58.

[14] For recent discussion of the implications of the continental situation to which this wedding was attached, see Paul Douglas Lockhart, *Denmark in the Thirty Years' War, 1618–1648* (London: Associated University Presses, 1996), 96–98.

but their presence in this year hardly demonstrated James's keen appetite for dramatic entertainment.

The Crown was not, then, invested in players as a class, nor could players have survived on the fees they were paid for court performances. We recall that any particular company, if invited to perform only once during the holiday season, received no more than a total of ten pounds per year for its royal services.[15] Indeed, since annual periods of revelry at court could hardly have supported most companies of players, if we seek a rationale for aristocratic patronage of public players we will see it arising not from the political concerns of the Crown at the Christmas court revels, or even from the bestowal of the names of King, Prince, and Queen on three companies in the new reign of James I. Rather, there is some justification, I think, in offering the notion of a kind of undefinable yet demonstrably strong commitment to public playing and players on the part of peers operating independently of any obviously political agenda. I suggest, in fact, that it was a personal interest in public drama on the part of individual nobles that may actually have helped create the configuration of the leading London dramatic companies first known to us in the last decade of Queen Elizabeth's reign.

On the face of it, members of the peerage (as opposed to the monarch) would not seem to be the natural allies of common players. Yet even if it seems significant that such well-known companies of the 1590s as the Lord Chamberlain's Servants and the Lord Admiral's Servants indeed bore the names of important officers of the Crown, the three reasons traditionally adduced for this association do not actually support familiar arguments that the "state" controlled public players in order to expedite monarchic propaganda or to repress sedition. For example, the assumption that the players' incorporation under high officers of the Crown would make actors easier to control is undermined by that very well-known instance in which members of the Lord Chamberlain's Servants presented *Richard II* on the eve of the Essex uprising. The followers of the Earl of Essex seem to have had no qualms in actually hiring the Lord Chamberlain's Servants for their own subversive aims; further, because the Privy Council lost no time after Essex's imprisonment in summoning members of this acting company to explain themselves, it would

---

[15] As one gathers from the accounts of William Henslowe, £10 would only have served to pay a playwright for perhaps two plays. Henry Chettle, for instance, received £6 in the spring of 1600 for *Damon and Pythias*. See *Henslowe's Diary*, ed. R. A. Foakes and R. T. Rickert (Cambridge: Cambridge University Press, 1961), 133.

seem that the state did not require (or could not depend on) anticipatory policing of players even by those officers of the Crown whose names the companies bore. In other words, the Lord Chamberlain does not seem to have effected any efficient control over the kinds of plays that the company actually bearing his name saw fit to present in a delicate and tense political week.[16]

A second reason adduced for this association of common players with aristocracy – for their noble nomenclature – may be paraphrased as follows. Whereas a high noble had little or no personal interest in common players, he may have deemed it "appropriate" to his status that he have a company of them performing plays in his name and wearing his livery. In other words, a company of common players could actually enhance a nobleman's status.[17] But this business of noble nomenclature for companies of common players appears to have prevailed well before the advent of Marlowe, Shakespeare, or Ben Jonson and other of their eloquent fellows began to impart some luster to playing and playhouses. Thus a perplexity attends the imagining of what, before the 1580s, was to be gained by an aristocrat when some group, garnished with his high noble name and livery, was enacting plays of the quality of *Cambises*. It is useful to remember that, even if partly educated, these nobles were accustomed to court holiday times when Plautine and Terentian plays might be performed on the quasi-perspective stages that were the traditional accompaniment of these Roman comedies.[18]

More of an assumption than a reason for theatrical patronage, a third view sees certain nobles, removed from the players, good-humoredly – and probably indifferently – allowing these fellows to bear their noble names and to wear their livery, occasionally summoning them to their estates or London houses when an "interlude" was to be offered for the

---

[16] For a more detailed discussion of the matter from this viewpoint, see Leeds Barroll, "A New History for Shakespeare and His Time," *Shakespeare Quarterly* 39 (1988), 441–64.

[17] For a recent such view, see G. K. Hunter, *English Drama 1568–1642. The Oxford History of English Literature*, vol. vi (Oxford: Clarendon Press, 1997), 11–12.

[18] For example, in the year that Shakespeare was born, the students at the prestigious Westminster School came to court and performed before Queen Elizabeth (and presumably the rest of the court) two Latin plays, Terence's *Heautontimoroumenos* and the *Miles Gloriosus* of Plautus. *Calendar of State Papers: Domestic Series, of the Reigns of Edward VI, Mary, Elizabeth, and James I* (London: HMC, 1856–72), 36:22; and J. T. Murray, *English Dramatic Companies*, 2 vols. (London: Russell & Russell: 1910), ii, 168. As regards the use of perspective, George R. Kernodle's neglected *From Art to Theatre* (Chicago: University of Chicago Press, 1944: Fourth Impression, 1964), 212–15, builds on L. B. Campbell's *Scenes and Machines on the English Stage during the Renaissance* (Cambridge: Cambridge University Press, 1923) which, of course, appeared almost simultaneously with E. K. Chambers, *The Elizabeth Stage*, 4 vols. (Oxford: Clarendon Press, 1923), where the matter is discussed in vol. 4, app. G.

private entertainment of their guests.[19] But this unexamined assumption also supposes that an earl or a baron was "lending" his name to the players to protect them from persecution by local authorities. This view of matters would seem, therefore, to beg the question: If an earl "lent" his name to a company to "protect" it from "the authorities," must he not have had some personal interest in the company in the first place?

It is, I think, because of the improbabilities of these scenarios that we must reformulate the whole issue of theatrical patronage. Indeed, I have perhaps belabored the obvious so as to clear the decks for our engagement with the central question informing this essay. That is, are there indications that nobles functioned as patrons for common players, companies, and playwrights, in much the same way and for the same reasons usually attributed to nobles who patronized other kinds of artists and artistic productions – that is, an interest in the genre per se? I suggest the answer is "yes," and the balance of this essay will be concerned with instances that might support this assertion. We can, I think, find aristocratic interest in public drama, which does indeed argue that particular nobles played a hand in the "rise" of some of the formal companies, although, as I have argued, for reasons other than the accumulation of added prestige.

The best-known – or most clear-cut – instances of the patronage of drama by nobles who were themselves interested in social prestige (perhaps transcending the obvious fact of their "inherent" nobility, their noble blood) warrants a passing attention, further to clear the decks. In the 1590s, the Countess of Pembroke, sister of Sir Philip Sidney, translated a tragedy written by Robert Garnier, one of the close-knit group of French Senecans who were in contact with each other between 1551 and 1590.[20] This French group shared a sense of the highly didactic purpose of drama, calling their tragedies *traités*, as did Garnier, or *discours*, as did Grévin, and intending their works to be as much read as watched. Lady Pembroke's translation of Garnier's *Marc Antoine* with its five acts and its choruses generated, as a result of Pembroke's personal prestige, a non-dramatic half-life to a form whose best-known English culmination would, of course, be *Samson Agonistes*, a century later. Writers

[19] But see the judicious remarks of Andrew Gurr, *The Shakespearean Playing Companies* (Oxford: Clarendon Press, 1996), 32–33.

[20] The most extended discussion of this situation both in England and in France is still that prefacing Sir William Alexander, *The Poetical Works*, ed. L. E. Kaistner and H. B. Charlton (London: Manchester University Press, 1921), xvii–clxxxvi.

contemporary with the Countess of Pembroke, because they worked in various genres, and because they may have been seeking – and have received – the Countess's patronage for maintaining this dramatic tradition, tried their hand at this form in which the emphasis seems to have been on the quality of the poetic line. The most telling exemplar of such deliberate effort was that of the public dramatist, Thomas Kyd, author of the wildly popular public play, *The Spanish Tragedy*, who rendered Robert Garnier's *Cornélie*, with its classical five acts and choruses, into English, dedicating the work to Lady Pembroke's aunt.

But it is the Mark Antony story, it seems to me, that may serve as our "radioactive trace" to the socio-literary influence of Lady Pembroke on the propagation of this genre of classical drama. The story of these lovers was by no means established in the canon of well-known love-stories before this time, Chaucer having alluded to it in his lugubrious *Monk's Tale* as only one of many "falls" – in this case, that of Antony. Therefore, when Samuel Daniel wrote an original closet drama on Cleopatra and patterned it on the formal Senecan model, and when he dedicated this *Cleopatra* to Lady Pembroke, it seems clear that the poet was writing in a vein calculated to appeal to the Countess. By the same token, Samuel Brandon wrote another such drama, adopting the viewpoint of Antony's second wife, and entitled *The Virtuous Octavia*. These plays, including Lady Pembroke's, were published in the early 1590s: Kyd's *Cornelia* in 1594 (dedicated to the Countess of Sussex to whom he promised a future translation of Garnier's *Portia*); Daniel's *Cleopatra* in 1594 (dedicated to the Countess of Pembroke); Lady Pembroke's *Antony* in 1595, and Brandon's *Virtuous Octavia* in 1598 (dedicated to Lady Lucia Audelay and Mary Thinne). Even Fulke Greville, who, with his school-friend Sir Philip Sidney had at Shrewsbury to "declaim and play one act of a comedy" (probably Terence) every Thursday, and who wrote a life of Lady Pembroke's brother Sir Philip, specifically rejected the notion of writing for the stage and worked on *Mustapha* in the mid-1590s (*Alaham*, still being in manuscript at his death in 1628).[21] Significantly, though both of these works were devoted to imperial figures of the Ottoman empire, Greville himself observed that he had also written – and disposed of for political reasons – a closet drama on Antony and Cleopatra, rendering more interesting the social circumstances attendant on Shakespeare's own *Antony and Cleopatra*, decidedly not a closet-drama, but also the first

---

[21] For Shrewsbury, see Ronald A. Rebholz, *The Life of Fulke Greville First Lord Brooke* (Oxford: Clarendon Press, 1971), 10. Rebholz's Appendices 1 and 3, discuss the dates of Greville's dramas.

known rendering of this hitherto recondite love-affair for the public stage.[22]

This phenomenon of classical drama-writing, often with its attendant search for high patronage, persisted into James's reign, with another such writer of "tragedy" seeking Jacobean patronage. William Alexander of Menstrie, who had been tutor to Prince Henry at the Castle of Stirling where the Prince was housed until 1603, came to England with the accession of James, and seems to have followed a path comparable to Greville's. Not created Earl of Stirling until 1633 nor even knighted until 1609,[23] he printed a closet drama, *Darius*, in 1603, dedicated to James VI, and then joined that play with a new one, *Croesus*, under the collective title of *Monarchic Tragedies*, in 1604, also dedicated to James. In 1607, when he expanded a second publication of that name to comprehend two additional dramas, *The Alexandrian Tragedy* and *Julius Caesar*, William Alexander described himself on the title-page as "Gentleman of the Prince's Privy Chamber." His highest political accomplishments are not detectable, however, until the reign of Charles who made him Secretary for Scotland in 1626 and bestowed on him a Scottish earldom seven years later.[24]

Alexander's sympathies with the circle of the Countess of Pembroke may also be inferred from his authorship of an addition to Book 3 of the *Arcadia* in the seventeenth century.[25] In this context, then, it may not be irrelevant to find Ben Jonson working, in tragedy, at least, along similar lines (while also complaining of the well-off William Alexander's neglect of him in favor of Thomas Drayton).[26] Though avoiding critical judgment on these works, one might relevantly note that both *Sejanus* and *Catiline*, the first published in 1603, the second in 1611, were divided into five acts set off by choruses, even though, by 1603, other stage models were available to Jonson whose own tragedies, whatever their virtues, were apparently not well received in the *public* theatre.[27] *Sejanus*,

---

[22] For further speculation regarding Shakespeare's relationship in these respects to the Cleopatra story, see Leeds Barroll, *Shakespeare Tragedy: Genre, Tradition, and Change in Antony and Cleopatra* (Washington, DC: Folger Shakespeare Library, 1984), 38–40, 280.

[23] See *Complete Peerage*, ed. H. A. Doubleday et al. (London: St. Catherine's Press, 1910–59), 12.1:278.

[24] See Thomas H. McGrail, *Sir William Alexander 1st Earl of Stirling* (Edinburgh: Oliver & Boyd, 1940) for a discussion of Alexander's political career which placed him in the genteel tradition of closet-drama writing.

[25] See Victor Skretkowicz (ed.), *The Countess of Pembroke's Arcadia* (Oxford: Clarendon Press, 1987), esp. lxiiiff.

[26] See *Ben Jonson*, 1, 77, 137, 160.

[27] As we recall, the choruses in *Sejanus* are implied and even consigned, it would seem, to another medium: "Chorus – of Musicians."

however, was dedicated to Lord Aubigny, the younger brother of the second most powerful noble in England, the Duke of Lennox, James's second cousin and immediate heir to the throne during the minority of the princes; *Catiline* was dedicated to the Earl of Pembroke, Lady Pembroke's son.

I have mentioned these bids by Senecan "closet" dramatists for sponsorship in order to work our way from the issue of patronage for specialized kinds of "drama" to the question of what patronage public professional drama – or "common" playing – might have elicited. To address this matter now, I should like first to recall traditional discussions of professional drama in the decade of the 1590s, oriented to the rise of the commercial playhouses on the Bankside and to the north of the City. These discussions foreground two playing companies: the Lord Admiral's Servants (associated with Edward Alleyn and Philip Henslowe), and the Servants of Henry Carey Lord Hunsdon, the Lord Chamberlain (the company associated with William Shakespeare and the family of the Burbages). Narratives that seek for the origins of these two companies – and thus for Shakespeare's earlier professional life – move backward through the great plague of 1592–93 to when two or three earlier companies seem to have comprised various combinations of those same actors.

One such pre-plague company, of course, was Lord Strange's Men, and it is the patron of this company, Lord Strange himself, whose activities best illustrate one kind of relationship between the emerging companies of actors and the nobility who favored them. "Lord Strange" was traditionally the name given to the son who would succeed his father as "Earl of Derby" after the latter's demise; thus Ferdinando Stanley, the patron of "Lord Strange's Servants," was called Lord Strange until October 1593 when his father, Henry Stanley, fourth Earl of Derby died. Naturally, Ferdinando, in October 1593, became fifth Earl of Derby, and his company of players was now known as "The Earl of Derby's Servants." Students of the drama remain interested in this group, we recall, because seven of them – Thomas Pope, Augustine Phillips, Will Kempe, George Bryan, Richard Cowley, John Hemmings, and William Sly – would, en masse, become the core of the playing company with which we first identify William Shakespeare in 1595, several of these individuals even being remembered in Shakespeare's will. Thus Strange/Derby's Servants have always held a special interest for historians of drama, but for us their careers may also reveal something about the nobility's interest in drama for its own sake.

As is well known, the new (Derby) name for this group turned out to be quite short-lived because Ferdinando died on 16 April 1594, only seven months after he had succeeded his father. His wife Alice had no son – and thus no heir to the earldom; as a consequence it passed to Ferdinando's younger brother who became the sixth Earl of Derby.[28] Given the association of the Derby earldom (most recently through Ferdinando) with the patronage of public players, one might quite reasonably expect that the deceased Earl's players (the group still best known to dramatic history as "Lord Strange's Men") would have sought to maintain their recently reworded appellation from "Lord Strange's" to "Earl of Derby's" Servants by trying to associate themselves now with the dead Ferdinando's brother, the new Earl. Puzzlingly, however, matters do not seem to have turned out this way. Rather, there was apparently an intervention that separated the dead Derby's players – whom I shall call the "Group of Seven" to remind us of their future constituency as the core of Shakespeare's company – from this new Earl of Derby, even though, as we shall see, he himself was extremely interested in plays and players. For as early as a month following the elder brother's death on 16 April, the Group of Seven and company are to be found at Winchester where they were paid as the "Servants of the *Countess* of Derby."

May 16: The same day and year [1594] it is agreed that there shall be given in reward by the Chamberlain of the city unto the Players of the Countess of Derby. vis viid[29]

This "Countess," of course, had to be Alice, the widow of the fifth Earl of Derby since the younger brother succeeding Alice's husband as Earl of Derby was not yet married. Further, this younger brother, four months later, would apparently have his own company of players, bearing his Derby name and acting in Norwich in September 1594.

It is important, then, if we are interested in patronage of public players by individual nobles, to look more closely at the Dowager Countess of Derby whose name the Group of Seven bore when they played in May 1594 in Winchester. She had been born Alice Spencer and was about thirty when her husband died.[30] Like her sisters, all of whom were from

[28] For information about the earls of Derby referred to in this essay, see *Complete Peerage*, 4:212–13. William 6th Earl of Derby (b. 1561) married Elizabeth de Vere (b. 10 July 1575) on 26 January 1595.

[29] See Murray, *English Dramatic Companies*, II, 406. Punctuation modernized.

[30] For details of the Spencer wealth, see Mary E. Finch, *The Wealth of Five Northamptonshire Families: 1540–1640* (Oxford: Northamptonshire Record Society, 1956). This wealth later enabled William Spencer, Sir Robert's second but first surviving son, to marry Penelope Wriothesly, Southampton's oldest daughter in 1615.

an extremely wealthy Northamptonshire family, she was an active patron
of the arts. She and her sisters were all kin, in fact, to the poet Edmund
Spenser and seem gladly or easily to have acknowledged this relationship and acted as his benefactors.[31] The poet dedicated his "Tears of
the Muses" to Alice, praising her "excellent beauty" and her "particular
bounties" to him.[32] Thus it is of some relevance to my general contention here that a countess who appreciated the elegant verses of an
Edmund Spenser was also assumed, by those who knew her best, to have
a fondness for staged spectacle. In 1602, for example, and now married to
Sir Thomas Egerton (later Lord Ellesmere), Alice would welcome Queen
Elizabeth to her home with an elaborate spectacle involving a mariner,
satyrs, nymphs, the spirit of Time, and so forth,[33] while in 1607 the *Ashby
Entertainment* would be written by John Marston at the request of Alice's
daughter, the Countess of Huntingdon, to entertain her mother.[34]

It was this "[Dowager] Countess of Derby," then, whose name the
"Group of Seven" bore in May 1594 in Winchester.[35] That the arrangement was interestingly temporary, however, is also indicated by the fact
that, barely two weeks later, on 3 June 1594, the same group would
appear bearing still another new name – in the first trace scholars have
found of a 1590s company known as the "Lord Chamberlain's Servants."
Yet few historians of the drama have felt it incumbent on them to explain
how any particular group of common players went about becoming the
Servants of a Lord Chamberlain – one of the most powerful officers
of the Crown. Further, there had already been one company of players bearing the name of the seventy-year-old Henry Lord Hunsdon, the

---

[31] For the general patronage of this group, see Thomas Heywood, "The Earls of Derby and the
Verse Writers and Poets of the Sixteenth and Seventeenth Centuries," in *Remains . . . of Lancaster
and Chester* 29 (London: Chetham Society, 1853), and Virgil B. Heltzel, *English Literary Patronage,
1530–1660*, unpublished typescript held in microfilm by the Folger Shakespeare Library.

[32] See A. C. Judson, *The Life of Edmund Spenser* (Baltimore: Johns Hopkins University Press, 1945),
5ff., an account which supplements *DNB* and *Complete Peerage*. For Lady Alice's age, see W. B.
Hunter, Jr., "The Date and Occasion of Arcades," *English Language Notes* 2 (1973), 47. Hunter
had Lady Alice's birth-date from Professor French Fogle who is engaged in writing a life of Alice,
Dowager Countess of Derby.

[33] For the text, see John Lyly, *Works*, ed. R. W. Bond (Oxford: Clarendon Press, 1902), 1.492ff. Bond's
assignment of this anonymous entertainment to Lyly is disputed by Chambers, *Elizabethan Stage*,
IV, 68, because the assignment is based on a forgery.

[34] See James Knowles, "Marston, Skipwith and *The Entertainment at Ashby*" in *English Manuscript
Studies: 1100–1700* 3 (1992), 137–92. Then, much later – twenty-seven years later, in fact – another
masque, also commissioned by her hosts for Alice Dowager Countess of Derby who would then
be seventy-five, was "Arcades" written by John Milton. For a partial text of this unpublished
entertainment, see John Milton, *Poetical Works*, ed. H. J. Todd (London, 1809), 6.151ff.

[35] These particular observations were first presented at the Folger Shakespeare Library conference,
"Court and Culture during the Reign of Elizabeth I: The Last Decade," October 4–5, 1991.

Lord Chamberlain, a company which toured at Dover and Maidstone between 1585 and 1590 and whose roster did not include the Group of Seven who at that time still belonged to a Derby. This (first) Lord Chamberlain's company had not been heard from, however, since 1589–90 when the group had been acting in Maidstone. The Lord Chamberlain Lord Hunsdon thus presumably had not himself "sponsored" a group of players since 1590, but suddenly, in June 1594, this high official was again lending his name to a theatrical company – a new one. "My Lord Admiral's Men and my Lord Chamberlain['s] Men" played together from the 3rd to the 13th of June at Newington Butts in the Surrey area of London, scarcely a month after the Group of Seven and their associates had been playing in Winchester as The Countess of Derby's Servants. However – and this is not often enough mentioned – no indication of the make-up of the new company would appear until the following March 1595, when William Shakespeare and Richard Burbage with one of the original Group of Seven, Will Kempe, collected moneys for the Lord Chamberlain's Players. Moreover, a complete list of these new Lord Chamberlain's Servants is not available for any year prior to 1598, and then via Ben Jonson's retrospect.[36]

   In describing the patronage of common players by nobles, then, we must ask how a group of such actors – theoretically among the lowest-standing members of early modern English society, and only two months after the unexpected death of their patron, the Earl of Derby – secured a Lord Chamberlain who had not sponsored a company of players for four years? Indeed, dramatic history has allowed too small a gap in time – two weeks! – to accommodate a process whereby the Crown (in the person of the Lord Chamberlain) decided to bring the London playing companies under control by placing them under the supervision of the Lord Chamberlain and the Lord Admiral.[37] We are speaking here of a high noble in an extremely busy position. His office being an anachronistic combination of royal household duties reaching back to the twelfth century and much wider sixteenth-century administrative responsitbilities involving constant access to the Queen, the Lord Chamberlain was by one contemporary described as

---

[36] See *Dramatic Records in the Declared Accounts*, 28–29: 207b. On 21 December 1596, the court pays John Heminges and George Bryan as representatives of the same company, and on 27 November 1597, Heminges and Thomas Pope do the collecting. The first complete list, however, is that recollected by Ben Jonson who in his 1616 Folio indicated the names of the original players of *Every Man in His Humour* produced at some time around September 1598. See Chambers, *Elizabethan Stage*, II, 197.

[37] See, most recently, Gurr, *Shakespearean Playing Companies*, 64–65.

the greatest governor in the king's house. He disposeth of all things above stairs. He hath a greater command of the King's guard than the captains hath. He makes all the [court] chaplains, chooseth most of the King's servants, and all the persuivants.

Among other things, he received ambassadors and conducted them into the Royal Presence, and he was ultimately responsible for all ceremony and entertainment.[38] Thus, for lowly players there was the laughably difficult problem of, as the phrase goes in Washington today, "developing an approach" to such a noble official of the Crown.

For this reason, and for lack of any obvious alternative answer, one must suspect intervention by the Dowager Countess of Derby, widow of the Group of Seven's former patron. That their company had once been allowed to bear her name suggests some degree of interest on her part in the players – an interest in performance to be manifested several times, as noted, in the future. Further, it is implausible that early modern English players would unilaterally discard the noble name of an earl that his countess had graciously allowed them to maintain, and equally implausible that another aristocrat such as Lord Hunsdon would permit himself to insult such a countess (or her influential relatives) by appropriating any group bearing her name, be they lowly carpenters, lowly stablemen, or lowly players. Accordingly, what happened to the company in the way of changing patrons most likely happened according to Alice Derby's own wishes. Whatever personal motivations existed anent the playing-company transaction are, of course, impossible to ascertain, but it is worth noting, finally, that Alice Derby was for many years to be in bitter litigation with her theatre-oriented brother-in-law, this sixth Earl of Derby, about the Derby properties, and this may explain the otherwise curious fact that the new Earl did not himself assume sponsorship of the professionally coherent and presumably accomplished company whose core was the Group of Seven as a renewed version of "The Earl of Derby's Servants." Perhaps, in the end, the most significant facet of this whole situation is that this did not happen.

Yet another interesting factor in this situation is that one of Alice Dowager Countess of Derby's several sisters, Elizabeth née Spencer,

---

[38] The Master of the Revels reported to the Lord Chamberlain. For the Lord Chamberlain, see Chambers, *Elizabethan Stage*, I, 36–42; and, more recently, Pam Wright, "A Change in Direction: the Ramifications of a Female Household" in David Starkey (ed.), *The English Court* (London: Longman, 1987), 153–54. For the Master of the Revels see Chambers, *Elizabethan Stage*, I, 36–42; and Barroll, "Drama and the Court." But the fullest description of the Revels Office (applicable also to the Elizabethan period despite its title) is now W. R. Streitberger, *Jacobean and Caroline Revels Accounts*, Malone Society Collections XIII (Oxford: Oxford University Press, 1986), ix–xxxv.

was married to George Carey, son of the Lord Chamberlain (Henry Carey, first Lord Hunsdon).[39] Elizabeth Spencer Carey was, like her sister, a patron of poetry and music since she too is remembered in one of Edmund Spenser's dedicatory sonnets before the *Faerie Queene*, in "Muiopotmos" which was dedicated to her, and in an ascription by John Dowland introducing his *First Book of Songs*, while her husband himself was a literary patron, having been generous to such writers as George Chapman, Abraham Fleming, and Edmund Spenser.[40] More importantly for the point in hand regarding the fate of the Group of Seven, however, George Carey, the Lord Chamberlain's son, was not only Alice's brother-in-law, but was also related to Charles Howard Baron Howard of Effingham (to be created Earl of Nottingham in 1596),[41] through the marriage of his sister Catherine. Catherine Howard, née Carey, was the first lady of Queen Elizabeth's Bedchamber and very close to her,[42] while her husband, as is well known, was Lord Admiral of England and thus a member, with the Lord Chamberlain, of Queen Elizabeth's exclusive Privy Council. It was this Lord Admiral, of course, who had lent his name to a playing company – "The Servants of the Lord Admiral" – which had been quite active throughout the 1580s, introducing the dramas of Christopher Marlowe in 1588, and featuring the famous creator of the stage-parts of Tamburlaine, Dr. Faustus, and the Jew of Malta: Edward Alleyn.

Whether or not there was a community of interest in public plays on the part of the three women I have just named – Lady Derby, her sister Lady Carey, and Carey's sister-in-law Lady Howard of Effingham – the fact is, as we have seen, that the Lord Chamberlain seems to have become in 1594, oddly, the patron of the Dowager Countess of Derby's Group of Seven. Indeed, our second record of this fact finds England's busy Lord Chamberlain surprisingly familiar with the company's day-to-day situation. We note a letter to the Lord Mayor of London signed with his name on 8 October 1594, four months after Hunsdon's adoption of this group, urging the Lord Mayor to allow Hunsdon's "companie of players" to play at one of the London inns, the Cross Keys, now that it is winter (and presumably difficult to attract audiences up to the north of the city where the Curtain and Theatre were located). Indeed it is interesting to

---

[39] See *Complete Peerage*, 6:630. Elizabeth Spencer married Carey 29 December 1574.

[40] Lady Carey had also been praised by Thomas Nash for her hospitality. The best account of Elizabeth Spencer Hunsdon and her husband as patrons is by Ernest A. Strathman, "Lady Carey and Spencer," *English Literary History* 2 (1935), 33–57.

[41] See *Complete Peerage*, 6:629 a and b; 9:786.   [42] Ibid., 9:786b.

see the Lord Chamberlain of England include the following minutiae about the players in this communication:

> They have undertaken to me that where heretofore they began not their plays till towards four o'clock, they will now begin at two, and have done between four and five, and will not use any drums or trumpets at all for calling of people together, and shall be contributories to the poor of the parish where they play, according to their abilities.[43]

It seems easier to assume that whatever intermediaries brought the group to the attention of the Lord Chamberlain were also instrumental in soliciting his intervention when it was needed by the actors, than that a Lord Chamberlain of England was himself so easily familiar with and accessible to common players bearing his name. It is not difficult, for example, to imagine one of the previously mentioned noblewomen, or even George Carey as instrumental here, given Carey's own record of arts patronage. On the other hand, if the eighty-year-old Lord Hunsdon, who had not "sponsored" a playing company for more than four years before this point, was indeed personally interested in his players, the argument of this essay is hardly compromised. Our search for instances of noble patronage of public players would, rather, have stumbled upon the personal involvement of the Lord Chamberlain himself! – but hardly for any detectable reasons of state.

Having reviewed the beginnings of the well-known situation in which the Lord Chamberlain's and the Lord Admiral's Servants became the two dominant London playing companies of the 1590s, I wish now to consider what degree of interest in public playing may be found in other members of the nobility during the two decades spanned by Shakespeare's dramatic career – interest that could be construed as "patronage." If there was a utilitarian pointlessness to any high peerage endorsement of common players or playing companies (even when the public theatre was at the height of its success), we must look beyond such impracticalities in seeking to determine why certain nobles may have been attracted to the idea of theatre itself, even in its so-called "primitive" form in the years before, say, 1576. Certainly there seems no theoretical objection to the possibility that individual nobles (or their spouses) might have been enamored of the milieu as much as or more than with the court presentations of Plautus and Terence or the gentlemanly enactment of contemporary

---

[43] From the *Remembrancia* as transcribed in *Dramatic Records of the City of London*, Malone Society Collections 1 (Oxford: Oxford University Press, 1909), 73. I have modernized punctuation and spelling.

Latin plays at the universities. Indeed, it is this personal involvement
which may serendipitously have created instances presently configured
as some impersonal "development of the early modern stage."[44]

For example, many members of the peerage other than the
Countess of Derby and her close female relatives – if indeed they were
concerned – showed interest in common plays and players. The ill-fated
Essex and other earls in his circle, in fact, suggest how consistent and
long-lived the accommodation to players by a noble family or a particular
noble could be. Essex's father had allowed an acting company to bear his
name until his own death in 1576, and – it has not been previously emphasized – that Earl's widow, Lettice, allowed this same company of
players to use *her* name, as the *Countess* of Essex's Servants, for two
additional years (1576–78) until her marriage to the Earl of Leicester
(21 September 1578) was revealed.[45] Now as Countess of Leicester,
Lettice was once more connected to a noble whose name is attached
to actors – in fact, to that very significant company, the Earl of
Leicester's Servants, which included James Burbage (father of Richard)
who had built perhaps the first London playhouse, the Theatre, in 1576.
Concomitantly, those players who, between 1576 and 1578, had been
using the Countess of Essex's name were probably the group that began
in 1581, the year after Lettice took on the name of Leicester, and when
young Robert, her son, having been styled Essex since 1576 (he was born
19 November 1566), became an M.A. of Oxford (6 July 1581) at fifteen.[46]
Nevertheless, "The Earl of Essex's Servants" (whose career might reward
further study) seem to have been performing as late as 1592 in Ipswich
and 1595 at Faversham, the young Earl of Essex then being twenty-nine.

Further, whereas two companies emerged from this closely related
aristocratic grouping of mother, son, and new husband, there exist other
signs as well of a special bent towards play-viewing in the circle that came
to surround the Earl of Essex. I am by no means suggesting some sort
of drama program – at the most, an affinity of related nobles for each
other that included an attraction to public play-performance.[47] Thus

---

44 If Prince Hamlet's obvious interest in plays, players, and the power of drama come to mind,
one might ask whether he was a wholly unrealistic portrait drawn from the wishful thinking of a
public dramatist or whether, in the end, he resembled some members of the peerage with whom
Shakespeare may have been distantly familiar.
45 "The Countess of Essex players" were paid for performing at court on Shrove Tuesday 1578
(see *Dramatic Records in the Declared Accounts*, 3:210b).
46 *Complete Peerage*, 5:141.
47 That there may have been a politically-motivated program which depended on drama in its
broadest sense, and with Essex's personal involvement is, however, interestingly suggested by

the general circle around Essex included his wife the Countess of Essex (born Frances Walsingham, the widow of Sir Philip Sidney), Essex's sister, Penelope Rich (married to Baron Rich), and her lover Charles Lord Mountjoy (later under King James created Earl of Devonshire), Essex's other sister, Dorothy, married to the Earl of Northumberland, and also Essex's play-oriented mother, Lettice Dowager Countess of Essex and Countess of Leicester (widowed again by the death of her second husband, the Earl, in 1588).[48] Also part of this group were Essex's long-standing friends. These were the Earl of Southampton and his wife, Elizabeth Vernon; the Earl of Rutland and his wife, Elizabeth (Sir Philip Sidney's daughter); and the Earl of Bedford and his wife Lucy, Countess of Bedford, perhaps the most active patron in the group.

Various members of this circle appear either singly or in company in connection with the viewing and favoring of common players and their plays. In 1598, for instance, Robert Whyte, conveying London news to his master Sir Robert Sidney (Philip's brother) now on the Continent, wrote of a supper on 14 February where the company included "my Ladies Leicester, Northumberland, Bedford, Essex, Rich, and my Lords of Essex, Rutland, Mountjoy, and others. They had two plays which kept them up till 1 o'clock after midnight."[49] Again in the fall of 1599, after Essex had returned early and disastrously – because against Queen Elizabeth's wishes – from his campaign in Ireland, we hear of two of the earls closest to Essex waiting out the time of this political crisis in London as the Privy Council debated what to do with Essex: "My Lord of Southampton and Lord Rutland come not to courte . . . They pass away the time in London merely in going to plays every day."[50]

This way of killing time is interestingly revealing, and perhaps too great an absorption in plays anticipates the errors to be made by some of the rebels (and by Hamlet) in plotting against a monarch. We recall that several years later, when some of the Essex conspirators, led by Baron Monteagle, paid to have *Richard II* performed on the eve of the Essex uprising, their actions, in contrast to the relative indifference of the Privy Council to the players who actually staged the drama, argued in these peers their own subjective sense of the power of staged drama and a consequent overestimation of its ultimate political efficacy. Nevertheless,

Paul E. J. Hammer, "Upstaging the Queen: the Earl of Essex, Francis Bacon and the Accession Day Celebrations of 1595," in David Bevington and Peter Holbrook (eds.), *The Politics of the Stuart Court Masque* (Cambridge: Cambridge University Press, 1998), 41–66.

[48] He died 4 September 1588. See *Complete Peerage*, 7:551.

[49] For the passage, see *L'Isle and Dudley MSS*, 2:322.   [50] See *L'Isle and Dudley MSS*, 2:401.

because some members of the Essex circle indeed assumed the emotive power of a performance by the players of a *Richard II*, we have, I think, located a kind of belief in staged drama which could imply patronage. In this particular case, certainly the least that can be said is that enough money to constitute the receipts of a full house was given by some nobles to players of an old play because these gentles believed this medium to be powerful enough to intensify a delicate political situation.[51] Naive, perhaps, but significant to the general point in hand regarding the possible aristocratic sources of patronage available to actors of public plays.

Another figure in the same circle – one, however, not involved in the Essex rebellion – Charles Blount Lord Mountjoy, future Earl of Devonshire and future husband of the divorced Penelope Rich – seems also to have in some way been drawn to drama. One of the members of the private dinner at which two plays were shown (see above), Devonshire was a literary patron. According to Sir Robert Naunton, he was "much addicted" to reading and "a good piece of a scholar."[52] Further, it was said of him by one of his retainers, Fynes Moryson, that though he "could read and understand the Italian and French" and though his "chief delight was the study of divinity," and more especially in reading of the Fathers and the Schoolmen, for "recreation," he delighted in "reading play-books."[53] Given the fact that an association with public plays would not necessarily enhance Devonshire's prestige, many contemporaries in the gentry and in the peerage having condemned his marriage to the divorced Penelope Rich, Moryson's is an extremely significant observation because no detectable political agenda seems to underlie the remark. It may merely have been a casual truth, indicating another instance in which not politics, but simply a love of plays motivates a connection with (printed) public drama.

Certain nobles even more intensely involved in the idea of common plays are, finally, to be found in the contacts of a branch of the Derby earldom other than that represented by Alice Dowager Countess. We recall that Alice's husband, Ferdinando Stanley fifth Earl of Derby, had died on 16 April 1594, only seven months after he had succeeded his father to the earldom. The successor was, as we have seen, the newly dead noble's younger brother (William Stanley) sixth Earl of Derby who,

---

[51] See n. 16 above.

[52] See Sir Robert Naunton, *Fragmenta Regalia*, ed. J. S. Cerovski (Washington, DC: Folger Books: Associated University Presses, 1985).

[53] See Fynes Moryson, *An Itinerary* (London, 1617), sig. 2F4 (STC 18205). Significantly, this work is dedicated to one of the other members of the later "Essex" social circle, William Earl of Pembroke.

at thirty-three, had a demonstrable, even a strong interest in stage plays himself. Four months after his older brother's death, and after the "retention" of his brother's playing company by Ferdinando's widow Alice, the new Earl had apparently acquired his own company of players who were acting as "The Earl of Derby's players" in Norwich by 15 September 1594.[54] That even the Earl himself became closely involved with his group is suggested five years later, on 30 June 1599, when Derby would be described by George Fenner as "busy penning comedies for the common players."[55]

By then, Derby had himself married: his Countess was one of the daughters of the Earl of Oxford and a niece of Robert Cecil, Elizabeth de Vere. The second testimony to Derby's close interest in playing, in fact, comes from her. In 1600 (?) she wrote a letter to her powerful uncle in which she told Cecil that she had been "importuned by my lord to entreat your favor that his man Brown, with his company, may not be barred from his accustomed playing place." The Countess continued:

if so vain a matter shall not seem troublesome to you I could desire that your furtherance might be a mean to uphold them for that my lord taking delight in them, it will keep him from more prodigal courses.[56]

Coincidentally, too, this Earl's wife had willy-nilly found herself connected to public drama before this in that her estranged father, Edward de Vere seventeenth Earl of Oxford, came from a family that had allowed players to bear the Oxford name since 1492, John Lyly having written for the Earl of Oxford's company in the 1580s. Indeed, because Francis Meres in his famous 1598 entries not only referred to Shakespeare but also observed that the Earl of Oxford is "one of the best for comedy among us," J. T. Murray reasonably speculated that Oxford too (like Derby) was writing such comedies (which also do not survive) for his own players.

Whether or not this is so, Oxford must have cared something about his company of common players, because one of his own acts of favor to them proved definitive in configuring the number of theatrical companies that existed in London at the accession of James in 1603. In brief, what

---

[54] See *Norwich*, ed. David Galloway, Records of Early English Drama (Toronto: University of Toronto Press, 1984), 105. They were also in Ipswich before 29 September of the same year. See *Dramatic Records*, Malone Society Collections II, part 3 (Oxford: Oxford University Press, 1931), 278–79.

[55] *Calendar of State Papers: Domestic*, v, 227, and Murray, *English Dramatic Companies*, I, 293–94.

[56] See *MSS of the Earl of Salisbury Preserved at Hatfield House*, 23 vols., ed. M. S. Giuseppi (London: HMC, 1883–1976) 13:609. A tentative date for this letter is 1601. For another instance of Derby's dramatic interests, see Murray, *English Dramatic Companies*, I, 293 n.

happened is that the company that had continued to bear Oxford's name throughout the 1590s crossed paths in 1602 with the players of another noble, the Earl of Worcester. The significance of this intersection is best understood in light of the situation for players in the city during the three years before the accession of James.

One of the two last known drama regulations promulgated for London by the Privy Council of England before the accession of James I reconfirmed a 1600 order aimed at restraining players and playhouse owners from infringing on the monopolies held by two playing companies, the Servants of the Lord Admiral, and the Servants of the Lord Chamberlain, both their patrons themselves being members of the Privy Council of England.[57] But three months following the reconfirmation of this regulation on 31 December 1601, the orders were actually changed. Edward Somerset Earl of Worcester, who had patronized a dramatic company in the provinces from the time he himself succeeded to his earldom in 1589, attained greater dignities in 1601 (his company still being active in the provinces). By 13 August 1601, he had replaced the Earl of Essex (executed February 1601) as Queen Elizabeth's Master of the Horse, attending his first Privy Council meeting on 26 June.[58] On 3 January 1602, the Earl's playing company performed at court for the first time. By 31 March, however, his players had merged – with the provincial company of the Earl of Oxford. And though this larger (or better) group continued to bear Worcester's name, it seems to have been the Earl of Oxford himself who affected all their fortunes for the better. Being first in precedence among all the earls of the kingdom, with the (honorific and hereditary) title of Lord Great Chamberlain of England, Oxford seems personally to have interceded with Queen Elizabeth regarding all these players, effecting the change that allowed this new group in 1602 to increase the former number (two) of companies allowed by the Privy Council in the London area.[59] The monopoly in London was now to be held not by two, but by three, companies (which, in James's reign, would, of course, become the King's, Queen's, and Prince's Servants). It is, however, the wording of the Privy Council records that indicates Oxford's role here, with Worcester, as Privy Council member, himself writing up their own edict. It notes:

[57] *Malone Society Collections*, ed. W. W. Greg (Oxford: Oxford University Press, 1907), I. i. 83-48.

[58] For Worcester's installation as Master of the Horse, see John Chamberlain, *Letters*, ed. N. E. McClure (Philadelphia: American Philosophical Society, 1939), I, 127. Worcester first attended a meeting of the Privy Council 26 June 1601. See *Acts of the Privy Council of England*, ed. J. R. Dasent, 32 vols. (London, 1890–1907), 31:465.

[59] For the Earl of Oxford's title, see *Complete Peerage*, 10:250.

the servants of our very good lord the Earl of Oxford, and of me, the Earl of Worcester, being joyned by agreement together in one company (to whom, upon notice of her Majesty's pleasure at the suit of the Earl of Oxford toleration hath been thought meet to be granted, *notwithstanding the restraint of our said former orders*) [italics added].[60]

Indeed, the new company was also assigned a playhouse, the Boar's Head – "the place they especially have used and do best like of."

Space does not permit further exploration of such a rich subject as the patronage accorded these three leading London companies, a study which should deal with the changes in their names during the first year of James's reign, but it may be appropriate to conclude this particular essay by speculating on how this affinity for plays by peers may have intersected the career of William Shakespeare, the central figure of English Renaissance drama and man of the public theatre *par excellence*.

Students of the period are, of course, familiar with the fact that the Earl of Southampton, Essex's close friend, apparently became William Shakespeare's patron – for poetry, at any rate – since this player-turned-poet, in 1593–94, dedicated *Venus and Adonis* and then *Lucrece* to the young Earl. It is thus interesting to note that even though Shakespeare cannot be associated with Southampton's highly political activity after that date, yet ten years later, after the rebellion, after Essex's execution, after Southampton's attainder and imprisonment in the Tower, and then his release by King James I and restoration-in-blood as "Southampton" in 1603, the Earl would cross Shakespeare's path again in the second Christmas season of the new reign.

During part of the holiday season of 1603–04, King James having left London to go hunting, his Queen Consort, Anna of Denmark, was the presiding royalty in the city. Accordingly, she was to be entertained at this time on two (known) occasions by the Earl of Southampton and also by Robert Cecil (now James's First Secretary), both of whom had decided to include a play as part of their individual entertainments. The play-situation, indeed, is the reason we know of these plans. A document indicates that Richard (or Cuthbert) "Burbage" had notified Sir Walter

---

[60] See *Dramatic Records of the City of London*, 85. Because now this company did not "tie themselves to one certain place and house" but was playing wherever it could in London in a process now said to be "as disorderly and offensive as the former offense of many houses," the Council "reasoned" that "As the other companies that are allowed, namely of me, the Lord Admiral and the Lord Chamberlain, be appointed their certain houses, and one and no more to each company, so do we straitly require that this third company be likewise to one place." Since it seemed that "the house called the Boar's Head is the place" that these players "have especially used and do best like of," the new edict "straitly charged" them to play there.

Cope, who seems to have been serving as Robert Cecil's administrative assistant, that the entertainment-cum-play that Cecil himself was planning for the Queen was going to encounter a problem. "There is no [worked-up?] play that the Queen hath not seen," the note to Cecil reports "the man Burbage" as saying, but an old play, *Love's Labor's Lost*, was being revived for Southampton's night.[61] The purpose of the assistant's letter to Cecil was to apprise him of the situation, but also to suggest the possibility that Cecil commandeer *Love's Labor's Lost* for his own reception, "Burbage" apparently waiting outside for direction. Whatever the decision (which is not known) this missive from Cecil's assistant to the First Secretary indicates to us a kind of continuity of relationship between a writer of common plays, or his company, with Southampton's household, the household, that is, of a member of a circle – the old Essex group – whose collective interest in public drama during the 1590s has already been demonstrated. Nor is there any reason to doubt that Southampton would have invited to his Christmas celebration those nobles with whom he had associated on that evening in 1598 when they all watched two plays together, especially since two of the Countesses at that party were now close to Southampton's royal guest, Lucy Bedford and Penelope Rich being, respectively, Ladies of Queen Anna's Bed and Privy Chambers.

Aside from Southampton, the Countess of Bedford herself interestingly intersects with Shakespeare's dramatic career – and long before her (presumed) presence at the Southampton Christmas celebration of 1604. She is, of course, well known to scholars as one of the important arts patrons of the time, though her presence at the 1598 party has not been much stressed. Even lesser known, however, is her dramatic patronage several years earlier, at the Christmas season of 1595. Then, at Burleigh-on-the-Hill, the opulent residence of her father, Sir John Harington, an elaborate Christmas was celebrated. According to Jacques Petit, tutor to the Countess of Bedford's younger brother, John Harington, and servant to Anthony Bacon (secretary to the Earl of Essex and a good friend of Penelope Rich), this holiday entertainment included two hundred guests.[62] Writing to Bacon, Petit observed the "great liberality" of the Countess of Bedford who was in attendance with her husband. Petit

---

[61] The question raised by Cope had to do with the pros and cons of preempting *LLL* for the Cecil evening. Given Cecil's power, this could be done, but this would leave Queen Anna playless on one of the evenings – and this situation was, apparently, Cecil's, not Southampton's problem. For these complications, see Barroll, *Politics, Plague*, 126–27.

[62] For Bacon's friendship with Rich, see the letter from her to Bacon quoted by Sylvia Freedman, *Poor Penelope* (Windsor: Kensal House, 1983), 117.

reported too that, on New Year's, Bedford invited professional actors to come to Burleigh-on-the-Hill from London, where they played *Titus Andronicus* for the guests. Indeed, Petit's letter is the only known reference to a performance of Shakespeare's *Titus* during his lifetime.[63]

As regards the name of the group performing on this occasion, however, one cannot uncompromisingly identify it as Shakespeare's company, the Lord Chamberlain's Servants. Though the publication of *Titus* in the First Folio suggests that the King's Servants now owned the play (at least by 1611 when Q3 was printed) and knew it to be Shakespeare's (simply because it appears among his works in the First Folio), the Lord Chamberlain's company (nor any other company) was not named in this instance by Petit.[64] Further, the scheduling is a bit close for an appearance by the Lord Chamberlain's Servants at Burleigh-on-the-Hill at this time since the company was to be paid for playing before the Queen on 26 and 27 December at Whitehall. Yet, under certain circumstances, as Ungerer has pointed out, the company could have made the trip. What does seem clear, however, from the viewpoint of noble patronage of public players, is that the Countess of Bedford went to the trouble of arranging for a company of actors to make a journey from London to Burleigh-on-the-Hill to present a common play (not by a Garnier or a Daniel) for the entertainment of an opulent holiday assemblage. That this play was *Titus Andronicus* with its pornography of violence suggests that there were indeed nobles whose interests lay in drama not as defined by Senecan recitation – a form favored by Hamlet himself – but by all the possibilities that this new kind of stagecraft could offer.

Given such an instance, coupled with Southampton's early patronage of Shakespeare's poetry and the Earl's later invitation to Shakespeare's company to be part of the entertainment for his 1604 assemblage in honor of Queen Anna, it seems significant that not only Southampton and

---

[63] See Gustav Ungerer, "An Unrecorded Elizabethan Performance of *Titus Andronicus*," *Shakespeare Survey* 14 (1970), 102–9. This performance has not figured in discussions of what some have said is a drawing by Henry Peacham of a performance of *Titus Andronicus*. June Schlueter, "Rereading the Peacham Drawing," *Shakespeare Quarterly* 50 (1999), 171–84, admirably reconstitutes the situation regarding the relationship of the drawing to Peacham and even to the Shakespearean tragedy itself. It is, however, perhaps useful to consider the possibility of Peacham's presence at this 1596 performance, Herbert Berry (see Schlueter, 184) having established the authenticity of his signature with the drawing, but dissociated him from the date "1594" (and the copying of the lines of the play).

[64] Q1 (1594) of *Titus* has a title-page indicating that the drama was "played by" the "Earl of Derby, Earl of Pembroke, and Earl of Sussex their Servants"; Q2 (1600) names these three groups but adds a fourth: the "Earl of Pembroke, the Earl of Derby, the Earl of Sussex and the Lord Chamberlaine their Servants" while Q3 (1611) indicates "As it hath sundry times been played by the King's Majesty's Servants."

Bedford, but also another noble friendly with the old Essex circle crosses the dramatist's path at a later date. In 1613, as is well known, Shakespeare, along with his fellow, the great actor Richard Burbage (also, apparently, a painter), would be asked to execute an *impresa* for the Accession Day Tilt of 1613 to be imposed on the shield of one of the participants. This was the Earl of Rutland, the brother of that prematurely-dead Earl of Rutland who had marched with Essex against Elizabeth.[65] There were many *impresas* needed for many shields on this Accession Day: for someone with the family connections of a Rutland to think of Shakespeare and Burbage as the artisans to decorate his own shield, however, seems more than random coincidence.

Finally, as regards Shakespeare the London playwright, there is around him the interesting aura of the Earl of Pembroke, member of a slightly younger generation in the peerage. Son of Mary Sidney, whose dramatic interests we have surveyed, Pembroke's largess to the arts is well known, but his interest in staged public drama, especially by Shakespeare's company (as opposed to his mother's more classical tastes in tragedy) albeit seldom cited, seems unquestionable. Although Pembroke was learned enough to value Ben Jonson perhaps primarily for his poetry, giving him twenty pounds a year for books, many of the Earl's actions suggest a particular interest in performance and staging. Notwithstanding his assistance to Inigo Jones to travel and study in Italy,[66] his emotional investment in the public theatre is strikingly emphasized by the words the Earl wrote in 1619. He had apparently befriended Richard Burbage – obviously not a poet but a player, and the creator of most of Shakespeare's great tragic roles – for, writing a letter to a friend relating the court news in 1619, Pembroke alluded to Burbage, who had died earlier that year: "All the company are at the play, which I being tenderhearted could not endure to see so soon after the loss of my old acquaintance Burbage."[67] Significantly, though this letter was written in June, Burbage had been dead since March.

---

[65] See E. K. Chambers, *William Shakespeare*, 2 vols. (Oxford: Clarendon Press, 1930), II, 153. There is often confusion concerning the identity of the Rutlands. Francis Manners sixth Earl of Rutland, who was made a Knight of the Bath at the creation of Prince Charles as Duke of York in 1605 – see *Dudley Carleton to John Chamberlain*, ed. Maurice Lee, Jr. (New Brunswick, NJ: Rutgers University Press, 1972), 67 – was not the son but the younger brother of the childless fifth Earl of Rutland who died 26 June 1612 (*Complete Peerage*, 11:259–62).

[66] For commentary on Pembroke, see Webb's "Memoirs" prefixed to Inigo Jones, *Stonehenge ... Restored*, ed. John Webb (London, 1725) – these remarks do not appear in the first, 1665, edition (Wing STC 654); Sir Sidney Lee in *DNB* 9.677ff.; Chambers, *Elizabethan Stage*, II, 308; and, most recently, Michael Brennan, *Literary Patronage in the English Renaissance* (London: Routledge, 1988), Bedford's friendship with Pembroke being discussed on p. 156.

[67] See, for the letter, R. C. Bald, *John Donne: A Life* (Oxford: Oxford University Press, 1970), 351.

Again, when Pembroke became Lord Chamberlain after the fall of
Somerset, one of the officials who, of course, now reported to him was
the Master of the Revels, so that after 23 December 1615 when he was
proclaimed Lord Chamberlain, Pembroke, in effect, was lord of the
London stage.[68] His favoritism towards the King's Servants was manifest
when he used his authority on 3 May 1619 – just a month before the
letter quoted above – to intervene in an unprecedented way with the
Stationers' Guild on behalf of (the dead) Shakespeare's acting company.
In a written communication Pembroke directed all booksellers and
printers to refrain from printing plays belonging to the King's Servants
without prior consent of the company, granting, in effect, a kind of copy-
right authority to the company, a move highly unusual for the times.[69]

Finally, and speaking more specifically to a Shakespeare connection
here, it is well known that the Earl was dedicatee of the First Folio – along
with his brother, the Earl of Montgomery. Thus it is not without interest
that not only Pembroke, old friend of Burbage, but also Pembroke's
brother, Philip Earl of Montgomery, husband of that Countess of
Montgomery for whom Lady Mary Wroth named her prose romance,
are *both* described in the Epistle Dedicatory by Heminges and Condell as
having been supportive to Shakespeare:

Since your Lordships have been pleased to think these trifles [Shakespeare's
plays] something, heretofore; and have prosecuted both them and their author
living with so much favor, we hope that . . . you will use the like indulgence
toward them you have done unto their parent.

Although this essay may fittingly end with the Earl of Pembroke and
the Shakespeare First Folio – an appropriate enough emblem for what
has here been generally urged – I do not think that what has been suggested about the patronage relationship between public play, players, or
playwrights and the aristocratic dispensers of largess has been conclu-
sive. A more comprehensive view requires further determination of what
is happening when that which we have come to call "theatre" conjoins
widely disparate social classes for seemingly disparate reasons. What is
clear is that there is no simple formulation for why nobles decided to act
as patrons for theatrical companies, to promote plays and playwrights
from particular companies, or to make use of individual public performances. In virtually all cases, however, it is the nobles who added luster

---

[68] For the date when Pembroke was proclaimed Lord Chamberlain, see *Calendar of State Papers . . . of
Venice*, ed. R. Brown et al. (London: Historical Manuscripts Commission, 1864–1990), 14:100.
[69] See Barroll, *Politics, Plague*, 39 n. 34.

and prestige to the companies – who in effect, helped to make the public theatre, as it were, worthy of aristocratic patronage.

The small selection of instances that I have presented here are at least illustrative of these points. In one case, as we have seen, the Earl of Derby – scion of one of the most distinguished earldoms of the realm, husband of the daughter of the Earl of Oxford who was also niece of the First Secretary of the monarch – is described as "busy penning plays for the common players": obviously Derby took pleasure in theatrical practice itself, whatever the social chasm between him and his avocation. At the same time Derby's father-in-law, the Earl of Oxford, a noble of great prestige who was also interested in public playing, elected to lend his name to a provincial company, as had his ancestors for many years, and later to help arrange that company's merger with the Earl of Worcester's Servants in an intervention that actually reversed an official regulation for limiting the number of acting companies in London. And in yet another series of disparate activities, aristocratic women such as Lucy Bedford undertook to solicit performances by public players at their homes, and to influence the selection of companies for annual performances at court; the Dowager Countess of Derby may even have been instrumental in determining the sponsorship of the Lord Chamberlain's Servants. And, of course, in the famous instance of *Richard II*, Lord Monteagle, acting somewhat naively in the interests of Essex, one of the most powerful earls in the kingdom in 1601, temporarily co-opted the public theatre in order to fuel sentiment for an armed oligarchic uprising against an entrenched monarchy.[70] In the end, then, aristocratic "patronage," conceived generically, seems an inadequate formulation for what such instances suggest about the diverse reasons for which individual nobles invested in the public theatre, and for what they contributed to its development in early modern England.

[70] In relationship to this instance it seems relevant that the entertainment referred to above (n. 49) in which the Essex group saw the two plays which kept them up until one o'clock was a dinner given by Sir Gilly Meyrick who was not only executed for his part in the uprising but was also connected with the *Richard II* performance: see "A New History."

From medieval to early modern

CHAPTER 5

"What revels are in hand?" Marriage celebrations and patronage of the arts in Renaissance England

David Bevington and Milla Riggio

To what extent, and in what ways, did disguisings, masques, and plays designed for royal marriages serve the state in Tudor England? How subservient to or independent of the manifestly political function of these occasions were the devisors of such courtly entertainments? What did patrons demand of their artists, and what role or roles did artists find for themselves in art forms that were conceived, in part at least, as ways of celebrating events of dynastic importance? Is there evidence of historical change?

We should like to address these large questions by focusing on two clusters of events at chronologically opposite ends of the Tudor reign. The first is to be found in the reign of Henry VII, when the King married his eldest son Arthur to Katharine of Aragon in 1501, his eldest daughter Margaret to James IV of Scotland in 1502, and a younger daughter Mary to Archduke Charles in 1508; we also glance at the marriage of Margaret of York to Charles the Bold in 1468, as an especially formative wedding in our terms. The second focus is on 1613, when James I married his daughter Elizabeth to the Elector Palatine Frederick.

Even though separated by over a century, these clusters of occasions give evidence of a striking continuity in traditions of courtly entertainment. Because the marriages being celebrated were instruments of foreign policy used to forge important alliances with Scotland, the Empire, Burgundy, and the like, no costs were spared in an effort to emphasize the political implications of the marital and dynastic union in each case. Intended to authenticate the history of England and its royal family in the context of European politics, these entertainments were overtly didactic and celebratory. The much lamented deaths of Prince Arthur in 1501 and of Prince Henry in 1612 provide an unintended historical parallel between the two periods we are studying, underscoring by their tragic seriousness the fragility of dynastic claims and hence the need for affirmations of continuity. The official account of

Arthur's marriage to Katharine of Aragon, *The Receyt of the Ladie Kateryne*, ends in a doleful account of Arthur's death and burial. Similarly, Henry Peacham's long mourning poem for Prince Henry in 1613 is appended to the official account of *The Manner of the Solemnization of This Royal Marriage*, by way of reminding the reader that a death's head should always stand on one's table as a token of human mortality even in the midst of rejoicing.[1]

Extensive parallels between the early sixteenth and seventeenth centuries are to be found in the elaborate schedules of entertainments devised for each occasion. Thomas Medcalf's commonplace book of about 1625 preserves the marriage contract of Frederick and Elizabeth (1613), illustrating the political weightiness of the settlement. Similarly, because it was the first alliance of the Tudor reign, the political significance of Katharine's betrothal to Prince Arthur in 1500 is attested to in the diplomatic correspondence and Privy Council orders of 1500.[2]

As set forth in these sets of documents, the royal festivities of the early Tudor reign and of 1612–13 show themselves as occasions for elaborate marriage sermons and epithalamia. In 1612, for example, Andrew Willet's *A Treatise of Salomon's Marriage, or a Congratulation for the Happy and Hopeful Marriage between the Most Illustrious and Noble Prince Frederick the Vth Count Palatine of Rhine . . . and . . . the Lady Elizabeth, Sole Daughter unto the High and Mighty Prince James*, typifies the kind of sermon written in a flurry of biblical citations to praise virtue in marriage and to tout the benefits of wifely obedience. Dedicatory poems and epithalamia by George Wither, Abraham Aurelius, and others adorn a paean to *Great Britain's General Joys* in 1612; Wither's *Epithalamia, or Nuptial Poems* were presented at Whitehall in February of 1613, along with similar epithalamia by John Trundell (*A Marriage Solemnized in An Epithalamion . . .*) and ballads. Similarly, in *The Receyt of the Lady Kateryne* we find plentiful illustrations of pageant shows and epithalamia devised to greet Katharine as she entered London and proceeded to the royal court (13ff.). When the Prince and Princess went

[1] Henry Peacham's long poem of mourning, with its series of allegorical visions and eulogies connected to *The Manner of the Solemnization of this Royal Marriage*, is to be found in the Folger Shakespeare Library; see n. 3. On *The Receyt of the Ladie Kateryne*, see n. 2 and 7 below.
[2] Medcalf's commonplace book, unpublished, is in the Folger Shakespeare Library. For diplomatic correspondence on negotiations concerning the marriage of Katharine and Arthur, see *Calendar of State Papers, Spanish*, ed. G. A. Bergenroth (London, 1862) and *Supplement to I and II* (London, 1868). For Privy Council orders and correspondence, see *The traduction & mariage of the princesse* (London: Richard Pynson [1500]), versions of which have been printed in *Letters and Papers Illustrative of the Reigns of Richard III and Henry VII*, ed. J. Gairdner (London, 1861–63), I, 404–17 and II, 203–5. All are cited by Gordon Kipling (ed.), *The Receyt of the Ladie Kateryne*, Early English Text Society (EETS) no. 296 (London, 1990), xi–xii. See also n. 7 below.

to St. Paul's to attend a marriage mass, they were instructed by sermons devised for the occasion (40ff.).

Tourneys and masques abounded in early Tudor England and in the Jacobean period alike, bringing to a climax the various marriage festivities. What Suzanne Westfall has called a "multidimensional entertainment" strove for amalgamation by enlisting the cooperation of many people, "from cooks to composers, from priests to players," commingling public and private space in a way that replicated in art the binary and paradoxical dimensions of courtly and aristocratic households.[3] Troupes of actors attached to these households traveled when necessary, as for example when Henry VII's players traveled to Scotland in 1502.

A work entitled *A Monument of Remembrance, Erected in Albion in Honor of the Magnificent Departure from Brittany and Honorable Receiving in Germany*, 1613, chronicles the honeymoon of the royal couple in a way that establishes their royal lineage in historical detail and explicates the union in terms of mythological and symbolical significances; it also pays homage to the dead Prince Henry. In *The Magnificent Princely and Most Royal Entertainments* of 1613, we find a record of entertainments for Elizabeth and Frederick after the newly married couple landed in Holland at the end of April, including their state progress through Mentz, Flushing, the Hague, Coblentz, and Heidelberg, celebrated on each occasion by elaborate allegorical devices. In structural outline and in particular detail, these entertainments recapitulate the order of events found over a century earlier, as chronicled in *The Receyt of the Ladie Kateryne*, 1501. The inertial force binding these occasions together over such a long period of time is a strongly conservative one.

The parallels and continuities are thus profound. We nevertheless wish to argue that the gap of time between the early sixteenth and early seventeenth centuries produced a significant shift in patterns of patronage. The earlier occasions are more artistically anonymous. Even when we know the names of the devisors of disguisings, we learn little of their aspirations and intellectual concerns. Their artistic individuality dissolves into the public event itself, much as medieval painters often subsume their individual identities into the representation of familiar religious subjects commissioned by the church. In the early seventeenth century, on the other hand, artistic identity is often sharply etched. Humanistic concerns of

3 Suzanne Westfall, "Public Privacy: Early Tudor Wedding Revels," presented at the annual meeting of the Shakespeare Association of America in April 1994. All the documents named in this and the previous and following paragraphs, and more, are to be found in an extensive collection of materials about the 1613 wedding in the Folger Shakespeare Library.

artistic integrity and independence become thematic subjects of masques by highly visible writers like George Chapman, Francis Beaumont, and Thomas Campion. Ben Jonson, who did not write for this particular occasion and therefore will not figure in this study, is nonetheless important for his insistence that the masque should center on the function of the poet as the one who preeminently could fuse dance, song, poetry, and scenic devices into a unified whole.[4]

The texts devised for Elizabeth's marriage to Frederick are meta-theatrically reflexive, and reveal a tension between artist and patron that is both productive and burdened with anxiety. Much has changed in the role of the artist who is called on to glorify the royal court. The public theatre too, we suggest, plays a significant role in defining ways in which dramatic art of the period learns to define and defend its own integrity and freedom. Shakespeare's towering importance as a dramatist brings him to the fore in such a debate over artist and patron. For that reason we precede our description of the entertainments and masques commissioned for early Tudor and Stuart royal weddings with an analysis of Shakespeare's dramatized portrayals of entertainment for a royal marriage.

I

When Duke Theseus, in Act 5 of *A Midsummer Night's Dream*, calls for entertainments to "wear away this long age of three hours/Between our after-supper and bedtime" on the day of his wedding to Queen Hippolyta, he expects masquing, drama, and music. "Come now, what masques, what dances shall have?" he asks. "What revels are in hand? Is there no play/To ease the anguish of a torturing hour?" From Philostrate especially he demands to know "What masque? What music?" Philostrate, "our usual manager of mirth," comes provided with a list of possible choices that includes a musical rendition of "The battle of the Centaurs" to be "sung/By an Athenian eunuch to the harp," an "old device" on "The riot of the tipsy Bacchanals," a satire on the Muses lamenting the death of learning, and of course "Pyramus and Thisbe" (5.1.32ff.).[5] The subjects of these proffered entertainments are, for the most part, appropriately Ovidian, even though the genres are not entirely clear.

[4] See Jack E. Reese, "Unity in Chapman's *Masque of the Middle Temple and Lincoln's Inn*," *Studies in English Literature* 4 (1984), 291–305.
[5] Shakespeare quotations are from *The Complete Works of Shakespeare*, ed. David Bevington, updated 4th edn. (New York: Longman, 1997).

The Bacchanals piece, we are told, is an old device that was "played" to help celebrate a previous state occasion, when Theseus "from Thebes came last a conqueror." The implication is that Theseus entered Athens in a formal "triumph" and was greeted by pageants and shows of the sort that invariably accompanied events of political momentousness in Tudor and Stuart England, such as royal weddings, royal entries, and the like. Perhaps "The riot of the tipsy Bacchanals" was the subject of a masque; the language is imprecise on this matter.

In any event, the whole passage sums up and gracefully parodies Renaissance England's fascination with royal celebrations, and describes the involvement of the arts in a way that sounds thoroughly contemporary: we are looking at the Renaissance English court thinly disguised as an Athenian court. Philostrate is the Master of the Revels. No doubt Shakespeare's artistically highlighted rendition makes too much of Theseus's supposed ignorance of what entertainment is in store for him; the records indicate that England's royalty was very much involved in planning and directing the work of the artists, dramatists, designers, and dancing masters whose services were retained for the occasion. Shakespeare does nonetheless give us a suggestive portrait of the way in which a court marriage provided the occasion for a richly varied array of festive entertainments, among which one could expect to find adult male actors putting on a play of their own that bears only a tangential relation to the wedding occasion itself.

"Pyramus and Thisbe" is a ridiculous play, and we do not mean to suggest that Shakespeare is parodying in it the achievements of professional players like himself and his colleagues. Bottom and company have never put on a play before; even if they are artisans, as were some adult professional players in London (James Burbage was a joiner), they are utterly naive about the means of contriving theatrical illusion in poetically evocative language. Indeed, the bumbling and amateurish literal-mindedness which prevents the "mechanicals" from even conceptualizing the possibility of theatrical illusion is itself the subject of Shakespeare's parody. Even so, the system of patronage by which these handicraft men are employed has potentially useful implications. "Pyramus and Thisbe" is entirely of the company's own devising; it is virtually written by them in concert, and is tailored to their own pathetic limits and acting abilities. Theseus may choose to see it or not, as he wishes, but Philostrate needs at least to have such popular entertainments at hand.

Theseus's royal condescension in allowing the performance may hint, then, that an English monarch ought to patronize popular dramatic entertainment by bestowing the royal imprimatur on an occasional play or two. Yet Theseus's doing so leaves the company free to present a play that has been written by and for them. "Pyramus and Thisbe" omits courtly compliment. It is not a play written as a flattering mirror of a court marriage, even though it was devised to be performed as part of the marriage festivities and with a very specific commercial hope of earning a set of pensions as a reward. Perhaps, despite the immeasurable distance in quality between "Pyramus and Thisbe" and *A Midsummer Night's Dream*, we can see the latter too as a popular dramatic entertainment vying for courtly attention and the sort of patronage that comes essentially after the creation of the work itself.

Shakespeare's representation of a wedding masque in *The Tempest* suggests a closer relationship to the court by 1611–13 and a greater dependency on its favor, though even here the artist portrays himself as essentially in charge of the event. Even if the play as a whole could not have been written to celebrate the wedding of James I's daughter Elizabeth to the Elector Palatine in 1613, perhaps two years after the play was originally written and produced, its attentiveness to courtly celebration of just such an occasion is manifest.[6] Certainly *The Tempest* provided suitable entertainment when it was chosen as part of the marriage festivities, in a competitive selection process that provides a link back to Bottom and his companions in 1595.

This time, the theme is much more overtly linked to royal marriage. The visitation of the three goddesses to bless the marriage of Miranda and Ferdinand is immediately translatable into a flattering wish of long life and happiness for any couple marrying at the Jacobean court (or indeed anywhere else). The genre is appropriately courtly; Prospero calls the show he produces a "revels" (4.1.148), and it contains many features that are well suited to courtly entertainment: allegory, invocations of mythological story, slightness of plot, symbolic costuming, a goddess descending by means of a chariot from the "heavens," celebratory song in honor of the institution of marriage, and, perhaps most tellingly, a kind of anti-masque. The dance of the reapers and nymphs is not called

---

[6] Stephen Orgel, "The Royal Theatre and the King," in Guy Fitch Lytle and Stephen Orgel (eds.), *Patronage in the Renaissance* (Princeton: Princeton University Press, 1981), 261–73, aptly describes how too much can be made of James I's having brought the major theatrical companies under royal patronage in 1603; the companies made their money chiefly through commercial performance, but were also glad to be summoned to court to assist in the celebration of a particular event, on which occasion "they selected (or were instructed to select) a piece that was appropriate to the occasion, and that might include some revisions to accommodate the fact of a royal audience" (267).

an anti-masque; in fact Shakespeare never uses the term. Nor does he describe Prospero's entertainment as a masque, though that term is one he uses elsewhere; Theseus speaks repeatedly of masques as appropriate to his wedding in *A Midsummer Night's Dream*, though none is forthcoming and may not even be on the menu. *The Tempest*, conversely, mentions nothing of a masque and yet gives us a kind of anti-masque presented by reapers who are "properly habited" in "rye-straw hats" and who perform a "graceful dance" with "fresh nymphs" (4.1.134ff.). The contrast between the richly costumed goddesses in the main action of Prospero's "revels" and the "sunburned sicklemen" who are bidden to "be merry" and "make holiday" in a "country footing" must have struck the play's viewers as a loving, familiar, and complimentary representation of the kinds of masquing entertainments that were so elaborately staged at court by Ben Jonson, Inigo Jones, and others.

At the same time, Shakespeare's (and Prospero's) revels are pointedly differentiated from the courtly masque in their mode of production and their implied system of patronage. No royal or aristocratic couples come out onto the floor to dance in what is, for the masque, the climactic moment of the occasion when those who are being celebrated become explicitly a part of the spectacle. No elaborate and costly preparation has gone into the costuming for those who thus take part as members of the court circle. The set is far less elaborate than in any of Jones's masques, with no moving parts, opening mountains, and the like. Most significantly, perhaps, the artist who creates these revels is himself the Duke of Milan and is thus both his own sponsor and creative genius. The Platonic role of philosopher-king, which got Prospero in such trouble back in Milan during his days of absentminded rule there, stands him in good stead in the artist's world of *The Tempest*. Here he can commission the show and produce it with Ariel's expert assistance. The materials come from his own artistic vision and power. He calls it "Some vanity of mine art" (4.1.41) and writes his own critical review afterwards about a "baseless fabric" that has "melted into air, into thin air" (4.1.150–51).

Implicitly, then, the masque in *The Tempest*, though never called that, represents a kind of edifying and deeply moving entertainment that is created by an independent artist who is beholden to his audience (including the court and also a much larger audience) chiefly for its power to approve or disapprove. The artist's push–pull relationship with his audience is signified in Prospero's proud and yet needful begging for applause in the Epilogue, where "Prospero" and the actor playing his part and the dramatist are all meaningfully indistinguishable one from the other. Whether or not *The Tempest* is Shakespeare's swan song to the theatre, the voice of the artist is certainly audible in the request of the speaker to be released from the "spell" of the island "With the help of your good hands." The appeal is directed with perfect lack of definition toward whoever may be listening, in the public theatre or at court. The tone of the Epilogue is notably lacking in the kind of sycophantic flattery one hears in John Lyly's court epilogues to *Campaspe* and *Endymion*, for example, or Thomas Heywood's 1633 epilogue to Marlowe's *The Jew of Malta*.

The voice at the end of *The Tempest*, then, speaks with dignity and respect to an audience on whom the dramatist and his company are deeply dependent – an audience that, in the main instance, is a paying audience indicating its approval not simply by a clapping of hands but by their willingness to fork over the price of admission at the door. That such an epilogue can be addressed indiscriminately to a paying audience and to the court bespeaks the kind of patronage that Shakespeare found in his commercially competitive theatre. A complex level of patronage thus distinguishes the commercial dramatist in the early seventeenth century from those who depended entirely or largely on the largess of the court. At the same time, the very possibility of such commercial success and of a hybrid commercial and privately patronized career like that of Shakespeare emerges from a social climate which accords the writer not only increased visibility but the possibility at least of some independence.

II

Before discussing the masques that were written specifically for the marriage of Elizabeth and James in 1613, let us go back a century or so to an earlier royal wedding for which we have documentation as to the kinds of events that were planned: the wedding of Katharine of Aragon, "the Ladie Kateryne," to Henry VII's son Arthur in late 1501. What kinds of entertainments were introduced into the festivities on this occasion, and how were they commissioned and sponsored? How was art called upon to serve the state in the early Tudor era, as sampled in this and similar occasions? Like the wedding of Elizabeth and James in 1613, this one in 1501 was intensely dynastic and political. Yet a long time intervened between those dates, a time in which English humanism gained considerable ground. Part of our contention in this essay is that the earlier event reveals a courtly world in which artists were far less inclined to explore their own roles as potential critics and humanists capable of commenting upon issues of courtly power and control and the relations of dramatic art to its surrounding social structure. Artists accepted a large degree of anonymity in that they did not expect to see their names appended to accounts of their work. Nor did they attempt to insert their own humanistic ideals and endeavors into the fabric of courtly revels designed by those in charge of the event. Just as painters accepted commissions to paint specific and commonplace religious topics like the Annunciation or the Crucifixion for a particular church and particular location, with matters of composition and of the details of subject matter (such as the expected attributes identifying a saint) specified in detail to the artist, dramatists and other writers who were chosen to take part in the large and communal task of devising a wedding celebration subsumed their personalities to a large degree into the enterprise as defined by the sponsoring organization.

A case in point is to be found in the seemingly official memorial of Prince Arthur's wedding to Katharine of Aragon in 1501. Entitled *The Receyt of the Ladie Kateryne* by its twentieth-century editor, Gordon Kipling, from the first words of the prologue, this account covers much more than the wedding itself. It starts with the departure of Katharine from her royal parents in Aragon, details her arrival in England, pays close attention to "thordre of the Citie of London" for her reception there, moves on in Book III to the celebrations surrounding the wedding itself and its festive aftermath (Book IV), and then turns unexpectedly to tragedy in an account of Arthur's untimely death and burial. The speeches delivered at various pageants as Katharine makes her way through London, by Saint Katharine, Policy, Noblesse, Virtue, the angel Raphael, Alfonso X of Castile, Job, Boethius, the Father of Heaven, a Prelate of the Church, and the like, offer her predictable sorts of advice and encouragement as she proceeds from the earthly kingdom of Policy to the spheres of moon, sun, and the heavenly kingdom – that is, from her Spanish beginnings to her new role as Arthur's consort.[7]

---

[7] Kipling, *The Receyt of the Ladie Kateryne*. The text, under the title *Here begynneth the note and tretise of the moost goodly behavor in receyt of the Ladie Kateryne, daughter unto Phardinand, the Kyng of Espayn, yoven in mariage gainct to Prince Arthure, son and heir unto our noble Soferynge of Englond, King Henry the vijth, in the xvij yere of his reign*, was edited by Francis Grose and Thomas Astle in *The Antiquarian Repertory* (London: for Edward Jeffery, 1808), 22:249–331. Another account is to be found in Arthur H. Thomas and I. D. Thornly (eds.), *The Great Chronicle of London* (London: printed by George W. Jones, 1938), 297ff., based on Fabyan's Chronicle and Rastell's Continuation, but the descriptions of the entertainments devised for the royal wedding focus on the jousts rather than on the disguisings; see especially 313–14.

Our interest is in the disguisings that adorned the wedding festivities. The texts, unfortunately, are not given verbatim, and so we cannot be sure that the reporter has not suppressed some controversial aspects of the entertainment or slanted his account in such a way as to represent the royal view of what was supposed to happen. Because the documents omit much dialogue and other verbal material of the sort we find in the revels for 1613, we can surmise that Henrician wedding entertainments were less text-based than those for the later sixteenth and early seventeenth centuries. Even so, the compiler's narrative suggests a good deal about how artists were employed in the service of the state on such a momentous occasion. As Kipling explains, the enterprise was a collaborative one involving the "master of the revels," who was chiefly a bookkeeper and purchasing agent, and the personnel of the Chapel Royal, who acted the pageants that were devised chiefly by a gentleman of their number, William Cornish. John English, too, as master of the King's Players (apparently the first fully identifiable company of players to form part of an English royal household), was an active participant and partner with Cornish; the court treasurer records a payment of ten marks "to John English for his pageant."[8] An acting troupe serving directly under the King was a recent innovation that built upon and expanded the elaborate provisions for revels within the households of the Yorkist kings Edward IV and Richard III. Such an internal troupe could provide important personnel for royal entertainments of the sort that the Henrician court needed in order to give symbolic weight to the Tudor regime.

Under this arrangement, the court seems to have had a dominant influence in specifying the contents and themes of the various disguisings arranged to celebrate the wedding. Even the earlier city celebrations in honor of Katharine's entry into London seem to have been orchestrated by royal will; although London had plentifully shown, on previous occasions (as in the so-called Reconciliation of Richard II with the City of London in 1392 over the city's refusal of a loan and Richard's vengeful retaliation), that it could offer pointed advice to the monarchy through its pageants and shows,[9] London's welcome to Katharine in 1501 seems to side entirely with the throne in its emphasis on the inestimable benefits accruing to Katharine by virtue of her being wedded to "the noble Prince Arthure," the embodiment of "Noblesse" and "everych Vertue

---

[8] Sydney Anglo, "William Cornish in a Play, Pageants, Prison, and Politics," *Review of English Studies*, n.s., 10 (1959), 347–60, and Kipling, *The Receyt of the Ladie Kateryne*, xix–xxiii.

[9] Glynne Wickham, *Early English Stages 1300 to 1660*, 3 vols. (London: Routledge and Kegan Paul, 1959–80), 1, 63ff.

Cardinall" (ii.254–63). The audience for these pageants is English; the occasion of Katharine's arrival is a cause for solidarity between crown and City.

Henry VII and his courtiers seem to have taken an active interest in every detail of the arrangements reported by the compiler of the *Receyt* narrative. The account of the first disguising, held on a Friday night after a week of festivities, introduces the event with an emphatic indication of royal directive:

The Kynges Grace, intendyng to amplifie and encrease the ryaltie of this noble and solempne fest with many and dyvers and goodly actes of pleasure, lett cause Westmynster Hall – the which is of great lengeth, bredith, largnes, and right crafty buyldyng – his wallis to be richely enhangyd with pleasaunt clothis of Arras, and in his upper part a riall and a great cuppbord to be made and erecte, the which was in lengeth all the brede of the Chauncery, and hit was vij settes, shelvys, "or" [gold] haunces of hight, furnysshid and fulfillyd with as goodly and riche treasure of plate as ever cowde lightly be seen, moch therof golde and all the remnante beyng gilte. (iv.130–40)

Here was presented on Friday evening, after the first royal jousts, "a goodly disguysyng," with the King, the Prince, the Duke of York, the lords of Spain, and a great company of other courtiers, along with the Queen, the King's mother, the Lady Princess, and "a goodly company of ffresshe ladies and gentilwomen of the courte and realme awayting on her," in attendance.

The "disguising" reveals its ancestral closeness to the masque, as such courtly entertainments were soon to be called. This one consisted of three pageants, each elaborate in its use of theatrical devices and each devoted to allegorizations of the marriage. The first featured a castle on wheels, drawn into the hall by lions (one gold and one silver), a hart, and an ibex – each animal simulated in its movements by two men inside. At the lower end of the hall, facing the royal and noble spectators under their cloths of estate at the upper end of the hall, Children of the Chapel sang sweetly from the four turrets of the castle. The castle represented Castile, and its four beasts were distinctively Spanish, especially the unusual silver lion (seen in the Spanish royal arms) and the Spanish ibex, as distinguished from the English antelope.[10] In a second pageant, an elaborately rigged ship sailed through the hall on its wheels to the vicinity of the castle, bearing a lady accoutered like the Princess of Spain and also two ambassadors named Hope and Despair, who made their way

---

[10] Kipling, *The Receyt of the Ladie Kateryne*, 154.

from the ship to the castle on behalf of the Knights of the Mount of Love, beseeching the ladies inside the castle to be favorable to them in love.

When this request was refused, a third pageant in the likeness of the Mount of Love passed through the hall to the other side of the ship, allowing its cargo of knights to alight from the mount and assault the castle with complete success. The descent of the ladies from the castle and their submission "to the pouer, grace, and will of thoes noble knightes" signaled the arrival of the time for dancing, first involving the knights with four ladies "aftir thenglissh fachyon" and four "after the maner of Hispayne," followed by the removal of the pageants and the dancing of Prince Arthur, Lady Cecil, the King and Queen, then the Princess of Spain, and still others, with the Duke of York and the Lady Margaret as the chief dancers (IV.142–244). By allowing the knights to prevail over the ladies, Cornish reversed the usual symbolic meaning of the *Roman de la Rose* and its many imitators, thereby substituting for the usual allegorical portrayal of male importunity a representation of English "noblesse" and a prevailing of English virtue over Spanish reticence.[11]

Notably absent, when we compare this evening's entertainment with Shakespeare's depiction of masquing in *A Midsummer Night's Dream* and *The Tempest*, is any consciousness of the role of the devisor and his place in the creation of courtly entertainment. Cornish's function is to devise a masque that will mesh with the ideological program of the entire series of events welcoming Katharine and her marriage to Arthur. The allegorical symbolism, even in its inverted form, is his *donnée*. The reworking of conventional symbolism for purposes of royal flattery is indeed anticipatory of a good deal of court-sponsored art under the Tudor kings, such as George Peele's deliberately outrageous retelling of the myth of Paris's choice in *The Arraignment of Paris* (c. 1581–84), according to which an Elizabeth figure reconciles the three competing goddesses (Juno, Minerva, and Venus) and subsumes their qualities of royal authority, wisdom, and beauty. Cornish as an artist is not visible; his function is to celebrate the state according to its wishes. His artistry goes into visual conceits of pageant wagons newly conceived and into verbal elaborations on received motifs of royal adulation. This is not to say that the art is lacking in genuineness or integrity, for the artist's views may well be consistent with the patriotic occasion he is helping to celebrate, but

[11] Gordon Kipling, *The Triumph of Honour: Burgundian Origins of the Elizabethan Renaissance* (The Hague: Leiden University Press for the Sir Thomas Browne Institute, 1977) 103–5, and Roger Sherman Loomis, "The Allegorical Siege of the Art of the Middle Ages," *Journal of the Archaeological Institute of America*, 2nd ser., 23 (1919), 255–69.

such harmony of purpose does preclude any kind of debate between the devisor and his royal patron.

Other disguisings conform to a similar model. The entertainment for Sunday evening commenced with an "interlude" in Westminster Hall, probably led by John English as master of the King's players, followed by a disguising of two pageants. In the first of these, a "herber" or arbor with a gate was brought into the hall so that twelve lords and gentlemen might emerge from it to dance at length. The second was fashioned like a lantern with many windows of fine lawn, containing twelve ladies who were ingeniously made visible by means of a hundred great lights. The ladies danced by themselves and then with the gentlemen (IV.313–46). The whole effect, manifestly appropriate for a wedding, was one of a coming together of the sexes at court in decorous harmony, the ladies' virtue underscored by the symbolism of the clear windows and the burning lights. A third disguising devised for the following Thursday presented two mountains in the lower end of Westminster Hall, chained together in an emblem of the amicable linking of England and Spain. One mountain featured many fresh green trees and the other rich ores; one was populated with twelve lavishly costumed courtiers and the other with twelve ladies, the highest among them being "arrayed aftir the maner of the Princes of Hispayne." The twelve couples came together as dancing partners, as the mountains were retired from the scene (IV.590–638).

A final disguising devised for the ensuing Sunday featured a many-windowed throne or tabernacle containing a cupboard of costly plate, and built in two storeys, providing room for eight gentlemen below and eight "fresshe ladies" above. This disguising also featured anti-masque characters (not labeled as such): two "woddosys" or wild men drawing in the wheeled pageant, and, flanking the throne, a merman ("in harnesse from the wast uppeward") and a mermaid, along with a Child of the Chapel singing "in every off the sayde mermaydes." As the gentlemen descended to the dance floor, they released many live rabbits, while for their part the ladies in their appearance on the dance floor released many doves and other birds into the hall (IV. 930–64). Music and dance provided the metaphor for marital containment of the potentially divisive elements hinted at symbolically in the libidinous wild men, the merman and mermaid that are both half-human and half creatures of the sea, lecherous rabbits, and Venus's doves.

In all these masques, truisms of sexual difference conventionally portrayed in medieval allegorical romances became the means of signifying the potentially stressful relations between England and Spain that the

state marriage was devised to resolve. The compliant and subservient
role of the artist must have seemed implicit to courtly participants as
necessary to the consistency of the overall design and to the integral connection between the marriage and foreign diplomacy. Since the marriage
was itself an artifact of national policy, the mythology devised to present
it at court took on the function of promulgating and idealizing that policy.
The artist was called upon to use his rhetorical skill in devising orna-
ments and conceits appropriate to such an official enterprise. Here was
at once his source of employment, his path of potential advancement at
court, and the fulfillment of his role as a loyal Englishman devoted to the
Tudor cause. This was not the only possible role for a serious writer in
the Henrician years; John Skelton demonstrates in *Magnificence* (1515–23)
and his other writings that a critical stance was certainly possible. Yet
Skelton was evidently not called upon to write masques or disguisings, as
Campion and Chapman were later on; Skelton seems to have been sponsored by the Norfolks, always in a disaffected relationship to the Tudor
throne. His role as courageously outspoken critic highlights through contrast the way in which the art of courtly ceremonial seems to have functioned at the center of power.

   Other celebrations of royal weddings during the early Tudor era tend
to confirm the pattern of sponsorship and patronage we have been discussing, though the records are comparatively meager. All owe a debt
to the splendid celebrations mounted in 1468 in Bruges for the wedding
of Edward IV's sister, Margaret of York, to Charles the Bold, Duke of
Burgundy, in dramatic ceremonials crafted to remind Margaret that she,
like Esther in the biblical story of Ahasuerus, was taking her place as the
third wife of a great prince. As Duchess of Burgundy, Margaret was to
become an important patroness of courtly entertainments.[12]

   John Younge's account of the betrothal of Henry VII's eldest daughter,
also named Margaret, to James IV of Scotland in January of 1502, described in John Leland's *De Rebus Britannicis Collectanea*, is more interested
in the tournament than in the disguisings. Although there was at least
one disguising with a pageant on 24 January, it is described only briefly:
"Incontinent after the Pryses were given, there was in the Hall a
goodly Pageant, curiously wrought with Fenestrallis, having many Lights
brenning in the same, in Manner of a Lantron, out of wich sorted divers
Sortes of Morisks. Also very goodly Disguising of Six Gentlemen and Six

[12] A full account of the wedding of Margaret of York to Charles the Bold is given in Olivier de la
   Marche, *Mémoires*, ed. Henri Beaune and J. d'Arbaumont, 3 vols. (Paris: Renouard, 1883–88).
   See Kipling, *The Triumph of Honour*, 33–35, 110–11, and passim.

Gentlewomen, which danced divers Dances." Insofar as we learn any details from this account, the evening sounds like a replay of the festivities for Arthur and Katharine, complete with the effect of a lantern. Payments from the Chamber Accounts indicate that at least two persons employed for the occasion, John Atkinson and John English, had been busy with the previous marriage ceremonials as well. Inevitably, perhaps, the ceremonials were less impressive than those for the King's son and his Spanish bride only two months earlier, in November of 1501.[13]

The betrothal of Princess Mary, Henry VII's younger daughter, to the Archduke Charles in 1508, described in a document called *The Solempnities & triumphes doon & made at the Spouselles and Mariage of the Kynges doughter the Ladye Marye to the Prynce of Castile, Archeduke of Austrige*, printed in London in 1508 by Richard Pynson, similarly focuses mainly on the jousts and tourneys, observing simply of dramatic entertainments: "There lacked no disguysynges, moriskes nor entreludes made and appareilled in the beste and richest maner."[14] To be sure, we do have a more circumstantial description in a unique Revels account discovered by Sydney Anglo with the descriptive title: "*This is the boke of the disguisings ffor the coming of thambassatours of Flaunderes anno xxiiij^o henrici vij*," describing a disguising presented at Richmond for the entertainment of the ambassadors negotiating the marriage terms and centered around a pageant car of a castle, a hawthorn tree, and a mount representing the marriage union of Castile and England in the vein of the two rock pageant cars used earlier to symbolize the English-Spanish marriage of 1501.[15]

The similarity of devices used in 1501, 1502, and 1508, and lack of further detailed information about disguisings in these great events, reinforce our impression that William Cornish, John English, and other

[13] John Leland, *De Rebus Britannicis Collectanea* (London: Benj. White, 1774), IV, 263; Sydney Anglo, *Spectacle, Pageantry, and Early Tudor Policy* (Oxford: Clarendon Press, 1969), 103–6; and Anglo, "The Court Festivals of Henry VII: A Study Based upon the Account Books of John Heron, Treasurer of the Chamber," *Bulletin of the John Rylands Library* 45 (1960–61), 12–45, esp. 24. For an account of the festivities connected with the actual marriage of James IV and Margaret Tudor in Scotland in 1503, focusing on the marriage as a means of confirming peace between Scotland and England as an important instance of the close link between sovereignty and marriage during this period, see Louise Olga Fradenburg, *City, Marriage, Tournament: Arts of Rule in Late Medieval Scotland* (Madison: University of Wisconsin Press, 1991), 67–149.

[14] *The Solempnities & triumphes doon & made at the Spouselles and Mariage of the Kynges doughter the Ladye Marye to the Prynce of Castile, Archeduke of Austrige* (London: Richard Pynson, 1508). Both the English and a longer Latin version published by Pynson have been reprinted by James Gairdner as *"The Spousells" of the Princess Mary*, in *The Camden Miscellany*, vol. 9 (Westminster: for the Camden Society, 1895). See p. 30 for the excerpt cited here. Gairdner's introduction offers a useful account of the political and diplomatic context of Henry VII's interest in the marriage negotiations.

[15] Anglo, "The Court Festivals of Henry VII," 24–25, citing Public Record Office, L.C. 6/50, fos. 143r–147v.

artists who created the disguisings were themselves subsumed anony-
mously into the work. Their artistic nature was expected to be "subdued/
To what it works in, like the dyer's hand," in Shakespeare's apt phrase
(Sonnet 111). These men were, as Gordon Kipling has shown, members
of the royal household, closely allied to its interests and in a position to
cooperate closely with others in the Chapel and the Great Wardrobe in
order to create spectacular musical entertainments ending in costumed
dance as an expression of Henrician official policy.[16] The fact that the
iconographical materials used by these artists in their marriage disguisings were also employed on later state occasions again points to a commonality of artistic traditions devoted to the service of the Tudor state.
An instance of this occurred on 7 October 1518 at Greenwich, two days
after the proxy betrothal marriage of Henry VIII's two-year-old daughter
Mary to the infant son of Francis I of France, when a political disguising designed to celebrate the Treaty of Universal Peace introduced a
pageant of a rock with five trees to symbolize Pope Leo X, the Emperor
Maximilian, King Francis I of France, King Henry VIII of England, and
King Charles I of Spain (who was to be elected the following year to the
imperial throne).[17]

The use of politically orthodox allegory by court artists like Cornish
under the Henrys does not lessen their achievement; it simply posits
a characteristically medieval stance of the artist toward his work as
addressed to a new Tudor regime intent on establishing its dynastic
legitimacy. The genre of the court disguising may have been largely
anonymous, but it was far from inert during the early Tudor era. Sydney
Anglo argues persuasively that although the major pageant sequences

---

[16] Gordon Kipling, "The Origins of Tudor Patronage," *Patronage in the Renaissance*, 117–64, demonstrates convincingly how, in a royal household greatly expanded to make patronage possible,
"Artists in his [Henry VII's] service became servants in his household, and just as his ushers,
guardsmen, and grooms enhanced his estate through their liveried and ceremonial attendances,
so his artists were expected to enhance his estate through their poetry, pageantry, and painting."
Hence royal patronage "always moved in the direction of magnificent visual display and political
eulogy" (164). Jan van Dorsten, "Literary Patronage in Elizabethan England: The Early Phase,"
in the same collection of essays, 191–206, shows how patronage had declined to a very low ebb
by the beginning of Elizabeth's reign, though the use of patronage to secure political ends by
Elizabeth's courtiers was still intense in a political context.

[17] Anglo, "Court Festivals," 25–26, citing Gonzaga Archives, Mantua, Busta 85 B.xxxiii, 10, fos.
104r–107r, *Calendar of State Papers Venetian*, II, no. 1088, and Edward Hall, *Chronicles*, edn. of 1809,
595. Anglo similarly refers to an anti-imperial play staged on 10 November 1527 consisting of an
arbor with a fountain and beside it a large olive tree symbolizing the new Universal Peace and
flanked by the two orders of St. George and St. Michael symbolizing England and France as
the makers of the peace; PRO *Revels Accounts*, E.36/227, fo. 53r–53v, and Hall, *Chronicles*, 735.
The occasion is discussed further in Anglo, *Spectacle, Pageantry, and Early Tudor Policy*, 124–36.
On the infant marriage, see H. F. M. Prescott, *Mary Tudor* (New York: Macmillan, 1962), 22.

variously devised for the Emperor Charles V, Anne Boleyn, Edward VI, Mary, Philip and Mary, and Elizabeth I are comparatively thin and diffuse in their theme and imagery when we compare them with the entertainments created for the wedding of Katharine and Arthur, celebrations of great court marriages during the period continued to be richly innovative.[18] The tournament and the court disguising, which had evolved in good part from Continental elements and especially from the Burgundian court,[19] developed a distinctively English form of artistic expression. Its fullest expression survives in the account of the wedding festivities of Katharine and Arthur in 1501, but other occasions appear to have been no less sumptuous.

Despite Henry VII's well-known dislike of extravagance, he appears to have regarded carefully planned expenditure on court disguisings as a pragmatic use of wealth.[20] The weddings of his children were his chief means of establishing himself as a major player in the foreign-policy contests of the early sixteenth century. Scotland to the north was both England's most troublesome neighbor and potentially important ally in the event of a union. The nine-year-old Archduke Charles, to whom the thirteen-year-old Mary was betrothed in 1508, was, as the grandson of the Emperor Maximilian and the son of Philip of Burgundy and his Queen Joanna, heir presumptive to Austria, Burgundy, and Castile; indeed, he became the Emperor Charles V. Even more than the other princes of Europe, Henry VII had reason to bolster the dubious legitimacy of his claim to the throne through a series of political marriages that had begun with his own marriage to Elizabeth of York.

From the evidence available,[21] then, it would seem that early Tudor marriage disguisings were created to address crucial dynastic considerations. And, whereas political considerations of course pertain also in

[18] Anglo, *Spectacle, Pageantry, and Early Tudor Policy*, 98ff.
[19] Kipling, *The Triumph of Honour*, and Anglo, *Spectacle, Pageantry, and Early Tudor Policy*.
[20] Kipling, "The Origins of Tudor Patronage," 117–64, argues persuasively that Henry VII was intent on displaying the magnificence of his royal household and regime through calculated patronage of literature, drama, painting, music, glasswork, tapestry, and every aspect of cultural life, in imitation of the magnificence of the court of Burgundy. Henry's patronage of the drama "may have been crucial in the development of the interlude and masque in England," and yet has been consistently undervalued (149). Henry was "the first English king to patronize troupes of players" (150). His major revisions in the Great Wardrobe and Chapel led to the formation of the Office of the Revels.
[21] Many records have been lost. Among them are *The Marriage of Queen Mary*, from July of 1558, ascribed to L. Lauder and W. Adamson and consisting evidently of a triumph and a play performed at Edinburgh in honor of Mary's marriage to Philip of Spain some years earlier in 1554. Also listed is *The Hatfield Mask for the Princess Elizabeth*, staged at Hatfield House, where Elizabeth resided, sometime between 1554 and 1556. Alfred Harbage, *Annals of English Drama 975–1700*, rev. S. Schoenbaum (Philadelphia: University of Pennsylvania Press, 1964).

1613, it does appear that in 1501 and the years immediately afterward the function of the court disguising was conceived primarily or indeed entirely in terms of dynastic political allegory. We find no hint of authors staking out their own position as humanists and artists. William Cornish, a central figure in courtly entertainments from 1494 to 1522, when he devised a transparently political play in honor of the Emperor Charles V's visit to England to conclude an alliance with Henry VIII against France as urged by Cardinal Wolsey,[22] stands wholly apart from Skelton, who occupied a very different world of loyal opposition and who appears to have disliked Wolsey with a special intensity. The iconography of the marriage disguisings, however innovatively employed, is in the tradition of medieval and chivalric allegorizing, inherited in good part from the Continent and especially Burgundy. The artists remain nearly or wholly anonymous (we know really very little even about Cornish) in the same creative sense as the compilers of most of the English Corpus Christi cycles. That is to say that individual creativity is vital, but is also contained within a framework of traditional symbolism and public function to which the artist devotes his talent.

We are not arguing that art need be stifled under such circumstances, or that it simply toadies to its source of patronage, any more than one would want to argue that medieval painters commissioned to execute works of art on prescribed subjects like the Annunciation or the Crucifixion were thereby deprived of artistic freedom. Blatant political patronage can of course stifle artistic expression, and indeed appears to have done so during the era of intense polemicism of the early Reformation, when John Rightwise had succeeded to the role of purveyor of political plays to the Tudor regime after the death of William Cornish in 1523,[23] but this constraint was triggered by extraordinary pressures. Our argument is instead directed to a fundamentally different concept of how the artist relates to patronage and how individual expression flourishes in a system we today can scarcely understand or view with sympathy. The artist's world of Chapman and Campion in 1613 is basically closer to our world of an artistic individuality that takes as its main subject its own protest against constraints imposed by patronage.

---

[22] See Anglo, "William Cornish," 357–60, Anglo, *Spectacle, Pageantry, and Early Tudor Policy*, 170–206, and Robert Lee Ramsay (ed.), *Magnificence*, by John Skelton, EETS extra ser. 948 (London: Kegan Paul, 1906).

[23] Anglo, *Spectacle, Pageantry, and Early Tudor Policy*, 238ff., describes the decline of court festivals in the era of Reformation politics. The mid-century reigns of Edward VI, Mary, and then Elizabeth were all times of unceasing religious controversy that left its mark on dramatic entertainment devised for the court.

III

The phenomenon of royal patronage exists in early Tudor England in a more lucid, even transparent, state of symbolic pageantry than in the more cerebral and artistically self-aware celebrations of 1613. Early Tudor marriage disguisings manifest in an essential form what Clifford Geertz sees as the cultural component of royal charisma: that numinous quality of royal will whose origins must be sought "in the same place as we look for that of gods: in the rites and images through which it is exerted."[24] Ernst Kantorowicz, in *The King's Two Bodies*, and David Bergeron, in his work on "Representation in Renaissance English Civic Pageants,"[25] similarly pay tribute to a symbolic world of late medieval Europe in which "medieval political theology" (in Kantorowicz's phrase) takes the form of ceremonial dancing and pictorial display in the courts of monarchs who seem attuned to a growing sense of the potential of ceremonial art to help fashion and adorn the political power needed for successful rule. The phenomenon is also part of the process described by Stephen Greenblatt, Louis Montrose, Stephen Orgel, Jonathan Goldberg, and others in which the artifacts of courtly entertainment gain a new prominence in literary and cultural studies because they display so usefully the process of cultural interchange between texts and the surrounding social and political context.[26] In this sense, what this essay undertakes to do is to juxtapose two notable instances, separated by more than a century of eventful time, and thereby suggest ways in which the process of cultural

[24] Clifford Geertz, "Centers, Kings, and Charisma: Reflections on the Symbolics of Power," in *Local Knowledge: Further Essays in Interpretive Anthropology* (New York: Harper Collins, 1983), 121–46.

[25] Ernst Kantorowicz, *The King's Two Bodies: A Study in Medieval Political Theology* (Princeton: Princeton University Press, 1957), and David M. Bergeron, "Representation in Renaissance English Civic Pageants," *Theater Journal* 40 (1980), 319–31. Other studies in the symbolic aspects of power include R. E. Giesey, *The Royal Funeral Ceremony in Renaissance France* (Geneva, 1960); G. R. Kernodle, *From Art to Theater* (Chicago: University of Chicago Press, 1944); Roy Strong, *Splendor at Court: Renaissance Spectacle and the Theater of Power* (Boston: Houghton Mifflin, 1973), and other studies cited in the following notes. David Norbrook has recently offered a quietly devastating critique of Kantorowicz, pointing out that Kantorowicz's two-bodies thesis arises out of a right-wing dislike of Whig progressive liberalism and a preference instead for a kind of medieval mysticism ("The Emperor's New Body? *Richard II*, Ernst Kantorowicz, and the Politics of Shakespeare Criticism," *Textual Criticism* 10 [1996], 329–57). The implications for New Historicist overreliance on this one work of Kantorowicz is disturbing, but in our view his description of a kind of medieval royal theology enacted through courtly dancing is still viable for our purposes.

[26] Stephen Greenblatt, *Renaissance Self-Fashioning: From More to Shakespeare* (Chicago: University of Chicago Press, 1980), *Shakespearean Negotiations* (Berkeley: University of California Press, 1988), and other studies; Louis Adrian Montrose, "'Shaping Fantasies': Figurative Gender and Power in Elizabethan Culture," *Representations* 2 (1.2, Spring 1983), 61–94, and other studies; Stephen Orgel, *The Illusion of Power: Political Theater in the English Renaissance* (Berkeley: University of California Press, 1975); Jonathan Goldberg, *James I and the Politics of Literature* (Baltimore: Johns Hopkins University Press, 1983), 231–39.

interchange and negotiation can develop over a period in which artistic self-awareness, cultural borrowing from other countries, and increasing sophistication of generic definitions all contribute to an enrichment and complication of the basic process delineated by Kantorowicz and Geertz. Charisma, in other words, has its own varying and developing history as well as its essential sociological and anthropological patterns.

In an important essay, Malcolm Smuts takes exception to the implicit and explicit assumptions of Geertz and others that Tudor public cere-mony relied heavily on artists and poets to express in allegorical terms the essence of royal charisma. Smuts's contention is that sheer pageantry, especially as embodied in the royal entry into London, was visually spec-tacular in a way that could be appreciated by public audiences who must have heard little or nothing of what was recited at various scaffolds on the pageant route. The role of the poet or dramatist as devisor of spoken texts was only marginally operative in the crucial business of conveying an image of royalty to the nation as a whole. When public spectacle grew less frequent and then fell into decline in the Stuart years, Smuts argues, an essentially medieval ritual gradually disintegrated.[27] We wish to carry this compelling argument further by suggesting that the world of literary allegory, binding artists to patrons in complex and self-reflecting patterns, turned increasingly inward – in the psychological sense of pre-occupying itself with the inner life of the court but also in the literal sense of staging its most important masques and pageants for select audiences at Whitehall. The loss of a medieval tradition of public spectacle brought into growing prominence an art form devised by artists for their wealthy patrons alone.

By the time of James I, masques at court had become extraordinarily elaborate and expensive. The set designs that Inigo Jones created in colla-boration not only with Ben Jonson but with George Chapman and oth-ers are legendary for their ingenious contrivances imported in part from

---

[27] R. Malcolm Smuts, "Public Ceremony and Royal Charisma: The English Royal Entry in London, 1485–1642," in A. L. Beier, David Camadine, and James M. Rosenheim (eds.), *The First Modern Society: Essays in English History in Honour of Lawrence Stone* (Cambridge: Cambridge University Press, 1989), 65–93. See also Smuts's important article on "The Political Failure of Stuart Cultural Patronage," *Patronage in the Renaissance*, 165–87, in which Smuts argues that the Stuarts "took virtually no steps to develop more effective supervision of court culture," so that stylistic innovation took place without centralized direction; it was more under the control of the artists themselves, as older artists and musicians were replaced by men schooled in Italian styles (169). Masques had long since developed to the point where the Office of Revels, nominally in charge, could no longer adequately supervise them; responsibilities "remained so fluid that we cannot always know for certain who decided on the themes and symbols used in these spectacles" (170). This process would seem to support the contention of this present essay that humanists found themselves in a position to assert their own agenda.

Renaissance Italy. Our interest in this essay is with the ways in which these developments brought along with them significant changes in patterns of patronage and the role of the artists who wrote the scripts.[28] The most immediately notable difference is that some of the artists were now well known and highly conscious of their status. For the festivities celebrating the marriage of Elizabeth and Frederick in 1613, the Jacobean court employed the talents of Thomas Campion, George Chapman, and Francis Beaumont, in addition to those like Shakespeare whose plays, already written and produced for public audiences, could be added to the roster. Borrowings from the public stage were, of course, far less expensive than masques especially produced at court, but by the same token they and their playwrights did not enjoy the same prestige in a serious game of Veblenian conspicuous consumption in which the masque became essentially a status symbol. Campion, Chapman, and Beaumont were paid specifically for shows designed to enhance the glory of the Jacobean court or, more often, some faction within that courtly society. To be sure, not all the entertainments devised for Frederick and Elizabeth were created by well-known writers; in the extensive records that have survived, a good deal is essentially anonymous in a way that must have resembled the efforts of those self-effacing royal householders in the reign of Henry VII. Still, to the considerable extent that major dramatists were drafted in 1613 – conscientious, proud authors intent on fashioning their own identities as men of letters – the encomiastic assignments were likely to generate friction. No instance demonstrates the problem more clearly than that of Chapman.

Chapman was commissioned to write a masque on behalf of "the two honorable houses or inns of court, the Middle Temple and Lincoln's Inn," to be performed at Whitehall before the King and his court on Shrove Monday, 15 February 1613. Chapman's description of the "whole show" has survived, incorporating not only a visual account of the festivities but Chapman's dialogue and songs.[29] The two accounts are in vivid, almost comic, contrast. The visual account pays homage to a "noble and magnificent performance" that began with a splendid procession on horseback to the court from the house of Sir Edward Philips, Master of the Rolls. The narrative is in fact dedicated by Chapman to Philips and

---

[28] David M. Bergeron, "Women as Patrons of English Drama," *Patronage in the Renaissance*, 274–90, looks at changes in court entertainment brought about by the increasing opportunity for women to appear in masques as dancers and even as allegorical figures in the masques proper.

[29] John Nichols (ed.), *The Progresses, Processions, and Magnificent Festivities of King James the First* (London: J. B. Nichols, 1828), II, 566–86.

addressed to him as a prime mover of the event. Chapman's dedicatory letter is the elegantly fawning sort often appended to patrons by their needy protégés; Chapman speaks of "the poor pains I added to this royal service, being wholly chosen and commanded by your most constant and free favor." Chapman is not slow to pay tribute also to "our kingdom's most artful and ingenious architect, Inigo Jones."

The procession Chapman describes is a sumptuous affair. Fifty gentlemen of the combined Inns of Court, "richly attired and as gallantly mounted," led the way with their footmen in attendance, followed at a fit distance by an anti-masque or "mock-masque" assortment of baboons attired "like fantastic travelers" and mounted on asses. The "choice musicians of our kingdom" came next in two triumphal chariots, and then the chief masquers in Indian habits, each attended by two Moors attired as Indian slaves and by torchbearers. The most elaborately adorned chariot was presided over by Plutus, god of riches. A full guard of two hundred halberdiers, two marshals, and the like, made up the rest of a procession that, in Chapman's view, was "so novel, conceitful, and glorious, as hath not in this land . . . been ever before beheld" (567–70). Upon their arrival at Whitehall, the assembly marched about the yard under the gaze of the King, bride and bridegroom, lords of the Privy Council, and the chief nobility who were standing in the gallery before the tilt-yard, and, having dismounted, were escorted into the performance hall.[30]

Chapman is no less lavish in his description of Jones's set, or, as Chapman calls it, the "works." Its chief feature was a great artificial rock erected in the lower end of the hall, complete with winding stairs and a silver octagonal temple honoring Fortuna. The huge rock proved capable of splitting in pieces with a great crack in order that it might

[30] The ceremonial sumptuousness of the occasion is described by Jerzy Limon, *The Masque of Stuart Culture* (Newark: University of Delaware Press, 1990), 142–57. Limon sees the masque as focusing on the element of earth as a constructive and harmonizing element in humours, influences on human life, and the like. Reese, "Unity in Chapman's *Masque*" (see n. 4), argues that Chapman's didactic intent is to insist that the great "correspondences" of degree, harmony, restraint, and decorum must be celebrated and that "Total allegiance to the king must be given' (304). If so, in our view, the theme seems remarkably close to what the Jacobean court wanted Chapman to say, and makes little allowance for the artistic restiveness that seems evident in Chapman's masque.

Though space does not permit us to discuss it here, the presence of "blackamoors" costumed as "Indian slaves" in Chapman's masque indicates a dimension of imagined otherness not present in the entertainments of 1501. Such a conflation of the native American with those of African descent reflects both the attraction to cultures regarded as exotic and a general level of vague confusion about the non-Europeans whose cultures would be disrupted by British imperial expansion. See D. J. Gordon, "Chapman's *Memorable Masque*," in Stephen Orgel (ed.), *The Renaissance Imagination*, (Berkeley: University of California Press, 1977), 194–202. Gordon's interest in colonization is linked to the concepts of honor, virtue, and law as ways of providing order and checking any subversive courtly ambitions to move beyond one's proper place.

reveal a mine of gold in which the twelve masquers were triumphantly seated; in an evening sky, the sun was seen ready to set behind it. In this sumptuous setting, Chapman's masque was essentially an ingenious rewriting or adaptation of mythology designed to shower praise on the Jacobean court: Plutus, formerly presented in the pagan world as blind, deformed, and dull-witted, was now made out to be sharp-eyed, handsome, and liberal by virtue of his love of honor, virtue, law, and true fame. Thus did Chapman lend his talents to the fashioning of a deliberately outrageous conceit, one that implicitly justified the extravagant expenditure of this masque (and others as well) by arguing that the money was spent in pursuit of courtly virtues and poetic excellence. Chapman's own potential role as beneficiary under such a system of benign trickle-down largess is markedly evident. He is the house intellectual for the occasion, an apologist for patrician wealth in which he is to share indirectly as a hanger-on.

At the same time, Chapman's querulousness as an under-appreciated humanist is no less in evidence, suggesting an author who is uneasy at prostituting his genius. Evidently not everyone at court thought Chapman had proved a good choice as poet for this royal occasion. He undertakes to answer "certain insolent objections made against the length of my speeches and narrations" (571). He creates a heroic role for himself not unlike that of Bussy D'Ambois and other of Chapman's eccentric protagonists: an unconventional defender of a true intellectual aristocracy that is too often bastardized by "every vulgarly-esteemed upstart" who "dares break the dreadful dignity of ancient and authentical poesy" and who presumes, "Luciferously," to "proclaim, in place thereof, repugnant precepts of their own spawn." "Truth and worth have no faces to enamour the licentious, but vainglory and humour." Chapman emerges from this self-serving characterization as the true defender of all poetic inventions that have in them "a fountain to be expressed, from whence the rivers flow," and that "should expressively arise out of the places and persons for and by whom they are presented, without which limits they are luxurious and vain" (572). His enemies are legion, and they are implicitly at the very court from which he hopes to derive nourishment and support.

This unstable mix of self-adulation and prickly defensiveness generates the fable of the masque itself. How is one to tell true invention from sham and self-glorification? Plutus begins the masque by mocking the very scenic devices of Jones that Chapman had appeared to praise in his physical description. "Rocks! Nothing but rocks in these masquing devices!

Is invention so poor that she must needs ever dwell among rocks?" (573). His mordant view of the court is of a place peopled with "stony-hearted ladies," their "repulsed servants," and "flinty-hearted usurers," all appropriate enough to a landscape of rocks much in need of transformation. Plutus cracks jokes about the legendary poverty of poets: "A man of wit! What's that, a beggar?" (575).

Capriccio, identified in "The Names of the Speakers" as this same "man of wit," is a satirical railing figure in the fashion of current satire, both humanist and scabrous clown. He confesses that he is himself "in needy pursuit of the blind deity, Riches." His lot as a man of wit is a hard one, in which he must "eat through main rocks" for his food, "or fast." His wit is a torment to him, like Sisyphus' rock, for he finds himself obliged to turn himself into more conceivable shapes than even Proteus might imagine (574). Though he conjures up in his imagination a better world of reward for poets, a "rich island" that implicitly flatters King James by attributing to him the reform of the world's abuse of riches, Capriccio's insistent vision is of the neglect of poets. Touchily he asks if the poet-critic can hope to be honored by the very society he criticizes: "is it impossible that I, for breaking a clean jest, should be advanced in court or council? Or at least served out for an ambassador to a dull climate?" He asks for understanding of the salient truth that "jests and merriments are but wild weeds in a rank soil, which, being well manured, yield the wholesome crop of wisdom and discretion" (576). Though, as satirist, he is "a dangerous fellow" who can either "puff up with glory all those that affect me" or else "spur-gall even the best that contemn me," Capriccio professes to be taking part in the present evening's entertainment with a benign view to providing "acceptable service" (577). Viewed in these terms, Chapman's masque is a fantasy centered on a needful and talented artist like himself. Small wonder that the masque did not please all its participants and viewers, who might be pardoned for having supposed that the masque should focus on them – as indeed it nominally does. For all its glorification of Stuart ideology, Chapman's masque is more nearly a manifesto of the disenfranchised intellectual.

Similar issues of the role of the artist at court arise in Campion's *The Lord's Masque*, also designed by Inigo Jones, and in Beaumont's *The Masque of the Inner Temple and Gray's Inn*, although arriving at different definitions of art's function as we might expect to find in the pronouncements of men who were temperamentally quite different from Chapman. Such differences, which limitations of space do not permit us to investigate here, only underscore what we have been attempting to demonstrate:

that the role of the artist at court became much more sharply defined and even contentious in the gap of time between 1501 and 1613, as artists became better known and increasingly aware of their potential moral authority as humanists and writers. Significantly, however, we also see a contrast emerge between the kind of patronage Shakespeare enjoyed at his public theatre and the politically sensitive system of largess at court to which Chapman and others were necessarily beholden. Shakespeare is no less aware than Chapman of his position as writer, but the parameters in which he is able to operate are more commercially defined and perhaps more artistically liberating. In generic terms, and in patterns of patronage, *The Tempest* is quite separated from the wedding masques prepared by Chapman and Campion. Those masques bear a strong generic resemblance to the disguisings prepared by William Cornish in the early sixteenth century, and are part of a continuous tradition of entertainment at court. At the same time, as this essay has attempted to show, shifting social and political considerations between 1501 and 1613 have changed the very conception of the artist's individual role in shaping the nature of courtly entertainment.

CHAPTER 6

The city as patron: York

Alexandra F. Johnston

It was once thought that the normal form of provincial early drama was the large Biblical plays performed by cities all over the country, "thystories of the old & new testament" as they are called in the York city council Minute Books.[1] The research of the last three decades has shown that there were very few such plays performed in a restricted number of cities almost exclusively in the north.[2] A question that has been rarely asked in the past but that is increasingly relevant to drama studies is why these few towns and cities were dramatic patrons and why they continued to be so in the face of economic decline and political pressure from more senior levels of government. In only two English cities do the texts of the plays and the records concerning their production survive – Chester and York. David Mills has recently written about the relationship of Chester and its people to the Chester Plays.[3] In this essay I will explore the complex relationship between the city council of York and what were, in the end, three major religious didactic plays and several ceremonial ridings that, one way or another, became their responsibility as the sixteenth century progressed.

York was an important provincial city in the fourteenth century, the center of a large and sprawling county with a hinterland whose business was attracted to the city by the annual dramatic event. It could be

I would like to acknowledge with gratitude the support I have received over the years from the Canada Council and its successor the Social Sciences and Humanities Research Council of Canada for my research into the dramatic records of late medieval and early modern England.

[1] *York*, 2 vols., ed. Alexandra F. Johnston and Margaret Rogerson, Records of Early English Drama (henceforth REED) (Toronto: University of Toronto Press, 1979), 34. Hereafter cited in the text parenthetically as *York*.

[2] See Richard Beadle (ed.), *The Cambridge Companion to Medieval English Theatre* (Cambridge: Cambridge University Press, 1994); Marianne Briscoe and John Coldewey (eds.), *Contexts for Early English Drama* (Bloomington: Indiana University Press, 1989); Eckehard Simon (ed.), *The Theatre of Medieval Europe* (Cambridge: Cambridge University Press, 1991).

[3] David Mills, *Recycling the Cycle: The City of Chester and Its Whitsun Plays* (Toronto: University of Toronto Press, 1998).

argued that the fundamental motivation for patronizing the play was purely commercial, since the crowds coming into the city to see them would also frequent the market stalls of the York craftsmen. But this reasoning becomes less compelling when one considers that York was served by three major fairs on Whitsun, the feast of SS. Peter and Paul (29 June) and the archbishop's fair at Lammas (1 August).[4] The feast of Corpus Christi, the day on which York stubbornly performed its Biblical cycle even when the Chester authorities had moved theirs to Whitsun, is a moveable feast, falling on the second Thursday after Whitsun. Depending on the date of Easter, it could fall any time from 21 May to 24 June, but the most common date was in mid-June. The tradesmen of York were unlikely to make a major effort to replenish the stock sold less than two weeks before at the Whitsun Fair when they knew that there would be two more special opportunities for trade at the end of June and the end of July. They were, besides, otherwise occupied on Corpus Christi Day since, even if they were not performing in the play, the ordinances of their crafts required that they walk with their pageant and until the 1470s also carry torches in the Corpus Christi procession that was held on the same day.[5] The only tradesmen likely to profit from the activities on Corpus Christi were the brewers and the victuallers who did have an unusual number of customers filling the streets of the city.

Some scholars have tried to suggest that the crafts undertook the performance of the plays because it provided an opportunity for them to display their craft to the audience.[6] Such an argument works for only a very few guilds such as the Building of the Ark that was the responsibility of the Shipwrights and the pageant depicting the ark at sea that was the responsibility of the Fishers and Mariners. But the argument can be much more cogently made that these crafts were given those plays because they had easy access to the needed set pieces. Similarly, the Bakers could provide the bread for their episode of the Last Supper and, less picturesquely, the Pinners the nails for the Crucifixion, and the Butchers the necessary blood for the Death of Christ. The only episode where there is any sense that the craft ascription is driving the text rather than the other way round is in the First Trial before Pilate where much is made of the lavish bed where Pilate falls asleep before Christ is brought

---

[4] David Palliser, *Tudor York* (Oxford: Oxford University Press, 1979), 181–82.

[5] For a discussion of the relationship between the play and the procession see Alexandra F. Johnston, "The Procession and Play of Corpus Christi in York after 1426," *Leeds Studies in English*, n.s., 7 (1973–74), 55–62.

[6] See, for example, Alan D. Justice, "Trade Symbolism in the York Cycle," *Theatre Journal* 31 (1979), 47–58.

before him. That episode was produced by the Tapiters, who made expensive bed hangings.

The arguments for the performance of the plays being based on commercial gain have been centered on the craft guilds who actually performed the pageants rather than on the civic government that produced the entire play. In a groundbreaking article, "The Illusion of Economic Structure: Craft Guilds in Late Medieval English Towns,"[7] Heather Swanson challenged the romantic notion that the "mysteries" or craft guilds of late medieval England represented the sturdy independence of the artisan class. Rather, she suggested that the guilds were the invention of the civic oligarchies as instruments to control commercial activity and her major examples are drawn from York. Her final sentence, "The most oppressive aspect of the guilds lay in quite another direction, in the way its members were expected to subsidize civic pomp, not least in the form of the Corpus Christi pageants,"[8] raised the whole question of the relationship between the civic government and the craft guilds in the production of civic drama. Some years later, R. B. Dobson took up Swanson's point and proposed a radical new approach to the creation of the *York Cycle*.[9] Basing his argument on the paucity of evidence for a guild structure of any kind in York before the Black Death in 1349, he dismissed the idea that the cycle as we know it could have evolved from the procession of Corpus Christi (itself only instituted in York in 1325 [*York*, 1]) and posited what he called the "big bang" theory of the origins of the *York Cycle* in which he suggested that the dramatic event with its extraordinary method of production was created by the civic elite at a time when they needed to assert their control over the commercial life of the city. He argued that by the appearance of the *Ordo Paginarum* (or detailed play list) in 1415 the "mystery plays . . . have already become intensely regulated from above, a more or less deliberate exercise in social control upon the city by its governing elite."[10]

But if this is so, there must have been either a pre-existing play text or a playwright who could be commissioned to take on the writing of the play. Many of us who have spent years studying the *York Cycle* as a literary artifact have struggled with the apparent contradiction between the fundamental unity of theology and imagery in the text and the idea

---

7 Heather Swanson, "The Illusion of Economic Structure: Craft Guilds in Late Medieval English Towns," *Past and Present* 121 (Nov. 1988), 29–48.

8 Swanson, "The Illusion of Economic Structure," 48.

9 R. B. Dobson, "Craft Guilds and City: The Historical Origins of the York Plays Reassessed" in Alan E. Knight (ed.), *The Stage as Mirror* (Woodbridge: Boydell and Brewer, 1997), 91–106.

10 Dobson, "Craft Guilds and City," 100.

that the plays had evolved over many years in the hands of small groups of artisans.[11] The *York Cycle* is part of the widespread movement of religious didacticism the aim of which was to stimulate what has been called "affective piety," dwelling on the humanity and suffering of Christ to stimulate a closer relationship with him and so enhance faith. It has parallels in such non-dramatic writing as *The mirrour of the blessyd lyf of Jesu Christ* written by the Yorkshire Carthusian Nicholas Love, based on the seminal Franciscan text of Pseudo-Bonaventure, *Meditationes Vitae Christi*. There are also parallels in all forms of late medieval art, including much of the medieval stained glass that still can be seen in the churches of York. The idea that the creation of the cycle of plays was a collaborative act between the civic oligarchy and playwrights inspired by the devotional movement all around them makes sense of all the known evidence.

The precondition of civic control also explains the method of performance in procession through the city streets that has so bothered scholars in the past.[12] The council held jurisdiction within the walls of the city, and in the crowded streets there was no large open space where a play and its audience could be fitted. The processional mode, moving from one small playing site to another throughout the city, solved the problem and ensured civic control. An act of creation for this method of production explains why the text so perfectly reflects the method of production where the motifs of traveling, of constant greetings and farewells are written into the text as the natural response to a performance that was constantly moving.[13] It also allowed the playwrights to fashion the plays with a verbal complexity and intimacy unparalleled in early drama because members of the audience were always close enough to hear each word that was said. The *York Cycle*, then, can be seen as the creation of two complementary impulses for political control and religious education. It is this combination of motivation that should be seen behind the city's

[11] See Richard J. Collier, *Poetry and Drama in the York Corpus Christi Play* (Hamden, Connecticut: Archon Books, 1977); Clifford Davidson, *From Creation to Doom* (New York: AMS Press, 1984); Alexandra F. Johnston, "The Word Made Flesh: Augustinian Elements in the York Cycle," in Robert Taylor et al. (eds.), *The Centre and its Compass: Studies in Medieval Literature in Honor of Professor John Leyerle*, Studies in Medieval Culture 33 (Kalamazoo: Western Michigan University Press, 1993), 225–46.

[12] See, for example, Alan Nelson, "Principles of Processional Staging: 'York Cycle'," *Modern Philology* 67 (1970), 303–20, later expanded in his *The Medieval English Stage* (Chicago: University of Chicago Press, 1974); Stanley J. Kahr, *Traditions of English Medieval Drama* (London: Hutchinson, 1974); Martin Stevens, "The York Cycle: From Procession to Play," *Leeds Studies in English*, n.s., 6 (1972), 37–61.

[13] Alexandra F. Johnston, "The York Corpus Christi Play: a Dramatic Structure Based on Performance Practice," in Herman Braet, Johan Noive, and Gilbert Toumoy (ed.), *The Theatre in the Middle Ages* (Leuven: Leuven University Press, 1985), 362–73.

own 1399 statement of the purpose of the plays that were to be played
"en honour & reuerence nostreseignour Iesu Crist & hounour & profitt
de mesme la Citee" ("in honour and reverence of our lord Jesus Christ
and the honour and profit of the said City" [*York*, 11]). The sponsorship
of the Corpus Christi Play displayed both the power and the piety of the
council.

The records of the dramatic activity of the city of York begin in the late
fourteenth century. Once the play was established, the mayor and the
twelve aldermen (who were almost exclusively in this period members
of the Mercers guild) acting as its producers, coordinated the work of
the individual crafts and sub-crafts in the presentation of the forty-eight
episodes depicting salvation history. Each craft was responsible for its
assigned episode, collecting "pageant money" from its members to buy
material for props and costumes, to rehearse, and to feed and pay the actors. The "hands on" coordination of each episode was the responsibility
of pageant masters elected by each craft. In the Mercers Guild (whose
records survive in the greatest detail), pageant master was an entry-level
position undertaken by the new and frequently younger members of the
guild.

However, it was the city council that was responsible for the overall
event. In 1476, a system of auditions was implemented to ensure the
quality of the production, "yerely in þe tyme of lentyn there shall be
called afore the Maire for þe tyme beyng iiij of the moste Connyng
descrete and able players within þis Citie to serche here and examen
all þe plaiers and plaies [and] pagentes thrughoute all þe artificeres belonging to corpus christi Plaie And all suche as þay shall fynde sufficiant
in personne and Connyng to þe honour of þe Citie and Worship of þe
saide Craftes for to admitte and able and all oþer insufficient personnes
either in Connyng voice or personne to discharge ammove and avoide"
(*York*, 109). It was also the council that decided whether or not the play
should be performed and when it would be performed. For example, in
1426, Friar William Melton, a charismatic preacher, urged that the play
be moved to the Friday after the feast so that the feast could be better
celebrated. This idea was apparently enthusiastically endorsed by the
larger body of the Commons (*York*, 43–44) but the council paid no attention and the play continued to be played on the feast day.[14] The council
was also the body that decided on the occasional substitution of one of
the confraternity plays – the Creed Play or the Pater Noster Play – for

---

[14] Alexandra F. Johnston, "The Procession and Play of Corpus Christi in York after 1426," *Leeds
Studies in English*, n.s., 7 (1973–74), 55–62.

the Corpus Christi Play, or on canceling the event entirely because of plague or civil disturbance.

As patron and producer, the council derived income from two sources. They designated the normally twelve stations or playing places along the traditional route and then rented them to citizens of the town, who in their turn made them available to the public. They also collected fines from guilds who failed to live up to the standard of performance set out in the city ordinances concerning the play. For example, in 1554 the Girdlers did not have their play ready in time "but taried an wholle hower & more in hyndrans & stoppyng of the rest of the pageantz folowyng and to the disorderyng of the same" (*York*, 312) and were fined for their action. One further play-related income for the city came from the rental of space adjacent to Micklegate Bar to some of the guilds for the storage of the pageant wagons and gear of nine or ten of the forty-eight pageant wagons. On the other side of the ledger, Corpus Christi expenses for the council consisted of a regular subsidy to the Innholders for the support of the pageant of the Assumption of the Virgin and the often sizable "mess bill" incurred on the feast day itself in eating and drinking, both for the council assembled at the Common Hall station and also for their wives who, from the early six- teenth century, held their own separate party at the last station on the Pavement.

It seems clear from the York evidence that once the play was estab- lished, the texts of each episode remained in the hands of the crafts. The "register" copy, the manuscript that has survived as BL Add MS 35290, was compiled some time in the third quarter of the fifteenth cen- tury when some form of processional performance had existed in York for close to a century. The most recent editor of the York text, Richard Beadle, believes it was compiled from the existing guild copies handed in to be compiled for an official copy.[15] Unfortunately, there is a lacuna in the records for this period so we have no direct evidence from the time of the original compilation. However, several pageants were not registered at that time and we do have the evidence from the 1560s of the council calling upon the delinquent crafts to submit their texts for registering. But this is not to say that the council was not concerned about the content of the play. A regular feature of the sixteenth-century performances was the presence of the city clerk or his deputy with the playbook at the first station (at the gates of Holy Trinity Priory, Micklegate), monitoring the

---

[15] Richard Beadle (ed.), *The York Plays* (London: Edward Arnold, 1982), 13–19.

performance and occasionally making notes in the margin to indicate new material or new stage business.

From very early in the history of the play, however, we can see the council taking a keen interest in its revisions of the play. In about 1415, two master lists of the pageants were compiled by the then town clerk, Roger Burton, and entered into the official Memorandum Book of the city. The first list, the *Ordo Paginarum*, describes the pageants as they then existed (*York*, 16–24). The second list seems to be a list of crafts and an extraordinary proliferation of sub-crafts and the episodes for which they were responsible (*York*, 25–26). These master lists were used as running tallies of what craft or sub-craft was responsible for each play, or part of a play. The so-called "*Ordo* gathering" has survived in a severely damaged condition but it is still possible to see the changes not only of craft ascription but also, from time to time, of play content. The episodes described in the *Ordo* correspond in broad outline, but not in detail, to the play text as it has come down to us. There is evidence to indicate, however, that about 1422, during the mayoralty of Henry Preston,[16] major revision took place. A detailed description of the wagon, props, and costumes for the Mercers' Judgment Play dated 1433 provides interesting evidence for the revisions (*York*, 55–56). The details of character that can be deduced from the costume evidence in both descriptions of the pageant indicate that it would have been impossible to perform the play as described in the *Ordo* with the 1433 set and costumes, but perfectly possible to perform the text in BL Add MS 35290 with the 1433 set and costumes. The revision to Judgment, then, was made between 1415 and 1433. Another, more significant change was made in the Passion sequence in the early fifteenth century. Thirteen crafts were responsible for the episodes beginning with the Betrayal and ending with the Division of Christ's Garments. These were divided into eleven episodes in the *Ordo*, but appear in only eight in the play text. One pageant, The Condemnation of Christ, brought together parts of four earlier pageants into a new mix. Ten years after the event, the crafts were still at odds about the financial support of the new pageant. In an agreement entered into the Memorandum Book in 1432 laying down the rules, it is clear that the city had ultimate authority over the recalcitrant crafts who apparently objected to the new order of things represented by the new text.

The *York Cycle* was brought into being and revised by a city at the height of its power. When Richard II created the city a county in its

---

[16] Preston was mayor 1421–22. See Francis Drake, *Eboracum* (London, 1736), 362.

own right in 1396 amidst much civic pomp and pageantry (*York*, 9), the
population of the city has been estimated at 15,000.[17] It was the second
city in the kingdom, the seat of an archbishopric, a great Benedictine
abbey (St. Mary's), the largest hospital outside London (St. Leonard's),
and major houses of all four orders of friars. One of these, the Augustinian
friary next to the Common Hall, housed a remarkable library that
challenged a similar great collection in St. Mary's.[18] York was a wool
manufacturing town and its guild of Mercers – the powerful civic oli-
garchs – were trading vigorously across the "middle sea."[19] But by 1548,
the population had fallen to "roughly 8,000" and the city had sunk to
sixth among the provincial towns. What emerges from David Palliser's
careful analysis of the reasons for the decline is the picture of a city that
had lost its economic base in the wool trade to the West Riding, its port
to Hull, and a large part of the "market" that fueled the service trades –
the religious houses – at dissolution in 1538. Only with the upturn in the
economy after 1560, the return of political stability to the north after the
rising of the northern earls in 1569, and the re-establishment of York as an
administrative center with the Elizabethan Council of the North and its
Ecclesiastical Commission did York regain its position as a major urban
center.[20]

The period we are considering, therefore, is a period of poverty and
decline and yet it is through this period that we can trace the active interest taken by the city council in the production of the plays. Although the
annual station rent fell from over six pounds in 1454 (*York*, 84–85) to a
mere pound in 1506 (*York*, 202) rising to a slightly higher 24s 10d by
1542 (*York*, 279), the council often took creative steps to ensure that
faltering crafts were helped to continue to take their part in the play.
In 1535, the Corpus Christi Play was not performed. That year the
Creed Play, sponsored by the Corpus Christi Guild, was played and
the city council decided to use all the money that the crafts would normally collect for their pageants to pay the legal expenses of a York man
in London (*York*, 256–57). We have, therefore, a record of a levy the

---

[17] Palliser, *Tudor York*, 202.
[18] For the library list of the Augustinian Friary see K. W. Humphreys (ed.), *The Friars' Libraries, Corpus of British Medieval Library Catalogues* (London: British Library, 1990); for that of St. Mary's see R. Sharpe, et al. (eds.), *English Benedictine Libraries*, Corpus of British Medieval Library Catalogues (London: British Library, 1996).
[19] Alexandra F. Johnston, "Traders and Playmakers: English Guildsmen and the Low Countries," in Caroline Barron and Nigel Saul (eds.), *England and the Low Countries in the Late Middle Ages* (Stroud: Alan Sutton, 1995), 99–114.
[20] Palliser, *Tudor York*, 202.

council collected from all the crafts that were preparing to present their pageants in the Corpus Christi Play that year (*York*, 257–58). Thirty-two of the possible forty-eight pageants seem to have been ready to go. Fifty years later, in 1585, the city underwrote the second production of a midsummer show to be produced by Thomas Grafton (see below), choosing to pay for it by levying the crafts for sums roughly equivalent to the pageant assessment. The order of the list of crafts and their contributions that Grafton submitted with his own bill reflects the order of the episodes sponsored by the crafts in the *Ordo* list. It is therefore possible to compare the two lists to assess which crafts were in continuing difficulty. The crafts and pageants that appear in neither the 1535 list nor the 1585 list are Shipwrights (Building of the Ark), Chandlers (Shepherds), Masons (Purification), Ironmongers (Simon the Leper), Shearmen (Road to Calvary), Winedrawers (The Appearance to Mary Magdalen), and Scriveners (Thomas of India). Of these, there is no information about the Shipwrights and the Winedrawers, although both those episodes could have been easily incorporated into contiguous pageants. In 1517 the city had ordered the common carters to pay towards the support of the Shearmen's pageant because "yei were of litill substance & was not able to bring furth yer pageant" (*York*, 214). There is no other evidence about this arrangement and we can only conclude that it was not sufficient to save the pageant of a craft completely dependent on the manufacture rather than the sale of wool. Shearmen literally sheared the newly woven cloth to remove the nap (*York*, 924). However, there is evidence that the council had some success facilitating the performance of the other four in the last years of the life of the plays.

During the reign of Edward VI and after the accession of Elizabeth, when the plays on the death and assumption of the Virgin Mary were suspended, the mayor and council ordered that the pageant money should be collected as normal by the crafts who had been responsible for the three episodes. The money was to be turned over to the mayor "to be further ordred by hym toward*es* setting forth of pageantz on Corpus chri*sti* day . . . wher he shall see most nede" (*York*, 297). In 1563, it was ordered that the pageant money of the Innholders that had gone towards the pageant of The Coronation of the Virgin (which they shared with the mayor) should go to the Chandlers for their Shepherd pageant. The order was repeated in 1569 in a document in which the Chandlers are described as "moch decayed" (*York*, 356). Here we see the mayor and council directing normal pageant income in a way that would shore up one of the few pageants in recurring financial trouble.

A different tack was taken by the mayor and council with the Laborers who were associated with the Masons in the play of the Purification of the Virgin. The Laborers had no guild structure through which to elect pageant masters and so the city oversaw the election of four masters, one for each ward for the Laborers' pageant. The results of the election appear in the Chamberlains' account book eleven times between 1523 and 1559. The pageant was entered into the register in 1567 (*York*, 231–32, 351 et passim).

By 1554, the Scriveners' Guild, hit hard by the dissolution of the religious houses, had dwindled to a single member, John Meltonby, and the council ordered that half the fine incurred by the Girdlers for not having their pageant ready in time (five shillings) should be paid to Meltonby to help him bring out Thomas of India. In an effort to rectify the problem, on 1 June of the same year, the council ordered that all who had been franchised by the name of cornmerchant should pay for the support of this pageant (*York*, 312). Since it is not mentioned again in the records, it is possible that the pageant continued to be presented with the help of the Cornmerchants.

The story of the Ironmongers pageant is less happy. During the 1560s the council turned its attention to that ailing pageant. This is one that was not registered in the late fifteenth century and in 1567, along with the Laborers' pageant, it was ordered to be surrendered for copying. This never happened and the play is irretrievably lost. The pageant had, however, been recently played. In 1562, the mayor and council ordered a merchant named John Granger to undertake to produce the Ironmongers' pageant and further ordered that all the regular contributors should pay their share of the pageant money (*York*, 340). Eight years later, in 1568, the council was continuing to worry about this pageant. General support does not seem to have been forthcoming. In March, the council challenged the Girdlers about their practice of selling ironware without contributing to the pageant (*York*, 355). On 26 September, the council worked out a way of coming to the rescue of one Leonard Temple who had performed the pageant for two years as well as repairing it to the total amount of 43s (*York*, 357). Ironically, after all its trouble to keep this pageant viable, there would be only one more production of the Corpus Christi Play. By the mid-1560s the council was itself deeply divided over religion and the performance of this survival of the Catholic past, along with the other two religious plays of York, the Pater Noster Play and the Creed Play, became one of the points of conflict between the Council of the North and the city, as well as among the aldermen themselves. Civic patronage of community drama was about to fall victim to the religious tensions of the early years of Elizabeth's reign.

The stories of the two other religious plays of York, the Pater Noster Play and the Creed Play, demonstrate the power and importance of religious confraternities in the city.[21] Although the Pater Noster Play may have had some morality-play features, it seems likely that it was based on the seven petitions of the Lord's Prayer. In their response to Richard II's survey of guilds in 1388, the Pater Noster Guild stated its major purpose to be the custodian of the play for the "health and reformation of the souls, both of those in charge of the play and those hearing it" (*York*, 693).[22] The document also states that, like the Corpus Christi Play, this play was performed "through the principal streets of the city of York." Although nothing is here stated, clearly the city council had to be party to the production of this play as it was to every other processional event since, as we have seen, the council had jurisdiction over the streets of the city. From the inception of its play, therefore, the Pater Noster Guild was dependent on the patronage of the city for its play to be performed. In 1446, the Pater Noster Guild merged with the St. Anthony's Guild and the name Pater Noster Guild disappears.[23] The play books remained in the possession of the guild chaplain, William Downham, who left them to William Ball, master of the Guild of St. Anthony in 1465 (*York*, 99).[24] In 1495, the city fined the master and brethren of the Guild for not bringing forth the Pater Noster Play "acordyng to ye wurship ofyis Citie" and ordered the guild to be prepared to perform it the next year (*York*, 178). It is possible that the play was performed every ten years between 1496 and 1536 since that year the council agreed on 19 April that Pater Noster should be played "by Course" on 1 August (Lammas Day). Preparations must have seemed inadequate to the council because on 19 June the play was postponed until the "Sunday next after Lames day" (*York*, 262). By this time, the city clearly felt a proprietary interest in this play. This sense of ownership was to be solidified when, eleven years later, the council managed, despite its protestation that the city was "in gret decaye,"[25] to acquire the property of the

---

[21] For a detailed discussion of the involvement of the York city council in the Creed Play and the Pater Noster Play, see Alexandra F. Johnston, "The Plays of the Religious Guilds of York: the Creed Play and the Pater Noster Play," *Speculum* 50 (1975), 55–90.

[22] "... in salutem & emendacionem animarum tam gubernancium quam audiencium ... " *York*, 6.

[23] Angelo Raine, *Medieval York: A Topographical Survey* (London: J. Murray, 1955), 93.

[24] Johnston, "Plays of the Religious Guilds," 73.

[25] York City Archives HB 18, fo. 15v. See Angelo Raine, *York Civic Records*, 8 vols. (Wakefield: Yorkshire Archaeological Society, 1946), IV, 139.

St. Anthony's Guild after the dissolution of the guild. With the property came the play books. The city had now acquired its second major religious play.

The third play, the Creed Play, probably written by William Revetour, chaplain of the Guild of Corpus Christi and deputy town clerk in the early fifteenth century,[26] was based on the twelve articles of the Apostles Creed and performed, like the Pater Noster Play, episodically along the same pageant route as the civic play and using some of the pageant wagons of the crafts. The play was left to the Corpus Christi Guild by Revetour in 1446 along with the "libris & vexill*is* eidem p*er*tinent*ibus*" (*York*, 68). A faded memo on the dorse of an account roll of the Guild for 1449–51 tells us a good deal more about the play. Revetour placed as a condition on his gift of the play and its properties that it should be performed every twelve years at least (*York*, 80). This requirement was changed by Revetour's executor John Fox and his fellow chaplains of the Corpus Christi Guild in 1455. The play was to be performed "in various places of the said city of York" (*York*, 765) every ten years and to be financed by the "inhabitants at these places" or the holders of the stations along the processional route. It is highly probable that the prominent citizens whose houses were the various sites for dramatic performances in York were members of the Guild of Corpus Christi.[27] Nevertheless, the city's apparent support of such a highhanded assumption of payment underlines its involvement in the production of this play as well. Corroboration that this was an acceptable method of financing this play comes from the Chamberlains' Accounts for 1525 when the city paid four shillings (a sum equivalent to the highest station rent at this time)[28] to the master of the Corpus Christi Guild for the performance at the Common Hall station (*York*, 238). This would by no means cover the cost of the whole production, so we must assume that payment was made to the Guild by the holders of the other stations.

In 1483, Richard III visited the city for the first time as king to have his son created Prince of Wales in the Minster. Richard was himself a member of the Guild of Corpus Christi, and on this occasion the city and the confraternity joined to honor the King with a special performance of the Creed Play on Sunday 2 September "a pon the cost of the most

[26] See Alexandra F. Johnston, "William Revetour, chaplain and clerk of York, Testator," *Leeds Studies in English*, n.s., 29 (1998), 153–72.
[27] See Meg Twycross, "'Places to hear the play': Pageant Stations at York 1398–1572," *REED Newsletter* 3 (1977), 10–33; and Robert H. Skaife, *The Register of the Guild of Corpus Christi in the City of York*, Surtees Society 57 (1872).
[28] Johnston, "Plays of the Religious Guilds," 60.

onest men of eu*ery* parish in thys Cite." On 6 September it was agreed
that for the honour of the city the mayor, aldermen and the council of
the twenty-four would attend the King at the production (*York*, 131). By
1495, the Creed Play had become more firmly entrenched within the
circle of patronage of the city. That year, after the St. Anthony's Guild
had defaulted with their production of the Pater Noster Play, the city
council determined that the Creed Play should be played instead. It is at
this time that the regular performance every ten years specified in 1455
seems to have been acted upon. However, the production was authorized
only after the mayor had seen the "prima pagina" on 1 May and agreed
that the banns for the play could be called first on 8 June and then
on 22 July for the performance on 23 August.[29] The Creed Play was
performed regularly thereafter at ten-year intervals in 1505, probably in
1515 (although no records survive for that year), 1525, and as a substitute
for the Corpus Christi Play in 1535. On 17 March 1545, in an act of
political prudence, the mayor was instructed by the council to discuss
with the master of the Corpus Christi Guild the "playng of the creyde
play[e] as he shall thynke good for the mooste p*rofett* & aduantage of the
sayd [cit] Citie" (*York*, 285). They apparently decided against producing
the Creed Play since the Bakers' accounts record the normal expenses
for their Corpus Christi pageant that year (*York*, 286).

   With the Act of Dissolution in 1547, the Guild of Corpus Christi ceased
to have any legal existence. In anticipation of this event, perhaps after the
discussion between the mayor and the master, the play disappeared from
among the possessions of the guild. The inventory drawn up in 1546 for
the King's commissioners makes no mention of the play books or the
properties that appear in all earlier inventories (*York*, app. II, 642–44).
The guild itself maintained a vestige of its former existence since it had
taken over the assets of the Hospital of St. Thomas the Martyr without
Micklegate Bar in 1478. The hospital eluded crown seizure of its property by inviting the mayor and the aldermen to become members of
the hospital. This they did on 28 April 1552, whereupon the master of
the hospital resigned and the mayor, Richard White, was elected master
and two aldermen became wardens.[30] In this way, the real property of
the guild passed to the city, but so did the identity of the ancient confraternity itself. When the Corpus Christi procession was revived under
Mary, the mayor, John North,[31] walked in the procession "as Master of
Corpuscrysty gyld" (*York*, 317). Ten years later, James Simpson, who had

---

[29] Johnston, "Plays of the Religious Guilds," 62.
[30] Skaife, *The register of the Guild of Corpus Christi*, 298ff.   [31] Drake, *Eboracum*, 364.

been sheriff of the city in 1547,[32] brought to the hospital "the Auncient booke [of the] or Registre of the Crede play to be saffly kept emonges thevident as it was before" (*York*, 348). In this way, the city of York acquired the third religious play anciently performed in the city.

The complex maneuvers of the York city council to preserve and encourage the performance of Catholic drama in the thirty years after Henry's break from Rome are only one aspect of the prolonged struggle by the people of York and many others in the north against the advancement of the new religion. At first there seems to have been little concern in York about Henry's break with Rome, but when the consequences of that break began to be felt with the suppression of such small religious houses in the city as St. Clement's and Holy Trinity (the site of the first station of the pageant route in Micklegate) by the summer of 1536 the city became restive.[33] In October, two months after the 1536 production of the Pater Noster Play, the Pilgrimage of Grace began in the East Riding under Robert Aske, and the Commons of York were quick to support it. After a show of reluctance, the mayor, William Harrington, a man long associated with the Liberty of St. Peter,[34] and the aldermen agreed to admit the rebels within the walls. Although the dean and chapter were more actively supportive than the city council itself, nevertheless the city was occupied by the rebels and a great council was held there with the support of several leading citizens, including aldermen such as George Lawson, who had been mayor in 1530.[35] The monks were restored to Holy Trinity and managed to remain together for another two years, but then, in David Palliser's words "Cromwell completed the process of monastic dissolutions. The six priories – St. Andrew's, Holy Trinity and the four orders of friars – surrendered in November and December 1538, while the two giants followed them a year later, St. Mary's Abbey on 29 November 1539 and St. Leonard's Hospital on 1 December."[36] Not only were the physical buildings part of the fabric of the city, the people who had inhabited them were part of the social and ceremonial fabric. The brethren of St. Leonard's had once been responsible for the pageant of The Purification of the Virgin (*York*, 19). The Augustinian friary and St. Leonard's had rented a station for the Corpus Christi Play together in 1454 (*York*, 85), and the abbot of St. Mary's frequently acted as arbiter in civic disputes.[37] Palliser estimates that ninety monks, nuns, and canons

---

[32] Ibid.   [33] Palliser, *Tudor York*, 234.   [34] Ibid., 108.

[35] Drake, *Eboracum*, 364.   [36] Palliser, *Tudor York*, 235.

[37] In the matter of the dispute between the Cordwainers and the Weavers over precedence in the Corpus Christi procession, see especially *York*, 169.

were turned into the world from York with pensions and some sixty friars without pensions. The dispersal of the religious and the physical destruction of the buildings "had a shattering impact on the city."[38] Yet because of the implication of the city in the Pilgrimage of Grace, the actions of Cromwell and his commissioners were not openly opposed, and when the King and Queen Katherine came in progress in 1541, they were greeted with fawning pleas for forgiveness and considerable pageantry (*York*, 271–77). The mayor and council met the royal party at the boundaries of their jurisdiction in the Wapentake of the Aynsty and fell as one to their knees while the Recorder, William Cankerd, delivered a speech of groveling apology for their misguided action during the Pilgrimage of Grace, saying:

we your humble Subiect*es* the May*er* Alde*r*men and co*m*mons of your grace ys City of yorke . . . for lack of syncere and poore knowlege of the verytie of god*es* worde and ignoraunt of o*u*r bounded duety to you o*u*r Soue*r*cign lord haue agaynst o*u*r naturall allegyance disobedyently and contrary your grace ys lawes for the common welth p*r*ouyded, greuously heynously and traitoryously offended yo*u*r high invyncible find most Royall maiesty yo*u*r imperyall crowne and dignitye in the most odyous offence of trate*r*us rebellyon (*York*, 274).

Open defiance was now replaced with canny resistance as we have seen in the maneuvering of the mayor and council over the even more socially disruptive dissolutions of the chantries and confraternities under Edward. Also during Edward's reign, thirteen parish churches were closed, but one way or another many of the medieval treasures in stained-glass windows in the remaining parish churches survived the iconoclasts.

Mary claimed her father's throne on 19 July 1553, too late for the festive season in that year. But the event was immediately hailed by the York city council. As soon as the news reached the northern capital her accession was acclaimed on 21 July with "grette fyers, drynkyng wyne and aylle, prayssing God."[39] In sharp contrast to the Recorder's address to Henry over a decade earlier, the corporation wrote to the Queen thanking God for "so noble, godly and most rightfull a Quene."[40] The city had almost a year to plan for the seasonal ceremonies of 1554 once again sanctioned by the crown. On 9 February with the new council barely sworn into office,[41] it was agreed "god willyng" that the Corpus Christi Play including the plays on the Virgin "late . . . left forth" should be played

[38] Palliser, *Tudor York*, 235–36.
[39] Ibid., 241, citing "Robert Parkyn's narrative" Bodley, Lat. Th. d. 15.
[40] Ibid., citing House Book, 21.
[41] The York civic year began with the election of the officers on St. Blaise's Day, 3 February.

(*York*, 310). In contrast to this long-term planning, a note of panic appears in the minutes for 20 April when the council hastily put in place "at the Chambre cost*es*" the procession and mass of St. George (with sermon) for 23 April that had been the responsibility of the Guild of St. Christopher and St. George, now dissolved. At the same meeting a procession on Whit Tuesday (15 May), perhaps associated with the Whitsun Fair, that had never before appeared in the civic records was ordered to proceed "accordyng to the old laudable custome at the charges of the Chambre" and the liturgical procession "on the morne aftr Corpus ch*ri*sti day shalbe lykwise made wit*h* torches & oy*er* solemptnyties accordyngge to the old vsage at chardg*es* of the Chambr" (*York*, 310–11). Everything was to be done according to the ancient custom and the council agreed to pay for it all. The evidence from the financial records is patchy in this period,[42] but when the receipts and expenses for 1554 are compared to 1542 (the most recent year for which we have full accounts) the contrast is striking. In 1542 the income from the station rents was 24s 10d; in 1554 the income from the same source was 34s 8d. In 1542 the city allowed only 17s. 8d. for expenses while in 1554 the bill for the ceremonial season (including 28s 5d for the St. George Riding) was £7 17s 9d – a truly extravagant amount for a city still struggling with economic depression.

But the revival of the old customs was not without incident. It was this year that the Girdlers were fined for holding up the play (*York*, 312). The authority of the mayor to shut down their shops was invoked to force three drapers to pay their pageant money for the support of their pageant and the torches surrounding the sacrament in the procession of Corpus Christi (*York*, 313), and Nicholas Haxop, baker, was presented by the searchers of the Bakers for refusing to attend their pageant of the Last Supper on Corpus Christi Day and fined forty pence, half of which, in accordance with the Bakers' ordinances, came to the chamber (*York*, 315). These acts of individual defiance, possibly motivated by Protestant zeal, were to prove portents of things to come.

A similar pattern of seasonal celebrations was repeated in 1555, 1556, and 1557. By 1558, however, the costs of such feastings had begun to take their toll. A long minute from the council meeting of 9 March 1558 cited the rising costs of food and drink and disallowed civic payment for the council banquets held on St. George's Day, Midsummer, and the "dynars and bankett*es* made to the lady*es*" on Palm Sunday, Whitsun,

---

[42] The York City Archives were kept for centuries in the lower level of the guildhall. The River Ouse flows by the foundations of the hall and the lower hall was subject to frequent flooding. It is remarkable that so much survives in a legible condition.

Corpus Christi, St. Stephen, and Midsummer. The meal on the day
of the election of the mayor was reduced to maynbread and beer or
wine. However, the "players & suche as taketh peyns ou*er* procession &c.
on saynt George day to be payd for their labou*r* of the chambr cost*es*"
(*York*, 326–27). A week later, the council agreed not to play the Corpus
Christi Play that year "the tyme instant beyng bothe trowblouse w*ith*
warres and also contagiouse w*ith* sykenesse" (*York*, 327). On 20 April,
although it was decided to set St. George aside for that year, it was agreed
that the Pater Noster Play should be played "th*c* Charg*c*s therof to be
borne of the money to be gatheryd by the occupac*i*ons of this Citie of
there pagyant money" (*York*, 327). The play was performed and the feast
at the Common Hall station was paid for by the chamber according to the
ancient custom. However, by 15 July the craft donations to the production
costs were still four pounds short and the mayor was instructed to "goe
ou*er* ageyne and ratebly gath*er* of eu*ery* occupac*i*on chardgeable to the
same." If the arrears were not made up the council was prepared to pass
a "furthr ordre" (*York*, 328). No further order appears, so presumably
the crafts did pay up. However, such reluctance may indicate that in the
late 1550s the council was more enthusiastic about the ancient Catholic
customs and plays than were some of the crafts.

   With the accession of Elizabeth, a more determined central admin-
istration initiated its long-range religious objectives early in the reign,[43]
but it took almost ten years before decisive action was taken in the north.
Although Nicholas Heath, the Marian Archbishop of York and one
of the strongest opponents of the 1559 Settlement, was deprived and
the province of York subject to a "general visitation of the northern
clergy . . . to enforce the Acts of Supremacy and Uniformity, including a four-day session at York,"[44] no overt changes took place in the
relations between the church and the city. Heath's successor, Thomas
Young, served as archbishop from 1561 to 1568 and president of the
newly re-established Council of the North from 1564–68. Young was not
a fervent Protestant and he was faced with a civic government in no
way committed to the new religion. Young wrote to a friend in 1564 that
only two of the thirteen members of the York city council were "favorers
of religion."[45] The others were not yet newly converted Catholics or

[43] The Settlement was declared in 1559 in what appears to be an active campaign to persuade the
   populace to accept Protestantism undertaken on the part of Elizabeth's councilors using their
   acting troupes. See Alexandra F. Johnston, "English Community Drama in Crisis: 1535–80," in
   Alan Hindley (ed.), *European Communities of Medieval Drama: a Collection of Essays* (Brepols, 1999,
   248–69).
[44] Palliser, *Tudor York*, 243.   [45] Ibid., 244.

recusants, rather they were "Catholic survivalists" for whom the new ways had little meaning and who clung tenaciously to the customs and beliefs of their childhoods. Nevertheless, they approached the new regime with caution. No performance of the Corpus Christi Play was mounted until 1561 when, on 27 March, it was agreed "that Corpus christi play shalbe played this yere with good players as hath ben accustomed Except onely the pagiantes of [thAssu] the dyenge Assumption and Coronacion of our Lady" (*York*, 331–32). Prudently returning to the form of the play performed under Edward, the council set out once again to sponsor a good performance of the traditional civic drama. Less prudently they proclaimed the play in "semely sadd apparell & not in skarlet" because "the late fest of Corpus christi is not nowe celebrat & kept holy day as was accustomed" (*York*, 333) and spent the enormous sum of £9 8d on their feast while watching the play (*York*, 339). Realizing that they now had three possible choices for their civic productions, the council, on 13 March 1562, considered performing the Creed Play on St. Barnabas' Day (11 June, a saint's day conveniently close to the traditional Corpus Christi date), but on 6 April agreed to produce "thystories of the old & new testament" or the Corpus Christi Play. No financial records survive from this year nor do the accounts of the Bakers. There is, therefore, no corroborative evidence that the performance took place. In 1563, the situation is similar, but it does appear that the play was performed from the wording of an agreement taken on 28 June, after a performance earlier in the month when four shillings of the money received "of the Inholdars shalbe payd towardes charges of Chandelars pageant" (*York*, 342). There is also a minute indicating that the expenses for the mayor and council at the play are to be "husbanded this yer by discrecion of my Lord Mayour" (*York*, 342). There is no mention of playmaking in the House Books for 1564.

On 6 January 1565 a disaster befell the city that was to destroy any plans that the council may have had to continue their production of religious drama. A thaw followed a heavy snowstorm and the subsequent flooding of the River Ouse carried away Ouse Bridge (and incidentally the ancient Council Chamber) effectively cutting the city in half. The first five of the traditional twelve stations for the plays were on the south side of the river and, perhaps more important, many of the pageant wagons (including the Mercers' magnificent Judgment wagon) were stored on Toft Green near the first station just inside Micklegate Bar. Even if the council had been prepared to have the play performed at a truncated number of stations, many of the sets were simply not available short of dismantling them, ferrying them across the river and then finding some-where else to store them after the production. The replacement for the bridge was not completed until the end of 1566, effectively prohibiting performances in 1565 and 1566. Although there is no evidence for per-formance in 1567, it is in that year, as we have seen, that the council called in the plays that had not yet been registered. Clearly, it had not given over its role of patron of civic drama.

But a figure who was to be central to the suppression of Catholic drama in the north, Matthew Hutton, was about to take up his new post as dean of Yorkminster. Hutton had come up to Cambridge in 1546 and became a fellow of Trinity during Mary's reign in 1555.[46] Here he became a member of the circle of Edmund Grindal, Bishop of London (1559–70), becoming his chaplain in 1561. Amongst his other patrons at this time was Robert Dudley, Earl of Leicester, one of Elizabeth's "godly" courtiers and patron of one of the most active touring companies. During his early years at Cambridge, Hutton experienced Mary's regime first hand. It left a strong impression on his Calvinist soul and, as Peter Lake has written, "It was the fragility of the protestant hold on the mass of the English people and the ever present threat of Rome that were to form the dominant concerns of Hutton's career."[47] Hutton was to spend much of the rest of his career in the north serving himself as Archbishop of York from 1595 to 1606. He certainly took up the challenge that he found on his arrival, enthusiastically pursuing his duties not only as dean but as secretary to the Council of the North and its Ecclesiastical Commission.

The mayor in 1568, William Coupland, a wealthy tailor who would on his death the next year leave a considerable estate including alms for 1,600 poor of the city, was among Archbishop Young's "non favorers" of religion. David Palliser refers to him as a "sturdy traditionalist."[48] Within ten days of his becoming mayor, the council agreed that the Creed Play should be performed instead of the Corpus Christi Play at the costs of the "Craft*es* & occupac*i*ons of this Citie as are chardged wit*h* bryngyng forth of the pageant*es* of Corpus christi" (*York*, 353). The Creed Play had not been performed since 1535. As we have seen, the mayor and the master of the Corpus Christi Guild in 1545 had considered it unwise to perform it in the last years of Henry's reign. Of the three plays in the hands of the city in 1568, it was probably the most doctrinally sensitive, associated as it was with both a credal statement and the guild founded to celebrate the Real

---

[46] Peter Lake, "Matthew Hutton – a Puritan Bishop?" *History* 64 (1979), 183.
[47] Ibid., 183.   [48] Palliser, *Tudor York*, 245.

Presence in the Eucharist. The plans did not go unchallenged. Within six weeks, word had not only reached Hutton but he had acquired a copy of the text from Coupland, read it, condemned it, and sent Coupland and the council a firm response. The letter itself is bound into House Book 24 and is written on paper in the spidery Italianate hand of Hutton's scribe. The dean begins by gracefully acknowledging the antiquity of the play but lamenting how it disagrees with the "senceritie of the gospell." His advice is that the play should not be played,

ffor thoughe it was plausible 40 yeares agoe, & wold now also of the ignorant sort be well liked: yet now in this happie time of the gospell, I know the learned will mislike it and how the state will beare with it I knowe not. (*York*, 353)[49]

After receiving the letter, the council agreed to abandon their plans on 30 March. On 27 April, Coupland went to the council declaring "that dyverse commoners of this Citie were muche desyerous to haue Corpuscrysty play this yere." But the council would not agree to such a performance unless "the book thereof shuld be perused/and otherwaise amendyd/before it were playd" (*York*, 354). No performance was mounted that year and the first hint of conflict over play production had appeared within the council itself.

In 1569, the Corpus Christi Play was performed for the last time under the watchful eye of the mayor William Beckwith, who would be one of the aldermen censured for their refusal to watch the Pater Noster Play three years later. The production was not without trouble. Fourteen stations outside the houses of specific people were decreed on 26 May but with the unusual proviso "that if the sayd persones will not pay for the sayd places as the lord mayour & Chambrelaynes shall thynk requisite than furthre ordre yerin to be taken at discrecion of my lord mayour and Chambrelaynes &c." Three must have refused to pay, since the next day three other locations were named (*York*, 356). That winter the northern earls rose in rebellion in favor of the old religion. Refusing to repeat the error their predecessors had committed at the time of the Pilgrimage of Grace, and perhaps influenced by the Protestant sympathies of the mayor, the York council firmly backed the crown and the leader of Elizabeth's forces in the north, the Earl of Sussex. The suppression of the rising was to mark the turning point in the religious climate

---

[49] Fr. Harold C. Gardiner, in his discussion of this passage, cited it from the published extract of the House Books (Robert Davies, *Extracts from the Municipal Records of the City of York* [London, 1843]), where the editor had misread "40" in the difficult hand of the secretary as "to." See his *Mysteries' End: An Investigation of the Last Days of the Medieval Religious Stage* (New Haven: Yale University Press, 1946), 73.

in York. There is no mention of playmaking in 1570 or 1571. It is perhaps significant that in 1570 the see, which had been vacant since Archbishop Young's death on 26 June 1568,[50] was filled, partly at Hutton's urging, by his patron Edmund Grindal. Grindal came to the northern province with a clearly Protestant agenda and it was inevitable that the civic patronage of Catholic drama would not long survive his arrival.

In 1572, William Allen, mercer, became mayor. Allen, described by Palliser as "the most firmly Catholic alderman,"[51] persuaded the council to authorize the production of the Pater Noster Play not played since 1558. Allen himself seems to have "pervsed" it and declared it fit for playing. The production was to take place on Corpus Christi Day (5 June), financed by the pageant money of the crafts and the members of those crafts (such as the Bakers) whose pageants were actually to be part of the play were to walk with their pageants to "see good ordre kepte." The traditional stations were named and by 2 June they all seem to have been paid for except the one outside the door of the house of Christopher Harbert, for which 3s. 4d. is noted as outstanding (*York*, 365–66). Christopher Harbert had come to York from Monmouthshire in 1550 and was, with Allen, a member of the Mercers' Guild dealing in "oil, soap, pots, wool, wood, bedding, haberdashery and grocery."[52] His imposing house near the Pavement still stands and its general location had been traditionally the site of the last station for all civic productions. Allen seems to have delighted in baiting his rival (a firm ally of Hutton and Grindal) by insisting that he pay for a station outside his door. On the day of the performance, Harbert and the older William Beckwith refused "to assocyate and assist his Lordship at the tyme of playeng of the Pater noster play" and were arrested and "commanded to warde / there to abide duryng my Lord Mayour pleasure." The next day they were released from prison but declared "vtterly disfranchised, and no more to occupie as ffree men of this Citie" (*York*, 366–67). Harbert appealed to the newly appointed Lord President of the North, Henry Hastings, Earl of Huntingdon, acknowledging, on 23 June, as part of his submission to the council, that he had sued Allen "before the Lord President and Counsell in theis North parties" (*York*, 367).[53] After paying a fine of forty

---

[50] Raine, *York Civic Records*, VI, 139.   [51] Palliser, *Tudor York*, 246.   [52] Ibid., 94, 193.
[53] Huntingdon could have been appointed any time after March 1572 when, as Claire Cross tells us in her biography, his appointment was the result of a "general exchange of offices" that saw the Earl of Sussex, who she tells us "had been a virtually non-resident Lord President in the north ever since Hunsdon had cast reflections on his competence during the Rebellion of the Earls," become Lord Chamberlain (Claire Cross, *The Puritan Earl* [London: Macmillan, 1966], 159–60). Angelo Raine notes that he was appointed in August, citing no authority (Raine,

shillings, Harbert was admitted back into the freedom of the city and restored to his rank as alderman. Beckwith, however, would not submit as easily and waited for the last month of Allen's term of office (January 1573) before he too admitted his part in the suit, paid his fine and was readmitted.[54] The next month Christopher Harbert was elected mayor.

Harbert's election as mayor could have been foreseen. A week after he had "humbly" submitted himself to Allen and the council, Archbishop Grindal requested a copy of the Pater Noster Play, which the council agreed should be sent. In November that year, with Huntingdon's arrival to take up residence in the city anticipated, the archbishop once again moved to put an end to an ancient custom. The feast of St. Thomas the Apostle (21 December), the traditional day for the Riding of Yule and Yule's Wife, fell on the fourth Sunday of Advent in 1572. Using the Sabbatarian excuse, Grindal banned the riding not only for that year "but also for all other yeres ensewyng" (*York*, 369).[55] Grindal and Hutton knew where the sympathies of the new president lay. It seems likely all three had had a hand in Harbert's rapid submission to his rival Allen. It was clearly a calculated move to reinstate him as alderman so that he could be elected mayor the next year. On 3 February 1573, the day of Harbert's election, the religious balance in York had decidedly shifted with lord president, archbishop, dean, and mayor all of one mind. For the first time that year, as "survivalism was yielding to conformity and recusancy," the council was required to submit regular returns of recusants, and Harbert took the first official civic action on Sabbatarianism.[56]

But the records for these years do not indicate that the craft guilds were convinced that their playmaking days were over. Although no plays were performed, the Bakers repaired their pageant in 1573 (*York*, 373) and their pageant house in 1574 (*York*, 376). The Mercers continued to elect pageant masters and the first of the redrawn craft ordinances

York Civic Records, VII, 56). This would be too late for the festive season in the north in 1572. However, new evidence discovered by David Mills in the letter book of the Protestant divine of Chester, Christopher Goodman, establishes beyond doubt that although Huntingdon did not take up permanent residence in York until December 1572, he had been appointed by early May. A letter from Goodman dated 10 May protesting the proposed performance of the Chester cycle is addressed "To the Lord President the Earl of Huntingdon." See David Mills, *Recycling the Cycle*, 146. I am grateful to Professor Mills for allowing me to use the added detail of the actual address to Huntingdon from his unpublished REED edition of the records of Cheshire.

54 Raine, *York Civic Records*, VII, 63.
55 Our only other knowledge of the Riding comes from a printed broadsheet found in the Bodleian Library which shows all the hallmarks of an attempt to Christianize an ancient custom associated with the winter solstice (*York*, 359–62). See also Alexandra F. Johnston, "Yule in York," *REED Newsletter* 2 (1976): 1:3–10.
56 See Palliser, *Tudor York*, 254, 248, 255.

that were to proliferate in the next few years are recorded in the third
Memorandum Book of the city (E 22) still referring to the playing of
pageants (*York*, 374–75). On 17 June 1575, one Christopher Learmouth
was paid twenty shillings for "makyng iij play book*es*" belonging to
"St. Anthonies" or the Pater Noster Play. This occasioned the realiza-
tion that "certayne of the same book*es*" were in Grindal's hands and the
council agreed "that the same shalbe required to be restored agayne." At
the meeting of 8 July, a motion was passed instructing Allen, Alderman
Maskewe, and two other councillors to

goe and requir of my L*o*rd Archebishop his grace all suche ye playe books as
p*er*teyne this cittie now in his graces Custodie and yat his grace will appoynt
twoe or thre sufficiently learned to correcte the same wherein by the lawe of
this Realme they ar to be reformed.(*York*, 378)

There was no response to this request.

The last attempt by the council to perform the Corpus Christi Play
comes during the mayoralty of Robert Criplyng in 1579. On 8 April, the
council agreed that the Corpus Christi Play should be played but that
the book (presumably the register, BL Add MS 35290) should be sent to
the archbishop and the dean "to correcte" (*York*, 390). The archbishop
and the dean apparently took no action and there is no further mention of the play that year. Two days after their request, in response
to an expressed desire from Huntingdon that the city establish a civic
preacher, the council sent out an order to all the crafts that they should
"assemble theym selfs togither forthwith and to aggree what evry company will gyve towards fyndyng of a preacher."[57] After a month's discussion, Criplyng signed a letter to Huntingdon saying that the city had
sufficient preachers and the crafts were "not willyng to gyve any money
towards the fyndyng of a preacher."[58] Whether or not the authorities'
refusal to allow the play and the city's refusal to support a preacher
had any connection, relations between Criplyng and the Council of the
North went from bad to worse. He was a Catholic sympathizer with
a recusant wife who "made no attempt to enforce the recusancy laws,
openly criticized a sermon by the Minster Chancellor, and was said to
have uttered 'very unsemely and fowle woords' against the clergy, which
had encouraged like-minded people to post street bills with 'filthie and
lewde speeches'."[59] By the end of his term, the Council had lost patience with him and took the unprecedented step of throwing him in jail
and appointing the reliable Christopher Harbert mayor pro tem. until

[57] Raine, *York Civic Records*, VIII, 7.   [58] Ibid., 9.   [59] Palliser, *Tudor York*, 254.

the mayor elect, Robert Asquith, could take office.[60] On the day of his election,

> the Commons did earnestly request of the Mayour and other this worshipfull Assemblee that Corpus christi play might be played this yere, wherapon my Lord Mayour [and theis] answered that he and his brethren wold considre of their request. (*York*, 392–93)

Nothing more is heard of the performance of the civic religious plays of York.[61] On 12 July that year it was agreed that the riding of the sheriffs that had accompanied the play and other ceremonial occasions should become an event in its own right (*York*, 393) and the next year this event at Midsummer Eve became an occasion when the aldermen were expected to supply men in harness to accompany the sheriffs (*York*, 396). The power and piety of the council once represented by the play was now represented by a military display and the civic preacher.

The struggle had clearly been a doctrinal one. There is no rhetoric against playing as such in the York story. Although, as we have seen, the financial records are discontinuous in the later sixteenth century, traveling players do seem to have been welcomed in the city. In 1581 the council agreed to performances by the players of both the Earl of Sussex and Lord Hunsdon in the first week of September, and each minute concludes "and to haue such reward as other players haue heretofore had in tymes past" (*York*, 397). Since only three sets of financial records survive from the eighteen years between 1558 and 1576 while twenty survive for the remaining twenty-seven years of Elizabeth's reign, we must assume on the strength of minuted statements such as this that the players did in fact play in York on their northern tours. Even Matthew Hutton seems to have approved of players. A paper account book from the Minster Chamberlains' "St. Peter's Part" or petty cash account of the dean and chapter (*York*, xxxv) survives from 1572 to 1600 and records four payments to players during Hutton's tenure as dean.

As the forces of reformation challenged the doctrine of the old plays, several English cities attempted to replace their traditional community religious drama with newly written community drama.[62] York was no

[60] Raine, *York Civic Records*, VIII, 25.
[61] However it appears from a fugitive note noticed by Eileen White in the Chamberlain's Book of 1593 that the play books had not entirely disappeared. That year the clerk noted "Lent Mr Richutton apothecarie the book for cred play." See Eileen White, "The Disappearance of the York Play Texts – New Evidence for the Creed Play," *Medieval English Theatre* 5 (1983), 107.
[62] For this development at Louth and Lincoln, see *Records of Plays and Players in Lincolnshire 1300–1585*, ed. Stanley J. Kahrl, Malone Society Collections VIII (Oxford: Oxford University Press, 1974), 5 and 67–68; at Shrewsbury, see *Shropshire*, ed. J. Alan B. Somerset, 2 vols., REED (Toronto: University of Toronto Press, 1994), 204–20, 243.

exception. In 1584, Thomas Grafton, a schoolmaster, asked permission to reintroduce drama into the summer festival by being granted license "to set forth certane compiled speaches and also to haue one pageant frame for that purpose" (*York*, 405). The plan was agreed to and eight stations chosen, all on the north side of the river including "at Mr Alderman Beckwith doore" (*York*, 406) suggesting that Beckwith's objection to the Pater Noster Play twelve years earlier had indeed been doctrinal. The pageant seems to have had a martial theme since part of the total bill of £3 6s 8d was for the riding of the "Champions in their apte and requisite manner" (*York*, 411–13). The next year Grafton seems to have proposed another more elaborate "Interlude" which was approved and the crafts were all assessed for the support of the event as they had been in the past for the Creed Play and the Pater Noster Play. Eight stations were again chosen but this time there was one in Micklegate as well as at Beckwith's door. Christopher Harbert was to entertain the ladies of the councilors at his house at the last station. This play involved considerable singing, the appearance of a crowned angel with spangles on his shirt, and a crowned queen. It also involved several masked figures. Grafton's bill provides us with a rare reference to the weather. Apparently it rained on the performance as he dolefully records, "Item, for 5 visards wee borrowed, and with the rayne were rotte in peeces" (*York*, 423). Perhaps the rain was taken as a portent since this is the last time pageants were attempted in conjunction with the Midsummer Show which became, as elsewhere in the country, an occasion for the mustering of the militia from the parishes and other martial displays.

Traveling players continued to visit the city with the occasional reference to companies being paid not to play (*York*, 481). On 22 September 1609, a group of citizens petitioned the council asking leave to build a playhouse where the companies could play. The council agreed, but by 11 December they had withdrawn their support because they feared "some of manuell occupacions in this Cittie who do intend to give over ther occupacions and fall to [and] an idle Course of life." The building had apparently been built but the council demanded that the supporters of the scheme "shalbe discharged for kepeinge of anie playehowse in this Cittie, as they will answere at their owne p*erell*" (*York*, 531).

Nevertheless, there seemed to be a continuing tradition of professional players in York. An actor was paid eleven shillings to recite an execrable poem written by one "Mr Penven the Poet" seeking a dredging operation in the River Ouse to James I during his visit in 1617 (*York*, 554–55, 558). This is the last time a mimetic interlude was part of a royal visit, but when the Cliffords of Skipton performed *The Knight of the Burning Pestle* in 1636, they sent to York for an actor named Adam Gerdler. The next year Gerdler was back with his brother or son Adam and the waits of York to be part of a performance of *Comus*.[63] But the city was no longer the patron of such activity. To conceive and foster drama such as the city of York had sponsored for two hundred years demanded a commonality of purpose, both doctrinal and civic. When the common ground of doctrine was swept away by the reformers, the civic purpose alone could not sustain the plays. The solidarity of the ruling oligarchy was broken and the plays became not symbols of civic unity and pride but rather of dispute within the council and among the citizens of York. The plays ended in York because the common will to continue them was no longer there. Civic pride and piety found other means of public expression that were safer and more acceptable to the increasingly diverse social and religious climate of late Elizabethan England.[64]

[63] Clifford Family Papers: Chatsworth House, Bolton Abbey 174 fo. 92v and 175 fos. 182–182v. I am grateful to my colleague Professor John Wasson for allowing me to cite evidence from his unpublished REED edition of the records of the Clifford papers.

[64] For a Table of York Crafts and Their Pageants 1535–1585, please see the *Shakespeare and Theatrical Patronage* website at http://icdweb.cc.purdue.edu/~pwhite/patronage/

CHAPTER 7

Theatrical patronage and the urban community during the reign of Mary

Mary A. Blackstone

In the early days of the Reformation, as his patron Thomas Cromwell strove to popularize Henry VIII's position against Rome, Richard Morison wrote a discourse for the King focusing on the law as "the piller that . . . holdeth up euery com*m*en welthe" and arguing that other rulers who had committed their laws to writing and codification had caused their "power to waxe great myghty and strong." In attempting to persuade Henry to do the same he linked a monarch's power with his subjects' knowledge of the law and spoke of "the euyll that cometh of ignoraunce, and of the goode that cometh of knowlage." He observed that in order to establish and maintain its power, the rituals and beliefs of the Catholic church were "inculked & dryuen into the peoples heddes, tought in scoles to children, plaied in plaies before the ignoraunt people, songe in mynstrell*es* songes, and bokes in englisshe purposely to be deuysed to declare the same at large." Rather than simple suppression and prohibition to counteract these methods, Morison argued that "a sick com*m*en wealthe wolde be ordred euen as men ordre ther bodye whan it is diseased. He that hathe an ache in his arme myndyng to put it awaie dothe not cut of tharme, but labourith to expell the ache preseruyng the arme for many good and necessary vses." He advocated the adoption of similar strategies including triumphs, processions, bonfires, and the noise of "all kyndes of instrumentes" to honor the successes of the King and his predecessors. With reference to the plays of Robin Hood and the Sheriff of Nottingham, he argued, "Howmoche better is it that those plaies shulde be forbodden*n* and deleted and others deuysed to setforth and declare lyuely before the peoples eies, the abhomynation and wickednes of the bisshop of Rome . . . and to declare and open to them thobedience

Research towards this paper was made possible by an administrative leave provided by the University of Regina and grants from the Social Sciences and Humanities Research Council of Canada and the Faculty of Graduate Studies and Research at the University of Regina. Thanks are also due to two graduate students, Maureen King and David Ackerman.

that your subiect*es* by goddes and mans lawes owe vnto your maiestie.
Into the co*mm*en people thynges sooner enter by the eies, then by the
eares: remembryng moche better that they see, then that they heare."[1]

Morison clearly entertained no doubts that the response of the
"ignoraunt people" would correspond with the intentions behind the
propaganda, and numerous scholarly studies have argued that Henry,
subsequent Tudor and Stuart monarchs, and members of their court
did employ the mechanisms of spectacle and theatrical patronage as
advocated by Morison – not only to promote the political and religious
beliefs associated with the Reformation, but also to establish a public
image and demonstrate their power and authority. The work of Paul
Whitfield White, for instance, reveals the extent to which theatre was
employed as Protestant and political propaganda under Henry VIII and
Edward VI.[2] Yet despite the demonstrable contribution of such propaganda to the new hegemony of the Reformation, circumstances leading
up to July of 1553 conspired to usher in correction and reversal in what
historians have identified as "the only successful sixteenth-century rebellion," a high point of tension in a century generally characterized by
crises on a number of fronts.[3]

---

[1] I cite here from a fair copy of the manuscript most likely prepared for the King (BL Royal MSS,
18.A.L., fos. 4a, 5b, 19a, 14b–15a, 15b, 17b, 18b–19a). A rough draft with substantial revisions
presumably reveals the process whereby Morison developed his argument (BL Cotton MSS,
Faustina.C.ii, fos. 5–22; partially transcribed by Sydney Anglo in "An Early Tudor Programme
for Plays and Other Demonstrations against the Pope," *Journal of the Warburg and Courtauld Institutes*
20 [1957], 176–79).

[2] Paul Whitfield White, *Theatre and Reformation: Patronage, Protestantism, and Playing in Tudor England*
(Cambridge: Cambridge University Press, 1993). For examples of other book-length works which
address theatre or spectacle as projections of a patron's political agenda and/or image see
also Sidney Anglo, *Spectacle, Pageantry and Early Tudor Policy* (Oxford: Clarendon Press, 1969);
David Bevington, *Tudor Drama and Politics* (Cambridge, MA: Harvard University Press, 1966);
Alistair Fox, *Politics and Literature in the Reigns of Henry VII and Henry VIII* (Oxford: Blackwell, 1989); John N. King, *Tudor Royal Iconography: Literature and Art in an Age of Religious Crisis*
(Princeton: Princeton University Press, 1989); Guy Fitch Lytle and Stephen Orgel (eds.), *Patronage
in the Renaissance* (Princeton: Princeton University Press, 1981); Eleanor Rosenberg, *Leicester: Patron
of Letters* (New York: Columbia University Press, 1955); Roy Strong, *The Cult of Elizabeth: Elizabethan
Portraiture and Pageantry* ([London]: Thames and Hudson, 1987); Leonard Tennenhouse, *Power on
Display: The Politics of Shakespeare's Genres* (New York: Methuen, 1986); Greg Walker, *Plays of Persuasion: Drama and Politics at the Court of Henry VIII* (Cambridge: Cambridge University Press, 1991);
Suzanne Westfall, *Patrons and Performance: Early Tudor Household Revels* (Oxford: Clarendon Press,
1989); and Alan Young, *Tudor and Jacobean Tournaments* (London: George Philip, 1987). Cautionary
notes regarding some of the approaches represented here have also been raised. See, for example,
Sydney Anglo, *Images of Tudor Kingship* (London: Seaby, 1992); M. D. Jardine, "New Historicism for
Old: New Conservatism for Old?: The Politics of Patronage in the Renaissance," *Politics, Patronage
and Literature in England 1558–1658*, *The Yearbook of English Studies* 21(1991) 286–304; and David
Norbrook, "Life and Death of Renaissance Man," *Raritan* 8.4 (1989), 89–110.

[3] David Starkey, "Introduction: Rivals in Power, the Tudors and the Nobility" in David Starkey
(ed.), *Rivals in Power: Lives and Letters of the Great Tudor Dynasties* (London: Macmillan, 1990), 21.

No other Tudor monarch had greater need for a strategy of theatrical propaganda than Mary. Suddenly, with her accession and the initiation of the Counter Reformation, individuals who had been resisting the Reformation found themselves in positions of authority and some who had spent years in exile or imprisoned outside the circle of power assumed positions at the center of court and Privy Council activities. Characterizing the turn of events as nothing short of miraculous, Reginald Pole upon his return from exile declared that despite policies and "armed power prepared to destroye her," Mary "being a virgin, helples, naked, and unarmed, prevailed" due to divine intervention.[4] Yet in order to secure her own power and achieve her principal agenda of restoring Catholicism, Mary recognized that such intervention would not be enough. She needed the immediate political experience and influence of government administrators and important local magnates under Edward and Henry. Consequently, the face of Mary's court and Council presented a fractured reflection of some of the complex perspectives and loyalties within the country at large.[5] Regardless of the success of Mary's Counter Reformation, the full effects of the previous twenty years would not be reversed with simple assertions of royal authority. The Reformation had initiated more than a change in religious allegiance. It had significantly affected the wealth of a range of individuals and institutions, profoundly changed an individual's access to knowledge and relative position within the micro- and macro-structures of authority, and fueled evolving personal and national concepts of identity and allegiance. It had, for instance, raised a number of commoners to positions of wealth and influence as key government bureaucrats, or scholars and propagandists like Morison (who, not surprisingly, moved to Strasbourg where a print campaign was launched against the Counter Reformation).[6] Some of these individuals seized on concepts such as "commen welthe" and developed them into agendas for social and political reform which were impossible

[4] John Elder, letter to Robert Stuart, 1 January 1556 as edited in *The Chronicle of Queen Jane, and of Two Years of Queen Mary, and Especially of the Rebellion of Sir Thomas Wyat. Written by a Resident in the Tower of London*, ed. John Gough Nichols, *Camden Society* 48 (1850) 157.

[5] In the spirit of arguments put forward by historians such as G. R. Elton ("Tudor Government: The Points of Contact, III. The Court," *Transactions of the Royal Historical Society*, 5th ser., 26 [1976]) and David Starkey ("Introduction: Court History in Perspective" in *The English Court from the Wars of the Roses to the Civil War* [London: Longman, 1992]), I have taken an inclusive approach to defining the Marian court by including not only members of the royal households and Privy Chambers but also members of her Council and members of the nobility and gentry whose access to the Queen's court and favor is reflected in documents such as the New Year gift list of 1557 (Starkey, *Rivals in Power*, 190; David Loades, *Mary Tudor: A Life* [Oxford: Basil Blackwell, 1989], 270–71, 358–69).

[6] S. T. Bindoff, *The History of Parliament: The House of Commons, 1509-1558*, 3 vols. (London: Secker & Warburg, 1982), II, 634.

and unacceptable in the sixteenth century but which eventually perco-
lated through contemporary discourse to prominence in the seventeenth
century.

With the benefit of hindsight, historians such as David Loades have
argued that the case for a mid-Tudor crisis has been overstated. Although
there were crises as in other reigns, there was no serious threat to state
or society because central and local governments continued to work
effectively.[7] In their study of monarchs and the court, David Starkey
and Kevin Sharpe have also asserted a continuity across the Tudor and
Stuart periods in which "all power rested in the king, 'who alone could
fulfil or frustrate ambition'." G. R. Elton as well as Starkey has argued
that Henry VII achieved a monopoly of power from which the Tudor
and Stuart court was born. Thus monarch and court became the center
of power and except during sessions of parliament, the history of these
periods "'may be more properly called the history of the court than that
of the nation'."[8]

No doubt Lady Jane Grey as well as Mary would have found these
assertions by turns reassuring and frustratingly demoralizing. Each would
have had occasion to anticipate Shakespeare's Richard II by asking,
"Am I not Queen?" Which comes first, the power or the position? How
do you maintain the one if the other is uncertain? Although Mary was
not unlike her predecessors or successors in facing serious challenges
from within her court as well as members of her Parliament, disaffected
local magnates, and the common people, her accession was certainly
more of a matter for "negotiation" than that of her father or brother.
Situated within the historical moment as Wyatt marched on London and
some of his followers assailed the very gates of her own court, Mary may
have understandably been somewhat less certain than twentieth-century
historians as to government control and the actual locus of power.

Michel Foucault's theoretical arguments might appear to be closer to
the mark when he cautions against

locating power in the State apparatus, making this into the major, privileged,
capital and almost unique instrument of the power of one class over another.
In reality, power in its exercise goes much further, passes through much finer
channels, and is much more ambiguous, since each individual has at his disposal

---

[7] David Loades, *The Mid-Tudor Crisis, 1545–1565* (London: Macmillan, 1992).

[8] Starkey, *The English Court*, 13; Kevin Sharpe, "The Image of Virtue: The Court and Household
of Charles I, 1625–1642," in *The English Court from the Wars of the Roses to the Civil War* (London:
Longman, 1992), 249; G. R. Elton, "The Court," 212, 214. The latter phrase is taken from David
Hume's *The History of England from the Invasion of Julius Caesar to the Revolution in 1688*, 9 vols. (London,
1811), VI, 293, where it is applied to the reign of James I, but it is cited as applied by Starkey (24)
to the entire period between the Wars of the Roses and 1642.

a certain power, and for that very reason can also act as the vehicle for trans-
mitting a wider power . . . Power must by [be, *sic*] analysed as something which
circulates, or rather as something which only functions in the form of a chain.
It is never localised here or there, never in anybody's hands, never appropriated
as a commodity or piece of wealth. Power is employed and exercised through a
net-like organisation. And not only do individuals circulate between its threads;
they are always in the position of simultaneously undergoing and exercising this
power. They are not only its inert or consenting target; they are always also the
elements of its articulation. In other words, individuals are the vehicles of power,
not its points of application . . . The individual which power has constituted is
at the same time its vehicle.[9]

Rather than centering power with a monarch and the court, Foucault
conjures up a chain or net-like structure through which it circulates.
He admits, however, that power is not "the best distributed thing in the
world," and his imagery draws attention to mechanisms such as patronage which Starkey has identified as the fundamental underpinning of
the court and its distribution of power. Given the importance of performance propaganda during Edward's reign and the apparent need
for counter propaganda under Mary, a study of theatrical patronage
and the network traced by touring performers as a cultural circuit of
power could be useful in determining the value of Foucault's approach
as an alternative perspective on power and control during Mary's reign.
In particular, such a study lends itself to Foucault's "*ascending* analysis
of power," which starts from the "infinitesimal mechanisms" of power
"at the most basic levels" and is

concerned with power at its extremities, in its ultimate destinations, with
those points where it becomes capillary, that is, in its more regional and local
forms and institutions . . . In other words, rather than ask ourselves how the
sovereign appears to us in his lofty isolation, we should try to discover how
it is that subjects are gradually, progressively, really and materially constituted
through a multiplicity of organisms, forces, energies, materials, desires, thoughts
etc.[10]

  Positioned at the regional extremities through their travels and distinguished at the social margins from vagabonds primarily through patronage, touring performers were at once constituted as subjects and potential
vehicles for constituting other subjects. As a point of departure for the full
analysis envisioned by Foucault, this chapter focuses on the intersection

[9] Michel Foucault, *Power/Knowledge: Selected Interviews and Other Writings 1972–1977*, ed. and trans.
    Colin Gordon, et al. (New York: Harvester Wheatsheaf, 1980), 72, 98.
[10] Foucault, *Power/Knowledge*, 97, 99.

of subject and touring performer in the urban community to identify key figures in the performance patronage network and examine the extent to which power, knowledge, and meaning circulated within the relationships which constituted what Suzanne Westfall has called "patronage theatre." By connecting elements of context and text it should be possible to consider key questions relating to the locus of power and control: how were the individuals encompassed by this network constituted and to what extent were they vehicles of power themselves; how did they see themselves and their relationship to society or the political system; to what extent was theatre[11] employed as propaganda and controlled as an homogenizing discourse; in responding to their context, how did individuals deal with conflicting ideas and multiple expectations for allegiance; and were individuals capable of expressing ideas divergent from the dominant ideology and/or engaged in collectively producing shared meaning encompassing community, court, and Queen.

LOCAL GOVERNMENT

In a country without a standing army or a locally distributed Crown bureaucracy, local government and civic authorities formed a critical link between the Crown and the common people in cities and towns. Maintaining order, enforcing the Queen's laws, and punishing offenders were important responsibilities for local officials. The tone of a royal proclamation issued just fifteen days after Mary was acclaimed Queen

---

[11] There may have been a distinct "politics of performance" associated with individual types of performance in early England. Clearly bearwards, musicians and players accessed their audience and presented their patrons through quite different performance media, but unfortunately contemporary record keepers upon whom we depend for our sources of information were unaware of our future interests, if not insensitive to the importance of such distinctions or simply uncertain as to what term should be applied to a performer they may not even have seen personally. Consequently, the terminology applied to performers in contemporary records is frequently imprecise and contradictory (even the term "players" may be applied to musicians as well as actors). In addition, during the sixteenth century the nature of performance undertaken by performers such as minstrels was undergoing transformation from a more diversified combination of skills to specialization and perceived sophistication by performers such as players and waits. See, for example, Timothy J. McGee, "The Fall of the Noble Minstrel: The Sixteenth-Century Minstrel in a Musical Context," *Medieval and Renaissance Drama in England* 7 (1995), 98–120; John Southworth, *The English Medieval Minstrel* (Woodbridge: Boydell, 1989), 142–55; and Walter L. Woodfill, *Musicians in English Society from Elizabeth to Charles I* (Princeton: Princeton University Press, 1953), 74–108. The focus of this paper is on theatrical discourse as polemic and propaganda, but given the above qualifications imposed by the context and our sources, the net has been cast widely to include performers who could have appropriated the elements of "playing" associated with theatrical discourse for the purposes of polemic or propaganda, including the Chapel Royal, minstrels, jesters, and waits as well as interluders and players.

in London suggested that she needed these officials as much as, if not more than, her Tudor counterparts:

> it is well known that sedition and false rumors have been nourished and maintained in this realm by the subtlety and malice of some evil-disposed persons which take upon them without sufficient authority to preach and to interpret the word of God after their own brain in churches and other places both public and private; and also by playing of interludes and printing of false fond books, ballads, rhymes, and other lewd treatises in the English tongue concerning doctrine in matters now in question and controversy touching the high points and mysteries of Christian religion.

Despite obvious anxiety regarding the degree to which her actual control extended to the literal and figurative extremities of the country, she would not compel her subjects to take up Catholicism "unto such time as further order by common assent may be taken therein," but she

> commandeth all and every her said subjects, of whatsoever state, condition, or degree they be, that none of them presume from henceforth to preach, or by way of reading in churches or other public or private places (except in the schools of the universities) to interpret or teach any Scriptures or any manner points of doctrine concerning religion; neither also to print any books, matter, ballad, rhyme, interlude, process, or treatise, nor to play any interlude except they have her grace's special license in writing to the same.[12]

This attempt to dominate the politics of knowledge and the important sixteenth-century mechanisms of communication and propaganda demonstrates that such control did not follow easily upon accession to the throne. Printing, preaching, and playing in some instances continued to reflect the sentiments of propaganda under Edward, but the relative mobility of the individuals connected with these mechanisms (much of the printing was instigated by exiles, and preachers, like players, were itinerant) made them especially difficult for the Crown to control.

  Local government, therefore, had a critical role to play in publishing and enforcing this and other royal proclamations. Several communities conscientiously fulfilled their responsibility and diligently educated the Queen's subjects through the apprehension and public punishment or imprisonment of performers. For instance, in May of 1554, after close

---

[12] *Tudor Royal Proclamations*, ed. Paul L. Hughes and James F. Larkin 3 vols. (New Haven: Yale University Press, 1969), II, 5–7. The proclamation also clearly places the responsibility for enforcement on "all mayors, sheriffs, justices of the peace, bailiffs, constables, and all other public officers and ministers" (7). These responsibilities are also stated in charters of incorporation for the period, in other proclamations and statutes, and in materials generated from within the towns such as the Norwich mayor's pageant of 1556.

questioning of one of Lord Russell's servants who was implicated in the matter, two minstrels at Norwich were set in the pillory and one had his ear nailed to the pillory "for devysing of vnfitting songes" against the "Masse and the godly procedinges of the Catholike faythe of the churche, and touching therein the homnor and dignytie of the Quenes highnes."[13] It is not surprising that in the heart of the Queen's East Anglian power base – and that of the Duke of Norfolk, an important member of her court – Norwich authorities were quick to suppress, interrogate, and publicly punish the perpetrators as a sign of their efficient and loyal service. Similarly, diligent enforcement was demonstrated by officials in Coventry in November of 1553 when four men engaged in "lewde and sediciouse behaviour" were sent to the Privy Council, questioned, and imprisoned.[14]

Clearly touring performers, like the Queen and her government, were dependent on local authorities to be the conduit through which they could reach the average individual. To augment the influence of a performer's patron, the good will of a local magnate like the Lord Warden of the Cinque Ports or a regional authority like a Justice of the Peace might be sought, but ultimately in cities and towns it was the mayor and aldermen who determined the nature of the performers' reception and the context – both literal and figurative – in which they would be seen. Upon a request for permission to perform, town authorities might not only sanction their performance but also provide a space and a reward over and above any money collected from the general audience. Marian records attest to the use of town facilities such as town halls and churches, obvious symbols of civic responsibilities and laden with local associations connected with Reformation and Counter-Reformation policy.[15] Marian records also cite instances of

[13] *Norwich 1540–1642*, ed. David Galloway, Records of Early English Drama (henceforth REED) (Toronto: University of Toronto Press, 1984), 34. It should be noted that Russell was himself connected with seditious ballad writers in 1553. The account of Edward Underhill, who was detained in August 1553 for writing an anti-papist ballad, credits Russell with providing him 20s. per week while in prison. See *An English Garner: Tudor Tracts 1532–1588*, ed. [Edward Arber] (New York: Cooper Square, 1964), 177–78.

[14] *The Acts of the Privy Council*, ed. John Roche Dasent, 32 vols. (London: HMSO, 1892–1907), *1552–1554*, IV, 368.

[15] For example, records relating to performers associated with specific patrons note performances in the town hall in Canterbury (*Records of Plays and Players in Kent 1450–1642*, ed. Giles Dawson, Malone Society Collections VII [Oxford: Oxford University Press, 1965], 12); in the guildhall in Bristol (*Bristol*, ed. Mark C. Pilkinton, REED [Toronto: University of Toronto Press, 1997], 62 – hereafter referred to as *Bristol*); Exeter (*Devon*, ed. John M. Wasson, REED [Toronto: University of Toronto Press, 1986], 147–48); and Oxford (*Selections from the Records of the City of Oxford, with Extracts from Other Documents Illustrating the Municipal History: Henry VIII to Elizabeth,*

"the Mayor's play," an initial performance hosted by the mayor and aldermen as a sign of respect to the patron.[16] On such occasions this became a local, everyman's equivalent of a performance at a household or the court with the officials' formal seating and attire contributing to the overall performance in which the assembled "commonality" participated. Under such circumstances, local playgoers would have seen touring performers as closely associated with the space and representatives of local authority, but this would have been a mutually reflexive relationship with local authority reinforcing the power and influence of the patron which in turn enhanced the authority of local officials.[17]

Like players, local governments depended on patrons for protection and support, and they clearly recognized that their position in the patronage chain was vital to the well-being of their community. Local records regularly itemize payments for entertainment of and gifts to local magnates as well as expenses for individuals making suits for a patron's support on specific matters relating to the welfare of the community. In 1555, for instance, New Romney paid for a man to ride to the Lord Warden of the Cinque Ports "to have his good wyll touchyng o[r] playe," a Whitsunday play potentially affected by Mary's 1555 prohibition of May games in Kent.[18] Consequently, the rewards and entertainment offered to performers often reflected the importance of the patron locally, regionally

---

(1509–1583), ed. William H. Turner [Oxford, 1880], 267); in the church in Harwich (Leonard T. Weaver, *The Harwich Story* [Dovercourt, Essex: L. T. Weaver, 1975], 16); Louth (*Records of Plays and Players in Lincolnshire 1300–1585*, ed. Stanley J. Kahrl, Malone Society Collections VIII [Oxford: Oxford University Press, 1974], 84); and Lyme Regis (Cyril Wanklyn, *Lyme Leaflets* [n.p.: Spottiswoode, Ballantyne, 1944], 39); and the mayor's house in Barnstaple (*Devon*, 41). Several of these spaces would have been laden with local associations connected with Reformation and Counter-Reformation policy. After the demise of its Corpus Christi pageants during the Reformation, Exeter hosted a performance by the Queen's interluders on the feast of Corpus Christi in the guildhall, whose first floor housed the Chapel of St. George, a focus for pre-Reformation religious rituals. See Robert Tittler, *Architecture and Power: The Town Hall and the English Urban Community c. 1500–1640* (Oxford: Clarendon Press, 1991), 41. In Louth, the performance by the Queen's players in the parish church came 20 years after a sermon in the church sparked the Pilgrimage of Grace through the suggestion that the Crown would close the church and seize its plate. The church with its newly completed steeple was such an important focus of local pride that an armed guard was set up to protect it. See Philip Hughes, *The Reformation in England*, 3 vols. (London: Burns & Oates, 1963), I, 300.

16 For example, in Dover (*Kent*, 42), Exeter (*Devon*, 148), and Bristol (*Bristol*, 61–63). For a description of such a performance at Gloucester, apparently in the reign of Elizabeth, see R. W[illis], *Mount Tabor, or Private Exercises of a Penitent Sinner* (London, 1639), 110–14.

17 For an important study of the appearance of players in town halls see Tittler, *Architecture and Power*, 139–50. Many of the developments noted by Tittler, however, took place in varying degrees and different time periods across the country. For many towns, the Marian period was a transitional stage in the development of customs and assumptions which became more commonplace in the later sixteenth and seventeenth centuries.

18 *Kent*, 137.

and/or nationally. For instance, in 1556 Norwich's mayor, Augustine Steward, gave the Queen's players 20s, the Duke of Norfolk's players 20s and the Earl of Oxford's players 12s 4d, but in the first year of Elizabeth's reign the tables turned and Lord Robert Dudley's players received 20s while the Duke of Norfolk's players received only 13s 4d – quite possibly an indication that the Howards' influence was not what it had been under Mary.[19]

A surprising number of local authorities, however, quietly took the politic long view in their treatment of traveling performers, at times sanctioning the appearance of strange bedfellows and/or providing comparative rewards which suggested sympathy with patrons who had openly opposed Mary's policies and authority. During the accounting year 1557–58, for instance, the city of Exeter rewarded not only the Queen's players (20s) and the Earl of Bath's minstrels (3s 4d), but also the Earl of Bedford's servants (7s 6d), Lord Audley's waits (5s), and Sir Peter Carew's minstrels (3s 4d).[20] To be certain, the Queen's players received the highest reward and are the only performers recorded as having performed before the mayor at the guildhall, but the records also suggest that due respect was paid to two patrons of local importance who had set themselves apart from Mary's court. Not only was the mayor present at a performance of the Earl of Bedford's servants (most likely his minstrels, who are known to have performed elsewhere in this period), but also he topped up an initial reward of five shillings, possibly because of an inadequate collection. Given the Earl's staunch Protestant agenda to the point of exile abroad and his minstrels' flirtation with inflammatory material earlier in the reign in Norwich, the mayor's hospitality at the very least highlights the delicate maneuvering necessary when negotiating between opposing patrons. During the turbulence of 1555, Exeter demonstrated no enthusiasm for the attempts of the local land owner, Sir Peter Carew, to muster an insurrection and Carew fled to the Continent. Yet in 1558, Carew's performers received the same reward as those of the Earl of Bath, a noble patron whose family had been one of Mary's earliest supporters. Both Bedford and Carew had since somewhat redeemed themselves by participation in the English campaign against the French, but the treatment of their performers in Exeter demonstrates that at least at the West Country fringes of Mary's commonwealth, power and influence were not seen as the exclusive prerogative of Crown and court.

[19] *Norwich*, 37, 45.   [20] *Devon*, 147–48.

In fact, some towns consciously asserted their own power and authority in opposition to the wishes of the Crown. Not long after Wyatt's rebellion, Rye's staunch Protestantism manifested itself in open defiance of royal policy. In 1554 the reintroduction of the mass in the local church sparked a disturbance and summonses of residents to appear before the Privy Council. Throughout the remaining years of the reign Protestants were in constant negotiation with authorities for power and control over the town.[21] In 1556 a Catholic mayor was imposed on the town, and this led in 1557 to imprisonment in the Fleet of a Protestant mayor elected in defiance of Privy Council instructions to re-elect the Catholic. Coincidentally, the Queen's players chose that particular time for their only visit to the town during the reign, although Mary's jester had visited in 1555. In other periods it was customary for the mayor of Rye to host a performance by traveling players, but obviously this kind of hospitality and ceremony was neither possible nor desirable in 1557. Ironically, the players received a reward of ten shillings despite the fact that the mayor had refused to comply with the Queen's request for aid in preparations for the war with France.[22] Obviously, viewed within this context any propaganda efforts on the part of the Queen's players to educate what Morison termed "the ignoraunt people" must have been qualified. The people were clearly capable of attaching their own meaning to current events in opposition to the attempts of a central authority to reconstitute their position on key issues. Both the citizens and the mayor of Rye were, in fact, prepared to assert the role of subjects in "constituting" the power of a sovereign.

Rye's overt resistance to policies of the Crown was exceptional, but the underlying sense of its own importance and the desire to determine its own identity were not. Local officials generally saw the preservation of social order as their first priority[23] with a closely related second being the

[21] *Acts of the Privy Council, 1552–1554*, IV, 387, 391, 395; *1554–1556*, V, 147, 155, 159.

[22] Rye Chamberlains' Accounts, East Sussex Record Office: Rye 60/7, fo. 166b; *Calendar of State Papers, Domestic Series, of the Reigns of Edward VI, Mary, Elizabeth, 1547–1580*, ed. Robert Lemon (London, 1856), 93; *Acts of the Privy Council, 1556–1558*, VI, 112, 166, 182, 185, 214, 238–39, 291–92; Graham Mayhew, *Tudor Rye*, Centre for Continuing Education Occasional Paper, no. 27 (Falmer: University of Sussex, 1987), 72–75. For instances dating from before Mary's reign when the Mayor entertained touring performers see "The Manuscripts of the Corporation of Rye," ed. Henry Thomas Riley, *The Fifth Report of the Manuscripts Commission* (London: Historical Manuscripts Commission, 1876), app., pt. 1, 495, col. a–496, col. a; and Rye Chamberlain's Accounts, 60/3, fos. 7b, 8b, 28b. I am indebted to Professor Cameron Louis for the use of records relating to Rye throughout this chapter.

[23] It should be noted that apart from prohibitions against players emanating from the central government, local officials introduced their own prohibitions during this period in London, Chester, and Newcastle. See *Dramatic Records of the City of London: The Repertories, Journals, and Letter Books*, ed. Anna J. Mill and E. K. Chambers, Malone Society Collections II.iii (Oxford: Oxford

enhancement of the city's image, prestige, and economic status – none of which were likely to be promoted by open confrontation with the Queen. Beyond the enforcement of proclamations, urban centers derived a degree of power from Mary's dependence on them in matters such as parliamentary subsidies and loans, mustering soldiers for the war with France, and overseeing the public burnings of Protestants. They also derived their importance and identity from their position as centers of trade and/or provincial market towns, from the resulting wealth of their citizens and institutions, and in some cases, from the increased wealth and responsibility they had assumed as a result of the dissolution. The mid-sixteenth century saw a marked increase in the interest of town officials in petitioning the sovereign for borough incorporation and the attendant administrative control, autonomy, and integrity it implied. The government responded with what Robert Tittler has identified as "a national urban policy": "After only 13 borough incorporations in the first 55 years of the Tudor dynasty, we find eight in the last seven years of Henry VIII, 12 in the nearly seven years of Edward VI, and a striking 24 in the slightly shorter reign of Mary."[24]

At the same time, civic officials made a complementary move to create a community identity and allegiance through the use of spectacle – including theatrical entertainment and the patronage of their own performers. The sponsorship of cycle and saints plays as well as other types of religious or folk drama had long been a focus of resources and a source of both revenue and communal pride in many towns. On a much smaller scale, even villages had established an early tradition of church ales, folk drama, or dancing, which could include touring to neighboring towns or households. During Mary's reign we see the revival of such entertainments in some towns which had discontinued them in response to the Reformation. For the most part, these revivals were short-lived, however, even within Mary's reign. In some cases such as that of New Romney's revival of its Whitsun drama, larger events and resulting prohibitions to avoid the assembly of crowds may have militated against these efforts, but in other cases these entertainments seem to have been superseded by secular entertainment specifically designed to produce a community identity and enhance respect for civic authorities. The

University Press, 1931), 295–98; *Chester*, ed. Lawrence M. Clopper, REED (Toronto: University of Toronto Press, 1979), 56; *Newcastle upon Tyne*, ed. J. J. Anderson, REED (Toronto: University of Toronto Press, 1982), 24–26.

[24] "The Emergence of Urban Policy, 1536–58," in Jennifer Loach and Robert Tittler (eds.), *The Mid-Tudor Polity c. 1540–1560* (London: Macmillan, 1980), 74–75; Robert Tittler, "The Incorporation of Boroughs, 1540–1558," *History* 62 (1977), 24, 40; and *Architecture and Power*, 75–76.

trend has been identified, in particular, with the Lord Mayor's shows
for London in the later sixteenth and seventeenth centuries.[25] It had its
beginnings, however, with civic spectacles in the 1530s and 1540s and
the climate of reform, which at least with respect to the matter of urban
policy seems, in fact, to have proceeded at an accelerated pace under
Mary. Her reign, for instance, saw the initiation in 1555–56 of a civic
pageant in celebration of Banbury's new charter and pageants for the
Lord Mayor of Norwich performed in part by the city waits.[26]

The text of the latter entertainment provides insights into a city's use of
theatrical spectacle for constructing an urban image and presenting the
way in which local authorities, the public, and local performers might
see themselves, their relationship to each other, and their relationship
with the Queen and her court. The first of three pageants focused on
a speaker representing Time, who drew comparisons with Rome and
proceeded to elevated praise of the Mayor, Augustine Steward,

> Suche one whome nature so did frame
> To seeke the peoples heallthe
> goodwill and wisdoomme tawhte ye same
> To Awgmennt the commomn wealthe.

The pageant alludes to the emblem "Truth the Daughter of Time"
(which had been applied to Mary by Pole and then used on her coins
and devices) and to the active role Steward and Norwich played in Mary's
accession to power.[27] Carol Janssen has argued that the use of this motto
along with the appearance of four virtues in the final pageant was inspired
by *Respublica*, a play thought to have been prepared by the Chapel Royal
for court celebrations surrounding Mary's coronation.[28] The Bishop of
Norwich not only presided over Norwich Cathedral, where several waits
sang in the choir, but also served as dean of the Chapel Royal and

---

[25] For example, see David M. Bergeron, *English Civic Pageantry 1558–1642* (Columbia.: University of South Carolina Press, 1971).

[26] *Banbury Corporation Records: Tudor and Stuart*, ed. J. S. W. Gibson and E. R. C. Brinkworth, *Banbury Historical Society* 15 (1977), 17; *Norwich*, 38–43.

[27] It would appear that Mary's "rebellion" was in part financed by church plate and money which had been stored in Steward's house, and the city supplied her with bakers, harness, bows, bow strings, and arrows in July 1553 (*Acts of the Privy Council, 1552–1554*, IV, 294–95, 298–99). Norwich had been the first city to proclaim Mary as Queen, but in 1555 support for Mary by civic officials proved to be at least a temporary embarrassment when the Mayor responded to current rumors by rejoicing somewhat prematurely at the supposed birth of an heir to the throne. See John Strype, *Memorials of the Most Reverend Father in God Thomas Cranmer, Sometime Lord Archbishop of Canterbury*, 2 vols. (Oxford, 1840), I, 526–27; II, 969.

[28] Carole A. Janssen, "The Waytes of Norwich and an Early Lord Mayor's Show," *Research Opportunities in Renaissance Drama* 22 (1979), 61–62.

participated in Mary's coronation. John Buck, the schoolmaster who created the pageant, could have accessed the Norfolk manuscript of *Respublica* possibly dating from the 1550s, and thereby consciously chosen to elevate the mayor and highlight his and the city's identification with Mary's power and agenda.

The next two pageants built on and qualified the image of the first by constructing a majestic pastiche of the city's most venerable and imposing elements, "a greate Castell with a greate gate thervnder like a Cytte gate & ouer the gate a greate Castell with towers made for Armes of the Cyttye & ye lyonn being cowched vnder the gate." In keeping with Morison's admonition, the appeal was first to the eyes with a symbol of the city's power founded partly on royal authority and partly on the accomplishments of the city and its people. To underscore its effect an orator, "Richelie app*a*rreilled," embodied "this wealle pieblicke" in outlining the qualities of good government necessary for it to flourish. Authorities should provide good example, "fere god and serue hym," provide for the poor, promote order and concord, administer wise justice, act impartially, and "Cause yoothe to be trayned and seasoned in Tyme / In vertew and Labour from synne vice and Cryme." To assist the mayor, the third pageant introduced the four virtues, Prudence, Fortitude, Temperance, and Justice, as guides who "yf yow keepe them no kinde of power/cann dommaige at annye owre." Thus the pageants emphasized his wisdom and virtue while communicating the role of citizens "of high and Lowe degree" in constituting his authority through election and holding him accountable for meeting their expectations. Unlike the Queen, the mayor was distinguished only temporarily from ordinary citizens by election, and emphasis on his exceptional virtue helped to establish his right to authority. Yet in both form and content, *Respublica* and the pageants shared similar concerns about the nature of good government in "Comon weales" and the role of the "Ignoram people" (a specific character in both entertainments) in providing advice on the virtues and expectations of good governors.[29]

Another parallel between the two popular and court entertainments is the involvement of performers in praising and counseling their own patron. Through their involvement in pageants which provided a kind of code by which their mayor could be judged, the waits were linked with a tradition of court artist/counselors including not only the Chapel Royal

[29] Nicholas Udall (attrib.), *Respublica: An Interlude for Christmas 1553*, ed. W. W. Greg, *Early English Text Society*, o.s., 226 (1952), 648. All references to this play are to the text of this edition.

in *Respublica* but also jesters, fools, players, and playwrights. The Norwich
waits, whose musical and theatrical talents drew considerable fame to the
city, were a source of civic pride. Like the Queen, members of the nobility,
and landed gentry, many urban communities had become patrons in
their own right by supporting a group of liveried waits. Some towns and
related organizations such as schools and guilds continued to hire local
minstrels, but by the middle of the sixteenth century, waits with their
evolving musical sophistication were the preferred civic entertainers.
Even a smaller town such as Rye could significantly enhance its image
and sphere of influence through its patronage of waits. In 1556–57, for
instance, the waits of Rye were specifically sought out by a representative
from New Romney to perform in their revived religious play. Eventually
waits would also tour like the performers of other patrons.[30] Even in
some communities too small to support a group of liveried waits, groups
of amateur performers could extend the town's sphere of influence by
taking the town play on tour to neighboring communities.[31]

   Thus urban communities participated at a number of levels in a complex network of patron/client relationships. Although the power and authority of local officials derived in part from the patronage of the Queen,
members of her court, and local magnates, it also derived from the town's
sense of its own integrity and identity. Much like a patron's performers,
town authorities were engaged in constituting not only subjects, out of a
responsibility to the Crown and to those who elected them, but also the
sovereignty of the Queen with its attendant responsibilities and rights.
This complex interdependence would have been publicly displayed
each time local authorities held "court" at "the Mayor's play," whether it
involved performers associated with the Queen and her court or a patron
outside her court. It was also displayed by a city's own performers who
were used to create and enhance a distinct identity and extend the community's sphere of influence or power base. However, before assuming
a correspondence between official intention and the actual response of
spectators engaged in assimilating the theatrical information carried by

[30] *Kent*, 137. For instance, in 1557–58 the waits of both Manchester and Derby visited the city of
  Nottingham where they received as much as if not more than minstrels associated with local gentry
  and even the Earl of Shrewsbury. See *Records of the Borough of Nottingham Being a Series of Extracts from
  the Archives of the Corporation of Nottingham*, ed. W[illiam] S[tevenson], et al., 7 vols. (Nottingham:
  Thomas Forman, 1882–1947), IV, 116–17. Perhaps the widest ranging waits were those of Norwich
  who traveled on an ill-fated voyage to Portugal at the special request of Sir Francis Drake in 1589
  (*Norwich*, 92–93).
[31] For example, during Mary's reign the Corpus Christi players of Sherborne, Dorset apparently
  toured to Lyme Regis where they appeared in the church. Joseph Fowler, *Mediaeval Sherborne*
  (Dorchester: Longmans, 1951), 323; Wanklyn, *Lyme Leaflets*, 39.

locally sponsored entertainments or touring performers, it will be necessary to look more closely at what Morison called "the co*mm*en people."

Within the performance patronage network of power relationships,
all participants except the Queen could function as subjects. Patrons,
their performers, and local authorities as well as other members of the
community were all in a position to be constituted as subjects through
theatrical propaganda emanating from the Crown. The focus here, however, is on the latter group of spectators, including "the co*mm*en people,"
a term with a wide range of connotations depending on its contemporary
application.[32] Morison characterized them as "ignoraunt people" for
whom theatrical propaganda was especially important because they
remembered "more better that they see then that they heere." Many
of these individuals might have justified the simple, malleable response
he apparently assumed, but judging from what we know about some of
them in the 1550s, such reactions are unlikely to have been universal.

Contemporary accounts of the great affection displayed towards Mary
at the beginning of her reign, "such and so extraordinary that never was
greater shown in that kingdom towards any sovereign,"[33] are borne out
in *Republica* by the character People, a hickish but loyal subject in whose
southeastern dialect Respublica is affectionately referred to as "Rice
puddingcake" (636). People offers wise counsel to Respublica on the
governance of the country, underscoring in particular the importance of
maintaining direct contact with the people, and he enthusiastically welcomes Nemesis, a figure specifically identified with Mary as the "goddes
of redresse *and* correction" (1).

Mary's early proclamation prohibiting unlicensed plays, however,
betrayed a fear that in "public assemblies" her "loving subjects" could be
stirred "to disorder or disquiet" by other subjects attempting to interpret
"the word of God" or "the laws of this realm after their brains and fancies." The full implications of the Reformation had released the specter

[32] The focus of this section, however, is informed by Michael Bristol's argument that in practice
there would have been little contemporary confusion as to which individuals were included in
this group: those individuals who were not "gentle" and who were not in positions of authority.
See his *Carnival and Theatre: Plebeian Culture and the Structure of Authority in Renaissance England* (New
York: Routledge, 1989), 42–44.

[33] *Calendar of State Papers and Manuscripts, Relating to English Affairs, Existing in the Archives and Collections
of Venice and in Other Libraries of Northern Italy*, ed. Rawdon Brown and Horatio Brown, 9 vols.
(London, 1864–97), VI, 1057.

of the common people appropriating these two reserves of knowledge and the mechanisms of printing, preaching, and playing which were critical to the sovereign's control of the power/knowledge dynamic. Such fears were, in fact, justified on a smaller scale by events like the disturbance at the reintroduction of the mass in Rye and on a larger scale by Wyatt's rebellion so that the government felt it necessary to remain vigilant throughout the reign. This did not stop people in the Queen's own Duchy of Lancaster from seizing a theatrical vehicle for asserting their own position in the power/knowledge dynamic. In 1557 the Queen's bailiff and a tenant who had been allowed to build a new house on crown lands in Widnes watched a mob of more than one hundred people tear it apart and use one of the main timbers to erect a maypole. The tenant reported these actions as "verey heynius riotus and after a Rebellius manner comytted againste the peace crowne and dignities of our said soueraigne Lorde and Ladie the King and Quenes maiesties."[34] It would appear that the riot developed because the Crown's tenant had built on land which had been in common use, but this incident dramatically demonstrates that even where royal patrons were concerned individuals at the social and geographical extremities of the patronage chain were not only constituted as subjects but also invested with the power to resist and respond. An incident such as Wyatt's rebellion might be seen as demonstrating the extent to which such resistance, when orchestrated by local magnates, could escalate from the extremities to confront and challenge the ultimate authority of the sovereign at society's perceived center. The Widnes incident, however, if it was concerned with the local issue of real control of a piece of crown land for the common good, provides insights into the focus of the less orchestrated negotiations engaged in by individuals at the regional level. Not unlike Wyatt whose espoused motive was to stop Mary's union with a Spanish prince and ultimately the feared domination of England by Spain, the Widnes mob also rioted to assert their right to locally identified and determined common space even in the face of royal prerogative. Although it may be less certain in Wyatt's case,[35] the motivation in both cases could have been less a challenge to Mary's position of authority than an insistence that she had the responsibility to govern a commonwealth with regard to input from her subjects.[36]

---

34 *Lancashire*, ed. David George, REED (Toronto: University of Toronto Press, 1991), 101–2.

35 Peter Clark, *English Provincial Society from the Reformation to the Revolution: Religion, Politics and Society in Kent 1500–1640* (Hassocks, Sussex: Harvester, 1977), 87–98.

36 Although outside an officially sanctioned theatrical context for carnival-like resistance, the Widnes incident can be seen as an assertion of ideas associated with "com*men* welthe," or

The use of the maypole as a quasi-dramatic, carnival symbol expressing resistance to the will of the Crown may have been intentional in
that fears of attendant public assemblies had prompted several suppres-
sions of May games,[37] but it also underscored more broadly the fact that
control of the theatrical medium was not simply the purview of touring
performers associated with the Queen and court. Whether attending
civic pageants, a mayor's play, or the real-life drama of public burnings,
such a crowd of "ignoraunt people" could impose its own meaning and
significance on the event and entertain a complex set of allegiances.
Any efforts at theatrical propaganda by Queen and court would have
to take into account audience members and subjects such as the weaver
John Careless, one of the four men apprehended in Coventry in 1553 for
"lewde and sediciouse behaviour." Careless died after two years' imprisonment in the King's Bench, but he was first imprisoned in Coventry
jail, where he was "in such credit with his keeper, that upon his word he
was let out to play in the pageant about the city with his companions.
And that done, keeping touch with his keeper, he returned again into
prison at his hour appointed."[38] During his imprisonment, Careless was
part of a close-knit Protestant community, and he wrote and received
several letters which were printed by John Foxe along with the transcript
of his examination. From all of this evidence there emerges a complex
individual. He displayed sufficient knowledge of the law to advise other
Protestants on how to respond when examined, but his compliance with
his jailer in Coventry was mirrored in a remarkable degree of compliance with the authorities that interrogated him. He could perform as a
good citizen in civic drama rooted in Catholicism while consumed with
a "merry" longing to sing and dance "before the ark of the Lord" as
a Protestant martyr. Furthermore, he could in one breath confidently
defend his reading of the word of God against examiners who would
re-educate him and in the next breath staunchly assert his loyalty to the
Queen and his willingness "to do her grace the best service that I can,
with body, goods and life, so long as it doth last" (and so long as his
religious beliefs were not compromised).[39] Careless asserted his loyalty,

"the expectation that society will sustain each of its members." The use of the maypole, in particular, connects this incident with Michael Bristol's argument that plebeian culture embraces
theatre because it provides a mechanism through which the "ethos of collective life may be
sustained and experimentally renewed" (213).

[37] *Dramatic Records of the City of London*, 295–96; *Acts of the Privy Council, 1554–1556*, v, 151.

[38] John Foxe, *The Acts and Monuments of John Foxe*, ed. Stephen Reed Cattley, 8 vols. (London, 1837–41),
VIII, 170.

[39] Ibid., 169–70, 172.

but he would not grant the Crown a monopoly over the power of the law, the word of God, or performance.

Careless' background as a performer and his flair for self-dramatization and articulation of his beliefs may explain why he languished in prison rather than rising to the martyrdom to which he aspired, but in the last moments of their lives, several of the Protestant martyrs engaged in overtly performative resistance. They seized the mechanism of punishment and transformed it into dramatic Protestant propaganda.[40] The resulting impact on "ignoraunt people" is a matter of debate, but at least with individuals like Careless it would surely have been a powerful common denominator in determining the relative success of theatrical propaganda presented by the performers of royal or courtly patrons. Careless may have been an uncommon commoner in the extent to which he felt empowered to read, write, and think independently and in his theatrical flair. However, in his negotiations with civic and royal authorities engaged in controlling, educating, and punishing a subject, he may not have been uncommon in assimilating apparently divergent loyalties to community, church, and Crown and, in particular, distinguishing between the Queen and her policies.[41] In asserting his own position of power in the process and demonstrating a capacity to integrate and reconcile complex allegiances he was not unlike some of Mary's more prominent subjects – including members of the court and Privy Council.

PATRONS AND TOURING PERFORMERS

So far, an examination of the performance patronage network has revealed that subjects and their local governments were active rather than passive participants in the circulation of power, knowledge, and

---

[40] See, for example, the account of the execution of Thomas Cranmer, who was displayed on a stage before his execution and who announced his performative intention that the hand which had written his false recantation would be the first to burn and followed through by thrusting it into the rising flames. In addition, Hugh Latimer encouraged fellow martyr Nicholas Ridley by telling him to "play the man. We shall this day light such a candle, by God's grace, in England, as I trust shall never be put out." In Hadley, Rowland Taylor's charismatic "performance" before his parishioners was put to an end only when one Robert King, identified as a deviser of interludes, assisted with the gunpowder to help him on his way. According to Foxe, King also officiated at Bury (Foxe, *Acts and Monuments* VIII, 90; VII, 550; VI, 696–700).

[41] Careless' expressed loyalty to the Queen despite his religious beliefs is not an isolated instance even amongst persecuted Protestants. Perhaps even clearer evidence that treason did not follow automatically upon heresy comes from Edward Underhill, a gentleman pensioner who could sing and play the lute and who composed a ballad against papists which circulated in print just after Mary's accession. Despite his determined Protestantism when questioned and his nearly fatal imprisonment, he was a staunch defender of Mary's person when her palace was attacked during Wyatt's rebellion. See *Tudor Tracts 1532–1588*, 170–98.

meaning. They could use the power inherent in the theatrical medium for their own purposes – sometimes divergent, sometimes complementary. Regardless of the extent to which they constituted a cohesive power base, however, a community's welfare still depended on its ability to function effectively within the larger commonwealth. For this it was partly dependent on patrons whose influence in turn depended on their power base in town and country as well as their relative position at court.

Local historian Charles Phythian-Adams has argued for the critical importance of integrating local history with national history in order to trace the "symbiosis between . . . provincial micro-structures and between them and the social and cultural macro-structure of the English nation." He suggests that for an understanding of matters such as national allegiance and identity and "the manner in which 'national' power is informally distributed and supra-regional influence is filtered down," we need to determine "spatially defined" "neighbourhoods," "the situation and distribution of noble and gentry estates within and amongst them," and "the ways in which the tentacles of patronage and clientage at different periods reached down to local dynastic grass-roots."[42] In an effort to identify mechanisms through which towns and their subjects were involved with the wider circulation of power in Marian England, this concept of neighborhoods can be applied to the spatially defined patterns traced by touring performers to examine them as signs of a patron's sphere of influence. Although the focus here is on the position of cities and towns within these cultural neighborhoods, they would also have encompassed more rural communities as well as the "communities" of household and court. The combination of aural and visual dramatic material, a patron's influence, and the mobility open to performers traveling under the patronage of a member of the nobility or gentry gave performers the potential to draw together geographically distant communities within their touring pattern. The frequency with which they revisited and reinforced this neighborhood as well as their local personal or patronage connections would obviously affect community response and the cohesiveness of the neighborhood, but by passing news and information from one town or household to another and by performing work which provided a shared set of signs and a common language, performers could circulate knowledge in such a way as to contribute to the patron's sphere of influence and local concepts of allegiance and identity.

[42] Charles Phythian-Adams, *Re-thinking English Local History*, Department of English Local History, Occasional Papers, ser. 4, no. 1 (Leicester: Leicester University, 1991), 18, 45–46.

In order to understand the significance of neighborhoods produced by Marian performers, it is necessary to begin by comparison with Edward's reign. The virtue of Richard Morison's advocacy must have been clearly understood by Edward's Privy Council to the extent that his theory was translated into personal as well as public policy. Three of his Privy Councilors patronized performers who established substantial cultural neighborhoods, and five others had performers who traveled within more limited neighborhoods.[43] By lending their names to touring performers, his most important and influential Privy Councilors created, first of all, mobile symbols of their own authority and power to protect or control clients. Collectively, they also extended the court to the provinces thereby creating a shared knowledge base and an immediate yet informal channel for locally reinforcing Council policies and authority. With Mary's accession, however, changes in the power structure resulted in the disruption of most of the neighborhoods established by performers in the previous reign. Whereas seven Edwardian patronage families had used traveling performers to establish spheres of influence under Henry,[44] only three such Marian families had any record at all of touring performers under Edward, and all three were continuing a tradition actually begun under Henry.

[43] All neighborhoods referred to in this chapter are derived from a database of records relating to traveling performers drawn primarily from the publications of Records of Early English Drama and the Malone Society published through 1997 as well as Ian Lancashire's *Dramatic Texts and Records of Britain: A Chronological Topography to 1558* (Toronto: University of Toronto Press, 1984). See related maps at http://uregina.ca/~blackstm/ and n. 105 below. The three major Privy Council patrons of touring theatrical performers under Edward were Thomas Cheyney, Lord Warden of the Cinque Ports (16 records, all from the Cinque Ports region); Edward Seymour, Lord Protector (16 records ranging from Dover to Lyme Regis to Bristol to Leicester to Cambridge); and William Parr, Marquess of Northampton (7 records primarily in the southeast but also including Cambridge and Leicester). It is possible that the latter group of players had been associated with Catherine Parr whose players had traveled a similar circuit up to her death in 1548 (3 Edwardian records, Maldon, Bristol, Dover). Performers associated with another court patron, Katherine Brandon, Duchess of Suffolk, also toured with some frequency (8 records in the southeast and East Anglia). Privy Council patrons whose performers appear to have toured less frequently during Edward's reign are Henry Grey, Marquess of Dorset (6 records in Norwich, Poole and Exeter); John Russell, Earl of Bedford (5 records, ports in Kent and Devon); Thomas Seymour, Lord Admiral (5 records, southern coastal towns and Cambridge); and John Dudley, Duke of Northumberland (5 records, the west and midlands). As with all neighborhoods referred to in this study, these will no doubt be altered as the process of discovering and editing records continues. It should also be remembered that the degree to which extant records accurately reflect the extent of Tudor touring patterns is inevitably qualified by the survival of records for particular locations and periods as well as the accuracy and assiduousness of contemporary clerks. In some cases such as that of Sir Francis Leek's players, town officials may not have seen it in their best interests to keep a detailed written record of their hospitality or they may not have provided official hospitality but simply turned a blind eye to performances.

[44] These included Thomas Cheyney, Edward Seymour, Henry Grey, John Russell, the Brandons, and the Parrs. Performers associated with John Bourchier, Earl of Bath travelled intensively, primarily in Devon, under Henry VIII, but appeared only three times in Edward's reign.

Operating from within a strong sphere of influence, Thomas Cheyney, the Lord Warden of the Cinque Ports established a formidable tradition of performance-patronage with regular and concentrated appearances by his touring performers in Kent and the Cinque Ports.[45] His adaptable political skills kept him in office under three successive Tudors until his death in December of 1558, so that at Mary's accession there was no discernible interruption in the intensity or consistency of his performers' travels. Perhaps partly because of his influence, the Cinque Ports contributed no participants to Wyatt's rebellion.[46] Canterbury and Faversham did contribute participants, however, and it is interesting to note that after the rebellion Cheyney's minstrels began regularly visiting Faversham following a thirteen-year hiatus. His minstrels had been visiting Canterbury every other year or so but after the onset of Protestant executions there they never returned. This may possibly be due to the minstrels' fear that public executions would be "a hard act to follow" or a mutual patron/performer decision not to encourage public gatherings, but it is consistent with the usual categorization of Cheyney as a "conservative politique" ("one who welcomed the return of the mass but was cool towards the papacy").[47] Although comparatively limited in geographical scope, Cheyney's was the most tightly drawn neighborhood under Mary and one with numerous other administrative, ceremonial, and performance links. Most likely because it was a major corridor of access to the Continent, Cheyney's cultural neighborhood also intersected with that of other patrons. However, in contrast with other periods, recorded incidents of a town's extension of hospitality to performers in honor of influential patrons – beyond the usual reward – were more isolated under Mary (for example, New Romney paid "for a drynkyng then at pellams" when the Lord Warden's minstrels visited and Dover rewarded the Earl of Sussex' players after a performance "at the wch were a greyt mayny of the comons with the meye & Iurates.").[48]

Marian records of performance patronage have surfaced for only two other Privy Councilors, and these are only isolated appearances for

[45] With respect to Parliamentary affairs Cheyney exerted considerable influence and control, in some cases overturning the nomination of Protestants to Parliament. This was particularly true in 1555 when Cheyney may have been reasserting his authority – and loyalty – after his decidedly ineffective role during Wyatt's rebellion. See Mayhew, *Tudor Rye*, 73, 294 n. 55; *Calendar of State Papers, Domestic*, 58–59; and Bindoff, *History of Parliament* 1, 634–38.
[46] Anthony Fletcher, *Tudor Rebellions*, Seminar Studies in History (Harlow, Essex: Longman, 1983), 78–79.
[47] David Loades, *The Reign of Mary Tudor: Politics, Government and Religion in England 1553–58* (London: Longman, 1991), 404–5.
[48] *Kent*, 42, 136.

the Earl of Bath's minstrels in Barnstaple in 1553–54 and the Earl
of Bedford's minstrels in Rye in 1554.[49] Both patrons had seats in
Devonshire where their performers toured during the 1540s, but performers associated with the Earl of Bath kept a low profile during
Edward's reign. Throughout most of his career John Russell, Earl of
Bedford, maintained strong patronage and clientage connections within
Devonshire, but his minstrels who had been touring there since he became Lord Admiral never appeared again in Devon after the summer of
1549 when he put down the Western Rebellion. By 1551–52 they ceased
to appear on tour altogether except for the one visit to Rye. At roughly the
same time performers associated with his son, the outspokenly Protestant
Francis, Lord Russell, began to appear in a somewhat different neighborhood including Devon from 1552–53. After his minstrels' involvement
with seditious material in Norwich in 1554, his performers appeared on
tour only twice (in Barnstaple in 1555–56 and Exeter in 1557,[50] when
Francis had returned from exile and succeeded his father as Earl of
Bedford). Given their brush with the authorities and what we know of
Francis' sympathies with Wyatt, an earlier appearance in Canterbury
some time between September of 1553 and September of 1554 leads to
speculation that the sort of influence and allegiance cultivated by these
performers was not what Mary – or his father – might have wished.[51]

A sustained and wide-ranging neighborhood of influence involving
primarily East Anglia and Kent had been established by the Duke of
Norfolk's theatrical performers prior to his imprisonment in the tower
towards the end of Henry's reign. He was released at the beginning of
Mary's reign and appointed Privy Councilor, but from before his imprisonment until after his death, no touring performers were associated
with him or his family. After his grandson's succession to the title in 1554,
his appointment as Gentleman of the Privy Chamber to Philip and his
first marriage in 1555 to Mary FitzAlan, daughter and heir of the Earl
of Arundel, the patronage of touring performers was revived with a similar East Anglian orientation and a gradually widening scope until in
1557–58 it included Exeter and Lewes (near the Arundel seat) as well as
Ipswich and Maldon. What is interesting about Norfolk's cultural neighborhood, however, is the degree to which the players' travels intersected

---

[49] *Devon*, 41; Rye Chamberlains' Accounts, 60/7, fo. 78b.   [50] *Devon*, 41, 147.

[51] *Kent*, 12. Evidence of Russell's continuing influence, over parts of Norfolk at least, in 1555 is
provided by a contemporary account crediting him with encouraging the people of Woburn and
Wickham Market to remain 'very protestauntes'. See "State Papers Relating to the Custody of
Princess Elizabeth at Woodstock, in 1554 . . .," ed. C. R. Manning, *Norfolk Archaeology* 4 (1855),
150.

with a different type of entertainment – the persecution of Protestants. Ipswich and Lewes saw executions in three of the four years in which they occurred so that when Norfolk's players visited those towns (the last two years of executions in Ipswich, and the last year in Lewes, when ten people were burned) their audiences would have been especially aware of the current religious policy and its implications. They would have faced similar though less intense awareness in Norwich, which they visited in the last of two years of executions, and in Exeter and Cambridge, both of which they visited for the only time after the one execution to be staged in those communities. While the intersection of players and martyrs may have been coincidental, it underscores the neighborhood context for player–public interaction. In 1557 and 1558, in particular, currently edited records for their travels include only one town (Maldon) which had not recently hosted an execution.[52] Like the sermons which accompanied the burnings, the players could have been useful in contextualizing or presenting a more positive performance alternative, but the very immediate dilemma faced in the performance context by both players and sensitized spectators highlights a similar dilemma faced by the more pragmatic members of Mary's court and Council who were anxious to support the authority of the sovereign but increasingly doubtful about the virtues of persecution and other aspects of Crown policy.[53] In this context, the cultural neighborhood created by the performers of a family closely associated with Mary and Catholicism could well have been a vehicle for diminishing credibility and the family's local influence.

The performers of one other Marian patron traced a somewhat wider ranging neighborhood. Although his father had been a patron of performers under Henry, the players of John Vere, Earl of Oxford, appeared only twice during Edward's reign. Between 1556 and 1558, however, they

---

[52] Data regarding Protestant burnings is derived primarily from John Strype, *Ecclesiastical Memorials, Relating Chiefly to Religion, and the Reformation of It, and the Emergencies of the Church of England, under King Henry VIII, King Edward VI and Queen Mary I*, 3 vols. (Oxford, 1872), III.ii, 554–56.

[53] On 3 February 1558 Thomas Cheyney, one of the most senior Privy Councilors – and the only Councilor/performance patron – wrote to the Queen expressing his concern that Kent was now weaker in "*manred*" than ever and begging to be allowed to resign his office of lieutenant of the shire. A number of factors may have influenced his decision – the recent loss of Calais and perceived danger of French invasion in Kent, excessive subsidies and forced loans, even current marital problems and old age. Local officials – even those in previously enthusiastic New Romney – were becoming increasingly unwilling to comply with and carry out government policy. The climate of persecution may also have been a factor. On 26 January he had received an order from the Queen to proceed against two individuals in Canterbury, and attached to his letter of resignation is a report noting that one had been executed (and "died blasphemously"), the other had been put in the pillory and the people of Canterbury had been cautioned "as to what they say of the King and Queen." The Queen does not appear to have accepted his resignation (Clark, *English Provincial Society*, 104, 106; *Calendar of State Papers, Domestic*, 98–99).

produced a neighborhood encompassing Norwich, Dover, and Bristol with the Earl's Essex seat at Hedingham Castle in the middle. Outside of Bristol and Dover, however, no location was visited more than once, and in this case there is an even more striking coincidence of player appearances and executions. Their two visits to Bristol coincided with the only two years in which executions took place there. Their visits to Oxford and Norwich came in the second of two years of executions. Since Canterbury witnessed an annual blood-bath and Ipswich enjoyed only one year without such entertainment, it is less significant that Vere's players visited there and more significant that their only visits which did not coincide with public executions in the same year were the two trips to Dover and the stop at Bridgwater. Although he was Lord Great Chamberlain and included on her New Year's gift list in 1557, Mary viewed Vere's enthusiasm for Catholicism with suspicion. His name topped the list of noblemen suspected of complicity in the 1556 anti-Catholic conspiracy.[54] Keeping in mind as well his Protestant father's patronage of John Bale,[55] the potential effect of his performers' cultural neighborhood, like the patron himself, remains ambiguous as a mechanism for fostering allegiance to the Queen and her policies.

More detailed analysis of factors such as cross-community relations, patron–client exchanges and ties of kinship would be required to determine the way in which each of the above neighborhoods actually functioned in the circulation of power among patron, performer, and specific communities.[56] However, the evidence derived from simply identifying the neighborhoods suggests a striking difference between the interaction of court and country at the level of performance neighborhoods in the reigns of Edward and Mary. Whereas some of the most prominent Edwardian Privy Councilors utilized the patronage of performers in extending their own image and that of the court into the provinces, only one of Mary's Councilors, Thomas Cheyney, had

---

[54] *Calendar of State Papers, Domestic*, 76; *Ambassades de Messieurs de Noailles en Angleterre*, ed. M. l'Abbé de Vertot, 5 vols. (Paris, 1763), v, 319. From the records, Oxford remains an ambiguous figure in his support for Mary and her policies. He reportedly declared his support for Mary in 1553 only under pressure from servants in his household, but he later involved himself in the persecution apparently to the extent of actually reporting individuals within his household. Extant records provide little supporting evidence for his suspected complicity in the 1556 plot, but other evidence from 1556 suggests that he, along with the Justices of the Peace for Essex, may have been perceived as less than diligent in pursuing individuals suspected of sedition. See James E. Oxley, *The Reformation in Essex to the Death of Mary* (Manchester: Manchester University Press, 1965), 210–37; *Acts of the Privy Council, 1554–1556*, v, 104, 141, 148, 310–12.

[55] White, *Theatre and Reformation*, 17, 195 n. 19.

[56] The results of such analysis will be presented in a book-length study of mid-Tudor patronage of traveling performers.

performers who maintained what could be called a neighborhood of influence. Having been established in the previous two reigns, it was intensive but limited in scope, and the fact that the minstrels avoided hot spots like Canterbury while Cheyney attended less than 20 percent of Council meetings leaves doubts as to the extent to which they might have been engaged in drawing communities in Kent closer to the court and its policies. Surprisingly, none of the Councilors categorized as "conservative catholic" ("one who welcomed the persecution and the return to Rome") patronized touring theatrical performers. Single appearances for the performers of other Privy Councilors suggest that they may have patronized performers but that touring performers did not regularly underscore their influence or promote public policy outside of their household. With the 'politique' Councilors (conformists "who had no enthusiasm for official religious policy"[57]) Lords Clinton and Wentworth (whose father Thomas was one of Bale's patrons) this is more understandable than with "conservative politiques" such as the Earl of Sussex, the Earl of Bedford, the Earl of Bath, and the Duke of Norfolk, all of whom had a previous tradition of touring performers. Successors to the latter three titles during the reign did develop neighborhoods of influence, but not all used them to foster allegiance to the court. Francis, Lord Russell and later Earl of Bedford was clearly not associated with the court and on at least one occasion his performers may have used their influence to promote opposition to the Queen and her policies.

Given the persistent concerns regarding control of theatrical propaganda as expressed in prohibitions and other official communications, it is hard to understand why only one Privy Councilor supported performers who developed a sustained touring pattern. There were clearly other more formal mechanisms for making the presence of the Council felt in the towns and collecting feedback on support for government policies at the extremities, but as Morison observed, none more effective than the indirect, visual medium of theatre in fostering a shared set of signs and knowledge. This must have been especially clear to the seasoned core of Mary's Council, most of whom had served under Edward, but the very pragmatism that made it possible for them to make the transition from the one Privy Council to the other may also have inspired as moderate a course as possible in personally promoting her policies. As her government, they were bound to implement her programs and enforce her authority, but their ultimate concern may have been more with their

---

[57] Loades, *The Reign of Mary Tudor*, 404–11.

own position and/or the stability of the country than with the Queen's specific agenda. A strategy of counter-propaganda may have been behind the intersection of Protestant executions and touring players associated with the Duke of Norfolk and the Earl of Oxford (although the motivations of the latter may be in question), but a strategy of public and personal association with the Queen's controversial policies through theatre may not have been particularly attractive to individual Privy Councilors.[58] As both patrons and subjects, some members of Mary's court may have been less eager than John Careless to demonstrate their readiness "to do her grace the best service that I can, with body, goods and life, so long as it doth last."[59]

The cultural neighborhood fostered by one other patron serves to highlight the implications of the limited scope and coverage of touring performers associated with the Marian court. In April of 1556, the Council found it necessary to write to the Earl of Shrewsbury, Lord President of the Council of the North, informing him that they understood

certain lewd persons, to the number of six or seven in a company, naming themselves to be servants unto Sir Francis Leek, and wearing his livery, and badge on their sleeves, have wandered about those North parts, and represented certain

---

[58] Similar conclusions have been drawn by Edward Baskerville with respect to print propaganda. See *A Bibliography of Propaganda and Polemic Published in English between 1553 and 1558, from the Death of Edward VI to the Death of Mary I. Memoirs. American Philosophical Society* 136 (1979), 9.

[59] This lack of commitment to the Queen and her policies was remarked upon by contemporaries such as the Venetian ambassador, who noted that Privy Councilors were "openly divided into two or three factions, so that were a change . . . by misfortune, to take place in the kingdom, with the exception of one or two, all the rest would be of doubtful faith, and adapt themselves to circumstances" (*Calendar of State Papers, Venice*, VI, 1071). The orientation of Protestant propaganda also suggests a perceived soft spot with the nobility and the Council by oscillating between a plea to "the ryghte honorable the nobilitie and ientlemen of Englande," to use their power to return a sick commonwealth to her former health and condemnation of members of the Council as "meane men" of questionable nobility and motivated by ambition rather than a genuine "loue to a commonwealth." W[illiam] Keth, *[W. Keth His Seeing Glasse.] Unto the Ryghte Honorable the Nobilitie and Ientlemen of Englande* (n.p., [1555]); [Laurence Saunders?], *A Trewe Mirrour of the Wofull State of Englande*, The English Experience no. 761 (1556; Norwood, NJ: Walter J. Johnson, 1975), B1b. See also John Bradforth, *The Copye of a Letter, Sent by John Bradforth to the Right Honorable Lordes the Erles of Arundel, Darbie, Shrewsburye, and Penbroke, Declaring the Nature of Spaniardes, and Discovering the Most Detestable Treasons, Which Thei Have Pretended Most Falselye agaynste Our Moste Noble Kingdome of Englande* (n.p., [1556?]). Twentieth-century historians have recognized similar tendencies within the Council but given them a more positive, pragmatic interpretation. For instance, speaking of the first Earl of Bedford, Diane Willen concludes, "As his whole career demonstrated, Russell was neither a committed Catholic nor a dedicated Protestant. He was in fact not at all motivated by ideological considerations, in this respect very much resembling colleagues like Richard Rich, William Paget or St. John . . . Russell and his colleagues, assured of general Christian principles, placed priority upon political stability and unity. Such men, at least during the Henrician period, distributed favours and made friends within all ideological camps." It would appear that Bedford and other Councilors may have further refined this approach under Mary. See *John Russell, First Earl of Bedford: One of the King's Men*, Royal Historical Society Studies in History Series, no. 23 (London: Royal Historical Society, 1981), 43.

plays and interludes, containing very naughty and seditious matter touching the King and Queen's Majesties, and the state of the realm, and to the slander of Christ's true and Catholic religion, contrary to all good order, and to the manifest contempt of Almighty God, and dangerous example of others.

The Council forbade Justices of the Peace to allow "plays, interludes, songs, or any such like pastimes whereby the people may any ways be stirred to disorder," and charged them with apprehending and punishing any offenders "as vagabonds, by virtue of the statute made against loitering and idle persons." They asked Shrewsbury to charge Leek with finding the players and delivering them for punishment, and they warned that if Leek encouraged any more traveling performers under his name he would answer for it.[60] With the exception of a prohibition noted in the York records against "players and Mynstrells namyng them self*es* to be Gentylmen Sarvaunt*es*,"[61] documentation of any further local actions relating to this incident has not been discovered, but the tone of the letter as well as its content casts the situation in a somewhat different light from that of the Norwich case involving Francis Russell's minstrels. This time the patron as well as his performers is specifically drawn into the affair, and both the letter and the prohibition as referred to in the York records convey an uneasiness about control of the patronage system itself. Given that the news had time to reach the Privy Council and make its way back to Shrewsbury, it does not appear that either he or the Justices of the Peace had been overly diligent in asserting their authority on the Queen's behalf. Leek was, in fact, a Justice of the Peace for Derbyshire himself, and this was not the first time during the reign that he had been taken to task for the retainers he was keeping.[62] At issue here is not only control of theatrical propaganda, but also control of the mechanisms of patronage, and regional and local government through which subjects at the geographical and social extremities could be constituted. Perhaps it is coincidental that, with the exception of Cheyney's performers, it was not until after this incident that performers associated with any court patrons – possibly including the Queen – began touring with any intensity. Yet even after April of 1556 court patrons – and members of the nobility in general   remained outside any theatrical network for the circulation

[60] Edmund Lodge, *Illustrations of British History, Biography, and Manners in the Reigns of Henry VIII, Edward VI, Mary, Elizabeth, and James I*, 3 vols., 2nd edn. (London, 1838), I, 260–62.

[61] *York*, ed. Alexandra F. Johnston and Margaret Rogerson, REED, 2 vols. (Toronto: University of Toronto Press, 1979), I, 322. For a Select Council report to the King on actions arising from this incident see *Calendar of State Papers, Domestic*, 82.

[62] He had appeared before the Exchequer in 1554 to answer to charges that he kept a number of liveried retainers who accompanied him to sessions of the peace and assizes (Bindoff, *History of Parliament*, III, 518–20).

of power and knowledge in large parts of the country. Substantial cultural neighborhoods were established in Kent and East Anglia but large parts of the west, the midlands, and the north remained outside the loop.[63] Thus, the picture so far produced by cultural neighborhoods is hardly a seamless landscape in which the micro-structures of urban communities are drawn to coalesce with court and sovereign by a united front of noble patrons. Still, this is only part of the picture. It must be augmented by reference to touring patterns associated with the country's most important performance patron, the Queen herself.

THE QUEEN AND HER PERFORMERS

From the Queen's perspective, there may have been good reasons for not encouraging her Privy Councilors and some other members of her court to involve themselves in a strategy of theatrical patronage. The distant and unenthusiastic relationship between the Queen and her Council suggested by the foregoing analysis extended well beyond the matter of performance patronage. In a letter of 1554 Cardinal Pole reported that she had "become very suspicious of the greater part of her Privy Council,"[64] and in May of 1557 the Venetian ambassador reported:

> Respecting the government and public business she is compelled ... according to the custom of other sovereigns, to refer many matters to her councillors and ministers. The truth is that, knowing the divisions which exist amongst them ... her Majesty, in order not to be deceived, and for the prevention of scandal, willed ... that Cardinal Pole should hear and have everything referred to him, it being evident that, whilst showing the utmost confidence in him, she distrusts almost all the others; and she says freely that in government affairs, most especially in cases of conscience and of offence against God ... she refers herself to the Cardinal, protesting that should errors be committed they will be attributed to him ... Besides, she is also greatly grieved by the insurrections, conspiracies, and plots formed against her daily, both at home and abroad, and although hitherto ... they have not caused any damage ... yet nevertheless, it being necessary ... to proceed to capital punishment or confiscation ... she knows that by these means the hatred and indignation she inspires

---

[63] It could perhaps be argued that the south and east were more open to Protestantism, and therefore performance propaganda needed to be concentrated there rather than spread out into the north and west. Such assumptions about the distribution of religious loyalties have been disputed, however. See D. M. Palliser, "Popular Reactions to the Reformation during the Years of Uncertainty 1530–70," Felicity Heal and Rosemary O'Day (eds.), *Church and Society in England: Henry VIII to James I* (London: Macmillan, 1977), esp. 45–46. It is clear, however, that Protestant executions were concentrated in the south and east (Hughes, *Reformation in England*, II, 261–64).

[64] *Calendar of State Papers, Venice*, v, 461.

are increased ... The consequence is that as until now the plots have been set-on-foot ... by the commonalty and persons of mean extraction ... so from the fickleness of that nation ... were they excited ... by some personage ... or nobleman of importance, there is no doubt they would create a great revolution throughout the realm ... the country ... showing a greater inclination and readiness for change than ever, provided it had a leader.[65]

Given her distrust of Councilors, her fear of insurrections and plots, and the perceived role of performance propaganda in spreading sedition despite prohibitions and the pursuit of offenders, the Queen could be expected to depend heavily on her own performers to establish a strong touring presence. In so doing they could serve as a corrective to her public image, a sign of her authority and potential patronage to her subjects, and a vehicle for communicating and inculcating ideas that would contribute to her control of the power structure.

Once again, the cultural neighborhoods produced by Marian performers may be best understood by comparison with those for Edward and Elizabeth. First of all, on the basis of currently available records, players patronized by Edward and Elizabeth were circulating in the countryside within seven months of their accession. Of course unlike Edward, who as Prince had had players touring extensively right up to the point of his father's death, Mary had not been in a position to patronize touring performers since the 1530s. This, however, does not explain the fact that it took at least two years and three months before her players began to extend their court activities with a sustained neighborhood in the country. Unlike Mary, Elizabeth had never patronized traveling performers, and yet the Queen's players were on the road much more quickly after her accession with an appearance as early as 12 May 1559.[66] Records relating to responsibilities and activities at court, including the royal marriage, provide no evidence that Mary's performers were exceptionally busy with either performance or other unrelated duties at court. Certainly the string of prohibitions of performance activity stretching from the early days of her reign through 1557 suggests that Mary and her Council saw public performance as a dangerous and divisive catalyst for dissent to be discouraged rather than encouraged, but such prohibitions did not inhibit her performers from touring later in the reign,

---

[65] *Calendar of State Papers, Venice*, VI, 1056–57.
[66] Rye Chamberlains' Accounts, 60/7, fo. 203. Edward's players were in Dover on or before 20 August 1547 (*Kent*, 40). These are the earliest specifically dated records so far edited. Because civic accounting practices do not always provide specific dates and accounting years span parts of first and last regnal years, both Edward's and Elizabeth's players could have toured earlier.

nor did similar prohibitions have a restraining effect on royal performers under Edward or Elizabeth. Concern about the hospitality her players might receive and the unsettled atmosphere in certain parts of the country do not appear to have been factors because her performers initiated a sustained touring pattern only after unpopular policies had extinguished the enthusiasm which had reportedly marked her accession.

Perhaps the strongest cause for hesitation may have been concerns regarding the effectiveness and/or loyalty of her performers, whom she had largely inherited from Edward.[67] These concerns were to some degree justified in 1556 when William Hunnis, Gentleman of the Chapel Royal, was implicated in plots against the Queen and imprisoned.[68] Under examination Hunnis implicated John Benbow, also of the Chapel Royal, although his role does not appear to have been treated as very serious. Thomas Cawarden, Master of the Revels and his assistant Sir Thomas Benger were also implicated in plots. They were both staunch Protestants, and Cawarden had been under continuous suspicion of plotting against the Queen since Wyatt's rebellion. As a result of the 1556 plot he was placed under house arrest and eventually imprisoned

---

[67] Edward's accession was marked by the introduction of five new faces to the group (possibly drawn from the Prince's players). However, of the six interluders listed in the first Chamber accounts delivered under Mary (George Birche, Richarde Cooke, Richard Skinner, John Birche, Thomas Sowthey, and John Browne), all were listed in the last surviving accounts for interluders under Edward (1551–52). Two players listed in the Edwardian accounts had left or died (Robert Hynstock and Henry Harryot) by 1553, and Cooke, Sowthey, and John Birch disappeared from the records after 1556. These last three players, along with Skinner and Browne, had been appointed by Edward. George Birch had been appointed under Henry. Although the fee lists running from Edward's reign into the 1590s list eight interlude players, the item appears to have been copied *pro forma* long after the interluders' demise. The Cotton MS Chamber Accounts (Vespasian, C.xiv, fo. 67–73b) noted by J. Payne Collier as listing four interluders during the reign of Mary, and cited as such by Chambers, would appear to date from Elizabeth's reign because of the inclusion of George Birch as receiving an annuity, which he was not granted until 1560. See John Payne Collier, *The History of English Dramatic Poetry to the Time of Shakespeare: Annals of the Stage to the Restoration*, 3 vols. (London, 1879), I, 161–63. For records relating to the royal interluders, as well as the chapel royal and minstrels, see Andrew Ashbee (ed.), *Records of English Court Music*, 7 vols. (Aldershot, Hants.: Scolar, 1986–93), VII (1485–1558), esp. 119, 313, 315, 317, 319–20. For a detailed discussion of the actors connected with the royal interluders under Henry VIII and his three children see E. K. Chambers, *The Elizabethan Stage*, 4 vols. (Oxford: Clarendon Press, 1923), II, 79–83.

[68] Under examination, co-conspirators revealed that Hunnis had been recommended to the group because of his previous connections with unfulfilled plots. The conspirator John Dethick "bore witness that there was no need to doubt this man, for *before* at the Juego de Canas or Barrieres, he had been *appointed*, with Allday, Cornwall, and others to the number of twelve, to kill the king and after him the Queen." See PRO SP11/7, nos. 38, 39, 42–47, 49; C. C. Stopes, *William Hunnis and the Revels of the Chapel Royal* (Louvain: A. Uystpruyst, 1910), 58, 64; and Ashbee, *English Court Music*, VII, 422–23.

in the Fleet.[69] The Queen was apparently so alarmed by threats from
within her court that she refused to appear in public and would not let
Cardinal Pole leave her side – even for his consecration as Archbishop
of Canterbury in March of that year.

Despite the connection of these individuals with court entertainments,
however, they were not directly involved in groups of royal performers
who toured under Mary or other Tudors. Although it is clear that a
strong Protestant agenda must have dominated royal performers under
Edward, neither her jester nor any of her minstrels or players were
connected with plots against Mary. Furthermore, at least two Protestant
playwrights apparently sought and received preferment at her court.
William Baldwin's play *Love and Lyve* was probably prepared for the court
at Christmas 1555–56. The previous Christmas, Nicholas Udall was paid
for plays he provided (possibly *Respublica*) and given a royal warrant for
necessary materials from the Master of the Revels. Later in 1555 he was
appointed Master of Westminster Grammar School.[70]

Either because of anxiety about their commitment to the Crown's
agenda or because of a failure to recognize the importance of a royal anti-
dote to seditious touring performers, royal dramatic performers were exceptionally slow to develop sustained touring neighborhoods. The King
and Queen's minstrels visited Hereford (the heart of her performers' earlier touring circuit when she was Princess) sometime between October
1553 and October 1554. Mary's minstrels appeared only twice more, in
1555–56 and 1556–57 and those of the King three more times between
1554 and 1557.[71] The King's and Queen's jesters appeared in Canterbury
during the 1554–55 accounting year. The Queen's jester (twice identified
as Lockwoode) appeared alone during the same year in Rye, Lydd,
and Gloucester, and twice more the next year, both in the southeast.[72]
After that, though, there are no more recorded travels by her jester.
The earliest her players appear to have begun touring was September

[69] W. R. Streitberger, *Court Revels, 1485–1559*, Studies in Early English Drama: 3 (Toronto: University
of Toronto Press, 1994), 208–10.
[70] *Documents Relating to the Office of the Revels in the Time of King Edward VI and Queen Mary*, ed. Albert
Feuillerat (Louvain: A. Uystpruyst, 1914), 159–60; Streitberger, *Court Revels*, 212, 215; William
L. Edgerton, *Nicholas Udall* (New York: Twayne, 1965), 65–67.
[71] *Herefordshire/Worcestershire*, ed. David Klausner, REED (Toronto: University of Toronto Press,
1990), 121; *Devon*, 41, 147; *Oxford*, 225, 267; *Banbury*, 16.
[72] *Kent*, 12, 106, 137; *Cumberland, Westmorland, Gloucestershire*, ed. Audrey Douglas and Peter
Greenfield, REED (Toronto: University of Toronto Press, 1986), 297; *Players at Ipswich*, ed. E. K.
C[hambers], Malone Society Collections II.iii (Oxford: Oxford University Press, 1931), 260–61;
Rye Chamberlains' Accounts, 60/7, fol. 101b.

of 1555,[73] although from that point until less than a week before Mary's death they produced a sustained and wide-ranging neighborhood.

The coverage afforded by her players was heaviest in East Anglia and the southeast, but it encompassed the southwest and points as far north as Beverley as well. The extent of their travels reflects little concern for economies of time or touring expenses to be derived from focusing on only one or two contiguous regions in any given year. Each year they traced a neighborhood encompassing the east and west as well as the midlands and/or the north. The frequency of visits to particular locations is not especially intense in that no town was visited more than twice, but considering that the neighborhood was produced over only three years at most, the distribution of the four towns which they did visit twice is interesting. Ipswich, Leicester, Beverley, and Exeter may or may not have been seen as strategic centers in their regions, but the timing of the players' appearances at these and other locations encourages speculation that their visits were not entirely uninformed by power negotiations involving their patron and communities within their neighborhood. The initiation of touring by Mary's players sometime between Michaelmas (29 September) 1555 and Michaelmas 1556 came at the height of the propaganda war being waged in print and followed upon a number of events which would have benefited locally from "contextualizing": in particular, her unpopular marriage to Philip, Pole's return and the reunion of the English and Roman Catholic churches, a number of conspiracies, and a call for a subsidy at the same time as the country was experiencing poor harvests – as well as the trials and initial executions of Protestant martyrs. Not surprisingly, then, the players visited Leicester and Exeter for the first time in the years in which they hosted their only burnings.[74] In Gloucester, Bristol, and Norwich, the players' only visits came in the first of only two years of burnings. The royal minstrels as well as the players appeared in Canterbury in the first year of executions and in Ipswich

[73] So far, their earliest touring records are from the 1555–56 accounting years in Canterbury, Gloucester, and Leicester. See *Kent*, 12; *Cumberland*, 297; *Records of the Borough of Leicester*, ed. Mary Bateson, 3 vols. (Cambridge: Cambridge University Press, 1905), III, 85.

[74] In Leicester, the timing of burnings and the players' visits may both have been influenced by the indictment of 28 St. Martin's parishioners for "displaying scorn towards the sacrament of the altar" (*Leicester*, III, 85, 92; A. G. Dickens, *Lollards and Protestants in the Diocese of York 1509–1558* [London: Hambledon, 1982], 305). It should be noted, however, that because the visits of players as well as burnings cannot always be precisely dated, the relative timing of these two events still requires further analysis in the light of overall touring circuits. In Exeter, for instance, where dates can be precisely determined, the players' visit on 17 June 1557 preceded the execution of Agnes Priest by nearly two months. Clearly the specific timing will have a considerable bearing on ultimate assumptions regarding strategy and reception of performance propaganda.

during the first two years of executions. In Oxford, the first of only two years of executions saw a visit by the King's minstrels (their only visit to the town) and the second saw visits by both the Queen's minstrels and her players (also their only visits to the town).[75] From another perspective, the players visited Rye in 1557 the day after their mayor was committed to the Fleet,[76] and the first of two consecutive years of visits to Beverley began in the year when Sir Francis Leek's players were suppressed.[77] On happier occasions, royal performers visited Barnstaple and Banbury in the same years in which the Queen granted charters of incorporation to the boroughs.[78] Finally, just after Pole's visitation of Lincolnshire and twenty years after the Pilgrimage of Grace began there, the Queen's performers appeared in Louth (1556–57) in their only visit to that shire during the reign.[79]

In some cases the records suggest that the Queen's players were warmly welcomed by local officials. Occasionally they note a specific place of performance associated with local authorities – the town hall in Canterbury, the church in Louth, and the guildhall in Oxford and in Exeter on Corpus Christi day. Oxford hosted a "drynkynge"[80] for the players and other towns hosted a mayor's performance, although this sign of respect was not reserved exclusively for the Queen's performers. In Bristol, for instance, in 1556 the mayor hosted the Earl of Oxford's players and Lord Berkley's players as well as the King and Queen's players. Although rewards were gradated according to the patron's social status, all three received the courtesy of a mayor's play. Thus the royal performers would have been seen by the local audience within the larger performance context created by the performers of two members of the nobility – as well as by the visiting preachers paid by the city at the same time and Protestant executions in the same year. As in other cities,

[75] *Cumberland*, 297; *Bristol*, 61; *Ipswich*, 260–61; *Leicester*, III, 85, 92; *Kent*, 12; *Oxford*, 267; *Devon*, 147.
[76] Rye Chamberlains' Accounts, 60/7, fo. 166b.
[77] A. G. Dickens has termed Beverley "a notable centre of unrest" throughout the reign. From April of 1554 through June of 1557 there were a number of citizens punished for railing against the sacrament and other related offenses. In April of 1556 two individuals, including a pensioned choirman of the Minster, were found to possess heretical books, so that the first visit of the Queen's players to the town coincided with another type of burning – the burning of seditious books. See A. F. Leach (ed.), *Report on the Manuscripts of the Corporation of Beverley, Historical Manuscripts Commission* 54 (1900), 178, 180; Dickens, *Lollards and Protestants*, 223 34, 227–29.
[78] *Devon*, 42; *Banbury*, 16.
[79] The record notes a payment to "ye quenes maties seruantes whenas they plaidd in ye churche," so they could be either her minstrels or her players. As her players appeared in Beverley in 1557 it is more likely that these are her players. Pole delegated the visitation to Bishop John White. He did not attend himself. *Lincolnshire*, 84; Hughes, *Reformation in England*, II, 239.
[80] *Oxford*, 267.

the players would also have been greeted by local authorities regularly engaged in official business with the Privy Council and/or Crown on matters of importance to the town,[81] so that any response to performance propaganda would ultimately have involved a complex intersection of three cultural neighborhoods with a range of interests and concerns in the local community and individual concepts of identity and allegiance.

A brief survey of the cultural neighborhoods traced by performers associated with the Queen and other patrons suggests a possible strategy of theatrical propaganda to counteract resistance to official policies by some local officials, patrons of 'seditious' performers, and individual subjects. But what was the actual effect of propaganda emanating from the court and to what extent would it have enabled the Crown to control the negotiations of power and meaning at the local level? The answer to this question would have depended on the way in which elements of the performance context intersected with the images and ideas through which players constructed their cultural neighborhoods.

COMMUNITY, COURT, AND "COMMEN WELTHE"

Comparatively few plays survive from Mary's reign, but one play, *The Interlude of Wealth and Health*, is thought to have been performed by the Queen's players at court during Christmas festivities in 1554–55,[82] and unlike *Respublica*, its performance requirements are such that it could have been in the Queen's players' repertoire when they first began touring the next spring. If it is a potential common denominator linking local communities and the community of the court, however, it casts doubt on the Crown's ultimate power to control performance patronage as a mechanism for drawing micro-structures of power and knowledge into the desired hegemonic macro-structures of allegiance and meaning.

Like Respublica, the two characters in the title roles of Wealth and Health, along with a third character, Liberty, are misguided and abused by three vices or false counselors before being rescued in a final scene, which concludes with praise of the ruling sovereign. Whereas Respublica is rescued by four ladies (Mercy, Truth, Justice, and Peace) and Mary's

---

[81] *Bristol*, 61–62; *Acts of the Privy Council, 1556–1558*, VI, 198–99, 208, 288, 303.
[82] T. W. Craik, "The Political Interpretation of Two Tudor Interludes: *Temperance and Humility* and *Wealth and Health*," *Review of English Studies*, n.s., 4 (1953), 98–108. Although apparently adapted superficially for publication in Elizabeth's reign (Catholic oaths given to the vices and a concluding blessing on Elizabeth – delivered by a character modeled on Cardinal Pole!), the play was first entered in the Stationers' Register in 1557. See W. W. Greg, *A Bibliography of the English Printed Drama to the Restoration*, 4 vols. (London: Bibliographical Society, 1970), I, 1.

alter ego (Nemesis), Wealth, Health, and Liberty are rescued by "a noble man" of "greet actortty" (450) called Remedy, who is also feared because he is "willing to fulfil his soueraines commaundement" and "not fraide to do right punishment" (454–55).[83] T. W. Craik has drawn attention to Remedy's red cap (834) and elegant gown (625) and the fact that he dwelled "not heare" (621) as an intended connection with Cardinal Pole (who had recently returned from long exile).[84] Unlike Nemesis who appears only at the point of judgment at the end of the play, Remedy appears early on and acts as a kind of paternal figure who knows in advance what the scenario will be and hovers to make sure things do not go too far. Whether intended as a courtly compliment to him or an explicit promotion of his image further afield, Remedy's function in the play clearly announces Pole's role as what the Venetian ambassador termed "the chief instrument in the realm"[85] while at the same time making him a symbol of the renewed role of the Catholic church in ministering to the needs of the country: as Remedy himself says,

> That none of you shall diminishe, nor amisse be tane
> I good remedy therfore may & will speake without blame
> For the comen welth, & helth both of the soule & body
> yt is mi office & power, & therfore I haue my actoritie.
>
> (585–91)

It is tempting to speculate that the players' resumption of touring after Pole's return to England reflects to some degree his understanding of the potential of performance as propaganda, but the most that can be said with any certainty is that many of the ideas expressed in *Wealth and Health* seem to reflect Pole's point of view.[86] When placed within a performance

[83] W. W. Greg (ed.), *The Interlude of Wealth and Health* (Chiswick: Malone Society, 1907); all further references to this play will be to the text of this edition.
[84] Craik, "Political Interpretation," 105–6.
[85] *Calendar of State Papers, Venice*, VI, 1068.
[86] Pole was certainly familiar with the use of spectacle and theatre for political ends as he participated in and attended such events in Italy (*Calendar of State Papers, Venice*, III, 408, 450, 579–82). His library contained the works of Seneca and Aristophanes. See A. B. Emden, *A Biographical Register of the University of Oxford A.D. 1501 to 1540* (Oxford: Clarendon Press, 1974), 733). Craik has drawn comparisons with Thomas Starkey's *A Dialogue between Reginald Pole and Thomas Lupset*, and many more could be made, even to the point of suggesting that the play was, in fact, inspired by the outline and thesis of the *Dialogue*. In his earlier days of acquaintance with Starkey, Pole appears to have subscribed to a number of ideas relating to social, political, and even religious reform. Many of the ideas later associated with advocates of the Reformation, such as the so-called Commonwealth-men, could be traced back to similar origins. Pole's reputation as an advocate for reform within the Catholic Church, in fact, provided the Pope with an excuse for revoking Pole's legatine commission in 1557, but the *Dialogue* is very much a work by Starkey and not Pole, so that correspondences between the play and ideas expressed by Pole at the time of his return

context, either at court or in the provinces, however, the play does not
stand as a closed text for inculcating the official doctrine of an authority figure. Instead, it demonstrates the potential for its performance to
precipitate a volatile mix of responses.

As a complex piece of political propaganda, the play bears considerable analysis, but focusing on its approach to simply one issue of critical
importance in late 1554 and 1555 will serve to crystallize its potential
impact on power relations. After reunification of the church with Rome,
Pole's next agenda item was the return of church lands, but already by
December of 1554 he was meeting staunch opposition, as anticipated,
from "the temporal nobility." Even the Queen's Privy Council showed
little enthusiasm, not surprisingly since they had for the most part benefited substantially by the acquisition of church lands themselves. *Wealth
and Health* may be seen as an appeal to "the people" who Pole thought
could "be reasonably expected to give it [his agenda] all favour and assistance," they "having suffered very great detriment, as since the abolition
of the obedience of the Church, they have been more and more oppressed daily."[87] The matter of social class was a non-issue in *Respublica*,
but in *Wealth and Health* the three main characters are specifically identified as noblemen and members of a court, at least initially, at odds with
each other. Thus their characterization as proud and haughty reflects on
both the nobility and the court. Wealth, for example, is "mutable" (52),
"cruell" (54), "wauerynge" (55), "fykle" (150), and the cause of "much
sorowe and care" (142). He openly declares that "by liberty now I doo
not set" (173). Using a proverb also cited by Miles Huggarde,[88] Shrewd
Wit mocks the noblemen's breach of the tradition of hospitality: "A man
may breke his neck as lyghtly / As his fast in your kechin, or selier truly"
(688–89). Against this, Good Remedy plays the role of the rescuer by
saving them from their woeful inability to choose counselors wisely, and
the resulting general decay, "dupedom," "revell and rout" (678). In his

to England and assumption of new responsibilities are probably more significant. In addition to
items cited below see, for example, "Cardinal Pole's Speech to the Citizens of London, in Behalf
of Religious Houses," in John Strype, *Ecclesiastical Memorials*, iii.ii, 482–510, and John Elder, *The
Copie of a Letter Sent into Scotlande* (London, 1555).

[87] From a letter sent to Mary by Pole, 2 October 1553, *Calendar of State Papers, Venice*, v, 421.

[88] First cited by Craik, "Political Interpretation," 106. There are many parallels between the play
and contemporary printed propaganda, with the same strands of thought and phrases being
appropriated and transformed by both sides. For instance, Huggarde identifies the seizure of
church lands as causing "the decaye of our common wealth," and he associates the evils of
the reformed church with foreigners, the drunken "Hance and Yacob." See *The Displaying of the
Protestantes, and Sondry Their Practises, with a Description of Divers Their Abuses of Late Frequented within
Their Malignaunte Churche* (London, 1556), fos. 85b, 110a, 116b.

sermon-like introductory speech to the three noblemen, Remedy echoes the tone and content of Pole's remarks to the Queen and the Council in a meeting on church lands in December of 1554. After noting that "the chiefe parte of all welth lyeth in great estates / Theyr substance and landes" (569–70), he reminds the noblemen that England's great wealth is derived from "ye grace of god which is our chief forderance" (584).[89]

The implication, made explicit in Pole's meeting, is that noblemen, therefore, should not begrudge returning church lands. In the end, Remedy offers forgiveness and shifts some blame to counselors. He feels "halfe ashamed, that long it hath be sayd / That noble men by such wretches hath ben deceiued" (896–97). However, the patronizing and unflattering portrait of Pole's opponents painted by *Wealth and Health* could not have been met enthusiastically by many members of the court – nor is it likely to have set many aristocratic households ringing with applause as it circulated in the provinces. Moreover, with this type of fractured official portrait on tour, it might explain why an analysis of cultural neighborhoods revealed so little use of theatrical patronage by members of the court to promote Crown policies. The traditional chain of patronage through which the sovereign distributes power to the nobility who in turn distribute favors further down the chain is in fact discredited as a result of the characterization of the nobility. Analysis of performance neighborhoods may lend credibility to Mary's distrust of her Councilors, but it may also reveal the potential weakness derived from a sovereign's ineffective use of patronage. The Venetian ambassador reported that "the country is much exhausted, above all the nobility and the commonalty . . . who chiefly contribute to the subsidies, this penury being caused not so much by the scarcity . . . as by the cessation of all sorts of supplies . . . and salaries . . . which the Court used to give, thus relieving many persons."[90] Concern for eliminating her debt may have inspired parsimony, but even when she did confer favors, David Loades has concluded that Mary seldom dispensed patronage "in accordance with her own future interests" or used "her patronage as an instrument of policy."[91]

---

[89] An eyewitness, Italian account of Pole's meeting is given by his secretary, Alvise Priuli, in a letter sent to Rome (BL Add MS 41577, fos. 161–66a). A summary is given by J. H. Crehan, "The Return to Obedience: New Judgement on Cardinal Pole," *The Month*, n.s., 14 (1955), 221–29.

[90] *Calendar of State Papers, Venice*, VI, 1068.

[91] Loades, *Mary Tudor*, 328–29. For a contemporary Englishman's perspective see Edward Underhill's complaint that despite "great thanks and large promises how good she would be unto us" after his defense of Mary during Wyatt's rebellion, "few or none of us got anything, although she was very liberal to many others, that were enemies unto GOD's Word" (*Tudor Tracts 1532–1588*, 191).

It must be noted as well that Pole, along with the playwright, may have mistakenly collectivized the response of "the people" on several issues, including church lands. Often thanks to the intervention of a noble patron, many civic officials and their towns – including towns visited by the Queen's players – had benefited substantially from the dissolution.[92] By the 1550s, towns were enjoying regular income from former church property and had absorbed it into an evolving collective identity. More importantly, however, both Pole and the playwright failed to appreciate the full ramifications of a more fundamental issue. Pole's Council opposition to the return of church lands had argued that "no outsider should have any say in the disposal of goods or lands in England without authority of Parliament ... [because] England was a *societas perfecta*, a complete civil society, having its parts, spirituality, Lords and Commons, duly knit together and a sovereign for head, just like any living human body."[93] This assertion of England's integrity in the face of potential foreign intervention expressed a sentiment shared not only by the nobility but also in modified form by local governments promoting a distinct civic image and the integrity of their own authority, and even by subjects like John Careless defending the personal integrity of their religious choice while affirming loyalty to city and Queen.

Ironically, the play also encourages this perspective to some degree by introducing a Dutch mercenary, Hance Beerpot, who is expelled with vitriolic comments on aliens by Remedy, the defender of "the comen welth, & helth both of the soule & body" (590). England was notoriously chauvinistic,[94] and both as a theatrical vehicle and a propaganda tactic Hance was guaranteed to elicit a powerful response. Controlling that response would have been another matter, however. Although there may have been times and places in England where Hance would have

---

[92] For example, Norwich acquired the Dominican Friary and the heavily endowed St. Giles hospital; see T. W. Swales, "The Redistribution of the Monastic Lands in Norfolk at the Dissolution," *Norfolk Archaeology* 34 (1969), 14–44. Both the city and the chief citizens of Exeter acquired church lands. The largest single purchaser was Maurice Levermore, who was mayor in 1555. See Joyce A. Youings, "The City of Exeter and the Property of the Dissolved Monasteries," *Report & Transactions of the Devonshire Association for the Advancement of Science, Literature and Art* 84 (1952), 135–37, 139. For other examples see *City Chamberlains' Accounts of the Sixteenth and Seventeenth Centuries*, ed. D. M. Livock, *Bristol Record Society* 24 (1965) xiii, xvii–xviii; Martha C. Skeeters, *Community and Clergy: Bristol and the Reformation c.1530–c.1570* (Oxford: Clarendon Press, 1993), 79–80; A. Crossley, "Early Modern Oxford," in *The City of Oxford, A History of the County of Oxford*, ed. Alan Crossley (Oxford: Institute of Historical Research, 1979), IV, 110–12; *Leicester*, III, 46–47; Tittler, *Architecture and Power*, 77–78.
[93] Crehan, "Return to Obedience," 224.
[94] See, for example, a foreigner's perspective, *Calendar of State Papers, Venice*, VI, 1066, 1085.

produced the desired hegemonic resonance,[95] at this particular time public feeling both inside and outside the court was running so high against the Spanish king, his entourage (some of whom were Flemish), and even the Italians in Pole's household, that the potential for decidedly divergent responses must have been enormous.[96] By 1557, in fact, Thomas Stafford's rebellious proclamation issued from Scarborough Castle may have voiced the increasingly common apprehension that the Queen, "being naturallye borne haulfe Spanyshe and haulfe Englyshe" had shown "herselfe a whole Spanyarde, and no Englyshe woman."[97]

More generally, as a mechanism for constituting subjects at either the court or the extremities, the play betrays little sensitivity to "the people" and the potential complexity of their perspectives. All moral interludes share a kinship with sermons, but this play's lengthy introductory debate, by "way of communicacion" (39), and Remedy's preachy dialogue place particular dramaturgical emphasis on an appeal to the ears over the eyes – without the advantages of the sermon's more closed format. David Loades has noted the mistaken emphasis which Mary and Pole placed on assertions of authority over passionate persuasion,[98] and Remedy's strong association with authority bears this out. *Wealth and Health* has no room for a counterpart to the character People in *Respublica*.[99] Instead,

[95] The intention might have been to construct a negative image of foreigners associated with the Protestant faith that would counteract the image of the foreign Pope. The character may be an attempt to draw attention to two generally popular Crown initiatives – the banishment of seditious aliens and the 1555 prohibition of Hanseatic merchants from virtually all trade in England. Furthermore, the 1549 uprisings in Norfolk and Devon had been put down with the aid of foreign mercenaries, including Germans, so that Hance may have inspired a negative reminder of Edward's reign if he appeared in Norwich, Barnstaple, and Exeter (Penry Williams, *The Later Tudors: England 1547–1603* [Oxford: Clarendon Press, 1995], 55, 121; *Calendar of State Papers, Foreign Series, of the Reign of Edward VI, 1547–1553*, ed. William B. Turnbull [London, 1861], 30–34). In a town such as Maldon, which had a substantial Germanic population, Hance could have had a polarizing effect, but his characterization attached such negative connotations to the idea of war that the piece would probably have been unplayable by 1557, well before the Queen's players visited Maldon in 1558. See W. J. Petchey, *A Prospect of Maldon: 1500–1689* (Chelmsford: Essex Record Office, 1991), 54–57; Ian Lancashire, 397.
[96] For contemporary responses to the Spanish in England see *The Chronicle of Queen Jane and Mary*, 81; *Calendar of Letters, Despatches, and State Papers, Relating to the Negotiations between England and Spain Preserved in the Archives at Vienna, Simancas, Besançon and Brussels*, ed. Royall Tyler, et al., 13 vols. (London: HMSO, 1862–1954), XIII, 56, 60, 72, 216; *The Diary of Henry Machyn*, ed. J. G. Nichols, Camden Society 42 (1848), 74, 79, 86, 96; and *The Accession Coronation and Marriage of Mary Tudor as Related in Four Manuscripts of the Escorial*, ed. and trans. C. V. Malfatti (Barcelona: n.p., 1956), 92–95. Contact with the Spanish was not limited to the court and London either. In 1553–54 Oxford, for instance, entertained three "strayngers of Spayne" (*Oxford*, 220).
[97] Strype, *Ecclesiastical Memorials*, III.ii, 516.
[98] *The Oxford Martyrs* (London: B. T. Batsford, 1970), 258–59.
[99] If Nicholas Udall was the author of *Respublica*, then it is instructive that he, like Morison, had immediate past experience with "the people's" insistence on a channel for reconstituting a

Remedy complains about the difficulty of maintaining Wealth, Health, and Liberty because "the people be so variable / And many be so wilfull, they will not be reformable" (539–40). Later he warns that "Craft wyll out and disceite wyll haue a fall" (937) and "god wyl punish the people when they be detelt" (798). That Remedy is anticipated with fear and associated with punishment and suspicion would only have served to highlight rather than counteract the more inflammatory and competitive performance propaganda connected with subjects like John Careless.

The absence of a role for the Queen in the play parallels her strategy, as noted by the Venetian ambassador, of governing through Pole, and it highlights the observation made by a number of scholars that there was no sustained effort to construct a particular public image for Mary like that suggested by Morison.[100] Taken in the context of the urban community and the dynamics of power relationships within the network of theatrical patronage, Pole's severe image was not an especially fortunate choice for the Crown's public face. His efforts to establish authority as a character as well as the principal agent of the Crown are reflected in attempts to dominate the politics of knowledge through suppression, censorship, and sometimes competing propaganda. However, viewed from the perspective of "the commen people" in the urban community, at least, the gap between intended response and actual negotiated meaning could have been substantial. Local government had a vested interest in demonstrating loyalty to the Crown and maintaining public order, but when faced with Crown policies which they saw as contrary to the "common welthe," they were prepared, with varying degrees of political tact, to assert a strengthening sense of power to constitute their own civic identity and integrity – and, implicitly, the role of the sovereign within the "common welthe." For the urban community, as well as for members of the nobility and gentry, inside and outside the court, patronage of performers and sponsorship of theatre and / or spectacle was one mechanism for asserting power. Performative resistance was another. The maypole

sovereign's policies. Just as Morison had been set to work in Henry's day to respond to the demands arising out of the Pilgrimage of Grace, so too Udall had been set to work on a response to the 16 articles tendered during the western uprising of 1549. Both writers invoked the rhetoric of "common weal" to portray a caring king and assert the importance of obedient and unified subjects (Morison, *A Remedy for Sedition*, A2a, A3a, A4, B3b, D2; "Udall's Answer to the Commoners of Devonshire and Cornwall," in Nicholas Pocock (ed.), *Troubles Connected with the Prayer Book of 1549, Camden Society* 37 (1884), 142, 147).

[100] This conclusion has been reached by a number of scholars examining a variety of evidence: Anglo, *Images*, 108–9; Loades, *Mary Tudor*, 209–10, 332–37; Young, *Tudor and Jacobean Tournaments*, 30. John N. King has offered an alternative perspective in *Tudor Royal Iconography: Literature and Art in an Age of Religious Crisis* (Princeton: Princeton University Press, 1989), 182–221.

erected by the Widnes mob and the merry martyrdom contemplated by John Careless – and more grimly dramatized by others across the country – were assertions of power by "the co*mm*en people." For subjects in positions of authority, there was non-participation in ceremonial or official functions. These could include cathedral services, to which the Bristol mayor and alderman had to be swinged by dean and chapter; Protestant burnings, for which the Privy Council had to order the sanctioning participation of local magnates; and possibly even the patronage of touring players, which all but one of Mary's Privy Councilors, even those with a prior tradition of patronage, avoided.

The unusually limited nature of cultural neighborhoods produced by performers associated with court patrons meant that such informal influence depended all the more on the Queen's players. This along with the apparent modesty of court spectacle and the potentially complex impact on tour of at least one court play suggests that Marian performance history, at least, cannot be told simply from the perspective of the court. Despite the Crown's attempts to control and censor the mechanisms of communication, a play associated with the Queen's own players opened the door to negotiated meanings which suggest that as in the case of printed propaganda,[101] the Crown's counter campaign was neither closely controlled and orchestrated nor especially sensitive to its audience. There may have been a strategy behind their travels, but for the players the theatrical potential of a character like Hance Beerpot may have outweighed any possibility of divergent political responses. The patron/client relationship demonstrated by *Respublica*'s performer/counselor approach contrasts with any later intended role for the players as one-way communicators between Crown and people. Yet, if Mary and Pole had been more sensitive to the full performance text of play and contextual response, they might have understood what Privy Councilors, local government, and individual subjects were trying to communicate. So far, the impact of the Reformation in England had had less to do with religion than with social and political reform.[102] Thus, a lack of enthusiasm for Mary's religion by individuals at court or among "the co*mm*en people" did not necessarily constitute a crisis or indicate a lack of concern for the "co*mm*en welthe" or allegiance to the Queen. The network of cultural neighborhoods traced by her interluders and those

---

[101] Loades, *The Reign of Mary Tudor*, 285.

[102] See, for instance, Christopher Haigh, *Reformation and Resistance in Tudor Lancashire* (Cambridge: Cambridge University Press, 1975), esp. 178–94; and Felicity Heal and Rosemary O'Day (eds.), *Church and Society in England: Henry VIII to James I* (London: Macmillan, 1977).

of other patrons was one of many mechanisms which Foucault would recognize as vehicles for the circulation of power and knowledge. The Queen's players gave the Crown a presence and influence within this forum at the local level, but it is doubtful that they dominated the resulting negotiations of meaning which constituted subject, sovereign, and "co*mm*en welthe." An agenda of conservative religious reaction married to major foreign alliances ran contrary to the spirit of reform reflected in her government's urban policy and evolving concepts of nationalism associated with "co*mm*en welthe" by even her own players. A claim by one of her subjects that the Queen "loves another realm better than this"[103] represented a much more fundamental threat to her power and the allegiance of "the co*mm*en people" than the religious independence asserted by John Careless. Elizabeth would recognize this and mobilize all the resources of her court, including spectacle and "patronage theatre," to marry her royal image with the English "co*mm*en welthe."[104] Through a much more developed and complex system of patronage, her openness to public appearances outside the court and the concept of Gloriana as an embodiment of the English nation, she found channels for both her subjects' participation in constituting the role and identity of their sovereign, and the Crown's greater control over evolving concepts of "co*mm*en welthe" and the allegiance of "the co*mm*en people."[105]

---

[103] Stated by William Harris in a Deptford tavern, 20 April 1556 (*Acts of the Privy Council*, v, 265).

[104] Mary appears not to have made much of the opportunity presented by royal entries for publicly constructing an image, English or otherwise. Elizabeth on the other hand consciously created images and appealed to the eyes as well as the ears. In her coronation entry, for instance, a pageant reminiscent of the Norwich show of 1556 featured two mountains representing "a decayed common weale" and "a flourishyng common weale," from which emerged Father Time and his daughter Truth. When presented with a "Byble in Englishe," the Queen "kyssed it, and with both her handes held vp the same, and so laid it vpon her brest, with great thankes to the citie therfore," thereby publicly linking herself with an English, Christian "commonweal" (Anglo, *Spectacle, Pageantry*, 350–51).

[105] Further information on patrons and their performers as well as maps for the analysis of patron/performer travels relating to this chapter may be found at the *Shakespeare and Theatrical Patronage* website at http://icdweb.cc.purdue.edu/~pwhite/patronage/ and at my own website at http://uregina.ca/~blackstm/

Patrons, players, and audiences

CHAPTER 8

Privy Councilors as theatre patrons

Andrew Gurr

There is not much evidence to tell us what kind of enjoyment Elizabeth's Privy Councilors got from watching plays. When the country itself was so divided over playgoing it would be surprising if they all had one mind on the subject. The official Privy Council support for playing in Elizabeth's time was always based on the ostensible need to provide the Queen with her annual entertainments. Something more than that, however, can be found in the motivation of some of the leading Councilors. Some odd items of evidence in the conduct of Elizabeth's two ministers who gave most support to playing, chimerical though most of them are, suggest that these men had stronger reasons for giving their support so consistently to the professional companies than the official arguments admit.

There were divisions over playgoing even inside the town councils which worked hardest to keep players out of their bailiwicks. While every Lord Mayor of London tried to stop it, many of the councils outside London were strikingly inconsistent. Bristol banned all playing in the city's guildhall in 1585, on the grounds that playing was too frivolous an activity for the town's official meeting-place. The town council renewed the order firmly in 1596, declaring "there shall not be any players in interludes suffred at any tyme hereafter to play in the yeald hall of Bristoll beinge the place of justice." This was issued in February. It imposed a fine of five pounds on any future mayor who broke the ban, to be deducted from the mayoral fee of forty pounds. None the less, in July of that same year Derby's Men appear in the records receiving thirty shillings and in August the Queen's Men were given two pounds, both for playing "in the Guildehalle." There is no record of the mayoral fee being deducted for this pair of acts of deliberate dereliction. What one mayor had ordained, his immediate successor ignored. Similar evidence of inconsistency amongst its membership can be found in the various Privy Council orders that relate to the professional playing companies.

In June 1584, George Whetstone's friend William Fleetwood, Re-corder of London, reported on a division in the Privy Council which pinpoints who the chief backers of playgoing were. Not surprisingly, they were the two Councilors most directly concerned with playing. One was the Lord Chamberlain, who was then Charles Howard, Lord Effingham, Lord Admiral, later the Earl of Nottingham. The other was his father-in-law, Henry Carey, first Baron Hunsdon, who seems then to have been working as Vice Chamberlain, probably in anticipation of Howard's promotion to Lord Admiral. These two had some support from Christopher Hatton, although he did not stand up with them on this occasion. Fleetwood wrote:

Uppon Sonndaye my Lo. [Mayor] sent ij Aldermen to the Court for the sup-pressing and pulling downe of the Theatre and Curten. All the LL. agreed thereunto, saving my Lord Chamberlen and mr. Viz-chamberlen [Howard and Carey], but we obteyned a lettre to suppresse theym all. Upon the same night I sent for the quenes players and my Lo. of Arundel his players, and they all willinglie obeyed the LL. lettres. The chiefestes of her highnes players advised me to send for the owner of the Theatre, who was a stubburne fellow, and to bynd hym. I dyd so; he sent me word that he was my Lo. of Hunsdons man, and that he wold not come at me, but he wold in the mornyng ride to my lord.[1]

The Theatre's owner, James Burbage, had once been a player in Leicester's company. He was now an impresario, landlord to the play-ers who used his Theatre in Shoreditch, and had evidently taken on the livery of Lord Hunsdon, as in some capacity his servant. What that capacity was, we cannot know, but it must have meant that the lord had some connection with the players, or at least with the new places for playing in London. Carey was patron of a traveling company, and Burbage was clearly no longer a traveler.[2] This association of the blunt, enterprising Burbage with the blunt, forthright Lord Hunsdon was one that lasted for the rest of their lives, and involved both of them in setting up the great duopoly of 1594, with the Lord Chamberlain making himself patron to Burbage's son's company, which included Shakespeare.

---

[1] Quoted in E. K. Chambers, *The Elizabethan Stage*, 4 vols. (Oxford: Clarendon Press, 1923), IV, 297–98.
[2] A company with Carey as its patron was recorded at Bath in June 1583 and Exeter in July of that year. In June 1585 what seems to have been a joint company of the Lord Chamberlain and the Lord Admiral (Carey and Howard) appeared at Dover, and later at Leicester, and at court in the next season. Neither company was used separately by their patron for the court seasons through this time.

Burbage's role in 1584 as a London impresario with his base in Shoreditch may be the reason why he had not been selected the year before to become one of the new company patronized by the Queen. Having been a player in Leicester's Men in the 1570s when they secured the first patent to protect the company, he had evidently left the Earl's service when he built the Theatre in 1576 in favor of a more congenial and London-based master, Henry Carey.[3] Fleetwood's letter implies that the Queen's Men were then playing at the Theatre, while Arundel's Men presumably were lodged at the neighboring Curtain. It is at least possible that for Burbage to play host to the newly established royal company was a mark of Privy Council interest in seeing that the new company got the best favors while in London. Later in 1584, as part of Charles Howard's attempt to settle the differences between the Lord Mayor and the players, and to secure a place in the city for the Queen's Men, they were given the right to play at certain specified city inns. But in June the aldermen's plea was about the suburban playhouses, and the Council's directive was sent to where the players evidently were more durably lodged, in the suburbs.

Fleetwood's version of Burbage's reaction is that he at first refused to believe that his patron as a Privy Councilor would have signed such an order. Only when he saw the signature and was warned about the consequences of disobedience did he give in. Orders issued by a divided Privy Council, however, rarely got their way. Carey, having joined Howard in openly disagreeing with the decision, may then have done some work behind the scenes to preserve Burbage's playhouse, because the order to pull the theatres down was not carried out.

The order may have been no more than a threatening gesture to indicate sympathy for the Lord Mayor. Over the years the Privy Council issued several orders to suppress and demolish the suburban playhouses. Besides the order of 1584, there was a notorious one in 1597, aimed chiefly at the Swan, and later ones aimed at the unlicensed playhouses such as the Curtain. Not one of them was ever carried out. How much this reflects the divisions within the Council and how much the practical difficulty of enforcing such orders is not easy to determine. The technical and legal difficulties of enforcing any demolition, and the deterrent effect of the likely costs involved in compensating the owners, must have been one practical consideration. The Council may simply have been

---

[3] Apart from helping his company to secure their status in law in the early 1570s, Leicester seems to have done little for them. See Sally-Beth MacLean, "The Politics of Patronage: Dramatic Records in Robert Dudley's Household Books," *Shakespeare Quarterly* 44 (1993), 175–82.

satisfied with making the kind of disapproving noises that successive
Lord Mayors begged for every year. More likely, though, the divisions
within the Council that are reflected in Fleetwood's letter, combined
with the point that the authority to execute such orders lay with the
Lord Chamberlain, the one figure least likely to insist on their enforcement, meant that the Council's officers were reluctant to act quickly,
and, in the absence of any further urging from the lords of the Council,
adopted the bureaucrat's resource of doing nothing.

It is a nice question how much Howard and his father-in-law were
exercised in 1584 by a real enthusiasm for plays, enough to make them
support the players against their enemies on the Council, and how much
by their principal Council duty, to provide Elizabeth with her Christmas
season of entertainment. Plays provided by the professional companies
were much cheaper and easier to obtain for court performances than
the masques which had been the predominant Christmas game until the
1570s. At court the school and chorister groups had usually provided
most of the plays that supplemented the masques, but by 1584 the boy
groups were rapidly losing favor to the adult players. Between 1564 and
1576 forty-two boy plays in all were presented at court compared with
twenty-seven adult company plays. Nineteen of the adult companies'
twenty-seven, however, were staged only in the last four of these seasons,
and the adult company share increased steadily up to the appointment
of the Queen's own company in 1583. The existence of the Theatre and
the Curtain from 1576 and 1577 also gave the players a more secure
basis for playing in London for long periods of time than the city inns
they had hitherto used. With those two kinds of backing, the professional
players were now rapidly creating the taste by which the Councilors could
appreciate them. Improvement in the quality of adult playing, marked
by the establishment of the Queen's Men, gave a strong reason for the
Privy Councilors to favor the leading professional companies against the
Lord Mayor.

Officially, the professional companies were controlled from 1578 by the
Lord Chamberlain's executive officer, the Master of the Revels. Edmund
Tilney had been appointed in 1578, and received his patent in 1581. He
was related to the Howards and also the Stanleys, two families which gave
patrons to the leading professional companies of the 1590s. Tilney's son
reported much later that the original appointment was fixed by Tilney's
cousin, Charles Howard. In 1578 Howard certainly had an interest in
the playing companies, having acted as the Chamberlain's deputy in
1574–75, and having started his own company subsequently. But it is

doubtful whether, not yet being a Privy Councilor, he had sufficient pull on his own to secure the post for Tilney.[4] If the claim is true, it is one of the earliest hints of Howard's long-running involvement in the control and promotion of the playing companies. Tilney was an excellent appointment. He took the work very seriously, and probably did more to help develop the companies than any of his successors.

The official reason for the Privy Council to give its protection to the professional companies was voiced in a letter dated 24 December 1578 from the Council to the Lord Mayor. It lists the companies that the Council thought suitable for performing at court. A Council minute notes

A letter to the Lord Maiour, &c, requiring him to suffer the Children of her Majesties Chappell, the servauntes of the Lord Chamberlaine, therle of Warwicke, the Erle of Leicester, the Erle of Essex and the Children of Powles, and no companies els, to exercise playeng within the Cittie, whome their Lordships have onlie allowed thereunto by reason that the companies aforenamed are appointed to playe this tyme of Christmas before her Majestie.[5]

This was a short-term order, giving the new Master of the Revels authority to license London performing by four companies of adult players together with two London choir-school companies. For the coming Christmas season it supplied six companies of known worth, all of which were experienced in performing at court.

Using the Queen's name and interests to authorize the professional companies became the standard reason for all subsequent protective orders. A minute of 3 December 1581 announced amongst its priorities, after the need to protect the country against plague, the further need to safeguard the royal pleasure against the opposition to playing:

Whereas certayne companyes of players hertofore useinge thier common exercise of playing within and aboute the Cittie of London have of late in respect of the generall infection within the Cittie ben restrayned by their Lordships' commaundement from playing, the said players this daye exhibited a peticion unto their Lordships, humbly desiring that as well in respecte of their pore estates, having noe other meanes to systayne them, their wyves and children but their exercise of playing, and were only brought up from their youthe in the practise and profession of musicke and playeng, as for that the sicknes within the Cittie was well slaked, so as noe danger of infection could follow by the assemblyes of people at their players, yt would please their Lordships therfore to grante

---

[4] See Richard Dutton, *Mastering the Revels: The Regulation and Censorship of English Renaissance Drama* (Iowa City: University of Iowa Press, 1991), 44–45. Charles Howard's son claimed in 1616 that his father had originally secured the office for Tilney.

[5] *The Acts of the Privy Council of England*, ed. John Roche Dasent, 32 vols. (London, HMSO, 1892–1907), XI, 73.

them licence to use their sayd exercise of playeng as heretofore they had don; their Lordships their upon for the consyderations aforesaid as also for that they are to present certayne playes before the Quenes Majestie for her solace in the Christmas tyme now following, were contented to yeld unto their said humble peticion, and ordered that the Lord Mayor of the Cittie of London should suffer and permitt them to use and exercise their trade of playing in and about the Cittie as they have hertofore accustomed upon the weeke dayes only, being holy dayes or other dayes, so as they doe forbeare wholye to playe on the Sabothe Daye, either in the forenone or afternone, which to doe they are by this their Lordships' order expressly denyed and forbidden.[6]

Subsequent orders reiterated this position, just as the successive Lord Mayors voiced the same arguments against any public playing in the city and the suburbs.

The available evidence upholds this of course as the Council's sole reason for protecting the players. There are no signs amongst any of the Privy Councilors at this time of any open or indeed any covert enthusiasm for playgoing. Besides the Earl of Leicester and the Lord Chamberlain, Sussex, both Carey and Howard were patrons of companies, but neither of the two latter seem to have used the groups to which they gave their names for their own pleasure, and both maintained a policy while they controlled the festive seasons of not using their own companies for court performances. It was the Lord Chamberlain's business to control playing at one end through the censorship of playbooks, a duty now exercised by Tilney, and at the other by ensuring that the best companies were on hand each Christmas. In the year following the establishment of the Queen's Men, 1584, the Council did work collectively to support the professional players. Thomas Radcliffe, the Earl of Sussex, the long-serving Lord Chamberlain and a bitter enemy on the Council to the Earl of Leicester's faction, died in June 1583. No successor was appointed, and that left that year's Christmas celebrations dangerously unsupervised. The Privy Council had to face the problem as a full committee when the season loomed. Seven Councilors, Burghley, Bromley, Bedford, Knollys, Hunsdon (Carey), Hatton, and Walsingham, signed a letter to the Lord Mayor on 26 November. They used the arguments of the December 1581 order, now specifying that only the Queen's new company was licensed to perform:

Forasmuch as (God be thanked) there is no suche infection within that citie at this presente, but that hir majesties playeres may be suffered to playe within the liberties as heretofore they have done, especially seeing they are shortly to

---

[6] *Acts of the Privy Council*, xiii, 269.

present some of their doeinges before hir majestie, we have thought good at this present to pray your Lp. to geve order, that the said players may be licenced so to doe within the Citie and liberties betwene this and shroftyde next; so as the same be not done upon sondaies, but upon some other weke daies, at convenient times.[7]

In the absence of the rightful officer, the Council was acting collectively. Clearly a new Lord Chamberlain was needed. It was a major Council post, its importance already signaled by the augmentation of the Revels Office in 1578 and the creation of the Queen's Men in 1583. Charles Howard was in some sense the heir apparent, but in view of the delay he was evidently not everyone's choice. His appointment to the Privy Council as Lord Chamberlain was announced at the beginning of the new year.

The Privy Council in 1584 was a complex organism. Most of its members were closely related by blood or marriage, and its numbers were small enough for it to maintain the appearance of consensus on most matters. But it had its factions and its rivalries, and some intense enmities.[8] Its Secretary, Francis Walsingham, had been appointed as a client of Lord Burghley, but he soon allied himself with the Council's charismatic antagonist figure, the Earl of Leicester, partly to develop what has been called the "war party" faction against the more moderate

---

[7] Chambers, *Elizabethan Stage*, IV, 295–96; *Dramatic Records of the City of London*, ed. E. K. Chambers, Malone Society Collections I (Oxford: Oxford University Press, 1907), 66.

[8] Some of the enmities were distinctly petty. In 1597, for instance, Howard was appointed Earl of Nottingham. This gave him precedence over the Earl of Essex, much to the younger earl's fury. What makes Howard's belated promotion to an earldom most intriguing is its connection with the death of his father-in-law, Henry Carey, the Baron Hunsdon, in July 1596, and the subsequent appointment of Carey's son and heir to the Lord Chamberlainship. Howard had worked long and happily with his father-in-law, handing over the Lord Chamberlainship to him in 1584, and joining him to set up the duopoly of new playing companies in 1594. Howard's equal status as a baron was offset by the difference in their ages, and the avuncular role that Carey played with him. But Henry Carey's son George inherited the Hunsdon title in 1596, and after an interim of some months while Lord Cobham held the post, he became Lord Chamberlain and a Privy Councilor early in 1597. Like Howard, George Carey had a distinguished military past, having commanded the land forces on the Isle of Wight at the time of the Armada. But he was quite a few years Howard's junior, and the younger man's barony is the most likely reason for Howard to have pushed for his own superior title in that year. There is no readier explanation for the timing of Howard's promotion. He urged it strongly for himself, and there is little other reason why he should have waited for recognition so long after his glories against the Armada. In 1596 he did win glory with his share in the Cadiz expedition. And in the wake of that fraught excursion his promotion to become Earl of Nottingham may have given him a secret glee at achieving a rank which gave him precedence in court ceremonial over his co-leader at Cadiz, the Earl of Essex. Certainly that enraged Essex. But his mind did not usually work in such malicious ways. His sense of self-importance was a constant factor in his thinking, and it is likely that the desire to rank above his brother-in-law George, now that George had his father's post on the Privy Council, weighed on him more than the thought of preceding Essex on state occasions.

position of Burghley and the Queen. There was little consistency in the factional alliances, though. Personal enmities, one of the better advertised of which was the Lord Chamberlain Sussex's overt hatred of Leicester, probably played their part quite as much as did political and family loyalties. It is never easy to identify what motivated particular actions in such a volatile organism. On the particular policy of attitudes to plays, the motives even of Leicester, the most positive supporter of his own playing company, and the man whose actions are in the main most readily identifiable, appear to have been dominated by his political needs.

Leicester's actions speak louder than his words over playgoing. Once, when he was appealed to on the subject in his role as Oxford's Chancellor, he conceded to the Vice Chancellor that he thought that visits by the professional players were not good for the students, although he did maintain that they could benefit from seeing and acting in academic plays. As Chancellor of Oxford, he confirmed the university's decision to ban "common stage players" in 1584, saying in a letter that he thought "the prohibicion of common stage players very requisite," although he would not like to see academic plays by students themselves banned. This was consistently the view of the University authorities, and had some backing from the Privy Council at large.[9] The ban was renewed in 1593, in the form of a letter from the Privy Council to the Vice Chancellor and Masters of the colleges. The letter was signed by both Cecils and others including Essex and Charles Howard, the Lord Admiral. The message was to be passed on to the mayor of Oxford to ensure that the ban held for a five-mile radius around Oxford. Cambridge did the same.

Leicester was not averse to seeing plays himself, though his taste seems to have followed his advice to Oxford, favoring academic plays over the "public offerings." He saw Gager's play *Meleager* at Oxford along with Henry Herbert, Earl of Pembroke, in 1585. His attitude to his own playing company was remote, except to give them political support. He had run a company since the late 1550s, and its lengthy record of touring up to 1588 shows what value a great lord could get from having a company wearing his livery made welcome in all the major towns. He gave them no money, and hardly ever seems to have made use of their services

---

[9] The celebrated dispute held in public at Oxford through the 1590s, when William Gager, John Rainolds, and others argued about the propriety of seeing plays, was in its way an extension of the debate about this stated position. On the whole, it was authority confronting the play-seeking students. See Chambers, *Elizabethan Stage*, IV, 245.

to entertain himself and his friends.[10] They added to his glory, not his pleasures. But he did give them tangible support on the Council.

In 1572 the six leading players in Leicester's company wrote to him asking for his protection against the forthcoming statute aimed at controlling vagabondage and unlicensed traveling. Whether it was the 1572 statute, or whether Leicester felt that his players did need some specific protection against his enemy Radcliffe, the Lord Chamberlain, he did use his power two years after their pleading letter, when he secured them a royal patent. Issued on 10 May 1574, this was the first written patent for a playing company ever to be allocated by the government.[11] For the players it was an invaluable piece of paper. When Tilney was appointed Master of the Revels four years later such patents became standard, but Leicester's was by some way the first. The initiative for such an innovation must have been Leicester's own: only he could have interceded with the Queen to secure such a unique license. Radcliffe, the Lord Chamberlain, might have done it, but he would have wanted it for his own company, not his enemy's. In part at least it gave Leicester's Men protection against the Chamberlain, as well as a means to bring the company to the royal notice. In the next Christmas festivities, 1574/75, Leicester's Men performed for the first time in ten years, playing more often than the other adult company and the three boy groups of that season. The Lord Chamberlain's own company did not perform, probably because the company's patron was sick and away from the court in 1574–75.

One major question that the long record of traveling the country and of playing at court by Leicester's company invites is whether the senior patrons of the professional playing companies, including the leading Privy Councilors, made any use of their companies to promote their own political positions. Like the other companies of these early years, Leicester's Men have left few traces of their thinking, apart from one demonstration of loyalty to their lord at Norwich in 1588 when a cobbler insulted Leicester's "ragged staff" emblem.[12] Leicester's prominent role on the Privy Council, his leadership with Walsingham of the more zealous anti-Catholics, his standing as political leader of the Puritan movement, and his consistent support of the "war party" on the Council have left

---

[10] Sally-Beth MacLean, "The Politics of Patronage," 177, notes an entry just after Easter 1559 recording a payment of 20s. to "your L players." There are no other signs that he made any direct use of them.

[11] The full patent is in *Dramatic Records of the City of London*, III.262–63.

[12] See *Norwich*, ed. David Galloway, Records of Early English Drama (REED) (Toronto: University of Toronto Press, 1984), 90.

no visible marks on the work of his playing company. His men wore his livery around the country, though, and the civic records of payments to the professional travelers suggest that mayors paid more attention to the status of their lord than the quality of their playing. How far this might have translated into loyal upholding of their lord's politics is a question for which the surviving texts provide no answers. Attempts have been made to see the repertoire of adult plays in these years, and particularly the plays of Leicester's Men, as upholding a rigorously Protestant dogma. Unfortunately, these attempts are undermined by the absence of reliable texts or even titles for the plays they performed.

It is plausible to claim, as Paul Whitfield White does, that "many Protestant leaders in the church and in the civil government came around to accepting playgoing as suitable recreation and recognizing once again its power as a medium of shaping public opinion."[13] Leicester, as the outstanding leader of the activists against the threat from Catholic Spain throughout the 1570s and 1580s, could have used his players to reinforce his case and his position. Equally, it is inconceivable that the players themselves would not have known what their patron stood for, and supported it in their plays. There is a strong possibility that on the one hand Leicester himself, or on the other the players and their writers, chose to present plays which supported the patron's public activities. But the dearth of play-texts leaves it as only an inference. The positive evidence for Privy Councilors finding plays useful rests mainly with their actions to protect the companies, and the few slight hints that individual Councilors consistently thought them worth protecting.

The figure who acted most positively and consistently through a lengthy career in government to support professional playing was Charles Howard. A committee man, lacking the charisma and the flamboyant self-advertising that went with it of a Leicester or an Essex, he is chiefly known as the man who was in charge of the English navy when the Armada set sail. This ignores both his uniquely long career in the service of two monarchs (born two years after Elizabeth, he died at the end of 1624 aged 88, almost outliving King James), and his mind for tactics and logistics that served the players even better than it served the navy. He was a tactician and committee man, a problem-solver rather than a strategist and commander. His skills were less colorful than his stately manner and his carefully noble dress. He was easy to ridicule for the smallness

---

[13] Paul Whitfield White, *Theatre and Reformation: Protestantism, Patronage and Playing in Tudor England* (Cambridge: Cambridge University Press, 1993), 173. See especially the chapter entitled "Changing Reformation Attitudes Towards Theatre," 163–74.

of his thinking over such clumsy devices as his remarriage early in the new reign, when he was sixty-eight, to Margaret, the nineteen-year-old daughter of the Earl of Moray and a cousin of King James.

This was a union that attracted inevitable mockery over the likely parentage of the several children that the marriage produced in the next fifteen years. His remarriage was a maladroit attempt to establish with the new King a relationship similar to that he had enjoyed with the dead Queen, which first secured his position at court. His first wife, Katherine Carey, was Queen Elizabeth's closest and most durable friend. She had died only a week before the Queen herself, six months before he married the young Margaret. The idea that in marrying a Stuart Charles Howard could establish a similarly close relationship with the new monarch, for all the discrepancy in the pair's ages, has never been regarded, either then or now, as a particularly adroit political maneuver.

He is generally seen as rather dull. He was a tall, and distinctly handsome man, who dressed elegantly but lacked airs or grandeur, and Robert Naunton said of him that he was "for his person as goodly a gentleman as the times had any, if nature had not been more intentive to complete his person than fortune to make him rich." That was certainly true of his early life at Elizabeth's court. In his fifties the Admiralty made him rich, but although he acquired a lot of properties he never bothered to put them on show. Above all, he was loyal to Elizabeth. Naunton summed him up as "a brave, honest and good man, and a faithful servant to his mistress, and such an one as the Queen out of her own princely judgment knew to be a fit instrument for her service, for she was proficient in the reading of men as well as books."[14]

Charles Howard, the second Lord Effingham, was born in 1536. A grandson of the second of the Howards who were the Tudor dukes of Norfolk, his father became Lord Chamberlain and (under Mary) Lord Admiral before him. His early career moved slowly, as his father groomed him to inherit his own offices. He started as an MP in 1562, undertaking minor duties till he succeeded to his father's title when the latter died in January 1573. As an MP, Howard became a member of Gray's Inn in 1564 and a Cambridge MA shortly before his accession to the peerage, in 1571. Both were fairly honorific titles, that went with social rank rather than personal interests, though he did become a collector of books and rare manuscripts once he could afford it. What he really gained in his early career was the promise of a secure status at court through his marriage in

[14] Robert Naunton, *Fragmenta Regalia*, ed. John S. Cerovski (Washington, DC: Folger Shakespeare Library, 1985), 68–69.

1563 to Elizabeth's cousin and friend, Katherine Carey, Henry Carey's daughter. Through all of his earlier years, which included some naval work and some courtly escort duties, he had no real say at court until his appointment to the Privy Council as Lord Chamberlain on 1 January 1584.

For this post he had been preparing himself through more than a decade. As a junior peer his naval services for the Privy Council may have been designed to prepare him for his eventual accession to his father's other main office, the Lord Admiralship, which, for a less than affluent nobleman, was the real prize. But his first real duty at court came soon after his father's death, in relation to his father's other main office. The only obvious reason why Howard should have been authorized through 1574–75 to stand in for his ailing cousin, the Earl of Sussex, as Lord Chamberlain was that he was recognized as the proper successor to the office once the current holder, Sussex, was out of the way.

That initial stint may have been what prompted Howard to start a professional playing company of his own. The first record of a company under his name appears in the provincial records in 1576, when he was forty.[15] It is quite possible that, following his stint as deputy Chamberlain, Howard chose to set a company up specifically to perform at court in the 1576/77 season, as they did, because the first appearance of his company's name in provincial records dates only from the following autumn. That suggests a positively interventionist policy. In that following autumn they played in the usual pre-court performance territories, Sussex and East Anglia, as if expecting a summons to court for the coming Christmas season. The Lord Chamberlain Sussex ran his own company, which performed at court in every year of his chamberlainship, and Howard may have felt the need to provide a similar resource, while he readied himself for his own accession to the chamberlainship. His company performed two plays, called *Tooley* and *The Solitary Knight*, at court in the 1576/77 season, after his term as Vice Chamberlain ended. They played at court again in the next season. A clerk at Bristol in 1577/78 was keen enough on the companies who visited the town to record the titles or "matter" of their plays, and for Lord Howard's he wrote that "their matter was the Q. of Ethiopia," presumably a play about Solomon's Queen of Sheba.[16]

---

[15] The only reasonably full biography of Howard is Robert W. Kenny's *Elizabeth's Admiral: The Political Career of Charles Howard Earl of Nottingham, 1536–1624* (Baltimore: Johns Hopkins University Press, 1970).

[16] J. T. Murray, *English Dramatic Companies, 1558–1642*, 2 vols. (London, 1910; repr., Russell and Russell, 1963), II, 214.

On the Privy Council, Howard, like his father-in-law Henry Carey, held to no single and overt line of policy, but generally backed Lord Burghley against Leicester and Walsingham.[17] Once he was made Lord Admiral, in 1585, he understandably gave more positive support to the "war party," but he was never seen as a regular ally to Leicester. His most consistent alliance, which ran throughout their time on the Council, was with his father-in-law, and was used to protect the players. Carey at first deputized for him as Lord Chamberlain, and then took the post over himself in 1585 when Howard moved on to the admiralship. They worked as allies in 1594, when they set up the duopoly of their own companies to replace the Queen's Men as the basic suppliers of Elizabeth's Christmas seasoning. The consistency of Howard's and Carey's policy over the professional players is a clear mark of Howard's tactical and committee skills.

His politica contemporaries did not rate him very highly, either as a politician or as a man of action. Mendoza, the Spanish Ambassador, reported to Madrid that Elizabeth thought Howard "a frank-spoken man," and so kept her secrets from him. The Catholics, concerned for the succession and maneuvering to secure a pliant heir to the throne, in 1600 reported that Howard was too dangerous to use, "a simple man and little able to guard a secret."[18] But these claims that he was honestly ignorant should be set against the evidence of his skills as a negotiator and committee man, especially as the controller of that expensive and ramshackle structure, the English navy. He was no sprinter, but his stamina was outstanding. On appointment to the admiralship he started his work preparing for the Spanish invasion immediately, using previously untested skills to manage difficult people. He later claimed that he had succeeded in making Sir John Hawkins, treasurer of the navy, and Sir William Winter, comptroller of the navy and the ordnance, both capable men but by 1585 the deepest and most convinced of enemies, to work together by the end of that year "as fast as buckle and girdle."[19] His responsibility for organizing the country's defenses against the Armada showed his stamina and even more his skill in working with and through committees. His capacity for mastering detail and getting things done

---

[17] An account of the Privy Council in this period is by Conyers Read, "Walsingham and Burghley in Queen Elizabeth's Privy Council," *English Historical Review* 28 (1913), 34–58. See also M. B. Pulman, *The Elizabethan Privy Council in the Fifteen-Seventies* (Berkeley: University of California Press, 1971).

[18] Kenny, *Elizabeth's Admiral*, 117, 249.

[19] Julian S. Corbett (ed.), *Papers Relating to the Navy During the Spanish War 1585–1587* (London, 1898), 251. Quoted by Kenny, *Elizabeth's Admiral*, 114.

was massive, and his control of the different officers under him, for all the charges of corruption that with very good reason were laid against the navy during the long Jacobean peace, when he had been twenty years and more in charge, is a testimony to his sense of duty and his effectiveness in that work.

He could keep control of himself while many others around him were exploding. The only clear testimony we have to his touchiness did not emerge until 1596, when he was trying to work with the Earl of Essex laying ostensibly secret plans for a voyage to check the Spanish navy's next threatened invasion. He showed he was capable of exploding then, in his outraged letter of resignation from control of what became the Cadiz expedition, claiming that he was being used as a drudge, and refusing to have anything more to do with it. In the end, of course, he did, and on the evidence that survives the expedition's partial success was due in larger part to his mollifying presence than to Essex's fiery one.[20]

As Lord Admiral, in the 1590s he had immense power. His authority stemmed largely from the prestige of defeating the Armada, but more materially it came from his huge profits in running a piratical navy. When he became Lord Admiral at the age of forty-nine, his influence at court, his personal prestige, and, not the least important, his finances were secured for life. Legalized piracy made the admiralty in the years of the wars against Spain by a long way the most enriching monopoly in the country. At the peak of his naval command, in the 1590s, his income from naval commitments and from licensing piracy has been estimated to amount to between £12,000 and £15,000 per year.[21] Personally, he never felt himself to be affluent, and he never built a great house in his own glory as did the Cecils and others. But the Admiralty income reinforced his power at court as much as his prestige on the Council strengthened his hand in committee work.

That double strength was backed with new offices that put his committee skills to work. One office of particular value to the players was his appointment as Lord Lieutenant of Surrey in July 1585. Since 1580 he had been on the commissions for the peace, which controlled the work of the magistrates and justices of the peace, for both of London's neighboring counties, Middlesex and Surrey, north and south of the river. These posts gave him considerable influence over the magistrates who controlled the suburbs of London and their playhouses. He used that influence consistently to help the playing companies. The only

---

[20] Kenny, *Elizabeth's Admiral*, 176–77.   [21] Ibid., 87.

concern the magistrates ever expressed about their playhouses was voiced by the Middlesex justices in 1612 over the cutpurses said to infest the Fortune. Since larceny was one of their main concerns, that is understandable. They never caused the players trouble over routine playing at their designated playhouses.

It is worth tracing Howard's influence on Privy Council policy with some care before noting the other hints about his affinity with playgoing. He seems from the outset to have had a clear idea of what should be done. Unlike his cousin Sussex, his own policy when he was finally made Lord Chamberlain at the end of 1583 was, as it had been when he deputized for Sussex in the 1570s, to give his name to a company of players, but not to use his own company at court. His new company was certainly not below standard, since they played at court twice in the 1576/77 season after Sussex took up the reins again, and again in the following year. After that he kept them away from the court until he gave up the chamberlainship to his father-in-law, Henry Carey, and moved on to the admiralship. His company was not at court through the 1584/85 season, while he was Chamberlain, but returned in the 1585/86 season, and their attendances grew in frequency thereafter. Their acquisition of Edward Alleyn from Worcester's started a career for Alleyn in Howard's livery that lasted into Jacobean times.

While he was Chamberlain in 1584 he undertook the negotiations with the Lord Mayor that were needed in the wake of the 1583 decision to establish a company patronized by the Queen herself. The job of treating with the Lord Mayor to get the Queen's Company the right to perform freely in London properly fell to the new Lord Chamberlain. He undertook that duty adroitly. In essence his plan was a logical implementation of the Privy Council's basic idea, which was to secure playing by granting the royal protection to the one great company consisting of the best players from each of the major companies of 1583. From the Lord Mayor he secured exclusive access for the Queen's Men to use the London playing venues, under specific constraints. The court *Remembrancia* have been lost for the period from March 1584 to January 1587, but the Lansdowne papers supply the gist of the deal. They include a petition from the Queen's Men to the Privy Council asking for help against the city fathers, together with the responses from the Lord Mayor and from Howard as Chamberlain. Howard offered the city sensible "remedies," including strict limits on the times and days when plays could be performed. Most specifically, evidently knowing the various dodges that the players were capable of trying, he declared "That the Quenes players only be

tolerated, and of them their number and certaine names to be notified
in your Lps. lettres to the L. Maior and to the Justices of Middlesex
and Surrey. And those her players not to divide themselves into several
companies."[22] One authorized company, of named players, were to have
the one license to perform inside the city. The various city inns where the
Queen's Men would be allowed to play were also specified. In order to
maintain such a firmly announced policy in subsequent years Howard
had to disadvantage the company that he himself patronized. The Privy
Council had set the Queen's Men up, and he saw to it that the Council's
policy was enforced.

   The Privy Council records from 1584 to 1603 show that this policy
was maintained consistently, with only the one change called for in 1594
by the fluctuating fortunes of the leading playing companies. The policy sponsored by Howard in 1584 was an adroit compromise between
the demands of the Lord Mayor and the convenience of the players and
London playgoers. From 1584 onwards the Council continued to declare
periodically that it tolerated public stages and public playing solely on the
grounds that it trained the professionals scheduled to perform each year
at the royal Revels. In reality the support was more positive. Through the
1590s the Council made a number of supplementary decisions that secured the place of both professional playing and professional playhouses
in the suburbs of London for the first time. It must have been Howard,
a much stronger planner and committee man than his father-in-law, the
Lord Chamberlain, and a potent figure in the relevant counties of Surrey
and Middlesex, who devised the plan that was implemented in 1594 to
establish two new leading companies and their theatres in perpetuity.
From the Armada onwards, Howard was a power in the land. There are
tantalizingly few hints about why he chose to protect playing so firmly.
The hints, though, suggest a personal commitment of some strength.

   What was done in May 1594 has been described in more detail
elsewhere.[23] In effect, the Lord Admiral and the Lord Chamberlain
worked together to set up a pair of new companies to replace the now
divided Queen's Men. Setting up two companies was a better guarantee
for the supply of the Queen's plays each Christmas than one had been.
They drew the player membership from some of the major companies
which had recently lost their patrons. They based the new groupings on
the two chief impresarios who owned playhouses in the suburbs, James

[22] Chambers, *Elizabethan Stage*, IV, 302.
[23] See Gurr, "Three Reluctant Patrons and Early Shakespeare," *Shakespeare Quarterly* 44 (1993),
    159–74; and *The Shakespearian Playing Companies* (Oxford: Oxford University Press, 1995), ch. 4.

Burbage and Philip Henslowe, and their heirs, Richard Burbage and Edward Alleyn. They resolved the chronic problem of relations with the city by banning all playing from city inns,[24] and instead specified as the only authorized playing places Henslowe's Rose and Burbage's Theatre. Henceforth the companies were denied any access to playing within the Lord Mayor's bailiwick.

The Burbage company did not like this constraint. For all his need to keep his playhouse tenanted, James Burbage evidently still favored the old habit of playing in London in the open air through the summer and in roofed city inns through the winter months. That must be the reason why, for all their Council-sponsored right to play at the Theatre, his company asked their new patron, the Lord Chamberlain, early in October of their first year, to write to the Lord Mayor requesting leave for them to play throughout the winter at the Cross Keys inn in Gracechurch Street, a roofed playing-space.[25] It was also the basis for Burbage's plan, when the lease on the land he had built his Theatre on came near to its expiry date, to build its replacement inside a roofed hall in the Blackfriars precinct.[26] That plan proved a disaster in the short term for the Lord Chamberlain's company, in the first place because Carey died in July 1596, before the Blackfriars playhouse was finished. He must have known of Burbage's plan, and must have given it his support. The hazards were substantial, as they proved to be after Carey died. Burbage was unlikely to have ventured so much capital on the new property if he did not expect the Councilor to give the plan his active support.

The Chamberlain's company went through a bad time in 1596 and 1597. Neither of Carey's successors, one as company patron and one as Lord Chamberlain, favored the company in the way that the old earl had. At the latter's death the new Lord Chamberlain became not Carey's son George, who did take over the title and the patronage of the company, but Lord Cobham, who promptly used his new office to force the notorious change in Shakespeare's latest hit, replacing the name of Lady Cobham's ancestor Oldcastle with Falstaff. Henry Carey's death was followed nine months later by Cobham's, when George Carey did inherit his father's role as Lord Chamberlain. But by then the limited extent of his support for his company had been signaled by him putting his signature to the

[24] The ban on playing in city inns or innyards must have been what prompted Francis Langley, far more interested in profit than in plays, to build the Swan upriver of the Rose and the Bear Garden, in 1595.

[25] Chambers, *Elizabethan Stage*, IV, 316.

[26] See Gurr, "Money or Audiences: The Impact of Shakespeare's Globe," *Theatre Notebook* 42 (1988), 3–14.

petition of Blackfriars residents to the Privy Council asking them to stop the new playhouse being used by his company. George Carey had his residence in the Blackfriars, next to the Revels Office and the new theatre, as did Lord Chamberlain Cobham, who had the main voice in the Council's reception of the petition. Neither man wanted a playhouse in his own back yard. James Burbage had worn Henry Carey's livery for at least the last twelve years, getting consistent support for his promotion of playing. When Burbage died in February 1597 his sons secured no such guarantees from Carey's son.

Howard took no direct part in these matters, but Henry Carey's death must have been a blow to his control of the Privy Council's actions over playing. Two allies on any committee are in a much stronger position than one man arguing for himself. That George Carey was a less reliable partner than his father became clear later in 1597, when the Privy Council made an order to have all the suburban playhouses pulled down. The order of 28 July 1597 to the Middlesex and Surrey magistrates banning playing and ordering the demolition of all the playhouses has caused much debate.[27] Its lack of consistency with Carey's and Howard's already well-implemented policy of maintaining a duopoly with designated playhouses is one question. Its relation to the Pembroke's company's trouble over *The Isle of Dogs* that same July is a second. And thirdly there is the strange record of Henslowe's doings, recorded in limited ways in his *Diary*, that tells what he did about the ban and the rival Pembroke's company. One implication is Henslowe's and Alleyn's likely collusion with Howard.

In 1597 Henslowe had a vested interest to defend, because Langley's Swan, where the Pembroke's men had started to play, was on the Rose's doorstep in Surrey. The Burbage sons were in no position to do anything, since both of their own playhouses were closed and their inherited capital was locked up in their father's abortive attempt to create the new hall. I suspect that the main opposition to Langley's new venture came from Henslowe, and that the Privy Council's action in 1597 was either a hamfisted response to his request to his patron for help, or else an ingenious move which he knew all about in advance. In February 1597 Langley made an agreement with a traveling company, Pembroke's, that they

---

[27] See Glynne Wickham, *Early English Stages 1300–1660*, 4 vols. (London: Routledge and Kegan Paul, 1959–80), II.ii, 9–29; William Ingram, "The Closing of the Theaters in 1597: A Dissenting View," *Modern Philology* 69 (1971–72), 105–15; see also Carol Chillington Rutter (ed.), *Documents of the Rose Playhouse* (Manchester: Manchester University Press, 1984), 118–25. The Order is printed in *Acts of the Privy Council*, XXVII, 313.

would play at the Swan. Five Pembroke's men gave Langley a surety of £100 each to guarantee that they would play at his playhouse for twelve months. These Pembroke's players were not by any means new to London. Four of the five guarantors had until recently been along the lane at the Rose as Admiral's men, a loss which explains why for three weeks from 12 February the Admiral's did not play. Robert Shaw, William Bird, Richard Jones, and Thomas Downton left Henslowe and Alleyn's company for Pembroke's, where they joined up with Humphrey Jeffes and Gabriel Spencer, who had probably been members of the original Pembroke's in 1592, since a "Gabriel" is named in the Pembroke's *2 Henry VI*, and a "Humfrey" in *3 Henry VI*. It was Spencer, still carrying the Pembroke livery on his travels, who joined the four ex-Admiral's Men to put up the five sureties for Langley. After four years of traveling they needed new material to satisfy London's appetite, and it was one of their new offerings, *The Isle of Dogs*, that got them into terminal trouble.

The Privy Council intervened again, on 15 August, putting the inquisitor Topcliffe to work investigating the genesis of the "lewd plaie." The Council's consideration of the matter, however, by then had gone through three weeks of a hot summer. It involved two distinct steps. The first, the Order of 28 July, coincided with the receipt of a letter from the Lord Mayor. Written on the same day as the Council's order, it repeated the familiar request for "the present staie & fynall suppressinge of the saide Stage playes, aswell at the Theatre, Curten and banckside, as in all other places in and abowt the Citie." The Council issued their order to the justices of Middlesex and Surrey in a form of words that seem to make use of the Lord Mayor's complaint. It banned all playing until October and specified that the Curtain and the Theatre in Shoreditch, and "the playhouses in the Banckside, in Southwarke or elswhere in the said county within iij miles of London" should be destroyed.[28] It has been suggested that the Council, which that day met at Greenwich, could not have received the Lord Mayor's letter, written in the city on the same day, but the wording is similar and the coincidence is striking. At least one man on the Council had experience of this kind of order from 1584, and he knew what its limitations were. The obvious assumption is that the order was really aimed at Langley and the Swan, intruders on Howard's policy of running only two companies at two playhouses. The plural "playhouses" specified on the Bankside firmly identifies the Swan along with the Rose.

---

[28] Quoted in Chambers, *Elizabethan Stage*, IV, 321–23.

At the Greenwich meeting eight Councilors were present: the Secretary, Robert Cecil, the Lord Keeper, the Lord Treasurer, Lord North, Lord Buckhurst and the Comptroller, together with Howard and George Carey, Lord Admiral and Lord Chamberlain. Cecil had Langley in his sights for his dealings over a large diamond that had been landed as part of a privateers' haul of loot from the Spanish, and which Cecil was trying to retrieve for the crown. Howard had no brief for Langley either, since the latter had pillaged Howard's own company for his players, and the new group was breaching the duopoly. And yet the order is precise in demanding that the Theatre, the Curtain, and the Rose be demolished as well as the Swan. Here we can only guess how much the two Councilors who were company patrons knew about the current state of their companies' affairs, because the Theatre had been out of use for three months by 28 July, and its former tenants were now using the Curtain. The Burbage heirs may have thought that the order to destroy their old amphitheatre could be a way to secure access to their new hall theatre, which the Council had forbidden them in November of the previous year. More positively, though, Henslowe must have thought that Langley's act of turning his four players into neighboring competitors needed a drastic reprisal.

In the event, *The Isle of Dogs* did that for him. Possibly recognizing that orders to demolish playhouses did not work, on 15 August the Privy Council imprisoned several of the Pembroke's players. The other players promptly returned to Henslowe, as if they knew they were safer there. He made them sign new contracts of service with him. The players put in prison were also signed up when they were freed on 3 October. Henslowe did not even observe the ban of 28 July for its full run, because the Admiral's was back playing at the Rose by 11 October, three weeks before the official end of the ban at Hallowe'en. Possibly hoping to secure a second patron's license as a bonus from the troubles, he recorded the new combination, "be gane my lord admerals & my lord of penbrockes men to playe at my howsse."[29]

The Council's honor was evidently satisfied by Langley's downfall. Howard and the younger Carey maintained the policy of supporting two companies and two specified playhouses consistently into the last years of Elizabeth's reign, with the changes that the companies' own shifts required. On 22 June 1600 the Privy Council issued an order explicitly

---

[29] *Henslowe's Diary*, ed. R. A. Foakes and R. T. Rickert, (Cambridge: Cambridge University Press, 1961), 60.

licensing the two new playhouses, the Chamberlain's Globe and the
Admiral's Fortune. It specified:

First, that there shall bee about the Cittie two howses and noe more allowed to
serve for the use of the Common Stage plaies, of the which howses one shalbe in
Surrey in that place which is Commonlie called the banckside or there abouts,
and the other in Midlesex. And foras muche as there Lordshippes have bin
enformed by Edmond Tylney Esquire, hir Majesties servant and Master of the
Revells, that the howse now in hand to be builte by the said Edward Allen is
not intended to encrease the number of the Plaiehowses, but to be in steed
of an other, namelie the Curtaine, Which is either to be ruined and plucked
downe or to be putt to some other good use, as also that the scituation thereof
is meete and Convenient for that purpose. Yt is likewise ordered that the said
howse of Allen shall be allowed to be one of the two howses, and namelie for
the house to be alowed in Middlesex, soe as the house Called the Curtaine by
(as yt is pretended) either ruinated or applied to some other good use. And for
the other allowed to be on Surrey side, whereas [there Lordshipps are pleased
to permitt] to the Companie of players that shall plaie there to make there
owne Choice which they will have, Choosinge one of them and noe more,
[And the said Companie of Plaiers, being the Servantes of the L. Chamberlen,
that are to plaie there have made choise of the house called the Globe, yt
is ordered that the said house and none other shall be there allowed]. And
especiallie yt is forbidden that anie stage plaies shalbe plaied (as sometimes they
have bin) in any Common Inn for publique assemblie in or neare about the
Cittie.[30]

This was largely a formal reaffirmation of the previous edicts, inserting
the new playhouse names and reaffirming that the limit was still only
the two companies. The Council was ignoring the fact that Tilney had
admitted Derby's and two new boy companies to perform at court the
previous Christmas.

One particularly curious aspect of Howard's role in the growth of professional playing in London is the fact that Edward Alleyn worked consistently as an Admiral's servant for three years with Strange's while the rest
of the players who wore the Admiral's livery played as a separate company. When he left his lord's company for Strange's Men the Admiral's
kept on touring the country in the Admiral's livery while Alleyn kept
his own suit as an Admiral's man when playing for Strange's. Wearing
another lord's livery showed a conspicuously faint loyalty to the patron
of his new company. Alleyn is unlikely to have felt, as has been con-
jectured, that retaining a personal patent from Howard with its right

---

[30] *Acts of the Privy Council*, xxx, 395; *Dramatic Records of the City of London*, i, 80; Chambers, *Elizabethan Stage*, iv, 329–31.

to wear his livery was just an insurance so that he could run his own separate company at some time in the future. As a Strange's man in 1592 he was already in the strongest company, with its own supportive patron. His choice must have been chiefly a show of personal allegiance, an old loyalty which happened also (though incidentally) to give him a license for working separately if need be. It was a unique arrangement, and certainly suggests an awkwardly ambivalent allegiance to the lord under whose patent he now traveled. The nearest equivalent to such an engagement was that of James Burbage, who flaunted Henry Carey's livery while running the Theatre in Shoreditch. But by then he had stopped playing himself, and there was obvious value in a playhouse owner being in the service of a Privy Councilor who supported playing, even before the particular lord became Lord Chamberlain.

The roles of James Burbage and Edward Alleyn in the establishment of the new duopoly in May 1594 form the kind of frustrating hole in the historical record where there are only a few rather chimerical inferences about human motivation. All we can be sure of is the conjunction of different interests working to the same end. The playhouse owner and the leading player both had an interest in securing Privy Council backing for the plan to allocate the shares in a monopoly of the prime source of income for players. Each man had a long-standing record of playmaking while in the service of one of the two men on the Privy Council who actively supported the professional companies. The Councilors needed to replace the old Queen's Men's monopoly with a fresh pair of companies, and each had a liveried servant, one of whom had a family interest in the only suburban playhouse on Bankside while the other owned the main playhouse in Shoreditch. For Alleyn, now reunited with the Marlowe plays of his earlier days in the Admiral's Men,[31] and Richard Burbage, allocated the Shakespeare plays he may have already acted in with Strange's and the early Pembroke's, along with half of the most experienced players of the time, it was as perfect a development as they could have hoped for. It suited Carey, his duty to provide the Christmas season of plays now assured, and Howard, his own company firmly established now after three years of traveling, under his name in the county that was his territory, equally well. Whose inspiration it was originally we can only guess. The two most inventive minds in this game as problem-solvers were Burbage and Howard, and Howard was the one with the authority to carry such a scheme through.

[31] See Gurr, "Three Reluctant Patrons," 174.

Howard's retention of Alleyn as his servant while he played among Strange's Men is only one of the more tangible indications that he gave his support to the players out of an interest warmer and more personal than his Privy Council duties called for. We know from Nashe's testimony that Carey gave positive backing to his playing company. We also know that Howard did nothing for Henslowe and Alleyn personally, although he did protect the building of the Fortune. Mostly the indications are of rather petty thinking, for in many ways he was clearly a petty-minded man. There are just a few hints of a greater generosity of mind, like the allocation of the Marlowe plays to his own company and Shakespeare's to the Chamberlain's, which might invoke the chimera of an honest and personal enthusiasm.

The fertile Leslie Hotson once suggested that in 1599 it was Howard who actually commissioned the company he patronized to write *Sir John Oldcastle*.[32] The basis for Hotson's conjecture was that the new Lord Cobham was then betrothed to Howard's daughter. The counter view, that Henslowe and the Admiral's company set the play up on their own initiative as a reprisal against the Chamberlain's Men, now ensconced next to the Rose at the new Globe, has been given more weight in recent years. But Hotson's conjecture need not be discounted entirely. There is a touch of pomposity in the redemptive picture of Oldcastle staged at the Rose which may be due to rather more than a belated gibe at the rival company's four-year-old mistake. The "gefte" which Henslowe records in his taciturn way as a present to the writers of the play may have started its journey at some distance from Henslowe's own pocket.[33] The Falstaff plays were hugely popular, and after four years and four plays featuring the royal jester his new name was now irrevocably fixed in London minds. It is not very likely that Henslowe, who commissioned the play but whose relations with Howard were distant, to judge from his pessimism in 1598 over the likelihood of Howard intervening on his behalf when he was canvassing for the Mastership of the Bears,[34] would have thought of such a means to please the company's patron. The lateness of the gesture and its timeliness for Howard's daughter's marriage suggests an impulse rather more personal than the desire to

---

[32] *Shakespeare's Sonnets Dated and other Essays* (New York: Oxford University Press, 1949), 155–58.
[33] *Henslowe's Diary*, 126.
[34] See *Henslowe's Diary*, 299. Henslowe reported to Alleyn that he had been to see the Lord Admiral over his candidacy, but held little hope of him lobbying in support of their case. The widowed Lady Essex had a similar grievance: that Howard listened to her complaints of poverty sympathetically, but then did nothing. He was a man who made his own judgments.

rub the other company's nose in its old mistake. It may indeed have been Howard who suggested the subject to the company.

As with most of the great lords of Tudor times, little survives to say what Howard's private mind was like. He stands in history as the right man at the right time, in 1588, and made little clear mark in the decades before and after that time of crisis. For all his massive income from his post as Admiral, he did not build houses to display his magnificence, as Cecil and so many others did. Instead he acquired several ready-made, most of them conveniently close to London and the court, maintaining and extending them, but never with memorable enterprise. He was in no way an exhibitionist or any sort of individualist.

Nor was he a sophisticated writer. Many of his papers survive, the vast majority relating to his pursuit of government business. His correspondence shows a practical man with a sharp turn of phrase, and an occasional dry wit. He wrote to Cecil in 1602 on Admiralty business, saying that he could not be at his office because he was sick and so had kept "aboard my bed."[35] He was more uxorious than his father-in-law, who famously kept a mistress, and his evident distress over his wife's final illness has to be set against the speed with which he remarried. He was well-read, and following the enthusiasm for antiquities generated by Sir Robert Cotton and his friends, he became a collector of books and manuscripts as soon as his income from the admiralty made it possible. He became dedicatee of several books, not least Hakluyt's second edition of his *Voyages* and other works of the kind that made his admiralship a logical recipient.

More significantly perhaps, he proved willing to allow others to benefit from his acquisitions. When Bodley started his library in Oxford, Howard was quick to become a donor. Amongst the collection that he gave to Bodley in 1604 were sixteen early manuscripts and thirty-four printed books. One of the more notable manuscripts was a fifteenth-century copy of the "Isabella Rule," the rigorous working orders of the English Minoresses, the "Poor Clares." Here is born another of the chimeras which infest any view of the details of Howard's life. The gist of the orders written in this manuscript, referring to the restrictions the nuns consented to over contact with the outside world in general and men in particular, is what Shakespeare gave the nun Francisca to recite to Isabella in *Measure for Measure* in late 1603 (1.4.10–13). The Minoresses

---

[35] *Cal. Hatfield MSS*, ii, 19, quoted in Kenny, *Elizabeth's Admiral*, 255.

were the Franciscan "votarists of St. Clare."[36] Whether Shakespeare got his access to the laws that are laid down in the "Isabella Rule" along with his heroine's name through Howard at some time before the manuscript was handed over to Bodley is another chimera.

[36] Darryl J. Gless, *"Measure for Measure," The Law, and the Convent* (Princeton: Princeton University Press, 1979), 262. See also R. W. Chambers and W. W. Seton (eds.), *A Fifteenth-Century Courtesy Book and Two Franciscan Rules*, EETS no. 148 (New York: Oxford University Press, 1914), 75–76. Gless lists (263) some of the rules cited by Francisca in the play.

CHAPTER 9

Tracking Leicester's Men: the patronage of a performance troupe

Sally-Beth MacLean

Any study of Elizabethan patronage in its first three decades will encounter a dominant figure in the glittering and controversial royal favorite, Robert Dudley, Earl of Leicester. From the early months of the Queen's reign until his death in September 1588, Dudley was a political force to be reckoned with, only occasionally lapsing in favor when his marriage to Lettice Knollys was discovered or when he overreached himself as governor of the Low Countries.[1] Appointed Master of the Queen's Horse shortly after Elizabeth's accession in November 1558,[2] his principal duties centered on the court where he had the Queen's ear and many opportunities to pursue his own self-aggrandizement as well as the suits of others alert to the special nature of his position.

Dudley was born to privilege as the fifth son of John, the first Duke of Northumberland, whose power during the later years of Edward VI's reign ended abruptly when an ill-advised attempt to put his daughter-in-law, Jane Grey, on the throne in her place roused the animosity of Mary Tudor. While his father and younger brother Guildford lost their heads as a result, Robert escaped with a chastening year or so in the Tower and the challenge of rebuilding his family's prestige and estates.[3] Released in October 1554 and pardoned early the next year, he was without property until the lands of the former monastery of Halesowen in Worcestershire and Staffordshire were settled on him in 1556, with the Queen's approval and through his brother Ambrose's generosity. Within two years, Dudley's Norfolk house at Hemsby was restored to him and he and his wife Amy were granted her inheritance of three Robsart manors

---

[1] Until Simon Adams' biography of Robert Dudley is published, the best source for personal events in his life is Derek A. Wilson, *Sweet Robin: A Biography of Robert Dudley, Earl of Leicester 1533–1588* (London: Hamilton, 1981).

[2] Dudley was appointed Master of the Horse 11 January 1558/59.

[3] Simon Adams analyzes the historical ambitions of the Dudley family in the West Midlands in his essay, "'Because I am of that countrye & mynde to plant myself there': Robert Dudley, earl of Leicester and the West Midlands," *Midland History* 20 (1995), 21–74.

in the same county. The sale of Halesowen in 1558 made Norfolk Dudley's principal base of operations, although Elizabeth's accession in November of the same year made Dudley a peripatetic courtier for the rest of his life, most often resident in the London area.[4]

Basking in the Queen's favor and, after his wife's timely death, hopeful of his chances of becoming the royal consort, Dudley rose rapidly to political power. Although he was not granted a peerage until 1564, he sought appointments that would benefit him financially and extend the range of his influence across the kingdom. Being the Queen's favorite was an expensive business but there was more at stake than managing life as a courtier. It seems clear that both Robert and Ambrose Dudley were anxious to achieve restoration of their father's estates and offices, most notably in the West Midlands where Northumberland had once campaigned for the lands of the Suttons, Lords Dudley. Initially, Robert acquired appointments in areas where his father had held sway – lord lieutenantships in Warwickshire and Worcestershire in 1559–60 and the outlying lordship of the manor at Beverley (1561–66) – while negotiating for high stewardship of the town of Warwick for two years before acquiring and then giving it in 1562 to his brother, newly created Earl of Warwick.

Dudley's appointment to the Privy Council in 1562 confirmed his strong position within the central government of the realm and more local offices in various parts of the realm accumulated: in the West Midlands, Justice of the Peace in Herefordshire (1562), Warwickshire (1562), and Worcestershire (1562, 1564); in the northwest, chamberlaincy of the county palatine of Chester (1565); in Yorkshire, High Steward and Receiver of Pickering Lythe and Constable and Master Forester of Pickering Castle (1564); in East Anglia, High Steward of Cambridge University (1563) and the bishopric of Ely (1565); and in the Thames Valley, Constable of Windsor Castle (1562), High Steward of Windsor (1563), Reading (1566), Abingdon (1566), and Wallingford (1569), and Lord Lieutenant of Berkshire (1569).[5] The chancellorship of Oxford (1564) was a key appointment, allowing him influence over university appointments and the education of the future clergy, gentry, and nobility, many of whom emerged favoring the moderate Puritan

[4] For further details of these early years, see Simon Adams, "The Dudley Clientele, 1553–1563," in G.W. Bernard (ed.), *The Tudor Nobility* (New York: St. Martin's, 1992), 241–65.
[5] Simon Adams provides a helpful summary of key appointments and a detailed analysis of the extent of Dudley's parliamentary patronage in "The Dudley Clientele and the House of Commons, 1559–1586," *Parliamentary History* 8 (1989), 216–74.

cause which Dudley pursued with increasing vigor over the next two decades.[6]

By 1563, Dudley's stake in the West Midlands was consolidated by a grant of lands centering on the lordship of Kenilworth and by his subsequent elevation to the peerage as Earl of Leicester in 1564.[7] At the same time, he was created Baron Denbigh, his influence now extending to four marcher lordships in Wales (Denbighshire and Montgomeryshire). In both these regions Dudley extended his landholdings energetically over the next decade. Yet only with the refurbishing of Kenilworth Castle in the early 1570s did he take up sometime residence in Warwickshire, in the heart of his father's former estate and close by his brother's seat at Warwick Castle. In 1579 he added the estate of Drayton Bassett on the border of Staffordshire and Warwickshire to his landholdings in the region.[8]

The 1570s also brought further appointments in new regions. Recognized as holding the most high stewardships in the period, Dudley added Bristol (1570) and Tewkesbury (by 1575) in the southwest, Great Yarmouth, King's Lynn (1572) and Norwich Cathedral (1574) in East Anglia, Andover (1574) in Hampshire, Harrow-on-the-Hill (after 1575) in Middlesex, and St. Albans (after 1579) in Hertfordshire, as well as the honor of Grafton in Northamptonshire (1570), not far from Kenilworth. By 1578, Dudley's purchase of the estate at Wanstead in Essex signaled expansion of his interests in the east where he added the lord lieutenancies of Essex (1585) and Hertfordshire (1585), and recordership of Maldon (after 1583) to his roster.

Dudley's territorial influence therefore was considerable, originating in the West Midlands and the East Riding of Yorkshire, but rapidly spreading to counties such as Cheshire and Berkshire, and eventually to

[6] See Lawrence Stone, *The Crisis of the Aristocracy 1558–1641* (Oxford: Clarendon Press, 1965), 736–40: "The success of Leicester and Burghley in their capacities as chancellors in purging the two universities of Catholic dons was probably one of the most crucial victories in a prolonged struggle for the allegiance of the political nation. The encouragement given by Leicester at Oxford to Puritans like Laurence Humphrey, President of Magdalen, and the caution and restraint exercised by Burghley in his dealings with the Puritans there, allowed both universities to become partly infected with Puritan doctrines, and thus to become important centers of Puritan propaganda among the young" (740).

[7] Simon Adams notes "his endowment on creation as baron of Denbigh and earl of Leicester in 1564 was the most generous single grant of a landed estate in the reign – he was also the only man Elizabeth promoted directly to an earldom" ("The patronage of the crown in Elizabethan politics: the 1590s in perspective," J. A. Guy [ed.], *The Reign of Elizabeth I: Court and Culture in the Last Decade* [Cambridge: Cambridge University Press, 1995], 29).

[8] Dudley's purchase of the lease of Drayton Bassett was a continuation of his dynastic land acquisitions in the West Midlands (see Adams, "'Because I am of that countrye'," 34).

Northamptonshire, Hampshire, and Hertfordshire where he never had property of significance. His biographer, Simon Adams, in reflecting on the pattern of his land acquisitions, notes "With certain important exceptions (the Welsh lordships and Wanstead, for example) Leicester's estate was largely composed of lands that had previously belonged to the Duke of Northumberland. The restoring of 'the Dudley estate' was one of his more under-appreciated ambitions."[9] On the one hand, Dudley seems to have been motivated to reclaim the past and to recreate himself as a representative of the landed aristocracy, with estates, an extensive affinity, and a household of retainers worthy of the tradition. Yet he was also proactive and restless in seeking political advantage in the form of offices and appointments that could extend his national influence and better furnish his coffers.

Dudley was a complex man. His interests were not purely selfish, whatever the scandalous accusations leveled by opponents.[10] As a key figure on the Privy Council and at court over three decades, Dudley pursued not only his own marital ambitions but also the cause of the reformed church in the face of Catholic resurgence encouraged by Philip of Spain and followers of Mary Stuart. Towards the end of his life, Dudley's dedicated support for England's intervention in the Netherlands against Spain won him both his supreme political cause and an appointment that unleashed his appetite for the grandiose. As leader of the expedition to the Netherlands, he commanded a vast retinue and was greeted by spectacular triumphs worthy of a monarch.[11] In accepting the governorship of the Netherlands, his personal goals overcame his political sense, an error in judgment that almost cost him the Queen's favor. Yet this chapter in his life is revealing – here is a somewhat contradictory blend of modernity and tradition, a courtier and skilful politician,

---

[9] Adams, "The Dudley Clientele and the House of Commons," 220.

[10] The hostile gossip culminated in the libelous tract, *Leicester's Commonwealth*, which has proved a work of remarkably enduring influence. See D. C. Peck (ed.), *Leicester's Commonwealth. The Copy of a Letter written by a Master of Arts of Cambridge (1584) with related documents* (Athens, Ohio: Ohio University Press, 1985). William Harrison, in his manuscript "Chronologie," provides another indication of contemporary attitudes towards Dudley: "the man of grettest powre (being but a subject) which in this land, or that ever had bene exalted under any prince sithens the times of Peers Gavestone & Robert Vere ... Nothing almost was done, wherein he had not, either a stroke or a commoditie; which together with his scraping from churche and commons ... procured him soche envie & hatred" (quoted in Simon Adams, "Favorites and Factions at the Elizabethan Court," in Ronald G. Asch and Adolf M. Birke (eds.), *Princes, Patronage, and the Nobility: The Court at the Beginning of the Modern Age c. 1450–1650* (London: German Historical Institute, 1991), 275.

[11] For full details of the extraordinary welcome given by the Dutch, see R. C. Strong and J. A. Van Dorsten, *Leicester's Triumph* (London and Leiden: Leiden University Press, 1964).

worldly-wise and focused on the most contemporary issues, distracted by coveted pomp and pageantry reminiscent of a medieval past.[12] It is not by chance that there was a large troupe of players in Dudley's entourage in 1585–86. From the first year of Elizabeth's reign, he included players in his patronage activities, probably for the same complex of reasons that he chose to take them to the Netherlands. Dudley's biography, briefly highlighted above, gives us the context in which to explore the interplay between this Renaissance patron and his players.

An enduring tradition inherited from the late Middle Ages still allowed members of the gentry and nobility, as well as the royal family, to act as patrons for performers of various types – bearwards, musicians, and players – who were typically paid for entertainment given to their patron's household during the festive season of Christmas and Shrovetide and then released to tour the countryside for at least part of the year. Aside from the royal troupes, most traveling companies seem to have mounted regional rather than national tours, the size of their rewards, and perhaps the range of their travels, usually depending on the extent of their patron's influence. Dudley's father had such a troupe of performers, on record in the southwest from 1531/32–53, and both Ambrose and Robert expanded upon this apparently modest employment of players.[13]

One of Robert Dudley's early initiatives after his appointment as Master of the Horse was to assemble a troupe of players. Not yet in possession of an estate or title, Dudley's twin instincts for self-promotion and tradition found expression in these performers. Sometime in late March or early April 1559, his household accounts make note of the first

[12] Wallace C. MacCaffrey, *Queen Elizabeth and the Making of Policy 1572–1588* (Princeton: Princeton University Press, 1981), 352, describes Dudley's entourage as follows: "He assembled around him an entourage which was more like the great household of a medieval baron than the headquarters staff of a Renaissance captain. For his immediate attendance he had a staff of about 75 persons, including a steward, secretary, treasurer, gentleman of the horse, comptroller, two gentlemen ushers, four gentlemen of the chamber, two divines, a physician, apothecary, and chirurgeon. Two noblemen, the Earl of Essex (his stepson) and Lord North, along with some 20 knights and gentlemen, accompanied him as volunteers, with their 40 servants. All in all the ordinary household of the Earl may well have numbered 200 persons."

[13] Published Records of Early English Drama (REED) collections for Barnstaple, Bridgwater, Bristol, Lyme Regis, Plymouth, and Poole include records for players under the senior Dudley's patronage. See the following REED collections: *Devon*, ed. John M. Wasson (Toronto: University of Toronto Press, 1986), 40–41, 234; *Bristol*, ed. Mark C. Pilkinton (Toronto: University of Toronto Press, 1997), 40, 43, 46; *Dorset/Cornwall*, ed. Rosalind Conklin Hays and C. E. McGee/Sally L. Joyce and Evelyn C. Newlyn (Toronto: University of Toronto Press, 1999), 211, 241; and *Somerset including Bath*, ed. James Stokes with Robert J. Alexander (Toronto: University of Toronto Press, 1996), 47. The accounts of Plymouth, 1549–50, record Dudley's minstrels under his title as Earl of Warwick, followed by two instances of players as Duke of Northumberland at Barnstaple. Because of the different locations involved and the limited number of records, it is unclear whether these accounts definitively distinguish between minstrels and players.

payment to "your L[ordship's] pleyers," with several further payments in May and June either at St. James' in London where he sometimes stayed or at his own new residence at Kew.[14] It is very possible that these players were in attendance for celebrations linked with Dudley's nomination as a Knight of the Garter (23 April) and installation in early June. There is no indication of the size of the troupe, although one player, Laurent, is fleetingly named.[15]

Although Dudley was to become one of the Elizabethan patrons most sought after by writers and scholars, it is noteworthy that the players were among the first to receive his official patronage. Certainly they would have served an immediate cause, helping to impress onlookers at court as part of their lord's retinue. It seems likely that Dudley aspired to compete with others whose impact was so vividly described by a contemporary witness: "I might speak here of the great trains and troops of servingmen also, which attend upon the nobility of England in their several liveries and with the differences of cognizances on their sleeves whereby it is known to whom they appertain. I could also set down what a goodly sight it is to see them muster in the court, which being filled with them doth yield the contemplation of a noble variety unto the beholder, much like to the show of the peacock's tail in the full beauty or of some meadow garnished with infinite kinds and diversity of pleasant flowers."[16] But Dudley was seeking popular support further afield as he strategized his rise to power. His career reflects his awareness of the links between court and country in the form of locally held offices that could benefit a royal favorite, especially one with the highest ambition.[17]

---

[14] The house at Kew was granted in December 1558. An earlier discussion of these household account payments can be found in my essay "The Politics of Patronage: Dramatic Records in Robert Dudley's Household Books," *Shakespeare Quarterly* 44 (1993), 175–82. For full transcriptions of the few surviving Dudley household accounts now held at Longleat House (1558–61) and the British Library (1584–86), see Simon Adams (ed.), *Household Accounts and Disbursement Books of Robert Dudley, Earl of Leicester, 1558–1561, 1584–1586*, Camden 5th Series, vol. 6 (Cambridge: Cambridge University Press, 1995).

[15] David C. Price, *Patrons and Musicians of the English Renaissance* (Cambridge: Cambridge University Press, 1981), 167, has suggested that Dudley engaged, at the generous rate of forty pounds a quarter, a company of players headed by Nicholas Culverwell in 1559. Although players were hired, there was no such quarterly payment: a closer look at the accounts shows that "Nicholas Culverwell and the Company" were the Company of the Staple, who make their appearance in the 1559–60 receipts and expenses in connection with the license granted Dudley for the export of 1000 sarplers of wool. See Adams, *Household Accounts*, 115–18.

[16] William Harrison, *The Description of England*, ed. Georges Edelen (Ithaca: Cornell University Press, 1968), 231. The *Description* was first published as part of *Holinshed's Chronicle* in 1577 (*STC*: 13568).

[17] Adams, in summing up Dudley's rebuilding of dynastic interests in the West Midlands, characterizes him thus: "However mixed his motives or however disparate his influence, Leicester's combination of enthusiasm for his country and pre-eminence at court brought

Dudley was ever a progressive patron. He must have seen that the players could provide contact with regions far from the court and central government, blending the benefits of promoting their patron's name and interests while earning performance income that would largely keep them off the list of his personal household expenses. In fact, after the spring and early summer of 1559, the first decade of the troupe's career is only known to us through rewards recorded in civic, court, and other private household accounts. It would seem, from the first three years' evidence when Dudley's household books do survive, that the players were paid primarily not for entertainment at home, but rather for promotional purposes across the country.[18]

An early piece of Dudley correspondence reveals the patron's personal intervention on behalf of his performance troupe. In mid-June 1559 he wrote a letter for the players to carry to the Earl of Shrewsbury as Lord President of the Council of the North, asking permission for their tour through Yorkshire, a region under Shrewsbury's jurisdiction: "my seruauntes bringers hereof vnto you, be suche as ar plaiers of interludes. And for the same have the Licence of diuerse of my lordis here. vnder ther seales and handis. to plaie in diuerse shieres within the realme vnder there aucthorities as maie amplie appere vnto your L[ordship], by the same licence. I haue thought, emong the rest, by my Lettres to besuche your good L[ordship] conformitie to them Likewise. that they maie have your hand and seale to ther licence, for the like libertye in yorke shiere. being honest men, and suche. as shall plaie none other matters (.I trust) but tollerable and convenient. whereof some of them have bene herde here alredie before diuerse of my lordis."[19]

In the ambitious range of this opening tour was Dudley looking for reconnection with lands and clientele previously associated with his father's estate? Possibly. Some of the earliest lands that Dudley was granted by the Queen in January 1559/60 and March 1561 were once

---

court and country together rather than drove them apart. In this respect his interest formed one of the major strands in the fabric of the Elizabethan political nation" ("'Because I am of that countrye'," 52).

[18] It is important always to bear in mind that the evidence from Dudley's household accounts is limited to the first three years of his career and only three of the last five.

[19] Lambeth Palace Library: MS 3196, bifolium (10 June 1559). I gratefully acknowledge the Archbishop of Canterbury and the Trustees of Lambeth Palace Library for permission to quote from this source and the kind assistance of the librarian and archivist, Dr. R. J. Palmer. Barbara Palmer reports that the antiquarian John Hopkinson, who made transcriptions from many of the Shrewsbury papers while they were still at Sheffield Castle in 1676–77, dated the letter 10 June 1559. Hopkinson's transcripts are now held at Bradford Record Office: 32D86/33 (the relevant letter copy is on fo. 8v).

part of his father's outlying holdings in the East Riding of Yorkshire.[20] Until REED research is completed in the northeast we will not know whether Dudley's players did venture that far, though if they did, they might well have chosen the route through Nottingham where they are known to have performed sometime in the summer of 1559.[21] They also toured East Anglia, the region where their patron's modest landholdings and his parliamentary seat were situated at the time.[22]

For the rest of the decade and into the next (1561–72), Dudley's men continued to visit the East Riding where the civic accounts at Beverley bear witness to above average rewards.[23] There may be a symbiotic connection between patron's concerns and players' itinerary discernible in this instance. Dudley was granted the lordship of Beverley, like his father before him, in 1561. Although he exchanged the manor of Beverley for properties in the West Midlands in 1566,[24] his influence continued, culminating in the grant of a new charter in 1573. The town clearly attributed its new status to their former lord's patronage efforts, the civic records paying tribute to "the new chartre graunted unto the Maior and Governors and Burgesses of Beverley by our gracious soveraigne Lady Queene Elizabeth at the sute and requeste of our most benigne lorde therle of Lacyter."[25] The following year the corporation set Dudley's arms in their guildhall.[26] August 1572 is the date of the last players' visit to Beverley but the level of their reward at the time is suggestive. Consistently Dudley's troupe had received an amount comparable only to that of the royal interluders (and sometimes surpassing theirs), but in 1572, the summer before incorporation, they won their highest amount from the burgesses, thirty shillings, plus more in perquisites such as wine.[27] The links between the town's suit for incorporation, the noble

---

[20] As indicated above, Northumberland had held lands in Yorkshire, notably the site of the monasteries of Watton and Meaux as well as the lordship and borough of Beverley, all in the East Riding and all returned to Robert in 1560–61.

[21] Nottinghamshire Record Office: Chamberlains' Accounts 1610B, fo. 9.

[22] Dudley, who had been MP for Norfolk in 1547 and 1553, was re-elected in 1559. For evidence of the East Anglia tour see *Norwich 1540–1642*, ed. David Galloway, REED (Toronto: University of Toronto Press, 1984), 45.

[23] Beverley Governors' Minute Book, East Riding of Yorkshire Archive Office: II/7/2, fos. 54v, 65; II/7/3, fos. 16, 36. My thanks to Diana Wyatt, editor of the REED Beverley records, for these references.

[24] See Adams, "'Because I am of that countrye'," 30, 33 and 58, n. 75.

[25] Beverley Corporation Account Roll, East Riding of Yorkshire Archive Office: II/6/30, mb 6, as quoted in *Report on the Manuscripts of the Corporation of Beverley*, Historical Manuscripts Commission Reports 54 (London, 1900), 183.

[26] K. J. Allison (ed.), *A History of the County of York, East Riding*, Victoria County History of England, 6 vols. (London: Oxford University Press, 1969), VI 75.

[27] Beverley Governors' Minute Book, East Riding of Yorkshire Archive Office: II/7/3, fo. 47.

patron's role, and the timely and generous welcome afforded his players are inescapable here.

Dudley's personal interests in land acquisition and offices were more pronounced in the West Midlands, but in this region there is less corresponding performance evidence available for the 1560s. Civic rewards to touring entertainers do not begin at Coventry until the mid-1570s, while Warwick's civic account book mentions only the Queen's and Worcester's players.[28] In Worcestershire, the surviving accounts of the principal city are summary in this period and those of Bewdley limited.[29] Similarly, Staffordshire's borough and household accounts are few in number, and those that do survive for Stafford make no mention of Dudley's players.[30]

The other principal region where Dudley collected some of his numerous high stewardships and lord lieutenancies in the 1560s was the Thames Valley, but here too the available evidence is very limited. From what we can discover, thirty years or so of touring records tell a story that may differ from expectations. Troupes under Dudley's patronage traveled annually with few exceptions from 1559 to 1588, the year of his death.[31] Although the Thames Valley might seem to have been a logical focal point for some of these tours, given the extent of the patron's regional influence there, the opposite seems to have been true. Instead, the players frequented more lucrative regions – East Anglia, the southeast, and the southwest. Of these East Anglia was the favorite. The players toured this always popular region for twenty of the thirty years, sometimes more than once. They performed at private residences as well as in boroughs along the way. A member of Dudley's affinity, Lord North, lived at Kirtling, near Cambridge, on the route to Norwich while Sir Thomas Kytson, a more conservative but conforming Suffolk county magnate, occupied Hengrave Hall near Bury St. Edmunds. Kytson, in particular, is known to have been a patron of the arts, employing the well-respected musician Edward Johnson in his household during the 1570s. Johnson was among the talents employed by Leicester for the extravagant festivities at Kenilworth in 1575 and it may be of related interest that Leicester's troupe was paid at Hengrave the previous year.[32] Where

---

[28] The 1546–69 Warwick Account Book is at the Warwickshire Record Office: CR 1618/WA1/1.

[29] See David N. Klausner (ed.), *Herefordshire/Worcestershire*, REED (Toronto: University of Toronto Press, 1990).

[30] As reported to me by Alan Somerset, the editor of the REED collection for Staffordshire (research in progress).

[31] For more details see REED's patronage website at http://eir.library.utoronto.ca/reed/.

[32] See *Records of Plays and Players in Norfolk and Suffolk*, ed. David Galloway and John M. Wasson, Malone Society Collections XI (Oxford: Oxford University Press, 1981), 166. For details of Kytson's musical patronage, see Price, *Patrons and Musicians*, 75–82.

the accounts of the North and Kytson households survive, we can trace the ready welcome assured the players, though they seem never to have come in company with Dudley himself.

A rare conjunction of patron and players on the road occurs in August 1571 at the time of a royal progress through East Anglia, stopping at Lord Thomas Howard's residence of Audley End on the edge of Saffron Walden. The town turned out in full regalia and with the obligatory bulging purse to greet the Queen. The town accounts confirm that Dudley's troupe, now known as the Earl of Leicester's Men, was part of the royal retinue, receiving a gift of 2s 6d while their patron was presented with a rather more expensive sugar loaf. In addition, and perhaps as emissaries in advance of the royal party the same year, they had received a performance reward of 8s 8d with the Queen's interluders.[33]

There is only one other clear instance of Dudley's movements intersecting with his players' in provincial England. The troupe made the lengthier trip to the southwest eleven times in their years on the road, either as a goal in itself or as an extension of a route through the southern coastal counties. In the spring of 1587, they paid a visit to Bristol where they played in the guildhall either just before or at the time of their lord's visit with his brother Warwick on 15–16 April.[34] Generally, they were well rewarded for these tours, receiving more on average than on other circuits, despite the fact that their patron had no special local appointments. Yet it is obvious from a comparison of rewards to other troupes that Dudley's political prestige carried sufficient weight with the towns of Devon that they were prepared to give his players more than any troupe other than the royal interluders.[35] Even in the first year of their formation, they were paid twenty shillings at Plymouth, more than the bishop of Exeter's troupe the following year and at the same level as the Queen's players three years later.[36] At Totnes they received twenty shillings in 1569–70; by contrast, one of the most active regional troupes, the players of a local magnate, Lord Mountjoy, were

---

[33] Saffron Walden Chamberlains' Accounts, Town Hall, 1570–71 accounts, pp. 75, 77.

[34] For details see *Bristol*, 129–31.

[35] The dominant nobleman in the southwest at the time was a strong Protestant sympathizer, a fellow member of the Privy Council and a member of Dudley's affinity. Francis Russell, Earl of Bedford, was Lord Lieutenant of Devon, Dorset, and Cornwall, and would readily have given his permission for Dudley's troupe to tour the region. See David Dean, "Locality and Parliament: The Legislative Activities of Devon's MPs During the Reign of Elizabeth," in Todd Gray, Margery Rowe and Audrey Erskine (eds.), *Tudor and Stuart Devon: The Common Estate and the Government. Essays presented to Joyce Youings* (Exeter: University of Exeter Press, 1992), 76–77.

[36] See *Devon*, 234–36 for the 1559–60, 1560–61 and 1562–63 accounts.

paid ten shillings in 1573–74, as were the equally active Worcester's Men in 1576–77.[37]

Another region frequented by Leicester's Men was the southeast. Here the towns were numerous and only small distances apart, as well as near London. The road through Canterbury, either directly to Dover and other Cinque Ports or through Sandwich along the coast was probably the most popular circuit for medieval and Renaissance entertainers. Leicester's troupe followed this circuit in sixteen of thirty years, at any season of the year. The favorite's reputation would have been well known here, even though there were other patrons more dominant in the region itself. Canterbury seems to have singled out the troupe for higher rewards, especially in the 1570s, although most other towns maintained a level consistent with other noblemen's players.[38]

There were only two regions which may have been seldom visited by Leicester's Men, the first being the Welsh border counties where, like the Thames Valley, his influence may have been felt for other reasons or where the rewards may not have been sufficiently appealing. Admittedly, Herefordshire has relatively few civic records extant and Shrewsbury's town payments are summary for most of the period. Only twice are rewards to the troupe noted in the border region, at Ludlow in 1573 and at Shrewsbury in 1581–82.[39]

Despite the frequency of the northeastern tours in the first decade, there is no indication that the road across the Pennines was taken to the northwest nor that the northwestern counties of Cumberland, Westmorland, or Lancashire were ever visited, apart from one isolated visit to the Earl of Derby's house at Lathom in 1587. However, there is little civic or household evidence for this period surviving to allow us to trace an itinerary in these counties. Dudley was Chamberlain of the County Palatine of Chester, as well as Baron Denbigh, and while the Earl of Derby may not have been a close affiliate, there was at least a family association with the Derby heir, Lord Strange. Dudley had a hand in arranging the marriage of Lord Strange to the youngest daughter of Sir John Spencer of Althorp in 1579 after which the couple spent at least some of their time in the north at various Stanley residences.[40] It is

---

[37] See *Devon*, 280–81.

[38] Faversham and New Romney also gave higher rewards to Leicester's men in some years; see *Kent: Diocese of Canterbury*, ed. James M. Gibson, 3 vols., REED (Toronto: University of Toronto Press, forthcoming).

[39] See *Shropshire*, ed. J. A. B. Somerset, 2 vols., REED (Toronto: University of Toronto Press, 1994), 1, 84, 233.

[40] French Fogle, "'Such a Rural Queen': The Countess Dowager of Derby as Patron," *Patronage in Late Renaissance England* (Los Angeles: William Andrews Clark Memorial Library, 1983), 10–11.

certainly possible that if we had more records, Leicester's Men would prove to have set their direction west as well as east in the northern reaches of the kingdom, at least to visit the Stanleys at home more than once.[41] Whether they would have tested their welcome at some of the recusant households in the Ribble Valley, for example, is questionable; many of these residences were at some distance from the main road north and may not have been sufficiently attractive. In fact, the scattered household accounts that do survive for the period suggest that most of the entertainers on tour in Lancashire were more localized, whether their host was recusant (like the Sherringtons of Wardley) or comfortably Protestant (like the Shuttleworths of Gawthorpe and Smithills).[42]

Given their patron's landed interests and offices in the midlands, especially in Warwickshire, the players can be expected to show up in the records of major centers like Coventry or Leicester. Although he never held a formal appointment there, Dudley had a special relationship with the city of Coventry, partly because of its proximity to his Kenilworth seat, but also because a member of his clientele, Sir John Throckmorton, was recorder there. The annual exchange of gifts was one expression of the bond that existed between patron and city; another was the higher civic rewards given to his entertainers – players, bearward, musicians – on their regular visits there.[43] In 1575, the second year for which Coventry's chamberlains' accounts survive, Dudley's players took away 26s 8d as an official payment, almost four times what his brother's troupe received and almost three times more than Lord Chamberlain Sussex's players. In this period both these troupes were performing at court, so we should not interpret these discrepancies as indications of lesser quality, either of patron or performance.[44] A special relationship existed between Robert Dudley and the city, which benefited the players too.

The 1575 payment to Dudley's players, which cannot be more closely dated, is especially tantalizing. This was the year of the royal progress

---

[41] Most of the relevant REED volumes have been published for the region: see *Cumberland/Westmorland/Gloucestershire*, ed. Audrey Douglas and Peter Greenfield (Toronto: University of Toronto Press, 1986); *Lancashire*, ed. David George (Toronto: University of Toronto Press, 1991); and *Chester*, ed. Lawrence M. Clopper (Toronto: University of Toronto Press, 1979). Work on the Cheshire volume, edited by David Mills and Elizabeth Baldwin, is nearing completion and advance reports do not include further news of Leicester's Men in the northwest.

[42] For household accounts of the 1560–88 period, see *Lancashire*, 151–81.

[43] See Adams, "'Because I am of that countrye'," 44–45, for further details of Dudley's engagement in Coventry's affairs and for sample gifts in the Coventry Payments Out Book and Chamberlains' and Wardens' Accounts, see *Coventry*, ed. R.W. Ingram, REED (Toronto: University of Toronto Press, 1981), 270–71, 310, 314.

[44] *Coventry*, 270. For performances by Warwick's and Sussex's troupes at court, see Scott McMillin and Sally-Beth MacLean, *The Queen's Men and their Plays* (Cambridge: Cambridge University Press, 1998), 14–16.

to Kenilworth, a nineteen-day extravaganza of festivities which might have recalled the players to augment the household and contribute to the dramatic presentations. Beyond the Coventry payment in the same year, we have little evidence that they were in the neighborhood. But we may question where they were, if not at Kenilworth, that year.[45] Their customary summer tour cannot be tracked elsewhere in 1575. It was not an exceptional year for Coventry's civic purse, however. In 1580, the troupe again tripled the amount given to others and continued to be rewarded at the highest level for the rest of the decade.[46] After their formation, only the renowned Queen's Men commanded more than Leicester's, but they were setting a new standard across the country.

Coventry was the most welcoming city in the midlands and the troupe performed often in the region – partial itineraries can now be traced for sixteen years out of thirty at this time.[47] This was the heartland of the patron's regional interests, but even a glance at the annual tours will confirm that Leicester's players had a much wider range for their travels – wider than any troupe's other than the Queen's Men, in fact – and that touring was a central and constant feature of their career. Their patron's early exercise of influence, even in the early 1560s, assured them of official sanction for their performances across the kingdom, and his special status as royal favorite guaranteed a higher level of reward.

There were a few disruptions in their provincial career. The players did become anxious shortly after the proclamation reviving the existing laws against unlawful retainers in 1572 lest their affiliation with their patron be challenged. Dudley had previously run into some trouble for infringing these laws, his instincts for grandeur sometimes straining even the Queen's indulgence. In 1565 he had been pardoned for such infringements and "licensed for life to retain 100 persons who were not in the queen's service, besides his household servants and officers serving under him."[48]

---

[45] The Coventry payment is unspecific in its time period. It falls among payments for a variety of performers some time after the entry for the Queen's guards coming to survey before the royal progress, but payments following for the previous 30 May and for Lent, even earlier, indicate that these accounts were not kept in chronological order (Chamberlains' and Wardens' Account Book II, Coventry Record Office: A 7 [b], p. 8).

[46] *Coventry*, 294, 298, 310, 317.

[47] REED research in some counties, such as Staffordshire, Hertfordshire, and Bedfordshire, has not yet been completed and work on Warwickshire's neighbor, the county of Northamptonshire, has not yet begun.

[48] For a careful analysis of the context and consequences of this proclamation and the statute 14 Elizabeth, c. 5 for the relief of the poor and against rogues and vagabonds, see Peter

Between 3 January 1571/72, the date of the proclamation, and 20 February 1571/72, the date when penalties were to take effect, Dudley's troupe wrote the following letter to their patron:

To the right honorable Earle of Lecester
their good Lord and master

Maye yt please your honor to vnderstande that fforasmuche as there is a certayne Proclamac*io*n out for the reviving of a statute as touchinge retayners as your Lordshippe knowith better than we can enforme you therof. we therfore your humble S*er*vaunt*es* and daylye Orators your players for avoydinge all inconveni*en*c*es* that maye growe by reason of the saide statutes are bold to trouble your Lordshippe w*i*th this our suite humblie desiringe your honor that (as you have bene alwayes our good Lord and master) you will now vouchsaffe to reteyne vs at the pr*e*sent as your housshold S*er*vaunt*es* and daylie wayters not that we meane to crave any further stipend or benefite at your Lordshippes handes but our Lyveries as we have had and also your honors License to certifye that we are your housshold S*er*vauntes when we shall have occasion to travayle amongst our ffrendes as we do vsuallye once a yere and as other noble mens Players do and have done in tyme past wherebie we maye enioye our facultie in your Lordshippes name as we have done hertofore. Thus beyinge bound and readye to be alwayes at your Lordshippes com*man*demente[49] we committ your honor to the tuition of the almightie

Long may your Lordshippe live in peace
   a pere of noblest peres:
In helth welth & prosperitie
redoubling Nestors yeres

Your Lordshippes S*er*vaunt*es*
most bounden
Iames Burbage
Iohn Perkinne
Iohn Lanham
William Iohnson
Roberte Wilson
Thomas Clarke[50]

The letter provides confirmation of aspects of the relationship between patron and players described earlier in this essay: the players essentially

---

Roberts, "Elizabethan players and minstrels and the legislation of 1572 against retainers and vagabonds," in Anthony Fletcher and Peter Roberts (eds), *Religion, Culture and Society in Early Modern Britain: Essays in honour of Patrick Collinson* (Cambridge: Cambridge University Press, 1994), 29–55, esp. 31–32.

[49] "com*man*demente" is written over another word.

[50] This is an undated formal copy of the letter, now bound as fos. 125–27v in the third volume of miscellaneous Dudley papers at Longleat House. Published by permission of the Marquess of Bath, Longleat House, Warminster, Wiltshire, Great Britain.

looked to Dudley for sponsorship in their annual touring, valuing the
currency that his name brought to their enterprise and wearing his livery
to make the sponsorship apparent. Now they were looking for closer
identification in the form of a license stating that they were his household
retainers, although they were at pains to assure him that they were not
seeking the type of quarterly wage that other resident members of the
household would expect.

Although Dudley's reaction is not on record, the troupe's resumption of their provincial touring in 1573 for another decade suggests
that he responded positively with the legal protection required. Unfortunately, there are no household account books corresponding to this
important creative period in their career, but acts of the Privy Council
and treasurer of the chamber accounts reveal that from 1572 to 1581,
Leicester's Men performed at court during Christmas or Shrovetide annually at least once if not more. The 1572 and 1573 performances in
particular would have served to emphasize their status as his household
retainers. In both years they were the dominant entertainers, performing
three plays each year. Although they may not have received quarterly
wages, the opportunities that their patron found for them at court were
of particular value, both for their prestige and their income. Dudley was
also willing to spend considerable amounts from his own purse to emphasize the relationship and to outfit his players in the manner befitting
his household ambitions. A rare wardrobe account covering the years
March 1571/72 through March 1573/74 contains routine expenses for
servants' liveries, but includes also an exceptional list of livery expenses
for the players entered on 24 December 1573, presumably in preparation
for their court performances at Whitehall on 26 and 28 December and
at Shrovetide. Approximately twenty pounds was spent on fine fabrics of
spectacular colors, calling to mind the "peacock's tail" image of retainers
mentioned earlier – nine yards of broad blue silk sarsenet, thirteen yards
of narrow crimson silk camlet, three yards each of white and blue Bruges
satin, fifteen yards of russet satin, two yards of red and white striped satin,
and purple and orange-colored taffeta.[51]

It would seem that the players made a good impression. Only three
months after the Shrovetide performance, Leicester's Men were granted
the first royal license to perform "Com*m*edies Tragedies Enterludes and
stage playes to gether with their musicke" anywhere in the kingdom,
including the city of London, provided that their plays be approved by

---

[51] Longleat House: Dudley Papers Vol. XII, fo. 31.

the Master of the Revels in advance and that they not be played during the time of common prayer or when the plague was at its height in London.[52] This is a celebrated landmark in the history of the English stage, among other implications, singling out the troupe of the Queen's favorite for special privileges so that they might provide "recreation of oure loving subiectes as for our solace and pleasure when we think good to see them."[53]

The precedent set by this license in 1574 presaged the foundation of the Queen's own troupe in March 1582/83. Dudley's players in this period were some of the stars of the Elizabethan stage. When Sir Francis Walsingham hired twelve of the finest actors in the country to create the Queen's Men in 1582/83, he drafted three of the five players named in the 1574 license – Lanham, Johnson and Wilson.[54] Burbage, who may have been the most entrepreneurial member of the troupe, opened the Theatre in Shoreditch in 1576 and thereafter may have confined his activities to London.[55] It seems likely that Leicester's Men would have performed on occasion at the Theatre, especially during the warm-up period before Christmas at court, when it was customary for the favored troupes to rehearse their presentations in and about London, but of this we have no sure proof.[56]

The loss of the key players to the Queen's troupe in 1583 was an unmistakable disruption in their customary pattern of alternating court performances during the festive season with the annual provincial tour. Most of the troupe members who held the royal patent must have performed the lost play, *Telomo*, at Richmond on 10 February 1582/83,

---

[52] The royal license, in Patent Roll 16 Elizabeth, pt. 9, was issued 10 May 1574. See *Dramatic Records of the City of London*, ed. E. K. Chambers, Malone Society Collections 1 (Oxford: Oxford University Press, 1909), pt. 3, 262–63, for the published transcription. The players named are the same as those who signed the 1572 letter, with the exception of Thomas Clarke, about whom nothing further is known (see Edwin Nungezer, *A Dictionary of Actors* [New Haven: Yale University Press, 1929], 92, and David Kathman's "Biographical Index to Elizabethan Theater," http://www.clark.net/pub/tross/ws/bd/kathman.htm, a website updating Nungezer's work).

[53] For a discussion of their prominence in the 1570s, see Scott McMillin, "The Queen's Men and the London Theatre of 1583," in C. E. McGee (ed.), *The Elizabethan Theatre X* (Port Credit, Ontario, 1988), 10–13.

[54] For a study of the political context for the formation of the Queen's Men, including Dudley's role, and their subsequent career, see McMillin and MacLean, *The Queen's Men and their Plays*.

[55] Nothing further is known of the fifth actor named in the license, John Perkin (see Nungezer, *Dictionary of Actors*, 274, and Kathman's website).

[56] See, for example, the Acts of the Privy Council entry for 24 December 1578, requiring the Lord Mayor of London to allow six companies, including Leicester's, "to exercise playeng within the Cittie, whome their companies aforenamed are appointed to playe this tyme of Christmas before her Majestie." *Acts of the Privy Council of England*, ed. John Roche Dasent, n.s., x (1577–78) (London, 1895; repr. Kraus, 1974), 436.

shortly before joining the Queen's Men in March. There are no further court or provincial appearances of Leicester's Men between February 1582/83 and June 1585 when another troupe under Leicester's patronage appears in the civic records of East Anglia. We may wonder if this was an entirely new company of actors or whether some of the twelve players specified (but not named) in a 1577 Southampton civic account escaped the draft and continued service as part of a reconstituted troupe.[57] Or were more of the players named to the Queen's Men drawn from the ranks of Leicester's? The records cannot be drawn out on these details. What can be deduced is the attitude of the patron himself.

No right-minded courtier would have resisted the draft of his players to a prestigious company in the Queen's patronage. Leicester's Men had, in spirit if not in fact, been functioning for some years as a quasi-royal company, with a range of touring and a level of reward to be equaled only by the Queen's Men. Their patron had the stability of the realm among his foremost concerns in these years and his familial, religious, and political sympathies were closest to those of Walsingham, who called the Queen's company into existence. The Dudley household account book extant for 1584–86 contains intriguing evidence that Dudley, in fact, took a close interest in the Queen's Men while also, predictably, ensuring that a company bearing his own name resumed touring.[58]

Several payments to the Queen's Men suggest that their former patron maintained his personal contact with them and that he may have taken a continuing interest in their court appearances and in the direction of their tours. Apart from his own troupe, they are the only players to show up in his accounts, just before their Christmas performances at court in 1584 and 1585, and before their summer tour in 1585.[59] The initial pattern of contact with his own troupe is reminiscent of the opening years of his career. The first evidence of their reformation comes in May 1585, when they receive several generous payments before setting off "into the Countrie" on a tour that took them through East Anglia, the Midlands and the southwest as far as Bath and Gloucester. Aside from possible previews in London in the late spring, their performances do not seem

---

[57] Southampton Book of Fines, Southampton Record Office: SC5/3/1, fo. 167.

[58] For a fuller discussion of this important household book, see my articles, "Leicester and the Evelyns: New Evidence for the continental tour of Leicester's Men," *Review of English Studies*, n.s., 39 (1988), 487–93, and "Politics of Patronage," as well as Simon Adams, "The Papers of Robert Dudley, Earl of Leicester: 1. The Browne-Evelyn Collection," *Archives* xx (1992), 63–85, and *Household Accounts*.

[59] For further details on Leicester's involvement with the Queen's Men, see MacLean and McMillin, *The Queen's Men and their Plays*, 18–24.

to have been intended for their patron's household although he spent time at both Wanstead and Kenilworth during this summer.[60] Nor is this unusual. Apart from the likelihood that the players had been involved during the extraordinary entertainments at Kenilworth in 1575, there are only two other instances in the thirty years of Leicester's patronage when surviving tour records may support their appearance for household events of prime significance. Leicester was favored with two visits from the Queen in 1578. The first was 6–16 May, providing the occasion for presentation of Sir Philip Sidney's *Lady of May*, a pastoral entertainment for Elizabeth as she walked in Wanstead garden.[61] There is no trace of Leicester's Men elsewhere in the spring of this year, so they may have been part of this first royal visit to Dudley's newly acquired residence in Essex.

The second royal visit in 1578 came two days after the occasion of his wedding to Lettice Knollys at Wanstead on 21 September. The players are on record elsewhere at Aldeburgh in Suffolk early in the same month but it is quite possible that they were in attendance, to delight the wedding guests and expand Leicester's household at the time of the royal visit.[62]

Although the players usually performed for the royal household rather than their patron's, this should not be considered surprising. Dudley was not a typical landed aristocrat, but rather a courtier whose first place was with the Queen at Christmas and Shrovetide. As a patron with a sharp instinct for self-advertisement, he would have looked for opportunities to engage his troupe in the activities of the royal household and their list of appearances is impressive: featured at Christmas 1560–62, in his earliest years as Master of the Horse, sixteen Christmas and Shrovetide appearances during their heyday from 1572 to 82/83, and a final performance in 1586.[63] When he did call upon his players to act as household retainers for personal reasons, it was more likely for exceptional events, such as

---

[60] The household accounts are closely detailed throughout this period with payments noted for other entertainers, usually musicians, on Dudley's own itinerary. See, for example, Adams, *Household Accounts*, 294, 296–97, for payments to the singers of Coventry and Birmingham, Lord Lumley's fool, and Lord Essex's taborer. If Leicester's Men had appeared at either Wanstead or Kenilworth, it is probable that their lord would have given them a reward at the time which would have been entered in these accounts.

[61] First printed in the third edition of *The Countesse of Pembrokes Arcadia . . . with sundry new additions* (London, 1598; *STC*: 22541). For further details see McGee and Meagher, "Preliminary Checklist," 98–99.

[62] See J. C. Coldewey (ed.), "Playing Companies at Aldeburgh 1566–1635," *Collections* IX, Malone Society (Oxford: Oxford University Press, 1977), 19.

[63] Standard sources for court appearances include *Dramatic Records in the Declared Accounts of the Treasurer of the Chamber 1558–1642*, Malone Society Collections VI (Oxford: Oxford University

the entertainments at Kenilworth. Of these few, the most remarkable on record was the triumphal progress through the Netherlands in 1585–86.

In 1585, Dudley finally achieved a long-sought goal. He and Walsingham had been arguing for a policy of intervention in the Low Countries in support of the cause against Spain for almost a decade. His personal ambition was to lead a force to relieve the embattled Dutch and to forge a Protestant alliance against the arch-enemy, Philip II. After years of frustrated lobbying and months of uncertainty about his own role, he was appointed commander of the expedition in October 1585.[64] The size of his personal household entourage at the outset was approximately one hundred, with a further seventy-two lords and gentlemen with their own retinues to swell the ranks.[65] This was the company that arrived in the Netherlands with Dudley in December of that year, but there were others who had set out ahead, notably a company of players. They were summoned to Leicester House in London and paid six pounds on 4 December before their departure for the Low Countries several days before their patron.[66] There is no doubt that the size of the troupe was increased for the purpose of the excursion abroad. A billeting list for the Hague entry on 6 January 1585/86 makes provision for fifteen players, as well as twelve musicians, and we can be certain that some of these fifteen were not regular members of Leicester's Men.[67] Both Robert Wilson, by then one of the Queen's Men, and Robert Browne, probably of Worcester's Men, appear abroad in the household accounts.[68]

The players were part of Dudley's splendid courtly retinue for his progress through Middelburg, Dordrecht, Rotterdam, and Delft to The Hague for Epiphany. Gaps in the surviving account book must have been covered by another book, destroyed in the Birmingham Library fire of 1879. A few extracts from the latter source show that the players

Press, 1962, for 1961); *Documents relating to the Office of the Revels in the time of Queen Elizabeth*, ed. Albert Feuillerat (Louvain, 1908); and *The Acts of the Privy Council of England*, ed. J. R. Dasent, n.s., vols. 7–32 (London, 1893–1907).

[64] For a fuller account of the expedition to the Netherlands and the events leading up to it, see MacCaffrey, *The Making of Policy*, 348–401.
[65] See Adams, *Household Accounts*, 22–23, 27–29, and 429 for precise details.
[66] MacLean, "Leicester and the Evelyns," 493.   [67] BL: Cotton Vespasian CXIV, fo. 320 col. b.
[68] For the entry relating to Browne, see MacLean, "Leicester and the Evelyns," 491, 493, and for Wilson see Adams, *Household Accounts*, 374. Adams' source is the transcript made by the Rev. Edward Hadarezer from the Stanton manuscript, a 1585–87 household account book lost in the 1879 fire at the Shakespeare Memorial Library, Birmingham (see Adams, *Household Accounts*, 5, 10–11). Both this and the 1584–86 account book were used for entries abroad in the first half of 1586. There is further evidence for Wilson's travels back and forth to England during the period in BL: Harleian 1641, fo. 19v. On 12 January 1585/86 he was paid £10 at court in Greenwich to carry letters to Leicester at Leiden (my thanks to Scott McMillin for this reference).

performed at least once during the Christmas season before some of them returned to England in the new year.[69] Will Kemp, who was clearly one of Leicester's Men, set out on 4 January but he was back with Dudley again by early May.[70] After the Christmas round of entertainments, at least some of the players may have been released for their English touring season which seems to have focused on the southwest via the Thames Valley in the early spring.

1586 was a remarkable year in the life of the patron and his players. It was his quasi-regal household they performed for at Christmas, and, as governor-general of the Netherlands, he may have recalled some of them by April for the St. George's Day celebrations at Utrecht with the traditional Garter ceremony and elaborate banquet following. Stow's *Chronicle* is the source for one of the entertainments at the banquet, a show of tumbling and dance titled "The Forces of Hercules" which "gaue great delite to the straungers for they had not seene it before."[71] A month later, embattled but still hopeful of his position, Dudley and his players transferred an annual custom to a new location, innovative and yet traditional in its purposes. When he makes his payment to his players at Arnhem at the end of May, it is not for a summer tour of the English provinces. Five players – Thomas Stephens, George Bryan, Thomas King, Thomas Pope, and Robert Percy – were dispatched, with the requisite letter of introduction from their patron, to tour parts of northern Europe where the courts of Frederick II of Denmark at Elsinore and Christian I, Elector of Saxony, made them welcome as representatives of their lord. This tour would have extended the reputation of Dudley and promoted the skills of English performers in new settings. Will Kemp and his boy Daniel Jones were to follow later, to augment or alternate performances at Elsinore in August and September.[72] German archives indicate that the troupe of five actors became attached to Christian's court at Dresden until July 1587, although Kemp and his boy presumably returned home sooner.[73]

[69] Adams, *Household Accounts*, 370. Leicester's Men are likely to have performed at the sumptuous banquet hosted by Dudley at Delft. Strong and Van Dorsten, *Leicester's Triumph*, 40–41, refer to town accounts for costs of two banquets, the other hosted by the town. Among the intermingled expenses were charges for "Dutch music of all kinds" as well as for singers and players.
[70] MacLean, "Leicester and the Evelyns," 490, 493.
[71] John Stow, *The Annales of England . . . vntill this present yeere 1592* (London, 1592; *STC*: 23334), 1214–15.
[72] MacLean, "Leicester and the Evelyns," 492, 493.
[73] E. K. Chambers, *The Elizabethan Stage*, 4 vols. (Oxford: Clarendon Press, 1923), II, 271–73. See also Thomas Heywood, *An Apology for Actors* (London, 1912; *STC*: 13309), sig. E1, and Johannes Bolte's transcripts from the Elsinore Register, "Englische Komödianten in Danemark und

What did these adventurous actors on the Continent perform? The
only entertainment of any description which we can perhaps associate
with them is "The Forces of Hercules." Brief as it is, Stow's commentary
may hold a few clues. A show featuring physical dexterity, music, and
dance would transcend language barriers while allowing for a variety
of delights with a dual political purpose – to display superior English
talents affiliated with the patron presiding and to compliment Dudley
himself, the new Hercules come to lend his strength to the Dutch cause.
References to the troupe who traveled to Denmark and Saxony suggest
that their performances at these foreign courts may also have highlighted
the arts of tumbling and music: they are called "instrumentister och
springere."[74] Even the early summer entry in Dudley's household account book describes Thomas King as "on of your Lordship mvssycions"
although neither his name nor that of any of the others appears on the
list of twelve musicians in Dudley's suite drawn up earlier in the year.[75]
There is no doubt that these instrumentalists and acrobats were actors
too. Pope and Bryan went on to become members of Lord Strange's
Men after Dudley's death in 1588, as did Will Kemp.[76]

   The acting talents of Leicester's Men may not have been fully on display during the continental tour because of inherent language problems.
But we may ask what evidence survives in the English records to indicate
their range of performance at home? Only a handful of play titles can
be found and no corresponding texts have yet been discovered. From
the provincial records comes only one title, *Myngo*, noted at Bristol
in 1577. There are more known from court records: *Predor and Lucia*
(Christmas, 1573); *Mamillia* (Christmas, 1573); *Philemon and Philecia*
(Shrovetide, 1573/74); *Panecia* (Christmas, 1574); *The Historie of the Collier*
(Christmas, 1576); *A Pastorall or A History of a Greek Maid* (Christmas,

Schweden," *Jahrbuch der deutschen Shakespeare Gesellschaft* 23 (1888), 101. It is clear from English
   civic records that another section of Leicester's troupe was again touring the provinces from at
   least January through the spring and summer of 1587.
[74] As quoted by Johannes Bolte, "Englische Komödianten," 101. See also Thomas Whitfield
   Baldwin, *The Organization and Personnel of the Shakespearean Company* (New York, 1961), 74–76, for
   another account of Leicester's Men on the Continent.
[75] Leicester Household Account Book, Christ Church, Oxford: Evelyn MS 258b, fo. [56]. See
   also Adams, *Household Accounts*, 351. The names of the twelve musicians, as recorded by Henry
   Goodyer in January 1585/86, are quoted by Strong and Van Dorsten, *Leicester's Triumph*, 122,
   from BL: Galba 108, fos. 98v–99. See also Strong and Van Orsten, 85–86, for a brief account
   of the activities of the Earl's musicians on the Continent: it should be noted that their discussion
   of the players is somewhat misleading because they did not know about the 1584–86 Dudley
   Household Account Book.
[76] Stevens and Percy have not yet shown up in later records (see Nungezer, *Dictionary of Actors*, 273,
   338–39, and Kathman's website).

1578/79); *Delight* (Christmas, 1580); and *A History of Telomo* (Shrovetide, 1582/83). Harbage and Schoenbaum tentatively classify the first four of these as romances, the *Greek Maid* as a pastoral (perhaps also a romance), and both *The Collier* and *Delight* as comedies.[77] Without the texts, it is impossible to be certain, but judging by the titles alone, these plays would seem to have been lighthearted productions appropriate for the festive season when they were featured. But is this all that can be said?

Their patron's personal interest in the political uses of theatre must be taken into account in considering the repertoire of Leicester's Men. Early in his career at court, Dudley was given a double reward for his intervention on behalf of the Inner Temple in a dispute with the Middle Temple. The more enduring benefit was the offer of the lawyers' skills in his service and the pledge never to give counsel against him. The other was both public and ceremonial, and very much to the man's taste. In 1561, the lawyers of the Inner Temple chose Dudley as their Christmas lord, Prince Pallaphilos. The revels celebrating Dudley's reign included a masque, *Desire and Lady Beauty*, and a tragedy, *Gorboduc*, which Marie Axton has perceptively analyzed for politically inspired themes.[78] Fortunately, texts survive for both, as well as a rare eyewitness account of the premiere performance of *Gorboduc* on Twelfth Night 1561/62 recently discovered by Norman L. Jones.[79] The eyewitness focuses much of his attention on the dumbshows which opened each act of the tragedy, although the 1565 and 1570 printed editions give no indication of their function or content.[80] The courtier concerned does, however. Like the dumbshow in Hamlet's *Murder of Gonzago*, *Gorboduc*'s mime sequences addressed controversial contemporary issues, including the rival marriage suits of Dudley and the king of Sweden. Unsurprisingly, the lawyers favored Dudley's cause, the second dumbshow of *Gorboduc* reinforcing what Axton has shown to be the message of the masque. Like the eyewitness, others attending the Inner Temple revels would have grasped

---

[77] Alfred Harbage (ed.), *Annals of English Drama 975–1700*, rev. S. Schoenbaum (Philadelphia, 1964), 42–51. The third edition, revised by Sylvia Stoler Wagonheim (London, 1989), 44–52, essentially repeats this information.

[78] Axton notes that the Inner Temple had been the Duke of Northumberland's Inn, undoubtedly an association that gave pleasure to his son who inherited his "lively appreciation of the possibilities of art and politics." See Marie Axton, *The Queen's Two Bodies: Drama and the Elizabethan Succession* (London: Royal Historical Society, 1977), especially 10, and her earlier study, "Robert Dudley and the Inner Temple Revels," *Historical Journal* 13 (1970), 365–78.

[79] The eyewitness account has been given a stimulating analysis by Norman L. Jones and Paul Whitfield White in "*Gorboduc* and Royal Marriage Politics: An Elizabethan Playgoer's Report of the Premiere Performance," *English Literary Renaissance* 26 (1996), 3–16.

[80] *STC*: 18684 and 18685.

the political subtext of these presentations but they were not the only audience intended.

On 18 January, Dudley sponsored a performance of both the masque and the play at Whitehall before the Queen. Axton's summary of the advice offered Elizabeth through the medium of theatre is also an illustration of Dudley's own purposes: "the Inner Templars offered the Queen advice upon the two most controversial political questions of the day: her marriage and the succession. The solutions were complementary, two aspects of a coherent policy. Both questions, the lawyers insisted, must be settled by the Queen in Council. The lawyers created for Elizabeth a Prince, presented him as protector of the established religion and offered him as the solution to the marriage question. All the power of emblem and allegory were used to suggest unanimity and concord in the choice of this Prince. The tragedy, by contrast, dealt with the question of disrupted succession, the difficulty of attaining concord between monarch and council when a natural course of succession was disrupted, the consequent civil war, and the improbability of choosing a legal successor under these circumstances. The contrast between the two entertainments was intended to be striking. Marriage was the approved course."[81]

A decade and more later, Dudley was still pursuing the same political issues with the aid of his theatrical protégés. George Gascoigne's *The Princely Pleasures at Kenelworth Castle*, published a year after the Queen's visit to Dudley in 1575, reveals that artful persuasion for marriage was the theme of several of the entertainments, with Olympian and Arthurian pedigrees provided for the Earl of Leicester, still her native, if aging, suitor.[82] It seems likely that Leicester's Men may have been engaged in some of these dramatic presentations, as well as in a play mentioned as one of the highlights of her second week at the castle in Robert Langham's *Letter*, another colorful eyewitness account: "So, after supper waz thear a play prezented of a very good theam, but so set foorth by the Actoourz well handling, that pleazure and mirth made it seeme very short, though it lasted too good oourz and more."[83] Was the "good theme" without

[81] Marie Axton, "Robert Dudley and the Inner Temple Revels," 374–75.
[82] For further details, see Axton, *The Queen's Two Bodies*, 61–66 and "Tudor Mask," 35–37. A unique copy of the 1576 edition of *The Princely Pleasures* was destroyed in the 1879 fire at the Birmingham Reference Library. For the later editions available (*STC*: 11638 and 11639), see C. E. McGee and John C. Meagher, "Preliminary Checklist of Tudor and Stuart Entertainments: 1558–1603," *Research Opportunities in Renaissance Drama* 24 (1981), 92–93.
[83] *Robert Langham: A Letter*, introduction, notes and commentary by R. J. P. Kuin (Leiden: University of Leiden Press, 1983), 55 (*STC*: 15190.5). Muriel Bradbrook devotes a chapter to Leicester's Men

purpose beyond entertainment? Given the context and the usual strategies of the patron it seems naive to assume so.

While we do not know the play which may have been performed by
Leicester's Men at Kenilworth, there was another familiar entertainment
offered to the Queen at Wanstead in May 1578 which may have engaged
their talents. Philip Sidney's *The Lady of May* has been called "the earliest
example in English of conventionalized pastoral drama," a genre destined for increasing popularity at court and in the public theatres.[84] Both
Marie Axton and William Ringler note that it was probably performed
by professional actors, skilled in dialogue and song. The surviving text
does make apparent that such seemingly escapist fare could resonate
with current concerns – various strands of interpretation include the
waning of Dudley's marital ambition and the debate over active support
for the Protestant cause in the Netherlands.[85]

Even when Dudley's royal aspirations had finally dimmed and his
dynastic goals encouraged him to make a risky marriage, he continued
to pursue other causes which associated themselves with drama of the period. In particular, the plays of Robert Wilson, a member of Leicester's
Men before the 1582/83 draft, are of interest for their political perspective. The three extant plays which can be ascribed to Wilson are
anti-Catholic and anti-Spanish in their international commentary and
Puritan in their criticism of the domestic church and the clergy.[86] Of
these, *The Cobbler's Prophecy* has been plausibly suggested as the play that
roused the Queen's anger in a performance at court in January 1587/88:
"after the Queen had heard a comedy, she flew into a passion with the
earl of Leicester, who was present, and told him that it behoved her at
any cost to be friendly with the king of Spain. 'Because,' she said, 'I see
that he has great preparations made on all sides.'"[87] Whether or not this
irritating comedy was Wilson's, the episode serves as another example
of theatre used for political purposes and associated with Leicester, who

at Kenilworth, but much of her discussion focuses on the mistaken identification of Langham
with John Lanham, one of the actors in the troupe (*The Rise of the Common Player: A Study of Actor and
Society in Shakespeare's England* [Cambridge: Cambridge University Press, 1962], 141–61). Robert
Langham has since been identified as a mercer of London and keeper of the Council Chamber
at the time.

[84] William A. Ringler Jr. (ed.), *The Poems of Sir Philip Sidney* (Oxford: Oxford University Press, 1962),
361.

[85] See, for example, Ringler, *Poems*, 361–62, and Marie Axton, "Tudor Mask," 37–41.

[86] Richard Dutton, *Mastering the Revels: The Regulation and Censorship of English Renaissance Drama* (Iowa
City: University of Iowa Press, 1991), 66–72.

[87] Quoted by Dutton, *Mastering the Revels*, 69, from the translation of Antonio de Vega's 9 January
letter in *Calendar of State Papers: Simancas*, IV: *Elizabeth 1587–1603*, ed. Martin A. S. Hume (London,
1899), 191.

worked indefatigably against Spain and for a moderate Puritan church at home. We know that Wilson was one of Leicester's Men until he joined the Queen's company; that he may have written the first of his surviving plays, *The Three Ladies of London* while in Leicester's service; and that he rejoined his former patron's troupe for the trip to the Low Countries.[88] The players' payments which surface in Dudley's 1584–86 household account book come at strategic times of year, when an interested patron might well want to preview the repertoire of troupes scheduled to perform at court during the Christmas season or be about to set out on their annual tour through the kingdom. Like Hamlet's close counseling of the players at Elsinore, it is feasible that a politically alert patron like Dudley may have engaged their efforts in furthering causes that he wished to promote at court or in the provinces.

Paul Whitfield White has shown that earlier Tudor acting troupes served the Reformation cause of their Protestant patrons with pious interludes and that similarly polemical drama continued into the early Elizabethan period.[89] He identifies Dudley as one of those likeliest to use his patronage of players to promote Protestant propaganda. Like others of similar religious persuasion, notably his brother Warwick, he "protected and supported advanced Protestant preachers, pamphleteers, and printers engaged in producing works treating the same ecclesiastical and theological issues found in the moral interludes." White suggests several plays by William Wager that may have been in the repertoire of Leicester's Men,[90] as well as the moral interlude *New Custom*, published in 1573, which seems to mirror Dudley's attitude at the time to the ongoing controversy about the use of vestments in the church.[91] These are plausible suggestions, but as he admits, they can only be guesswork, given our lack of hard evidence in the form of dedications or prayers to patrons in the extant texts of the period.[92]

---

[88] Dutton notes (71) that the standard datings of *The Three Ladies* (1581/84) may mean that it was written for Leicester's Men and Scott McMillin, *The Queen's Men*, 32, thinks it probable. David Kathman's biographical essay for the New Dictionary of National Biography (forthcoming) dates *The Three Ladies* as 1581, but places *The Cobbler's Prophecy* in the early 1590s.

[89] Paul Whitfield White, *Theatre and Reformation: Protestantism, Patronage and Playing in Tudor England* (Cambridge: Cambridge University Press, 1993) and "Patronage, Protestantism and Stage Propaganda in Early Elizabethan England," *Yearbook of English Studies* 21 (1994), 39–52.

[90] White, *Theatre and Reformation*, 64–66, 180.

[91] White's case for *New Custom* as a Leicester's play is given in "Patronage, Protestantism and Stage Propaganda," 51–52.

[92] Eleanor Rosenberg, *Leicester: Patron of Letters* (New York: Columbia University Press, 1955), 306–07, identifies William Gager, author of the Latin tragedy *Meleager*, as the playwright most closely associated with Dudley, but this was in the realm of academic drama at Oxford, rather than the popular stage.

Although hampered by the loss of play texts and continuous family papers, we are still unusually fortunate in the evidence we do have for analysis of Dudley as a patron of players. Conscious of the inherited tradition and fully aware of his privileges as royal favorite, he embraced the patronage system on his own terms, in the course of his career playing a key role in promoting theatre for the new Elizabethan age.[93]

---

[93] For touring itineraries for Leicester's Men and related maps and source materials, please see the *Shakespeare and Theatrical Patronage* website at http://icdweb.cc.purdue.edu/~pwhite/patronage/

CHAPTER 10

Patronage and the companies of boy actors

Michael Shapiro

On 31 July 1996, *The New York Times* published an article in its education section entitled "$114 Million Campaign Lifts a Black College to the Elite of Fund-Raisers."[1] The title referred to Spelman College's unprecedented success in fund-raising under the leadership of its president, Dr. Johnetta Cole. One of her strategies is to give donors, both black and white, a stole of kente-cloth, "a multicolored West African weaving," which Dr. Cole describes as "the stripe of royalty." Bestowing this gift on her donors, which designates them as "the royalty of this institution," transforms their tax-deductible but still no doubt generous contributions of cash or commodities into an exchange of gifts, a ritual of reciprocity. As Dr. Cole observes, "Gift giving is fundamentally a way [of] establishing a relationship."

Dr. Cole is surely correct, and her success at establishing many such relationships speaks for itself, and may involve the parties in subsequent gift exchanges. In all such relationships, friends of Spelman College (or any nonprofit institution) donate money or property in return for expressions of appreciation, for recognition of their generosity, for honors to themselves or others, for memorials to relatives or friends, and in some cases, for objects of little material worth but of high symbolic value. From a purely materialistic, cost-accounting perspective, aside from possible tax benefits to the donor, the institution gets the better of the exchange by far: the stoles of kente-cloth cost a fraction of the donations received. But what is missing from the cost accountant's perspective is the incalculable pleasure of patronage, the inner satisfaction of feeling magnanimous, especially when the gift fosters projects dear to the donors' hearts, helping either to create something new or to preserve or enhance something old. Participation in gift exchanges

---

[1] William H. Honan, "$114 Million Campaign Lifts a Black College to the Elite of Fund-Raisers," *New York Times*, 31 July 1996, B6.

helps us to formulate and express our personal and social identities: by gifts shall we know ourselves and be known to others.

I

Much has been written of late about the difference between exchanges of gifts and exchanges of commodities, not only from an anthropological perspective but also with regard to early modern Europe. Some commentators regard sixteenth-century England as a locus of transition from a feudal culture, in which gift-giving was a way of articulating relationships based on reciprocal service, to a market culture, in which goods and services were commodified, that is, exchanged according to their monetary value as established by economic forces.[2]

In a recent dissertation, Barbara Sebek has elucidated the debate in the late Tudor period between advocates of what are often seen as two different systems of exchange. Gift exchange is easily idealized, for it is said to create what Sebek calls "perpetual bonds of friendship."[3] In such works as Arthur Golding's translation of Seneca's *De Beneficiis* (1578), it is contrasted with traffic in commodities and evaluated as superior, for being the tangible expression of what can neither be seen nor measured. Participants in gift exchange are bound in continuing if not inalienable relationships. They are linked by moral bonds based on trust and conscience, which are not enforceable by law, for their gifts betoken an exchange of good turns or favors between friends. Unlike the temporally limited obligations of contract and trade, gift exchange, as Seneca explains, insures endless reciprocity to the mutual benefit of both parties:

For him that lendes me monny, I must paye no more than I have taken: and when I have payd it, I am free and discharged. But untoo the other [one who gives a benefit] I must pay more: and when I have requyted him, yet neverthelesse I am still beholden to hym. For when I have requyted I must begin new again.[4]

---

[2] See, for example, Wallace T. MacCaffrey, "Place and Patronage in Elizabethan Politics," in S. T. Bindoff et al. (eds.), *Elizabethan Government and Society* (London: Athlone Press, 1961), 97–126; and Linda Levy Peck, *Court Patronage and Corruption in Early Stuart England* (Boston: Unwin Human, 1990), 1–29.

[3] Barbara Sebek, "Cracked Commodities, Cursed Gifts: Transacting Women and Conceptualizing Exchange in Early Modern England," unpublished Ph.D. dissertation (University of Illinois, 1994), 1–84. The quoted phrase appears on 50.

[4] Seneca, *[De Beneficiis, or] The woorke of the excellent Philosopher Lucius Annaeus Seneca concerning Benefyting, that is too say the dooing, receyving, and requyting of good Turnes*, trans. Arthur Golding (London: John Day, 1578), sig. E4.

In short, such relationships require continuous giving, receiving, and repaying.

Seneca seems to have in mind an exchange between or among equals, whereas in feudal and early modern culture, the exchange of gifts was often part of a hierarchical social structure. Whether or not the language of mutuality is preserved, gift exchange becomes intricately involved in networks of patronage, in which differentials of power, prestige, status, and class are often crucial elements.[5] It would seem naive to regard gift exchange, whether in Seneca's or Golding's lifetime, as devoid of self-interest, for the underlying purpose of such exchanges is to generate mutual obligations and benefits of incalculable worth and infinite duration, far more likely to serve the deeper interests of the parties than a temporally limited, legally enforceable traffic in commodities of carefully defined and therefore limited monetary value.

To understand early modern patronage in terms of gift exchange, one must not be misled by the idealizing rhetoric of Golding's Seneca and other traditionalist opponents of the developing cash-based market economy, although such rhetoric tells us what patrons and clients wanted to think about their transactions. Indeed, then as now, gift and commodity systems of exchange not only coexisted but constantly interpenetrated one another, essentially because the distinction between making money and offering service was far from clear cut. It was costly to perform service, as Elizabeth's courtiers knew, and hence some mechanisms to recoup costs needed to be devised so that loyal subjects might serve their sovereign without depleting their own or her resources. Monopolies, patents, reversions, wardships, a host of privileges and offices granted by the Queen would repay such loyalty and engage the recipients in a series of reciprocal gestures of service and reward. In short, the sovereign could bestow lucrative favors upon those who had

---

5 In looking at gift exchange in a number of cultures, Marcel Mauss, *The Gift: The Form and Reason for Exchange in Archaic Societies*, trans. W. D. Halls (London: Routledge, 1990 [first published in 1950]), 39 et passim, speaks of the three obligations: to give, to receive, to reciprocate. C. A. Gregory, *Gifts and Commodities* (London: Academic Press, 1982), stresses competitive aspects of gift-giving in which power, authority, and status are gained and lost (55) and in which domination and control are established (19). Gregory distinguishes gift and commodity systems but sees them as complementary and as capable of transmuting into one another. Annette B. Weiner, *Inalienable Possessions: The Paradox of Keeping-While-Giving* (Berkeley: University of California Press, 1991), also sees gift exchange as agonistic, but believes that it is motivated less by reciprocity, or "the hoary idea of a return gift," than by "the radiating power of keeping inalienable possessions out of exchange" and hence increasing one's own spiritual energies to achieve "hegemonic dominance over others" (150).

pleased her with gifts and service, in part so that they could afford to continue to please her with more gifts and service. Like the royal patron, those of her appointees who wielded some power or controlled access to power, or who from our point of view simply performed bureaucratic services, generally expected to receive gifts and service from supplicants, and so on down the line.[6]

Early modern theatre illustrates the blurring of distinctions and inter-twining of service and profit, gift-giving and commodification. Although theatre historians often narrate an evolution from gift exchange to com-mercial transaction, a rigid dichotomy seems simplistic. Playing, for actors, was always a business for which they expected to be paid, even though they styled themselves as the servants of such and such an aristo-crat to acknowledge a role they occupied for part, if not all, of the year. Wearing the livery of an aristocratic patron became, after 1572, a way for acting troupes to exempt themselves from vagrancy laws intended to prohibit the wandering of "masterless men." The official patrons of such troupes, as well as the other aristocrats in whose banqueting halls such troupes often performed, regarded the plays they paid for as gift offerings to them, or from them to their guests. Maintaining or hiring small acting troupes was an integral part of the elaborate ethos of hospitality or housekeeping, and such practices continued long after the theatre became part of London's commercialized entertainment industry.[7] Although London-based troupes began as early as the mid-sixteenth century to perform in purpose-built theatres before paying customers eventually numbering in the hundreds if not thousands at a single performance, touring by acting troupes, with its dependence on the patronage of provincial elites and municipal authorities, continued until the closing of the theatres in 1642. So did court performances by London-based companies, performances commissioned by the highest patron of the land and for which the actors were amply rewarded.

If theatre in the early modern period is, as Walter Cohen calls it, "a socially composite organization," a hybrid of the feudal and capitalist forms I have described as gift and commodity systems, the work of

---

[6] MacCaffrey, "Place and Patronage," 97–126. See Richard Dutton, *Mastering the Revels: The Regulation and Censorship of English Renaissance Drama* (Iowa City: University of Iowa Press, 1991), 41–44.

[7] Suzanne Westfall, *Patrons and Performance: Early Tudor Household Revels* (Oxford: Clarendon Press, 1990), 122–51. On the ethos of housekeeping in the period, see Felicity Heal, *Hospitality in Early Modern England* (Oxford: Clarendon Press, 1990), 1–191.

the children's troupes is a particularly vivid example.[8] Most previous scholarship on the boy companies has stressed either their ritualistic function in a gift-exchange system, or their profit-seeking in the commercial entertainment business. Here, we have two legitimate but very different meanings of the term "patronage," one based on reciprocal gestures between patrons and clients, the other based on the hope of making money by attracting paying customers. Much of the scholarship on the children's troupes has too sharply, in my view, differentiated the two modes, or at best has focused too narrowly on the evolution from the former to the latter. It is surely the case that the general movement from the court performances in the early Tudor court to the "private theatre" performances in Paul's and Blackfriars after 1599 represents a drift from gift exchange toward commercialization, but the transition is by no means perfectly linear and the two systems continually mix. In the pages that follow, I propose to recast the history of the children's troupes, stressing the dynamic interplay between these two modes of patronage.[9]

II

A relatively pure example of theatrical gift-giving is the performance of *Sapientia Solomonis* by the students of Westminster grammar school on 17 January 1566 before Queen Elizabeth, her guest Queen Cecilia of

[8] Walter Cohen, *Drama of a Nation: Public Theater in Renaissance England and Spain* (Ithaca: Cornell University Press, 1985), 151. As Cohen's subtitle makes clear, his emphasis is on the public theatre, which he characterizes as capitalistic and "fundamentally artisanal." He acknowledges the influence of the children's troupes on the repertories of adult companies and on the development of hall theatres, but dismisses them as "having done no lasting damage to their adult rivals" (266). Douglas Bruster, *Drama and the Market in the Age of Shakespeare* (Cambridge: Cambridge University Press, 1992), examining what he calls "a poetics of the market" (11), both situates the theatre within a rapidly developing market economy and traces the dramatists' responses to such changes, but in so doing he makes little, if any, distinction between public and private theatre plays, or plays by adult or children's troupes. Dutton, *Mastering the Revels*, 31–32, describes the newly built London theatres as sites of "capitalist entrepreneurial enterprise" but points out that they were used by companies forced to work, at least in part, within a "traditional patronage system." In short, he concludes that "free enterprise was conditioned by the vital necessity of maintaining aristocratic protection."

[9] For the history of the children's troupes, I draw on several standard accounts: E. K. Chambers, *The Elizabethan Stage*, 4 vols. (Oxford: Clarendon Press, 1923), II, 1–76; Harold N. Hillebrand, *The Child Actors*, University of Illinois Studies in Language and Literature, XI (1926), nos. 1–2 (repr. New York: Russell and Russell, 1964); Alfred Harbage, *Shakespeare and the Rival Traditions* (New York: Macmillan, 1952); and Michael Shapiro, *Children of the Revels* (New York: Columbia University Press, 1976). The most recent of such works is Andrew Gurr's, *The Shakespearian Playing Companies* (Oxford: Clarendon Press, 1996), 218–29, and 337–65. Although I think Gurr overstates the commercialism of the children's troupes, especially the earlier ones, I cite this book frequently because of its cogency and because it incorporates relevant recent scholarship.

Sweden, and possibly members of her Privy Council. This production apparently fulfilled the statutory requirement dating from about 1560 that the Westminster grammar school students produce a Latin play each year. The previous year, the Queen attended a performance of a Roman comedy at the school, probably Plautus' *Miles Gloriosus* and perhaps also Terence's *Heautontimorumenus*. The text used was an adaptation of a work by Sixt Birck, a German schoolmaster, dramatizing the relationship of Solomon and the Queen of Sheba in a way appropriate for schoolboys. It was originally printed in 1547. Whoever adapted the play for the Westminster students also added several hundred lines and introduced new characters: three morality play abstractions and a low-comic prankster named Marcolph derived from comic slaves of Roman comedy and morality play Vice-figures. The Westminster text also includes a prologue and epilogue making explicit the allegorical connection with Elizabeth and Cecilia.[10]

There is much about the Westminster performance of *Sapientia Solomonis* that makes the play seem like a gift offering. For one thing, Elizabeth was clearly the school's patron, having restored her father's foundation shortly after her accession. At some point on this occasion she received one of several elaborately executed manuscript copies of the text, written in red and black ink and bound "in vellume with the Queenes majestie hir armes & sylke ribben stringes."[11]

The production seems not to have been heavily subsidized by the Revels Office, the branch of the royal household responsible for selecting plays for royal entertainment and assisting their production at court. There is no record of expenses either in the Chamber Accounts or the Revels Accounts for *Sapientia Solomonis*, although there was a payment to the Children of Paul's for performing a play before Elizabeth and Cecilia at the latter's lodgings in the Savoy. Nor for that matter is there any record of payment by the Revels Office for transportation of its materials to Westminster, as there was the previous year. Instead the archives of the abbey contain a bill for "expenses for the furniture and setting forthe of A play entytled, Sapientia Solomonis." These expenses total 52s 10d and that amount was paid by the school or the abbey by way of reimbursement to "Master Brown," probably Thomas Browne, then headmaster of the school. There is no other recorded payment to Browne himself for his work in staging the production. In fact, the bill

---

[10] Elizabeth Rogers Payne (ed.), *Sixt Birck, Sapientia Solomonis* (New Haven: Yale University Press, 1938), 24–45.
[11] Ibid., *Sapientia Solomonis*, "The Bill for the Westminster Performance," between 40 and 41.

records a payment by the school to the officers of the revels of 13s 8d
and stipulates a charge "for the conveiance of thapparell from the revelles
unto westminster, & from thence unto the revelles againe."[12] Although
assisted by the Revels Office, this production was evidently staged some-
where on the grounds of the school or the abbey with which it was
associated rather than in a banqueting hall in one of the royal residences
in or around London. The Revels Office loaned costumes but did not
pay for their transportation.[13]

Under the first Tudor monarchs, children's troupes from various institutions began performing plays at court. Henry VII and Henry VIII had
been entertained by the Children of their own Chapel Royal, a group of
boy choristers maintained primarily to supplement the adult members
of the Chapel Royal in providing music at worship services. In 1527/28,
Henry VIII and his guests were also entertained by the grammar school
students of St. Paul's, who also performed Latin plays before Cardinal
Wolsey and his guests. Nicholas Udall brought his grammar school students from Eton to play before Cromwell in 1538, and his pupils from
Westminster grammar school to play before Mary in 1554 and evidently
on other occasions.

But it was Elizabeth who, in the first half of her reign, was most often
entertained in her own palaces by various troupes of children. Among
such companies were her own Chapel Children, the juvenile division of
her Chapel Royal, but more frequent entertainers were the boy choristers from St. Paul's Cathedral, from the Chapel Royal at Windsor, and
from Westminster Abbey. The Revels Accounts often record expenses for
mounting these productions or transporting materials from the Revels
Office to one of the Queen's residences, suggesting royal subsidization,
if not patronage. The Chamber Accounts record payment on such
occasions to the masters of the troupes – usually Sebastian Westcote
(or Westcott) of Paul's, Richard Ferrant (or Farrant) or William Hunnis of

[12] Ibid.
[13] On one other occasion, Elizabeth may have attended a play at a location other than one of the
royal banqueting halls. On 29 December 1601, Dudley Carleton wrote to John Chamberlain:
"The Q: dined this day privatly at my Lord Chamberlains; I came even now from the blackfriers
where I saw her at the play with all her candidae auditrices." The letter is quoted and discussed
by C. W. Wallace, *The Children of the Chapel at Blackfriars, 1597–1603*, Nebraska University Studies,
1908 (repr. New York: AMS, 1970), 95ff.; cf. Chambers, *Elizabethan Stage*, ii, 48 n. 6; Hillebrand,
Child Actors, 166. Wallace, who argues that the Queen herself established the Children of the
Chapel at the Blackfriars theatre, sees this passage as evidence of her attendance on at least one
occasion. Chambers and Hillebrand disagree. Without subscribing to Wallace's entire theory, I
am persuaded by Carleton's casual reference to "the play," which he too seems to have attended,
that Elizabeth might well have made a visit to a private theatre on this occasion.

Windsor and later the Chapel Royal, and John Taylor of the Westminster Choir – in the amount of £6 13s and 4d per play. The fixed sum suggests that the fee was not related to expenses incurred in the production, but was a grant made either to reward the sponsoring institution or to compensate the master and others for services rendered. Eventually, some of these companies established their own theatres, ostensibly so that they could "rehearse" the plays they were likely to bring to court. Rewards for playing at court and income from rehearsals for court performance strike modern scholars as the objects of commercial transaction, but it is possible that men like Mulcaster, Westcote, and Ferrant sought ways to finance the increasingly lavish productions they felt obliged and perhaps honored to present to Elizabeth if asked to do so by the Revels Office.

The earliest record of a "private theatre" for a boy company concerns the hall of the Merchant Taylors, a space used by the students of the grammar school maintained by the guild, who performed under the direction of Richard Mulcaster, headmaster from 1561 to 1586. Admission cost a penny and was evidently open to the public. In March 1574, however, the masters of the guild forbade the use of their hall for plays, on the grounds that "everye lewd persone thinketh himself (for his penny) worthye of the chiefe and most comodious place withoute respecte of any other either for age or estimacion in the comon weale."[14] Andrew Gurr sees this incident as "an early illustration of playgoing's commercial pressures, where the price of a seat buys a social positioning as much as a physical space," and refers to "Mulcaster's *commercial exploitation* of his boys."[15] Mulcaster's students may have performed in the guildhall as rehearsals for their appearances at court on 1–3 February 1573 and 2 February 1574 or in preparation for an audition before the Master of the Revels, as the Westminster grammar school boys had done in 1564/65. At any rate, the troupe continued to perform at court even after the order forbidding it to use the guildhall, appearing on 15 February 1575, and 6 March 1576, but not again thereafter until their last appearance on 12 February 1583. What is not known is whether the ban remained in force or was rescinded, what effect it had on court appearances, and whether or not the troupe found alternative space. The critical issue is whether or not the troupe found alternative space, whether these guildhall performances were regarded as preparations for bringing a theatrical gift-offering to court, or as business ventures camouflaged to provide a legal fiction and perhaps to enhance their commercial appeal.

---

[14] Quoted by Chambers, *Elizabethan Stage*, II, 75.
[15] Gurr, *Shakespearean Playing Companies*, 220, my emphasis.

Most likely they were both gifts and commodities, both rehearsals and "rehearsals," depending on whose perspective one adopts.

The most frequent payee for court performances in the first half of Elizabeth's reign was Sebastian Westcote, almoner and choirmaster at Paul's from 1547 to 1582. He seems to have continued the theatrical tradition established by the previous almoner and choirmaster, John Redford, under whom he had served for a year or so as a vicar choral. There is no record of theatrical performances by the Children of Paul's during the Edwardian regency (1547–53), and relatively little such activity during Mary's reign (1553–58), presumably because the restoration of Roman Catholic liturgy meant more work for the cathedral's musical establishment. Westcote did lead the children in an appearance before the then Princess Elizabeth at Hatfield House, her official residence, on 12 February 1552. Princess Elizabeth's Household Accounts for 1551/52 list payments of 20s to the King's drummer and fife, 30s to Mr. Heywood, and a disproportionate sum of £4 19s "to Sebastian, towardes the charge of the children with the carriage of the plaiers garmentes."[16] Unfortunately, there is no way of knowing how much of Westcote's share was intended to cover such costs as transporting costumes or properties, how much went for the children's expenses, how much went to the Cathedral, and how much to Westcote himself. Perhaps because of the favor gained from previous appearances before Elizabeth prior to her accession, Westcote and the Paul's boys were frequent entertainers at court after she became queen in 1558. They may have been the troupe which appeared at court as early as August 1559 or Christmas 1560, but their first unambiguously recorded appearance was during Christmas 1561. For the next two decades, they were the most popular troupe of adults or children to entertain the Queen, appearing on about two dozen subsequent occasions. For these productions, Westcote was payee and presumably producer/director. Although we cannot tell how much money he personally made from such appearances, his will indicates that he had acquired some wealth and property, although as almoner and choirmaster of St. Paul's, Westcote had other sources of income beyond the reward received for bringing plays to court.[17]

Another form of royal patronage is the protection he received from those who objected to his religious views and practices. In the 1560s,

---

[16] Quoted by Hillebrand, *Child Actors*, 116. The troupe may have been the company who entertained Princess Elizabeth and Queen Mary at Hatfield House, although the evidence (Thomas Warton's *History of English Poetry* [1871], III, 312) does not permit identification of the actors involved.

[17] Westcote's will is printed in Hillebrand, *Child Actors*, 327–30.

during the vigorous attempts to establish Anglican practice in all churches, Westcote was often in trouble with ecclesiastical and municipal authorities for Catholic sympathies if not outright recusancy. He was threatened with excommunication and hence dismissal, and at one point was briefly imprisoned in Marshalsea. He nevertheless retained his post at St. Paul's, and while there is no direct evidence of royal protection, he was at one point defended by Robert Dudley, the Earl of Leicester, himself a royal favorite. As Dudley was generally regarded as sympathetic to the institutionalizing of the Protestant reformation, his protecting of Westcote may have been requested by his own patron, Elizabeth.[18]

Westcote was also given extraordinary powers to impress, or draft, talented boy choristers from any choir in the land, and on one occasion the Privy Council interceded when someone else tried to impress one of his choristers. In short, Westcote's relationship with his sovereign can be construed in terms of gift exchange. The money he received for providing theatrical entertainment, though no doubt useful and welcome, is, like the protection from zealous reformers, evidence of an ongoing relationship with the sovereign in what might be seen as a reciprocal system of obligations, where the monetary reward was seen as one of the gifts exchanged rather than as a cash payment for services rendered.

Like Mulcaster, Westcote had his children rehearse before paying spectators in some sort of theatre on the Cathedral grounds. Such a playhouse is suggested by Westcote's will, which records bequests "to Shepard that kepeth the doore at playes" and to "Pole the keper of the gate," presumably one of the gates of the churchyard.[19] In 1575, the Repertory of the Court of Common Council recorded a complaint to the Cathedral authorities that "one Sebastian . . . kepe the playes and resort of the people to great gaine," a complaint which suggests that some kind of playing space was used by choristers for the master's personal profit.[20] Whether maintained solely for profit or out of a desire to please the royal patron, Westcote established and maintained a fee-charging playhouse, somewhere on the grounds of St. Paul's Cathedral.[21]

---

[18] Trevor Lennam, *Sebastian Westcott, the Children of Paul's, and "The Marriage of Wit and Science"* (Toronto: University of Toronto Press, 1975), 21.

[19] Quoted in Hillebrand, *Child Actors*, 330.   [20] Ibid., 123.

[21] Possible locations for the playhouse at St. Paul's have included St. Gregory's parish church, the almonry or a hall therein, the hall of the college of Minor Canons, the Chapter or Convocation House, a hall in one of the buildings under the almoner's control just outside the precinct, and a hall or makeshift theatre in one of several properties leased to Westcote. Lennam, *Sebastian Westcott*, concluded that "the precise location of the Paul's playhouse remains obscure" (44). A specific location was proposed by Reavley Gair, "The Staging of Plays at Second Paul's: the Early Phase,

Richard Ferrant, following the lead of Mulcaster and Westcote, also established some sort of theatre for the Children of the Chapel Royal to use in preparing to audition or in rehearsing for court performance. He did so by renting space in 1576 in the precinct known as Blackfriars, a former Dominican priory. Any theatre located there – as on the grounds of St. Paul's Cathedral – was thus exempt from the jurisdiction of the mayor and alderman, the municipal authorities who strove to curtail, if not eliminate, theatrical activity in London throughout the early modern period.

Ferrant was moving a step beyond previous Masters of the Chapel Royal. The monarch's own boy choristers had entertained their royal patron under the leadership of William Cornish as early as the reign of Henry VII.[22] Court performances by the Chapel Children are also recorded under subsequent masters – Richard Bower, who held the post from 1545 to 1561, Richard Edwards who served from 1561 to 1567, and William Hunnis, who served from 1567 to 1597, with some sort of temporary leave from 1576 to 1580, during which time the post was effectively filled by Ferrant. Ferrant had been master of the Children of the Chapel of St. George, Windsor, since 1564. In Shrovetide, 1567, an acting company of Windsor boy choristers under his leadership appeared at court, as they continued to do nearly every year until 1575.

1599–1602," in G. Hibbard (ed.), *The Elizabethan Theatre VII* (Toronto: Macmillan, 1977), 21–47; and *The Children of Paul's: the Story of a Theatre Company, 1553–1608* (Cambridge: Cambridge University Press, 1982), 44–56. Gair placed the theatre in the southwest quadrant of the precinct in a private house under the almoner's control. This "little house," he argues, was a two-story structure built across the northwest corner of the cloister and was the only playhouse ever used at any time by the chorister troupe. For reactions to Gair's theory, mostly skeptical, see reviews by Ejner Jensen, *Comparative Drama* 18 (1984–85), 82–84; and Peter Hollindale, *Review of English Studies* 36 (1985), 80–81, as well as more detailed responses by Michael Shapiro, "The Children of Paul's and Their Playhouse," *Theatre Notes* 36 (1982), 3–5; and Herbert Berry, "Sebastian Westcott, the Children of St. Paul's, and Professor Lennam," *Renaissance & Reformation* 14 (1978), 77–82. Gurr cites Gair's work on the playhouse, but tactfully concludes, "Where exactly it was in the precinct and what was its shape and capacity are not clear from the surviving documents" (221–22 n. 10).

   We do not know how long a playhouse had been in existence at Paul's prior to the complaint against Westcote in 1575, so that we cannot be sure whether to credit him or Mulcaster, whose playhouse was in existence by 1574, with the establishment of the first English "private theatre," that is, the first indoor or hall theatre to charge admission. Both Mulcaster's and Westcote's playhouses were probably in existence by the mid-1560s, when the two masters regularly brought their troupes to court. Gurr suggests that Westcote saw a chance to fill the market niche which the Merchant Taylors' Boys had occupied until "the close-down on Mulcaster's commercial exploitation of his boys" (220).

22 Gordon Kipling, "Henry VII and the Origins of Tudor Patronage," in Guy Fitch Lytle and Stephen Orgel (eds.), *Patronage in the Renaissance* (Princeton: Princeton University Press, 1981), 149–64.

On 6 January 1577, the court records document a joint performance of a play entitled *Mutius Scevola* by the choristers of the Windsor chapel and the Children of the Chapel Royal, and for several years thereafter Ferrant was associated with the latter troupe in their frequent court appearances.

We do not know where the Chapel Children had rehearsed prior to Ferrant's establishment of the first Blackfriars theatre in 1576. They may have used a hall available to the Chapel Royal, until Ferrant, for un-known reasons commercial, political, or aesthetic, moved the troupe's rehearsal space to the portion of Blackfriars he rented from William More and converted into a playhouse. After Ferrant's death in 1580, Hunnis bought his widow's lease to the playhouse, a move which evi-dently required More's approval. The Earl of Leicester, who we recall had been Westcote's protector, intervened on Hunnis's behalf to support his claim, declaring that Hunnis "meanes ther to practise the Queens children of the Chappell, being nowe in his chardge, in like sort as his predecessor did for the better trayning them to do her Majestie service."[23]

Although Hunnis did acquire the lease in 1580, the playhouse was used for the next four years by a combination of Chapel and Paul's cho-risters playing not directly under his supervision but rather under the sponsorship of the Earl of Oxford and his associate John Lyly. Andrew Gurr thinks that the use of the names of both Chapel and Paul's sug-gests that the actual choristers of neither institution were involved, and that a specially recruited group of juvenile actors performed under the joint rubric, or separate, or other rubrics as the occasion demanded. Gurr's hypothesis is consistent with his thoroughly commercial view of the enterprise, which he, like Alfred Harbage, evidently finds salutary in the case of the adult companies but reprehensible when ascribed to the children's troupes. What seems to underlie this view appears to be an assumption that adult troupes, like Shakespeare's, were theatrical collectives comprising equal sharers (which not all were), but that the children's troupes were vehicles enabling the masters and managers to "run . . . [their] boys for profit," as Gurr puts it,[24] that is, to get rich on the backs of a juvenile labor force.

At one point in the early 1580s, Henry Evans, a scrivener, became involved in the management of the troupe. Some commentators suggest that he was the principal agent of the further commercialization of the boy companies. Evans had evidently been close to Westcote, possibly

---

[23] Quoted by Hillebrand, *Child Actors*, 91. [24] Gurr, *Shakespearean Playing Companies*, 223.

in the production of plays by the Children of Paul's, to judge from his subsequent interests in boy companies. Westcote mentioned Evans in his will as his "loving frend," designated him as "overseer" of the will, and urged him "to be carefull for my sister Elizabeth Wescote widow in her affayres and busyness as tyme shall serve."[25] Acting on his own, or else in partnership with Oxford and Lyly, Evans acquired the lease for the first Blackfriars theatre from Hunnis and sold it to Oxford around June 1583. In 1584, however, William More regained his lease on the Blackfriars property and evicted the children's troupe, probably a combination of Paul's and Chapel boys playing under Oxford's name. Perhaps it was Evans's past association with Paul's that permitted the troupe, or the Paul's contingent, to shift its operations back to the playhouse on the Cathedral grounds, now under the control of Westcote's successor, Thomas Giles.

Throughout the 1580s, Lyly's plays were performed by the amalgamated or separate children's companies both at court and in the private theatres at Blackfriars and Paul's, and the early printed texts often include different prologues and epilogues for the different venues. Whatever the venue, these extradramatic speeches strike the same courtly posture, gracefully sounding the tropes of *sprezzatura*, the self-deprecating ploy advocated by Castiglione for use when a courtier is entertaining his patron. To judge from the tone of these extradramatic addresses written for court or private theatre performances, as well as Lyly's interest in dramatizing the relationships between remote and celibate sovereigns or deities and their mortal subjects and admirers, the ambience at the first Blackfriars theatre in the early 1580s and at the playhouse in Paul's in the latter 1580s approximated that at court, and that approximation may indeed have been the basis of whatever commercial success the Children of Paul's achieved in their own playing space.[26]

The question asked of the court and private theatre productions of the 1570s must be raised again with respect to plays written by Lyly and others for the children's troupes in the 1580s. Were productions staged by the Evans-Oxford-Lyly partnership during the early 1580s at the first Blackfriars playhouse and then later at Paul's intended as part of a gift exchange or were they commercial ventures? In arranging for his own children's troupe to perform at court, Oxford was from one point of view striking the classic pose of courtier – entertaining his sovereign by

---

[25] Ibid., 329, 330.
[26] Shapiro, *Children of the Revels*, 38–51; cf. Dutton, *Mastering the Revels*, 61–65, who stresses differences between court and private theatre audience responses.

means of his own efforts or through his good offices in order to establish
a relationship, a relationship which might (re)gain royal favor and with
it provide him with influence, access to influence, and lucrative gifts,
privileges, and offices. Lyly, as author of these plays, assisted his own
patron, Oxford, and later hoped, on the basis of a veiled hint from
Elizabeth, that his reputation as a court entertainer might secure for
him the reversion to the Mastership of the Revels, a position in which he
could prosper and continue to entertain his sovereign and benefactor.[27]
In short, Evans, Oxford, and Lyly probably pursued different goals, and
their motives in producing plays at court and in private theatres probably
included a desire both for immediate financial gain and for access to royal
patronage.

As separate troupes or as an amalgamated company, the enterprise
went downhill after the loss of the Blackfriars lease. One reason for
the decline may have been the establishment in 1583 of an adult troupe,
the Queen's Men, more directly under royal patronage than either
of the two leading children's troupes. This company was created by
Edmund Tilney, the Master of the Revels, out of the best adult talent available. The Queen's Men gave three performances at court in
1583/84, when the Chapel Children and Oxford's boys gave one each,
and the following year the troupe gave four. No other adult troupe appeared at court until the Lord Admiral's Men did so in 1588/89. The
creation of the Queen's Men solved several problems: it appeased the
municipal authorities by limiting the number of adult companies allowed
to "rehearse" in London; it ended the competition for court appearances
among patrons of other adult troupes, it centralized the authority of the
Master of the Revels over the theatrical industry, and, as Richard Dutton
has suggested, it permitted the Revels Office to "provid[e] high quality
entertainment for the court relatively cheaply."[28]

Whether the new policy of favoring the Queen's Men with court performances was a change in policy or a reflection of changing court tastes,
the children's troupes seemed to go into decline. The Chapel Children
did not perform at court under their own name after 2 February 1584,
and Oxford's boys, perhaps an amalgamation of Paul's and Chapel choristers, appeared at court for the last time during the following Christmas

[27] G. K. Hunter, *John Lyly: the Humanist as Courtier* (London: Routledge and Kegan Paul, 1962), 68–88.

[28] Dutton, *Mastering the Revels*, 51; for a thorough study of the Queen's Men see Scott McMillin and Sally-Beth MacLean, *The Queen's Men and their Plays* (Cambridge: Cambridge University Press, 1999).

season, 1584/85. The Children of Paul's came to court regularly each
Christmas season from 1586/87 to 1589/90, but in 1591 the publisher
of the quarto of Lyly's *Endimion* declared that "the Plaies in Paules were
dissolved."[29] Most scholars believe that the troupe was silenced as a result
of its participation in the Marprelate controversy, although there is no
evidence as to what was deemed offensive. Gurr suggests that sporadic
records of provincial appearances by both children's troupes during the
1590s indicate that the troupe(s) "tried to make some money by touring,
itself a mark of their transfer from academic to commercial guidelines."[30]
But these half-dozen or so recorded provincial appearances seem too few
and far between to represent serious commercial intentions, and might
also represent the use of forged charters or other fraudulent efforts by
other troupes to appropriate the names and exploit the reputations of
the London boy companies. By the early 1590s, both children's companies were dormant, and there is no record of performances by the
troupes either in their own London playhouses or at court until the end
of the 1590s, when both the Paul's boys and the Chapel Children were
resuscitated.

III

The two leading children's troupes resumed playing in 1599 and 1600
as somewhat more commercialized enterprises than they had been a
decade earlier. The directorates of both revived companies involved entrepreneurs who surely expected a return on the money invested in the
companies. Despite this drift toward commodification, some aspects of
the troupes' activities in the decade or so between resuscitation and
demise within a decade or so, nevertheless seem to perpetuate features
of gift exchange. Both resuscitated troupes maintained a nominal, if not
stronger, affiliation with a prestigious religious choir and rehearsed, or
"rehearsed," in playhouses associated more or less directly with the chorister companies prior to 1591, and both entertained Elizabeth during
the winter revels at court.

The resumption of playing at Paul's is usually dated sometime after
May 1599, when Edward Pearce succeeded Thomas Giles as choirmaster. Giles, who was terminally ill, retained the choirmaster's house and
salary, which has led Gurr to suggest that Pearce was compelled by

---

[29] Endimion, "The Printer to the Reader," in *The Complete Works of John Lyly*, ed. R. Warwick Bond,
3 vols. (Oxford: Clarendon Press, 1902), III, 18.
[30] Gurr, *Shakespearean Playing Companies*, 226.

necessity to revive the idea of "marketing the choir as a company of players in the old playhouse,"[31] that is, reinstituting the practice of playing at Paul's. Whatever Pearce's motives, presumably under his supervision, to some degree, playing continued, even after Giles died in July 1600. Court appearances followed within a year of revival, and are duly recorded in the Revels Accounts. During the winter revels of 1600/01, the company played at court, as it did several more times until its demise in 1607. Its last court performance, 30 July 1606, was of a lost play entitled *The Abuses*, on the occasion of a visit by James's brother-in-law, Christian of Denmark.

The degree of control Pearce exercised over the troupe is problematic, as is the issue of whether the actual choristers under his control were identical with the acting troupe which styled itself the Children of Paul's or whether the latter was an entirely separate group of boys recruited and trained only for acting. Pearce, like his predecessor Giles, had the power to impress boys into the Paul's choir, which usually numbered around ten or twelve. The acting company evidently used a larger group. *Antonio's Revenge*, for example, requires seventeen actors, if one believes, as Gurr does, that boy companies did not normally double roles.[32]

In the latter part of 1600, about a year after the resumption of playing at Paul's, the Children of the Chapel Royal also began performing in their own playhouse in Blackfriars. This second Blackfriars theatre was located in a different part of the priory from that used by the combined Chapel-Paul's-Oxford children's company between 1576 and 1584. Most scholars believe that the moving force behind the revival of the Chapel Children was Henry Evans, formerly associated with Westcote and later with Oxford, Lyly, and the children who performed at the first Blackfriars. In September 1600, Evans leased from the Burbage family a part of the Blackfriars, which they had four years earlier hoped to turn into a theatre to be leased to the Lord Chamberlain's Men. When influential residents of this affluent neighborhood protested, the plan was

---

[31] Ibid., 339.

[32] Ibid., 340. These lists are printed by Hillebrand, *Child Actors*, 110–12; two names in the 1598 list also appear in the text of Marston's *Antonio and Mellida*, which suggests that these two choirboys, at least, were also part of the acting troupe. See also Gair, *Children of Paul's*, 131. Whether or not the children's troupes doubled roles is moot: Roslyn L. Knutson, "The Devil in the Details: *Histriomastix* and the Number of Players in Paul's Boys, 1599–1603," unpublished paper, suggests that the children's troupes might have doubled roles in order "to use the company's experienced players efficiently and develop the skills of the inexperienced players"; even with doubling, she finds that some plays produced within four years of the company's revival require 13–18 speaking actors and about a half dozen extras. I am grateful to Prof. Knutson for sharing work in progress.

abandoned, so that the Burbages were probably pleased to find a tenant, one whom the neighbors evidently found acceptable. Evans' partners in this enterprise included his son-in-law, Alexander Hawkins, Edward Kirkham of the Revels Office, and Nathaniel Giles, choirmaster of the Chapel Royal following the death of William Hunnis in 1597. Like all previous choirmasters, Giles held the right to impress boys into his service. Just as Pearce did at Paul's, Giles used his impressment privileges to augment the twelve boy choristers of the Chapel Royal, for several plays call for eighteen to twenty actors to be onstage at once and one of the legal documents refers to a troupe of eighteen or twenty.[33]

Henry Clifton, the father of one of the children impressed, protested (successfully) to the Privy Council to have his son returned. He charged that Giles recruited a group of boys entirely separate from the choirboys to serve as actors at Blackfriars.[34] The opposite is suggested by the wording in the revised writ of impressment issued to Giles in 1606, forbidding him to permit his choirboys to be "used or imployed as Comedians or Stage players, or to exercise or acte anye Stage playes Interludes Comedies or tragedies, for that it is not fitt or decent that such as shoulde singe the praises of God Almightie shoulde be trayned upp or imployed in suche lascivious and prophane exercises."[35] Thereafter, but perhaps no earlier, it is possible that an entirely different set of actors with no connection to the Chapel Royal performed at Blackfriars, which might explain subsequent references to the troupe as the Children of Blackfriars.

Like the Children of Paul's, the Chapel Children, under its various names, performed at court during the winter revels in 1600/01 and nearly every year thereafter until 1608/09. At that time, the company lost its playhouse in Blackfriars, which was taken over by an adult troupe, the King's Men. The former tenants migrated to a theatre in Whitefriars, and changed the troupe's name from the Children of the Queen's Revels to the Children of the King's Revels. Court performances by a troupe using the latter name are recorded during the winter revels of 1609/10 and 1611/12, while a reconstituted troupe styling itself as the Queen's Revels performed four or five plays at court during the winter of 1612–13 and began traveling thereafter.

Despite the regularity of court performances after 1600/01, the revived children's troupes were part of a theatrical world which had changed significantly during the 1590s. For one thing, adult troupes now appeared at court far more often than the boy companies, who had begun to be edged

---

[33] Wallace, *Children of the Chapel*, 75–76; Hillebrand, *Child Actors*, 203.
[34] Hillebrand, *Child Actors*, 160–63.   [35] Chambers, *Elizabethan Stage*, ii, 52.

out in the 1580s by the Queen's Men and then became inactive for most
of the 1590s. After 1594, the virtual monopoly held by the Queen's Men
became a "duopoly," as Gurr puts it,[36] in which the Lord Chamberlain's
Men and the Lord Admiral's Men, now performing in their own amphitheatres, divided the London theatrical business between them. This
limitation of permitted troupes to two seems to have been loosely enforced, perhaps restricted to "public" theatres, and was never invoked to
prevent the revival of playing at Paul's or Blackfriars, so-called "private"
playhouses. Moreover, as these playhouses were located on the grounds
of St. Paul's Cathedral and in the liberty formerly controlled by a
Dominican Priory, they were exempt from municipal control, as were
adult companies performing outside the city limits either in Shoreditch
or Bankside.[37]

As the theatre industry grew, so did the authority of the Master of
the Revels. Traditionally responsible for providing the court with entertainment, he was subsequently authorized to license companies, then
playhouses, and by 1606, any texts to be printed. There is no evidence
that the Revels Office supplied costumes and properties for court productions by the newly revived children's companies after 1599 as it had
done throughout the earlier part of Elizabeth's reign. C. W. Wallace
thought he had found such evidence in an account by a German visitor,
the secretary to the Duke of Stettin-Pomerania, who visited Blackfriars
in 1599. According to this observer, the Queen had a theatre built
["*erbauet hat*"] and had supplied it with an abundance of expensive ap-
parel so that the musically talented choirboys could play a weekly comedy
in order to prepare for court appearances. Most subsequent commentators discount this claim of royal patronage, at least to the degree of having
the theatre built expressly for the Chapel Children, but the supplying of
costumes by the Revels Office remains a possibility.[38]

It is not even clear how much jurisdiction the Master of the Revels had
over the children's troupes. Gurr suggests that his authority extended only
to "public" playing, which meant only over the adult troupes performing
in open-roofed amphitheatres, and not over playing in academic or chorister theatres, considered "private" performances as they were held in

[36] Gurr, *Shakespearean Playing Companies*, 65.
[37] Stephen Mullaney, *The Place of the Stage: License, Play, and Power in Renaissance England* (Chicago: University of Chicago Press, 1988), 47–55.
[38] Wallace, *Children of the Chapel*, 105–25; Hillebrand, *Child Actors*, 164–66. The passage also mentions an admission price of 12d, the presence of a select group of spectators, and a musical prelude, but its assertion of royal patronage seems to most historians to be exaggerated, if not altogether misinformed.

halls or indoor venues often belonging to their sponsoring institutions.[39]
Tilney never issued patents to the revived children's troupe, nor did he officially license their playhouses. Pearce and Giles, the two choirmasters,
did receive royal patents giving them the power to impress boys into
service. Nevertheless, Tilney regularly invited their companies to entertain Elizabeth and then James at court. One of Tilney's assistants,
Edward Kirkham, a Revels Officer since 1581 and Yeoman since 1586,
was listed as official payee for a few court performances by children's
troupes, and may have also functioned as a manager, an investor, or as a
representative of the Revels Office. At the dissolution of the Blackfriars
operation, Gurr believes he "was acting like a government receiver in a
bankrupt company."[40]

In 1604, the Blackfriars children's company received the first patent
ever issued to a boy company. Signed by James and Anne, it permitted this troupe to call itself the Children of the Queen's Revels. Queen
Anne evidently wished to set up a household establishment parallel to
the King's. This project included her own acting company, the Lord
Chamberlain's Men having become the King's Men, as well as her own
Lord Chamberlain and, under his jurisdiction, several other officers, including the equivalent of her own Revels Office. A patent of 1604 made
Samuel Daniel something like Anne's Master of the Revels, with responsibilities to provide her with theatrical entertainment, providing that the
texts first obtained his "approbacion and allowaunce."[41]

Daniel was an unfortunate choice, for he soon found himself in trouble
over his own Blackfriars play, *Philotas* (1605), which seemed to allude to
the Essex case, a still dangerous topic. The company also offended the
King, first over alleged anti-Scots allusions in *Eastward Ho!* (1605) by
Jonson, Marston, and Chapman, then over highly personal anticourt
satire in Day's *The Isle of Gulls* (1606), and finally over mockery in a lost
play of James's drunkenness, silver mines, and love of hunting. James's
displeasure over these attacks may have finally led to the troupe's loss
of royal patronage in 1606. Two years later, when the company staged
unfavorable representations of the French court in Chapman's *Conspiracy
and Tragedy of Charles, Duke of Byron* (1608), all playing in London was
temporarily suspended.[42] As Richard Dutton suggests, the prevalence of

[39] Gurr, *Shakespearean Playing Companies*, 56, 337–39.   [40] Ibid., 355.

[41] Dutton, *Mastering the Revels*, 159–60; Leeds Barroll, "The Court of the First Stuart Queen," in
Linda Levy Peck (ed.), *The Mental World of the Jacobean Court* (Cambridge: Cambridge University
Press, 1991), 202–05.

[42] Janet Clare, *"Art made tongue-tied by authority": Elizabethan and Jacobean Dramatic Censorship*
(Manchester: Manchester University Press, 1990), 118–31, 138–45. Roslyn Knutson, "Falconer

"railing" at Blackfriars and the impudence involved in satiric thrusts at King James and his Scots friends may have qualified as a kind of licensed abuse when launched by a company patronized by Queen Anne, and possibly performed before her in her husband's absence.[43]

Despite the Blackfriars troupe's closer connection to court, first through the Chapel Royal and later through the Queen's direct patronage, Paul's at least initially provided a more elitist ambience. On the basis of a single allusion, uncorroborated by any other source, W. R. Gair has argued that Lord Stanley, Earl of Derby, was active in reviving the Paul's boys. He has also stressed the influence of William Percy, whose manuscript plays indicate his hope that they would be produced at Paul's, although there is no evidence of such productions and no other record of Percy's involvement in theatrical activities at Paul's. Finally, he exaggerates the role played by John Marston, then of the Middle Temple, and one of the first playwrights for the newly revived company, in establishing what Harbage had earlier, and with disparaging intent, called a coterie theatre.

Gurr accepts the idea of a small, elitist playhouse at Paul's, but suggests that around 1603, the production of city comedies by Middleton and others indicated a switch on the part of the Paul's boys in the direction of citizen culture, a veering toward the values and concerns of middle-class Londoners and away from the sharp and often personal satiric "humours" plays performed at Blackfriars. Unfortunately, the repertories of the Paul's and Blackfriars troupes are not as clearly distinguishable in ideological attitude as Gurr implies.[44] Their differences are further blurred by ambiguities of tone, as well as by the uncertainty of dates of performance and by the crossing-over of plays from one troupe to the other.

What both troupes do share is a drift toward increased commercialization. Legal records of the period reveal the presence of entrepreneurial types in the companies' directorates and we can observe a corresponding concern with financial return. Testifying during a libel suit arising from a lost play by George Chapman, *The Old Joiner of Aldgate*, performed at

to the Little Eyases: A New Date and Commercial Agenda for the 'Little Eyases' Passage in Hamlet," *Shakespeare Quarterly* 46 (1995), 1–31, sees "the little eyases" passage in the folio text of Hamlet as a friendly warning from an adult troupe to the Blackfriars children's company in 1606–08 about the danger to the entire London theatre industry caused by the boy company's arousing of royal displeasure through satiric railing.

[43] Dutton, *Mastering the Revels*, 190–93; for the concept of festal abuse, see Shapiro, *Children of the Revels*, 38–58.

[44] Gurr, *Shakespearean Playing Companies*, 342–43, 352–56.

Paul's in 1603, Pearce minimized his role in the troupe's management, perhaps to evade responsibility for any damages awarded the plaintiff. He claimed that the burden of the company's management had fallen on the shoulders of Thomas Woodford, a businessman who entered the picture in 1603 or 1604 and who subsequently fell out with Pearce.[45] Kirkham, Yeoman of the Revels, was also involved in the affairs of the company, as he was at Blackfriars, but in what capacity is unknown. Pearce's ability to revive the company even after its demise, and hence his centrality to the operation, is suggested by the annual payment of £20 he was offered in "dead rent" in 1608–09 from the rival children's troupes at Whitefriars and perhaps Blackfriars so "that there might be a cessation of playeinge and plays to be acted in the said howse neere St. Paules Church."[46]

Much more is known about the front-office affairs of the troupe playing at Blackfriars because of the greater litigiousness of its directorate and the frequent changes in its personnel. As an aftermath of the Clifton affair, Evans withdrew, more or less, from the active management of the Blackfriars theatre and at least ostensibly passed his interest and authority on to his son-in-law, Hawkins. Around 1604, two new investors joined the syndicate, William Rastell, a merchant, and Thomas Kendall, a haberdasher. Giles and Kirkham likewise seem to have withdrawn. Later, Robert Payne, John Marston, and Robert Keysar, a goldsmith, joined the syndicate. Like Evans, most of these men did so as businessmen seeking profit and most of the legal action concerns the recovery of their investments from one another or from the troupe's assets.[47]

In 1608, after a lengthy closing of the playhouse on account of plague, Evans returned the Blackfriars lease to the Burbages. Keysar moved the company to the theatre in Whitefriars, which in 1607–08 had been the home of another troupe of boy actors, the shadowy Children of the King's Revels, a thoroughly commercial enterprise having not even the slightest connection with any sponsoring academic or religious institution. The same can be said for Beeston's Boys, a company of boys or youths run entirely along commercial lines as an adult company between 1637 and 1642.

In 1610 a patent was granted to Keysar's new syndicate, which now included Philip Rosseter, a royal lutenist, and several marginal theatrical

[45] C. J. Sisson, *Lost Plays of Shakespeare's Age* (Cambridge: Cambridge University Press, 1936), 12–79; see also Clare, "*Art made tongue-tied*," 90–93; and William Ingram, "The Playhouse as an Investment, 1607–1614; Thomas Woodford and Whitefriars," in Leeds Barroll (ed.), *Medieval and Renaissance Drama in English II* (New York: AMS, 1985), 225–28.
[46] Chambers, *Elizabethan Stage*, II, 22–23.　　[47] Hillebrand, *Child Actors*, 171–206.

figures, for a company to be called the Queen's Revels Children. By this time, the actors who had once been part of a boy company were growing long in the tooth. Nathan Field, who had acted in *Cynthia's Revels* in 1601 at Blackfriars at the age of thirteen was now twenty-two, as Gurr points out.[48] Some of the actors joined adult troupes, such as the King's Men, and some merged with a group of adult actors in a new troupe, the Lady Elizabeth's Men, formed around 1613. Rosseter and his associates held on to their patent for the Queen's Revels Children and evidently used it when touring the provinces. But, as Gurr reports, in 1617–18 three different troupes claiming the same title arrived in Leicester.[49] In the provinces, if not at court or in London, juvenile troupes claiming some former role as purveyors of entertainment to royalty and nobility apparently still had commercial value.

IV

While a movement toward the commercialization of the children's troupes is obvious from the foregoing account, the perception of these companies as somehow part of a ritualized gift exchange system also seems to have been part of their appeal. Certainly, as I have tried to show, aspects of both gift and commodity systems could coexist and in-terplay, but on precisely what terms? When I wrote on this subject some two decades ago, I concluded that the commercial success of the chil-dren's troupes depended on the extent to which they could project the image of themselves as purveyors of theatrical entertainment to the court and nobility. The model I used at the time was the label sewn into my cloth cap, a gift my brother brought me from London: the hatter had officially been designated as a purveyor of headwear to the royal fam-ily "by appointment to Her Majesty the Queen," and his merchandise displayed his own coat of arms and Latin motto.[50] Whereas I tended to see this model as a harmonious blend of patriotism and profit-seeking, others would have described it as exploiting a sense of elitism or snob-bery among consumers eager to gain or maintain social status, if not an out-and-out commercial ploy.

In recent years, my views on the children's companies of early modern London have changed somewhat, perhaps a result of my own recent

---

[48] Gurr, *Shakespearean Playing Companies*, 358. Shen Lin, "How Old Were the Children of Paul's?" *Theatre Notes* 45 (1991), argues that the troupe at Paul's, if indeed composed of choristers, need not have aged collectively, as "new choirboys were being enrolled at all times" (127).

[49] Gurr, *Shakespearean Playing Companies*, 361.   [50] Shapiro, *Children of the Revels*, 16.

forays into fund-raising and a greater appreciation of the symbolic power of gift-giving and its role in shaping one's sense of self. What I once saw as a "harmonious blend" of opposing forces now seems to me to be an even more complex site of conflicting impulses, never fully resolved and constantly in flux. Despite the growing tendency toward commercialism, the children's troupes began and ended as part of a system of patronage, which was itself changing in the period, but which expressed itself through ritualized exchanges of gifts. Gift exchanges, as I have argued, are signs of ongoing relationships, and the more important the relationship the more likely the exchange is to be ritualized. Even in the early Jacobean period, when the children's troupes underwent significant commercialization and sought the patronage of paying spectators, their plays were still surrounded by an aura, albeit fainter than it had been in the first half of Elizabeth's reign, of a gift offered to a powerful spectator whose continued patronage was of paramount importance.

CHAPTER 11

The audience as patron: The Knight of the Burning Pestle

Alexander Leggatt

The Drama's Laws the Drama's Patrons give,
For we that live to please, must please to live.
Samuel Johnson, "Prologue at the Opening of the Theatre
in *Drury-Lane* 1747"

Halfway through the fifteenth-century morality play *Mankind* there is a great offstage roar from the devil Titivillus: "I come with my legs under me!" With the audience's appetite thus whetted, the Vices delay his appearance by setting a condition: "We shall gather money unto, / Else there shall no man him see." They are quite specific in their demands: "He loveth no groats, nor pence of tuppence; / Give us red royals, if ye will see his abominable presence" (454–65).[1] They then proceed to take up a collection. The device exploits the popularity of the devil figure – there is no hint that the audience will have to pay extra to hear Mercy's sermons – and in so doing it gives voice to the tacit contract between actors and audience: if you want to see the show, you have to give us money. The ostensible purpose of *Mankind*, announced in the speeches of Mercy, is to edify the audience and help them towards salvation. But the Vices bring out the play's other purpose, to make money for the acting company, and with characteristic subversiveness they reveal that what the audience really wants is not edification but entertaining devilry.

By stopping the performance until the collection is taken, the actors exert control over the audience: the show will proceed on the actors' terms or not at all. But this is also a game of chicken. A recalcitrant audience, bored with devils and preferring edification, or simply objecting to the surcharge on principle, could at this point stop the show in its tracks by refusing to contribute. Actors and audience have a hold over each other; it is a classic example of what David Bevington and Milla Riggio elsewhere in this collection call "The artist's push–pull relationship with

[1] G. A. Lester (ed.), *Three Late Medieval Morality Plays* (London: Ernest Benn; New York: W. W. Norton, 1981).

295

his audience" (131). This moment in *Mankind*, by making money-gathering part of the script, acts out the consequences of the commercialization of theatre, the dependence that actors and audiences have on each other's cooperation. No money, no show is a principle that operates two ways. The collection for the appearance of Titivillus is possible only because the actors, and the playwright who devised the moment, are confident of the popularity of what they have to offer, and so they can be unusually brazen in their demands. But in laying bare the game of power they are playing with the audience, they are taking a risk: what would happen if the audience rebelled?

Just such a rebellion is built into the script of Beaumont's *The Knight of the Burning Pestle*. In fact it is the essence of the play. The company putting on *The London Merchant* is barely three lines into the prologue when a Citizen in the audience objects to the title, objects to the play, and, joined by his Wife, insists on a play of his own devising, a pro-citizen romance, with a leading actor of his own choosing, his apprentice Rafe. Like the author of *Mankind*, Beaumont makes us think about the contract between stage and audience that in normal circumstances is silently accepted, and he uses the same device: one party breaks the rules by insisting, brazenly and excessively, on its rights. Playwrights and actors can dictate the nature of the entertainment, because they are devising it; but the audience can also dictate the nature of the entertainment, because they are paying for it. As the actors abuse their power in *Mankind*, the audience abuses its power in *The Knight of the Burning Pestle*. The difference is that in *Mankind* the real audience really pays, while in *The Knight* the audience that rebels is not the real one, but a joke audience, scripted by the playwright and played by members of the acting company. However, the real audience watching the rebellion is made to think of its own role and responsibilities, of the implications of the principle that Samuel Johnson was to state: the drama's laws the drama's patrons give.

The play was likely acted in 1607, at the Blackfriars playhouse, by the Children of the Revels. Both date and auspices are significant for the experiment Beaumont is conducting. The children's companies exemplified in their own history a conscious change from court theatre to commercial theatre. Like the Children of Paul's, the Chapel Children (ancestor of the Blackfriars company) had become increasingly commercialized in the 1570s, charging admission to rehearsals for plays that were to be performed at court.[2] It may have been in practical terms a small

---

[2] Michael Shapiro, *Children of the Revels* (New York: Columbia University Press, 1977), 13–15. On the general commercialization of childrens' theatre see 13–16, 21–26.

step from public rehearsals to ordinary public performances; but it meant in principle a major change in the company's sense of its audience. They went from doing plays for the Queen to doing plays for anyone who would pay to see them. Their descendants, the Blackfriars company that played *The Knight*, originally had a court connection through the Chapel Royal, but lost it through the nature of their repertoire. On 4 February 1604 King James had issued a patent entitling the company to call itself the Children of the Queen's Revels. But the company gave offense by the satiric strain in its plays: jokes about Scotsmen and thirty-pound knights in *Eastward Ho* (1605) did not go down well at court, and John Day's *The Isle of Gulls* (1606) was considered topical enough to warrant several arrests. The actual chapel choristers were gradually withdrawn from the company, and on 7 November 1606 James issued a commission that had the effect of severing the choristers of the Chapel Royal from the company at the Blackfriars, which was now called simply the Children of the Revels. By 1608, after further indiscretions, they became the Children of the Blackfriars.[3] The court connection, increasingly nominal, disappeared largely as a result of the company's own actions; and it is a reasonable inference that they did satiric plays that created scandal because such plays brought in a curious public. They were bad politics but good box-office.[4]

It was in the shadow of these events, with royal patronage having recently been withdrawn, that the company performed *The Knight of the Burning Pestle*, a play that in its opening line turns away "From all that's neere the Court"[5] and focuses instead on the paying, public audience. In place of the old-style, obsequious prologue declaring the company's total dependence on royal favor (Lyly's Prologue to *Gallathea* is a typical example), Beaumont substitutes a comic dramatization of its dependence on the public. That dependence is a crucial part of the story of theatrical patronage. In her introductory essay to this collection, Suzanne Westfall describes the period in question as one in which "the theatre was rapidly becoming commodified and patronage shifted from the upper strata of society to include the general public" so that "By the end of the sixteenth

---

[3] Shapiro, *Children of the Revels*, 27–28. For a recent account of the history of this company, see Andrew Gurr, *The Shakespearian Playing Companies* (Oxford: Clarendon Press, 1996), 347–65.

[4] Gurr, *Shakespearian Playing Companies*, 350–51, offers a different explanation, based on Queen Anne's patronage of the company in the early years of the new reign. She had a court of her own, and a mind of her own, and the French ambassador commented on her habit of attending plays that poked fun at her husband.

[5] All references to *The Knight of the Burning Pestle* are to the text edited by Cyrus Hoy in vol. 1 of *The Dramatic Works in the Beaumont and Fletcher Canon*, gen. ed. Fredson Bowers (Cambridge: Cambridge University Press, 1966).

century . . . companies like Shakespeare's clearly had two patrons – both
the monarch and the paying public" (p. 41, above). The total process
is a long one, still not quite finished: the example from *Mankind* shows
how early the paying public was seen as a factor, and the brochure for
the 1999 Stratford (Ontario) Festival, a theatre enterprise largely dependent on the box office, lists the Governor-General, the representative of
the Crown in Canada, as its "Patron." But the Elizabethan-Jacobean
period was one in which the pace of change accelerated and people who
wrote about theatre became sharply aware of two intersecting systems,
implying two ideas of what the word patron could mean. Elsewhere in
this collection, Michael Shapiro shows these intersecting systems at work
in the boys' companies, and David M. Bergeron, using the Shakespeare
Folio as an example, shows how the concept of the paying public had
extended from playgoers to readers. In 1615 J. Cocke, in his character of "a common Player," wrote, "howsoever hee pretends to have a
royall Master or Mistresse, his wages and dependance prove him to be
the servant of the people."[6] Other essays, here and elsewhere, have explored what it means to be the servant of a royal or aristocratic master,
or mistress; my concern is with what it means to be the servant of the
people.

   The power of the audience as patron and paymaster was connected,
Andrew Gurr has argued, with the establishment of purpose-built playhouses: "Whereas when travelling the players could sustain themselves
with the same plays repeated in constantly changing venues, once the
venue was fixed the repertory had to keep changing. As the chief deter-
minant of this novelty there had to be an intimate interaction between
the settled expectations of the playgoers and the fare they fed on. The
result was a constant, pressurised evolution in the players' repertoire of
plays, a kind of aesthetic Darwinism."[7] While the influence of an aristocratic patron on his company's repertoire can be elusive and hard to
demonstrate,[8] an audience is direct. It packs the house, or it stays away.
Audience taste dictated that *Doctor Faustus* stayed in the repertoire up
to the closing of the theatres while *Sejanus* died at its first performance.
For a playwright who was not content with writing to order, but wanted
to do work that interested him personally, this presented a challenge. It
is the perennial problem of the serious artist: how does one resist the
tyranny of the audience and maintain the right to work on one's own

---

[6] Quoted in E. K. Chambers, *The Elizabethan Stage*, 4 vols. (Oxford: Clarendon Press, 1923), IV, 256.
[7] Andrew Gurr, *Playgoing in Shakespeare's London* (Cambridge: Cambridge University Press, 1987), 115.
[8] See Gurr, *Shakespearean Playing Companies*, 32–35.

terms, when the audience is paying the bills?[9] For one of the gentlemen who comments on the forthcoming play in the Induction to Day's
The Isle of Gulls, the answer, for the crucial first performance at least, is to
bring one's own audience. He asks if the author is properly prepared for
his opening: "And where sits his friends? hath he not a prepard company
of gallants, to applaud his iests and grace out his play?" (sig. A2r).[10]

Ben Jonson was not content with such limited solutions. Possessed of
the most self-conscious literary ambition of any playwright of his time,
he mounted a sustained attack on the audience's power, countering it by
insisting on his own authority. In *Every Man out of his Humour* he anticipates the advice of Day's gentleman and provides his own claque, except
that he goes one stage further and builds the claque into the script.
Mitis and Cordatus offer a running commentary on the play, with Mitis
raising objections and Cordatus, "The Authors friend . . . of a discreet,
and vnderstanding iudgement" (The Character of the Persons, 11–13),[11]
squashing them. Mitis is obligingly submissive. But when Jonson, towards the end of his career, returns to the device in *The Magnetic Lady*, his
mounting irritation with the audience shows in the figure of Damplay,
who not only refuses to accept correction but declares, "I care not for
marking the *Play:* Ile damne it, talke, and doe that I come for . . . I will
censure, and be witty, and take my Tobacco, and enjoy my *Magna Charta*
of reprehension, as my Predecessors have done before me" (III. Chorus,
19–25).

Damplay makes it sound as though his right to be a nuisance is part of
the British constitution; but earlier he has revealed that its real origin is
financial: "I see no reason, if I come here, and give my eighteene pence,
or two shillings for my Seat, but I should take it out in censure, on the
Stage." The Boy who represents the company retorts that Damplay is
demanding more than he paid for: "Your two shilling worth is allow'd
you: but you will take your ten shilling worth, your twenty shilling worth,
and more" (II. Chorus, 59–65). This echoes the Induction to *Bartholomew
Fair*, where the contract with the audience is literal: "It is further agreed
that euery person here, haue his or their free-will of censure, to like or
dislike at their owne charge, the *Author* hauing now departed with his
right: it shall be lawfull for any man to iudge his six pen'orth, his twelue

---

[9] Richard Monette, Artistic Director of the Stratford (Ontario) Festival, has summarized his
dilemma as follows: "I'm here to make art, not money; but I can't make art if I don't make
money."

[10] John Day, *The Isle of Gulls* (London, 1606).

[11] All references to Jonson are to *Ben Jonson*, ed. C. H. Herford and Percy and Evelyn Simpson,
11 vols. (Oxford: Clarendon Press, 1925–52).

pen'orth, so to his eighteen pence, 2. shillings, halfe a crowne, to the value of his place: Prouided alwaies his place get not aboue his wit" (85–91).[12] Despite his claim that he has departed with his right, Jonson is actually keeping the audience in its place, measuring how much it has paid and how much censure it is allowed. But at least Jonson at such moments acknowledges the commercial basis of theatre. In the prologues to *Epicoene*, *The New Inn*, and *The Sad Shepherd*, he presents the play as a feast, and himself as the cook, with no suggestion that the guests pay for their entertainment. This allows him to insist that though he is pleasing the audience's taste, he himself has the right to determine what that taste should be: "If any thing be set to a wrong taste, / 'Tis not the meat, there, but the mouth's displac'd" (*The New Inn*, Prologue, 8–9). Jonson may seem to be more honest in the opening to *The Magnetic Lady*, where the Boy presents the theatre as a shop selling wares for sale; but the metaphor is not sustained beyond the first few lines, as though Jonson is reluctant to face its implications. He would rather see himself as provider of a feast to appreciative guests than as simply one party to a commercial transaction.

Mankind presents itself as a means of divine grace, *The New Inn* as an act of hospitality. In both cases the audience pays – though the author of *Mankind* is more willing to admit this than is the author of *The New Inn*. *The Knight of the Burning Pestle* demystifies theatre by presenting it as a cash transaction. In this respect, the Bell Inn episode is crucial. Rafe's attendant, George, speaking in the idiom of romance, tells his master,

> I have discovered, not a stones cast off,
> An ancient Castle held by the old Knight
> Of the most holy order of the *Bell*,
> Who gives to all Knights errant entertaine:
> There plenty is of food, and all prepar'd,
> By the white hands of his owne Lady deere.
>
> (II.349–54)

The reality beneath this old-fashioned knightly courtesy is revealed the following morning:

TAPSTER. Maister, the reckoning is not paid.
RAFE. Right curteous knight, who for the orders sake
    As I this flaming pestle beare about,

---

[12] As David M. Bergeron reminds us, the address to the reader in the Shakespeare Folio takes the same position in strikingly similar language: "Judge your six-pen'orth, your shillings worth, your five shillings worth" and so on (p. 61).

We render thankes to your puissant selfe,
Your beauteous Lady, and your gentle Squires,
For thus refreshing of our wearied limbes,
Stiffned with hard atchievements in wilde desert.
TAPSTER. Sir, there is twelve shillings to pay.
RAFE. Thou merry Squire Tapstero, thankes to thee,
For comforting our soules with double Jug . . .

(III.139–49)

Rafe appears not to hear the Tapster, not because he wants to avoid payment but because he is in a different play. His chivalric romance will not admit such gross considerations as tavern bills, and so in his play the Tapster has not said what the audience has heard him say. By the same token, in the normal conditions of theatre nothing is said about its commercial basis. We'll strive to please you every day, give me your hands if we be friends – the stage–audience relationship is one of mutual courtesy. The gatherers go silently about their work;[13] they have no lines in the script. Beaumont gives them lines.

What follows is more complicated. The Host makes Rafe hear him by speaking in his own language: "Thou valiant Knight of the *burning Pestle*, give eare to me, there is twelve shillings to pay, and as I am a true Knight, I will not bate a penny" (III.157–59). Rafe hears, but misunderstands: "Sir Knight, this mirth of yours becomes you well" (III.165). The demand for payment is so far removed from his mental world that he takes it as a joke. The Host threatens to "cap" (arrest) Rafe and the Citizen, warned by his Wife that the threat is serious, intervenes: "Cap *Raph*? no; hold your hand sir Knight of the *Bel*, theres your mony, have you any thing to say to *Raph* now? Cap *Raph*?" (III.176–78). The Citizen's intervention is like and unlike the moment in *The Taming of a Shrew* when the Duke orders the arrest of Phylota and Valeria, and Sly, watching the play, suddenly explodes: "I say wele have no sending to prison" (xvi.47).[14] Like it, in that a member of the onstage audience intervenes to prevent an unpleasant turn in the action; unlike it, in that Sly's intervention changes nothing (as the Lord assures him, Phylota and Valeria have already run away), while the Citizen actually invades the play world to solve a problem that seemed otherwise insoluble. The Citizen's intervention breaks a stalemate that threatened to stop the play dead; Rafe and the Host were

[13] For one of the few discussions of these necessary functionaries, see Gerald Eades Bentley, *The Profession of Player in Shakespeare's Time 1590–1642* (Princeton: Princeton University Press, 1984), 93–101.
[14] Geoffrey Bullough (ed.), *Narrative and Dramatic Sources of Shakespeare*, 8 vols. (London: Routledge and Kegan Paul; New York: Columbia University Press, 1966, 1).

fixed in opposed positions from which neither would budge. His cash, like the collection in *Mankind*, allows the play to continue. It is like putting another nickel in the slot to see the rest of the show. But the money, we notice, changes hands in silence; the Host says nothing to acknowledge it, and neither does Rafe. Beaumont dramatizes both the commercial basis of theatre and the general agreement to bury it in silence.

He also plays, characteristically, with levels of illusion. Within the play's overall fiction, the Citizen is paying real money to discharge an imaginary tavern bill; the joke is on him. But if the audience takes it that way the joke is finally on them, since the Citizen is ultimately an actor whose money is play money. It is the audience that has paid real money to see an actor pay fake money, and to find the sight amusing. Beaumont later gives the joke another twist in the Crakovia episode, when Rafe, having received from the Princess the sort of pure chivalric hospitality he thought he received at the Bell, insists on tipping everybody as though the castle were an inn. Once again the Citizen provides the money, and once again Rafe accepts it in silence.

The Bell episode is prophetic of what we now call the hospitality industry, in which hotels and restaurants use words like host, hostess, guest, and hospitality – not to mention patron – to mask a purely commercial transaction. This is what Jonson does when he calls the play a feast. The Host has to insist on payment because he has a business to run. So does the theatre management. The Boy who represents the company trying in the face of the citizens' interruptions to put on *The London Merchant* fluctuates between tact and exasperation in his handling of these recalcitrant customers; but when the Wife orders Mistress Merrythought offstage to make room for another Rafe scene he is finally pushed beyond endurance: "you'le utterly spoile our Play, and make it to be hist, and it cost money" (III.294–95). Questions of artistic coherence and integrity can be argued back and forth, but in the end the company has to protect its investment. The citizens may have bought their places, but the company bought the play. The Boy later utters what sounds like a threat to make the Citizen financially liable for the entire fiasco: "Well sir hee shall come out, but if our play miscarry, sir you are like to pay for't" (IV. Interlude, 17–18).

The Boy takes the issue down to what is now called the bottom line. There is also an artistic bottom line. The citizens' rebellion is directly counter to the principle stated by Probee, the author's spokesman in *The Magnetic Lady*: "our parts that are the Spectators, or should heare a *Comedy*, are to await the processe, and events of things, as the *Poet* presents them, not as wee would corruptly fashion them" (IV. Chorus, 10–13). After years of battling the audience with wit and irony Jonson finally says, flatly, sit down and shut up. In *The Knight of the Burning Pestle*, far from waiting the process and events of things, the Citizen interrupts three lines into the Prologue, orders, "Downe with your Title boy, downe with your Title" (Induction, 9), and goes on to specify the entertainment *he* wants. This is a basic threat not just to the company's investment but to its authority, to the playwright's authority, to the whole theatrical occasion. This is what happens when one element in the mixture that makes theatre gets out of control.

The citizens' rebellion has more specific implications. They are not just Everyaudience, the generalized "we" to which criticism so often resorts as a matter of convenience when discussing audience response. They are middle class, and in demanding seats on the stage they are taking places normally reserved for "the most important patrons"[15] at the private houses. They illustrate Ann Jennalie Cook's observation that "where placement depended on payment, money could overturn rank."[16] Their basic challenge to the play – "down with your title" – is embodied in a challenge to social class that is equally basic. We might almost take this moment as symbolic of the displacement of the aristocratic patron by the paying public. They present an equivalent challenge to the hierarchy of gender. The Wife, even before she mounts the stage, establishes herself as She Who Must Be Obeyed:

WIFE. Let him kill a Lyon with a pestle husband, let him kill a Lyon with a pestle.
CITIZEN. So he shall, I'll have him kill a Lyon with a pestle.

(Induction, 42–44)

The presence of a woman on stage, even more than that of a citizen, would have seemed "unconventional and immodest."[17] (Jonson would later compound the joke in *The Staple of News*, having a whole party of

---

[15] Gurr, *Playgoing*, 30.
[16] Ann Jennalie Cook, "Audiences: Investigation, Interpretation, Invention," in John D. Cox and David Scott Kastan (eds.), *A New History of Early English Drama* (New York: Columbia University Press, 1997), 309. Compare the 1574 complaint of the masters of the Merchant Taylors guild, forbidding the use of their hall for playing: "everye lewd persone thinketh himself (for his penny) worthye of the chiefe and most comodious place withoute respecte of any other either for age or estimacion in the comon weale" (cited by Shapiro in this volume, p. 279).
[17] Sheldon P. Zitner, commentary to the Revels edition of *The Knight of the Burning Pestle* (Manchester: Manchester University Press, 1984), 58. Diana E. Henderson reads the Wife's role as part of a general misogyny in the drama of the time, a satiric attempt "to discredit female spectatorship" ("The Theater and Domestic Culture," in *A New History*, 180–81).

gossips mount the stage to pass judgment, mostly foolish, on his play.) The Wife is a bit apologetic at first, aware of her dubious status: "By your leave Gentlemen all, Im'e somthing troublesome, Im'e a stranger here, I was nere at one of these playes as they say, before" (Induction, 49–51). But her very inexperience gives her the confidence to demand whatever she wants. Her domestic authority is suggested when the Citizen seems sympathetic to Merrythought's rough treatment of his wife, and his own Wife quickly brings him back into line (III.520–29). She is given the Epilogue, which Rosalind, similarly privileged at the end of *As You Like It*, admits is not the fashion. She ends the play by issuing her last order: "come *George*" (Epilogus, 10–11).[18] Beaumont links the rebellion of the citizens to carnivalesque, saturnalian inversions: the reversal of class, the woman on top. Child actors had played such games before: in the pre-Reformation ceremony of the Boy Bishop, and (Michael Shapiro speculates) in plays acted by choirboys around Holy Innocents Day.[19]

This particular rebellion is not just a seasonal carnival impulse. For one thing, it is part of a scripted drama, thereby participating in the commercialization of carnival which, Andrew Gurr has argued, undermined its subversiveness.[20] Within that context, which ironizes it as carnival, it is local and specific, aimed, as popular revolts in the political sphere often were, at correcting a particular abuse. The abuse in this case is the perceived anti-citizen bias of *The London Merchant*. The Citizen demands, on the spot, a play of his own devising, a romance with an adventurous citizen hero; he even has a title, *The Grocers Honour*. Beyond this he and his Wife think not in terms of the overall coherence of the script but in terms of particular, favorite effects. Here Beaumont's commentary on the requirements of an audience opens out beyond the class issue. The playwright may think of himself as providing a coherent, carefully crafted artistic experience. In *The Magnetic Lady* the Boy warns the audience,

A good *Play*, is like a skeene of silke: which, if you take by the right end, you may wind off, at pleasure, on the bottome, or card of your discourse, in a tale, or so; how you will: but if you light on the wrong end, you will pull all into a knot, or elf-lock; which nothing but the sheers, or a candle will undoe, or separate.

(Induction, 136–41)

Beaumont's onstage audience, instead of seeing the play as a single coherent experience, comes looking for particular, local effects. They

---

[18] For a sympathetic account of the Wife's role, showing her disruptiveness as creative and liberating, see Laurie E. Osborne, "Female Audiences and Female Authority in *The Knight of the Burning Pestle*," *Exemplaria* 3 (1991), 491–517.

[19] Shapiro, *Children of the Revels*, 8–9.   [20] Gurr, *Shakespearean Playing Companies*, 13.

want displays of skill from the actors: the Wife, admiring the boy who dances in the Interlude at the end of Act III, asks him if he can tumble or eat fire (10–16). When Rafe appears as the May Lord, the Citizen is critical of his costume: "hee's reasonable well in reparell, but hee has not rings enough" (IV. Interlude, 23–24). Over and over, the Wife demands fight scenes featuring Rafe: "I pre'thee sweet heart let him come fight before me, and let's ha some drums, and some trumpets, and let him kill all that comes neere him, and thou lov'st me *George*" (II.128–31). Lee Bliss sees this as a matter of the Wife's personal psychology: "Nell's almost stream-of-consciousness responses betray latent sexual preoccupations and an all too overt demand for violence as well as spectacle."[21] It is also an established popular-theatre taste, out of place at the Blackfriars: battle scenes were a staple of more old-fashioned public playhouses, notably the Red Bull.[22] Her demand for drums and trumpets is equally out of place, since they were unsuitable for the small space of the Blackfriars, and the boys' company preferred woodwinds.[23] Since every leading actor needs a juicy death scene, the Citizen demands, against the Boy's protests that they are trying to perform a comedy, that Rafe come on stage and die. As there is topical theatrical satire in the Wife's demand for battles, Rafe's death-groan may echo the Folio Hamlet and the Quarto Lear, both of whom utter the same sound "O,O,O . . ." which the more genteel tradition of Shakespearean editing has suppressed. But behind the local jokes is a more basic comment on audience mentality: an audience comes expecting, not a carefully crafted total experience, but a series of favorite ingredients. To the Citizen's list we might add ghosts, devils, mad scenes, poisonings, car-and-helicopter chases, nude scenes, and explosions.

The playwright may labor for weeks or months over the script, but the audience comes to see its favorite actors. The title pages of Elizabethan playbooks are more likely to name the acting company than the author, though in the Jacobean period the authors start to encroach. The citizens provide their own star, Rafe. They always refer to him by name, and they are impatient when he is offstage. (When's Burbage coming? When's Kemp coming? Sly, in *The Taming of a Shrew*, asks, "*Sim*, when will the foole come againe?" [v.186].) The play they want to see is essentially a series of star turns for Rafe, and it does not bother them that the Rafe

---

[21] Lee Bliss, *Francis Beaumont* (Boston: Twayne, 1987), 43.

[22] Alexander Leggatt, *Jacobean Public Theatre* (London and New York: Routledge, 1992), 70–75. On battle scenes in earlier popular drama, see Scott McMillin and Sally-Beth MacLean, *The Queen's Men and their Plays* (Cambridge: Cambridge University Press, 1998), 129–30.

[23] Gurr, *Shakespearean Playing Companies*, 131.

scenes become increasingly disconnected. While they frequently get so involved in the illusion that they forget they are watching a play – when Jasper threatens to kill Luce, the Wife asks her husband to raise the Watch and send for a local magistrate (III.92–93) – at other times they think of the actors simply as actors, making no identification of them with their characters.[24] The Wife is particularly taken with the boy who plays Humphrey: "didst thou ever see a prettier child? how it behaves it selfe, I warrant yee, and speakes, and lookes, and pearts up the head?" (I.91–93). The citizens champion Humphrey throughout, though in the play his role is that of the idiot the heroine shouldn't marry, and their response is the equivalent of wanting Slender to marry Anne Page. So far as they do judge the total action of *The London Merchant*, they judge it by values they have brought into the playhouse with them, and these are not the values of the play. The play, conventionally, champions young love against parental authority; for them it is the other way around, and they are particularly rough on the hero, Jasper.[25] To return to Jonson's image, they have the thread by the wrong end.

The citizens bring their own theatrical tastes and moral values to bear on *The London Merchant*, at whatever cost to artistic coherence or authorial intention. The fun provokes a question: isn't this in the end what all audiences do? No one brings a blank mind to the theatre, no spectator can be totally passive. This particular audience may be unsophisticated, but in a sense they are within their rights. Above all, they have paid to be here, and are willing to go on paying to get the show they want. They are anticipating Jonson, and calling his bluff: to his insistence that the audience should censure no more than it has paid for, they retort that they can, and will, pay more. The Citizen pays extra to give the Bell and Crakovia scenes the turn he wants. He has definite views about Rafe's musical accompaniment, and backs them with hard cash:

CITIZEN ... *Rafe* playes a stately part, and he must needs have shawmes;
   I'le be at the charge of them my selfe, rather then wee'l be without them.
PROLOGUE. So you are like to be.
CITIZEN. Why and so I will be: ther's two shillings, let's have the waits of
   South-warke.

(Induction, 96–101)

Setting up the scene in which Rafe reviews his troops at Mile End, the Wife promises, "my husband shall lend you his Jerkin *Rafe*, and there's

[24] See Bliss, *Francis Beaumont*, 44–45.
[25] Osborne, "Female Audiences and Female Authority," 512, sides with the Wife's objections to Jasper's brutality, and sees them as an invitation to interrogate the idea of the romantic hero.

a scarfe; for the rest, the house shall furnish you, and wee'l pay for't" (v.61–63). She contributes in smaller ways, tipping the boy who dances at the end of Act III: "there's two pence to buy you points withall" (III. Interlude, 15–16). This aspect of the play was brought out fully in the 1990 Stratford, Ontario production, directed by Bernard Hopkins and Pat Galloway. The citizens were in modern dress, and George paid on the spot for everything he asked for with money from his wallet. In the end he handed over his credit card, and the audience reacted as an earlier audience would have reacted to Faustus bargaining away his soul. They had paid for their own tickets with credit cards, and to them the Citizen's commitment was poignantly real.

In dramatizing their willingness to pay for their entertainment, Beaumont insists, provocatively, that the citizens have a point. But in the last analysis paying for a play is not the same as paying for a cabbage. Kathleen E. McLuskie and Felicity Dunsworth point out the limitations of the market concept of playgoing: "the market for plays was *not* comparable with the market for commodities. The product, play performances, was not a commodity, in that there was not a stable method of production (it could involve a variety of producers; it could be produced from scratch; it could be recycled and adapted), and there was a highly unstable relationship between product and price."[26] *The Knight of the Burning Pestle* dramatizes, with comic extravagance, the fluidity of the theatrical occasion, the amount of improvisation and adaptation it involves, and above all the moment-by-moment negotiation that makes it differ radically from the single encounter at the cash register when goods are exchanged for money. In these negotiations the company has its rights, no less than the citizens. They paid for the play, they cast and rehearsed it, and they have an obligation to the rest of the audience who have come in good faith to see a play called *The London Merchant*.

In the ensuing conflict of forces, and the complex relationship it establishes between the company's play and the citizens' play, Beaumont toys with a basic question of theatre, the relationship between artist and audience. There is always a gap: what the audience expects is never quite what the actors provide, and the signal the actors think they are sending is often not the signal the audience receives. Backstage conversations between actors and audience after a show will confirm this. ("I loved the bit where you . . ." "What bit was that?") Given the inevitability of the gap, Beaumont – widening it to make the experiment more radical – raises

[26] Kathleen E. McLuskie and Felicity Dunsworth, "Patronage and the Economics of Theater," in *A New History*, 439.

the basic question, how do theatre artists reconcile their sense of their work with the audience's sense of it? Can the gap be bridged?

The Prologue begins by washing his hands of the problem. The prologue he delivers emphasizes the limits of *The London Merchant*, drawing a circle of constriction, stressing what the play will not do; it ends with an impromptu prose line that turns the whole Rafe business over to the citizens:

From all that's neere the Court, from all that's great
Within the compasse of the Citty-walles,
We now have brought our Scaene: fly farre from hence
All private taxes, immodest phrases,
What ere may but shew like vicious:
For wicked mirth never true pleasure brings,
But honest minds are pleas'd with honest things.
Thus much for that we do: but for *Rafes* part you must answere for your selfe.

(Induction, 108–16)

He says, in effect, we're doing our play, you do yours. But the Boy has too many artistic ideas of his own to preserve a completely hands-off policy. As the Citizen rebels against the taste of the company, the Boy cannot help criticizing the taste of the Citizen:

CITIZEN. What shall we have *Rafe* do now boy?
BOY. You shall have what you will sir.
CITIZEN. Why so sir, go and fetch me him then, and let the Sophy of *Persia* come and christen him a childe.
BOY. Beleeve me sir, that will not doe so well, 'tis stale, it has beene had before at the red Bull.

(IV.25–30)

For once the Boy prevails. His objection implies that the Rafe play, like *The London Merchant*, is taking place on his stage, before his audience, and he feels some responsibility for it. He has even named the play himself, countering the Citizen's suggestion of *The Grocers Honour* with *The Knight of the Burning Pestle*. The Wife agrees, not detecting the veiled sarcasm of the new title: given the phallic association of the pestle (pizzle) and the pox-association of burning, this is a title on the order of *Blazing Saddles*. It is also the title of Beaumont's play. This at once privileges the citizens' play over the company's and declares that the citizens' play is funny in ways they do not suspect. They get their play, but they get it on the actors' terms.

As the Boy cannot quite keep aloof from the citizens' play, *The London Merchant* cannot be completely unaffected by the citizens' interruptions, which are frequent and substantial. The actors carry on with the dialogue as though nothing had happened; but while they do not acknowledge the interruptions, they have to pause, usually for several lines at a time, to let them take place. In those pauses we see the actors' acknowledgment of the audience's activity, something that in normal performance is taking place all the time without a break in the action. No actor can be unaware of the audience (ah, they got that bit, they didn't get that bit, now they're coughing). The actors' determination to keep going is seen at the beginning of Act II: though the citizens have just demanded Rafe, the Merchant and Humphrey enter instead. But later, when the citizens politely ask Mistress Merrythought to leave the stage and make room for Rafe, she departs without a word. (This is the intervention that provokes the Boy to protest that the play cost them money.)

More mischievously, the two plays start to work together. Rafe frightens Mistress Merrythought, who thinks he and his attendants are giants; in a panic she loses her money, and Jasper picks it up. The citizens demand that Rafe fight Jasper, and he does; but Jasper beats him. If the two plays can be seen in competition, the company's play at this point has the edge. There may even be a point when an actor finally replies to the audience's criticism. When the Wife lectures Merrythought for his treatment of Mistress Merrythought, his voice is heard offstage singing:

> *I come not hither for thee to teach~*
> *I have no pulpit for thee to preach~*
> *I would thou hadst kist me under the breech~*
> *As thou art a Lady gay.*
>
> (III.541–44)

He could be replying to her, and if so it would be the only moment when the players make a direct counterattack on the audience. She certainly thinks he is insulting her, and is quite offended. But the fact that he is offstage, and could equally well be addressing his own wife, leaves the question in doubt and makes the comedy more teasing.

As the play goes on the citizens become a little less aggressive, a little more relaxed, as increasingly they get what they want. At the same time the Rafe scenes become more and more disconnected from *The London Merchant*, and from each other. This may imply that the two plays cannot finally be reconciled, and work best apart from each other; and by the same token the company and audience have in the end to ignore each other. This does not augur well for theatre, however, and it is tempting to look for some final harmony, some reconciliation of play with play

and of stage with audience. Lee Bliss sees common interests between the
plays, "a rapprochement in tone, duplicating with variations comedy's
triumph of life over annihilation," and a final similarity between their
heroes: each is "a plucky apprentice-lover who meets with adventures
that test his worth." Finally, she suggests that Merrythought's reference
to "all we, thus kindly and unexpectedly reconciled" (v. 330–31) could
include the citizens.[27] The Wife's address to the rest of the audience
certainly offers communal harmony: "I thanke you all Gentlemen, for
your patience and countenance to *Raph*, a poore fatherlesse child, and if
I might see you in my house, it should go hard, but I would have a pottle
of wine and a pipe of Tobacco for you" (Epilogus, 3–6). But this is an
appeal to the audience, not to the acting company whose work she has
disrupted, and at least one critic finds it hard to imagine the gentlemen
accepting her invitation.[28] Merrythought's "all we" is deliberately open.
Harmony remains a possibility, but no more than that.

   What reconciles all the disparate elements of the play – *The London
Merchant*, *The Knight of the Burning Pestle*, the citizens, and the acting company – is Beaumont's own art, which has invented them all. Only the
offstage audience is beyond his control, and we will return to that problem. What Beaumont offers is not a secure harmony of the various
components of theatre, but a mischievous interplay whose final effect
is elusive. We may think he invites a straightforward mockery of the
citizens, and some critics read the play that way.[29] Others respond more
positively to the citizens' energy and generosity of spirit, and point out
that their play is a lot more fun than *The London Merchant*; this seems
to be the prevailing view in recent criticism.[30] Beaumont allows a variety of judgments: his own commitment is not to one play or another
but to the interplay between them.[31] (There is a modern equivalent
in the interplay of two operas in radically different styles in Strauss's
Ariadne auf Naxos.) His art is full of paradoxes: its interruptions and im-
provisations are fully scripted, and the Blackfriars company will have
rehearsed them. In a play that shows the breakdown of authorial control
(we do not even know who allegedly wrote *The London Merchant*) the author

[27] Bliss, *Francis Beaumont*, 50, 53. See also David A. Samuelson, "The Order in Beaumont's *The
    Knight of the Burning Pestle*," *English Literary Renaissance* 9 (1979), 316.
[28] Zitner, *Knight of the Burning Pestle*, 28.
[29] Gurr claims the play is written "in a mood of elitist satire and genial contempt for citizens"
    (*Shakespearean Playing Companies*, 102).
[30] See Ronald F. Miller, "Dramatic Form and Dramatic Imagination in Beaumont's *Knight of the
    Burning Pestle*," *English Literary Renaissance* 8 (1978), 67–84; Bliss, *Francis Beaumont*, 46–47; and
    Zitner, *Knight of the Burning Pestle*, 20–37.
[31] See Bliss, *Francis Beaumont*, 47.

writes even the interludes, which would normally be left to the acting company.[32]

Our assumptions about how theatrical illusion is created are increasingly challenged. At the beginning, the Boy gives a realistic sense of the lead-time needed to bring a play on stage: "you should have told us your minde a moneth since" (Induction, 31). Yet Rafe appears in fully prepared scenes, which are ready as soon as asked for, and which involve a supporting cast that grows as the play goes on. He brings his attendants Tim and George with him; but the Host, the Tapster, Barbaroso and his victims, the Princess of Crakovia, the troops at Mile End – where did they come from? When the Host sends word to Nick the Barber to play Barbaroso, should we see Nick (who never appears in his own person) as a member of the acting company, or a character in *The Knight of the Burning Pestle*? And where does *his* supporting cast come from?

Some critics have tried to sort the play out in literal terms. This entails seeing Rafe as a master of improvisation, dramatist as well as actor, and seeing the acting company improvising along with him, cooperating at first but ultimately getting their revenge on him.[33] Considerable wit and ingenuity have gone into these reconstructions of the inner action; but in the end it's like asking how Mia Farrow gets onto the screen in *The Purple Rose of Cairo*. Beaumont is playing with impossibilities – instant gratification, illusions that become realities – until "A satiric attack upon contemporary theatrical tastes becomes, in effect, an onslaught upon the epistemology of the stage itself."[34] There is in all this an element of sheer play, and it may seem over-solemn to suggest that Beaumont also has a point to make. But we cannot lose sight of the way the fun begins, with the Citizen's interruption of the Prologue and his utter rejection ("down with your title") of the play the company has announced for that day. Beaumont's point, I think, is that when one element of theatre gets out of balance like this, when the audience takes its demands to extremes, then theatre does not just become impossible: it spins off into a dizzying void of absurdity. There is a warning here about the excessive power of the audience as patron that is offered far more lightly, and cuts far deeper, than all Jonson's lectures.

The final irony is that the first audience of *The Knight of the Burning Pestle*, in the words of the publisher's letter prefixed to the first edition, "utterly

[32] As Zitner points out, Rafe and the citizens increasingly invade the interludes (*Knight of the Burning Pestle*, app. C, 170–72).
[33] See Bliss, *Francis Beaumont*, 48–49; and Samuelson, "The Order," 313–15, 316.
[34] Miller, "Dramatic Form," 68. Miller's article is a particularly full and persuasive discussion of the whole question.

rejected it." Beaumont's joke about rebellious audiences blew up in his face. He must have expected better at the Blackfriars: the children's companies presented themselves as playing for an elite, sophisticated public,[35] a public that had shown its favor to satire and irony in the past, and ought to have enjoyed this particularly sophisticated example of it. Jonson, presenting *Cynthia's Revels* to the Blackfriars audience, expressed his confidence in them:

> If gracious silence, sweet attention,
> Quicke sight, and quicker apprehension,
> (The lights of iudgments throne) shine any where;
> Our doubtfull authour hopes this is their sphere.
> (Prologue, 1–4)

Yet Walter Burre, *The Knight's* first publisher, accuses the audience of "want of judgement, or not understanding the privy marke of *Ironie* about it (which shewed it was no ofspring of any vulgar braine)" though to spot the irony in this play would seem about as difficult as seeing a church by daylight.

The Boy who has to deal with the citizens keeps appealing to the Blackfriars audience, separating them from these upstarts. Usually he apologizes: "if anie thing fall out of order, the Gentlemen must pardon us" (II.262–63); "it is not our fault gentlemen" (IV.49). The Blackfriars audience are "Gentlemen"; Nell is quite out of place. At one point the Boy appeals for help: "I pray Gentlemen rule him" (III.296). The audience of course does nothing and the play goes on; they too are powerless to stop the Citizen. And if they are enjoying the fun they would not want to stop him; by their silence they become complicit.

Was that the problem? At first glance the play's irony is clear, and ought to have been enjoyable. But is the way that irony operates too intricate, in its play of mockery and enjoyment of the citizens?[36] Did the audience, which might have accepted a straight anti-citizen satire, find itself overtaxed? Did they even feel that in setting up their failure to control the Citizen, Beaumont was telling them: you're as bad as he is? There has been much throwing about of brains over the play's failure: Andrew Gurr suggests that there may have been too many citizens in the audience, and they were not amused;[37] Michael Shapiro, that the audience saw no attractive aristocratic figures to identify with.[38] But I think it comes down in the end to Lee Bliss's suggestion that Beaumont

---

[35] See Gurr, *Shakespearean Playing Companies*, 73.   [36] See Zitner, *Knight of the Burning Pestle*, 38.
[37] Gurr, *Shakespearean Playing Companies*, 74.   [38] Shapiro, *Children of the Revels*, 76–77.

was simply asking too much.[39] Besides, it is always dangerous to be first in the field with a new form, and *The Knight of the Burning Pestle* is evidently the first full-blown dramatic burlesque in English. By the 1630s the audience seems to have been ready for it, and under the auspices of Queen Henrietta's company at the Cockpit in Drury Lane it came back into the repertoire, continuing to hold the stage after the Restoration. It has had many twentieth-century revivals (including one in which the young Noel Coward played Rafe) and its descendants include such hits as *The Rehearsal, The Critic*, and *The Real Inspector Hound*. But in 1607 the audience was not ready, and like its onstage counterparts it rebelled. Linda Hutcheon has argued that irony depends on the existence of a discursive community with a body of shared understanding. Irony does not create such communities; rather it is the existence of the community that makes irony possible.[40] In 1607, it would seem, the discursive community for *The Knight of the Burning Pestle* did not yet exist.

When a play has no clearly understood basis for appealing to its audience, other, more trivial factors may intervene. There was a warning for Beaumont in Day's *The Isle of Gulls*, produced at the Blackfriars the previous year. In the Induction, three gentlemen take over the stage, each with a demand to make of the forthcoming play: one demands satire, the second bawdry, the third bombast. Day shows that gentlemen, no less than citizens, could be obstreperous, and the boy who represents the company complains about the trivial causes that can turn an audience off:

"tis growne into a custome at playes, if any one rise (especially of any fashionable sort) about what serious busines soeuer, the rest thinking it in dislike of the play, tho he neuer thinks it, cry mew, by Iesus vilde; and leaue the poor hartlese children to speake their Epilogue to the emptie seates."

(sig. A3r)

There was, it seems, a particular danger in an audience that saw itself as fashionable and elite. Like the show-off gallant whose playhouse behavior Dekker satirizes in *The Gull's Hornbook*,[41] they were more concerned with their own social performances than with the play, and they were sufficiently insecure to take the lead from anyone who looked impressive.

For whatever reason, the audience let Beaumont down, dramatizing all too clearly the point of his warnings about dependence on the paying public. The play was rescued by the company manager Robert

[39] Bliss, *Francis Beaumont*, 36–37.
[40] Linda Hutcheon, *Irony's Edge: The Theory and Politics of Irony* (London and New York: Routledge, 1994), 89–101.
[41] See Shapiro, *Children of the Revels*, 70–71.

Keysar, who preserved the manuscript, and the printer Walter Burre, who after a decent interval published it. Beaumont's own reaction to the failure is unrecorded. But he never wrote a play like this again, and when Fletcher's *The Faithful Shepherdess* failed – also at the Blackfriars – Beaumont's commendatory verses to the printed text include a sharp attack on the audience. This time the comedy is not genial but angry:

> One company knowing they judgement lacke,
> Ground their beliefe on the next man in blacke:
> Others, on him that makes signes, and is mute,
> Some like as he does in the fairest sute,
> He as his mistres dothe, and she by chance,
> Nor wants there those, who as the boy doth dance
> Betweene the actes, will censure the whole play:
> Some like if the wax lights be new that day:
> But multitudes there are whose judgements goes
> Headlong according to the actors clothes.
> ("To My Friend Maister *John Fletcher* upon his Faithfull
> Shepheardesse," 19–28)[42]

The Citizen's wife enjoyed the boy dancing between the acts; the Citizen scrutinized Rafe's costume. Once again the audience is looking for incidental effects, and is not ready to appreciate the play as a whole. But Beaumont, picking up Day's point and anticipating one of the jibes in the Induction to *Bartholomew Fair*, is especially scathing about those who censure by contagion, having no judgments of their own. No judgment is in fact the underlying problem of the Blackfriars audience, the audience that rejected both *The Knight of the Burning Pestle* and *The Faithful Shepherdess*. (Fletcher's preface is particularly severe on the audience's naive expectations about pastoral.) In his experimental dramatic burlesque Beaumont played, cleverly and imaginatively, with the problems raised by the audience as patron. But with the failure of both his play and Fletcher's, he must have come to the conclusion that the problems were too real to be funny.

In the passage that forms the epigraph to this essay, Samuel Johnson summarizes the challenge presented by one kind of patronage, dependence on the paying public, as in his magisterial rebuke to Lord Chesterfield he outlined the frustrations of the other kind, dependence on the caprices of the powerful. Aristocratic patronage has to be traced largely through the historical record, through inferences drawn from

---

[42] From the text edited by Cyrus Hoy in vol. III of *The Dramatic Works in the Beaumont and Fletcher Canon*.

incomplete and sometimes contradictory evidence. Other essays in this volume, and a growing body of scholarship elsewhere, show that much can be achieved in this vein. This essay has dealt with that other and, in its own way, equally difficult patron, the audience, through evidence that presents its own difficulties. *The Knight of the Burning Pestle* is a play-text, as open to interpretation as an archival record, and it has no simple message. Beaumont saved that for his address to Fletcher, quoted above. The play, as plays do, speaks with many voices, its pervasive irony means that it is constantly turning ideas against each other, and it is dependent for its effect on the unpredictable conditions of performance, including the very audience that it takes as its subject. It survives for us as a source of teasing, paradoxical reflections on the theatrical occasion, made possible by destroying the occasion itself. In this, as in its initial failure, it can be seen as an experiment with volatile material, one in which (anticipating *The Alchemist*) the laboratory itself blows up.

Index